REPORTS

OF THE

COMMITTEE OF INVESTIGATION

SENT IN 1873 BY THE MEXICAN GOVERNMENT TO
THE FRONTIER OF TEXAS.

TRANSLATED FROM THE OFFICIAL EDITION MADE IN MEXICO.

NEW YORK:
BAKER & GODWIN, PRINTERS,
No. 25 PARK ROW.
1875.

PREFACE TO THE TRANSLATION.

This book is a translation, ordered by the Mexican Government, of the reports presented by the commission which it sent to the frontier, to investigate the depredations committed on both sides of the Rio Grande. The President of the United States, in compliance with a recommendation of Congress, had previously dispatched an investigating commission to the Texan border,·to inquire in to the robberies complained of in Texas, and alleged to have, been perpetrated by Indians and citizens of Mexico. That was the origin of the appointment in the neighboring country of a similar commission. The Mexican Government wanted to have the matter investigated on its side, and as impartially as possible, for it felt the necessity of being prepared against the plots of some malicious claimants and other ambitious private parties in this country.

The result of the Mexican investigation is shown in these reports, now published in English for the information of the American people. It proves that the complaints of the Texans are groundless, inasmuch as the cattle stealing done among them is not the work of any residents in the adjoining country, but of Indians belonging to the United States, and their own outlaws disguised as Indians. If either of the two nations can complain of Indian and other depredations—as it is now demonstrated—it is Mexico, some of whose entire States have been ruined by Indians and banditti from the United States, who still depredate there to a certain extent, robbing horses and perpetrating other outrages. The origin of those evils on both banks of the river, it is clearly proved, consists, in a great measure, in the encouragement given to the Indians for plunder by the traffic carried on with them ever since 1835, tolerated and consented by the American authorities, and in which the Indians exchange their booty, most frequently from Mexico.

Besides the lack of foundation in the Texan claims, the absurdity of their amount, in consequence of an enormous exaggeration, is evidenced by the official data showing the value of all the property in the counties referred to by the claimants. They complain of having lost much more than they ever could possess, while they still certainly retain a good deal.

The work of the Mexican border Commission has been wonderfully laborious. They visited all the towns and many ranchos not remote from the Rio Grande, all along the river on its right bank, as far up as La Resurreccion, a distance of about 450 miles. Wherever public archives could be found, they ransacked them most industriously, with a view to find some traces of the facts under investigation. They examined nearly 300 witnesses, whose testimonies, with other documentary evidence annexed to the reports, cover 17,688 pages in manuscript.

The official edition, from which this translation is taken, has an appendix containing a tabular statement of the names, domiciles, &c., of 278 witnesses examined on the principal questions, besides other tabular and detailed notices of Indian incursions into the Mexican frontier States (covering 42 folio pages), and some few interesting data about the removal of the Kickapoos from Mexico, and Indian hostilities in that country. One of the documents inserted in that appendix is a message sent to the Legislature of Texas, by Gov. E. J. Davis, dated Austin, April 19, 1873, bitterly lamenting the frightful demoralization of the State, since, according to the Governor's calculations, more murders had been committed in it, during three months, with a population of little more than 800,000, than in the State of New York (excluding the city of New York), with more than three million souls. The Governor also alludes to the culpable suppression of the cattle registry in one county—a fact, we may say, which tends to prove that cattle stealing in that section had its protectors there, and not in Mexico.

For the convenience of the reader who may want to be
informed about the foundation of the Texan complaints against
Mexican Indians and robbers, rather than other matters interesting the Mexican frontier, we beg leave to refer him to
the first report in its whole, up to page 223, and more particularly to the second one, under the headings, "Indian Depredations in Texas" (page 341), and "Robbery of Cattle and
Horses" (page 383). As of general interest, we also would
especially recommend the portion entitled "Indian Policy of
the United States," commencing at page 427.

TABLE OF CONTENTS.

———•••———

INVESTIGATING COMMISSION

OF THE

NORTHERN FRONTIER.

————◆————

THE Commission appointed by the Executive of the Union, in conformity with the law of 30th September, 1872, was installed in Monterey on the 14th November of the same year, and, agreeably to the instructions received, adjourned to Matamoros to commence their work.

They then traveled along the line of the Bravo to Mier, and are satisfied that the data thus acquired are sufficient to give an idea of the vexed questions of the frontier, with exception of that of the Indian depredations, which will require careful study and examination, after which the Commission will make a special report.

Desirous of hearing the complaints of the sufferers of injuries received, the Commission issued copies of the regulations of the 21st November, and invited the citizens of Mexico and Texas to present their claims before them. They then set about to collect all the facts relative to cattle stealing on the United States frontier, whether favorable or adverse to the Mexican Republic. Besides this, and in compliance with the law of Congress, their duties extended to the hearing and investigation of the complaints of American citizens, and to this end the above-named regulations were issued, as follows :

Investigating Commission of the Northern Frontier.

*   *   *   *

" The object of the Commission being to form a clear judgment of the question, they have resolved to be guided only by the strictest impartiality and justice, and hence invite all persons residing in territory pertaining to the United States, or who own property there, and consider that they have the right to complain of robberies or depredations committed by bands organized in Mexican territory, to present their claims before the Commission, with all the necessary proofs."

The Commission soon became convinced that the provisions of the regulations were wholly inadequate to the requirements of the case. They desired particularly to hear the complaints of the citizens of Texas, but none of those who appeared up to the present had complained of damages done to their cattle, attributing their injuries to the criminal acts of persons residing in Mexico.

Apart from this, a conscientious investigation necessitated vast study. The questions on the frontier are extremely complex, and it would be impossible to examine all the details under their various aspects, if the means of study and investigation were solely limited to the information obtained in the form of complaints, from persons prompted by self-interest.

These diverse considerations gave rise to the necessity of compiling official "*expedientes*." In these documents are collected all the material for the history of the relations between the frontiers since 1848, and as a natural consequence, the facts are free from any personalities which would have resulted from a decision of private claims, had these been the only means by which the Commission could arrive at a clear understanding of the case.

In carrying out this system, the Commission was compelled to study, investigate and classify the result of their labors.

They accepted with pleasure this position, which enabled them to act with entire independence, and to assume the whole responsibility of their proceedings. The Commission does not hesitate to say that they accept this responsibility, because they are satisfied that they have made every effort to sift the truth, whether favorable or otherwise to the Mexican Republic.

In taking upon themselves this immense responsibility, in which was at stake not only the credit of Mexico, but the honor of the members of the Commission, a system of minute investigations became necessary, and the Commissioners did not shrink from using every measure, in collecting testimony, to carefully weigh the qualifications of the witnesses, their reputation for veracity, and the value of their assertions and claims.

Independent of these reasons, there was one no less powerful motive why the Commissioners should proceed with the utmost circumspection. In the course of their investigations, accusations were made against various persons, on either side of the river, of complicity in the robberies of cattle and horses. The Commissioners had to judge of these accusations, and their judgment was equal to a sentence; and although the sentence could inflict no physical punishment, it at least would cause moral suffering to those who were proved guilty of connivance in the robberies, or at least protection of the cattle thieves. This sentence had to be passed without giving the accused the opportunity of defending themselves, a fact which was not a little repugnant to the consciences of the Commissioners. In the impossibility of calling upon the accused to defend themselves, the Commissioners constituted themselves into counsel for the defendants, not for the purpose of exculpating them, should they be guilty, but for the better opportunity of forming an opinion of the true merits of the case. To this end, the Commission instituted a method of private investigation, and when at all doubtful of the testimony procured, and of the good faith of the witnesses, they proceeded to collect testimony for the defendants.

The Commissioners persisted in this system, when, by observation, they became convinced that pecuniary interests formed no obstacle to this mode of procedure, whilst, on the contrary, it was not impossible that erroneous testimony might be given under false impressions, through personal enmity or other causes calculated to adulterate the truth, and of this they soon had ample proof. Hardly had they commenced their work, when Mr. T. H. Hines, citizen of the county of Cameron, Texas, and Justice of the Peace in the 3d District, was accused before the Commission of complicity in the robberies of horses in Mexico and of cattle in Texas. The details of the accusation gave to the case the impress of exceptional gravity, and included acts of public notoriety which assumed the character of proofs, and gave to the accusation a certain air of truthfulness. From the private investigations instituted by the Commissioners, they discovered that Mr. Hines was a man of respectability, and bore an excellent character; that the witness was a man of no character, and that the testimony had been given from a feeling of personal enmity, with malicious intent to injure Mr. Hines.

Mr. Hines was not the only person who, in the opinion of the Commissioners, had been falsely accused. The same witness at that very time accused several other persons. He charged José Turner with receiving horses stolen in Mexico and collecting droves on Mr. Hines' account; Juan Thompson, administrator of the estate " Santa Anita," Texas, with conniving with some of the inhabitants of Cuevas, from whom he received horses stolen in Mexico, giving in exchange therefor cattle stolen in Texas; and J. Siebert, city marshal in Brownsville, with complicity in the cattle robberies; nor did this witness limit himself to accusations against these persons, but brought similar charges against various others.

As regards José Turner, his good character for respectability is well established, and as for the others, the Commissioners refuse to accept the testimony, if for no other than for the culpable perjury of the witness.

Besides this man, there was another who also made himself notorious for his falsehoods; and even had these not become patent, as they did, the fact that, in refutation of these charges, his own securities, persons of acknowledged probity, declared the witness to be a person addicted to falsehood and of bad repute, would have been quite sufficient to have caused the Commission to decline his testimony.

These cases have been mentioned, not as the only ones of this nature, but as a sample of the most notorious, and to illustrate the system of investigation pursued in the collection of proofs.

Wherever false charges were suspected or the slightest falsehood noted, the Commissioners used due diligence to procure proofs of the same, so that side by side stands the accusation and the evidence for the defense; and in every case where falsity has been proved, the Commissioners have not hesitated to admit the calumnious nature of the first.

Added to these considerations, which arose from a sincere desire to learn the truth, and compelled the Commission to move leisurely in their work, was another, which strengthened their determination to persevere in this system. They were impressed with the belief that there were strong temptations on the part of many to present before the Commission false testimony, and a tendency to impose upon their good faith, hoping that the Commissioners would rest satisfied with the evidence given, and close their work, leaving the accused under suspicion, and their own proceedings open to censure or enveloped in mystery. But under the system of investigation pursued by the Commission, it was impossible to inaugurate any such plan, without laying themselves open to discovery.

Notwithstanding all their diligence, the Commission was not satisfied that the testimony had been sufficiently filtered. The result of the investigations showed the necessity of the presence of many of those condemned by the tribunals, or accused by public opinion, of complicity with the cattle thieves, on both frontiers, since 1848, as being the only witnesses who could give evidence in many important details.

Practical observation convinced the Commissioners of the unscrupulousness of the witnesses, who, probably, in declaring against others, were doing the utmost to conceal their own complicity. In accepting this evidence, therefore, it was necessary to do so with a certain reserve, and to this end, it was determined to classify the witnesses coming under this head.

Another class of witnesses were totally unknown to the Commission; they were ignorant of their antecedents, and doubtful of the degree of credibility with which they might be accredited. In regard to such, it was necessary to require securities among persons known to the Commissioners, and many men of noted respectability appeared before the Commission and gave testimony as to the character of the witnesses, and as to the amount of credit which their evidence deserved.

The witnesses who testified before the Commission may be divided into the five following classes :

1st. Persons of known respectability, whose depositions required no security.
2d. Persons of veracity, but who being unknown to the Commission, were required to give security.
3d. Persons unknown, whose declarations could not be certified to, not having securities.
4th. Persons of bad faith, condemned by the tribunals or accused by public opinion as accomplices of the cattle thieves.
5th. Persons who were totally undeserving of credit.

The number of witnesses coming under the four last classes is comparatively few.

Under the first four are collected all the proofs of testimonial evidence.

Citizens who have been in official positions have made deposition before the Commission, the municipal and county police, proprietors, merchants, clerks, laborers, persons accused of complicity in the cattle robberies, criminals condemned by the tribunals. The testimonial proofs laid before the Commission, are quite sufficient to form a judgment on the case ; nevertheless, the Commission, notwithstanding all the careful diligence employed in collecting this evidence, determined to give to this class of proofs a secondary importance, and were satisfied with this resolve at every step, and determined to adhere to it.

There were various reasons for coming to such a determination : testimonial evidence is extremely dangerous when not submitted to debate and contradiction, and for this reason, that proofs received in this manner, without official citation and with no audience, are lacking in importance.

Ignorance on the part of the witnesses gives a well founded

motive for objecting to their evidence; and in many instances this ignorance reached such a point, that the witnesses had not even the faintest idea of time, and although honest in their intentions, and truthful in the main, they fell into errors which, at least, cast a doubt upon their testimony. Lastly, although the witnesses might not be ignorant, nevertheless, their testimony was weakened, from the fact that the occurrences, through lapse of time, or probably because they made no deep impression on their minds at the time they took place, afterward caused the witness to fall into error. Under these circumstances, the Commission is of opinion that testimonial evidence in this class of investigation is of itself incomplete and unreliable, and cannot be employed as a basis on which to pass judgment.

Acting from this standpoint, the Commission, although not discarding testimonial evidence, used every effort to secure proofs from the strongest circumstantial evidence. Legislation, administrative measures, the judicial records, the civil and criminal statistics and various publications were to the Commission mines rich in evidence from which invaluable deductions might be made, not only in determining the question from its general aspect, but also in furnishing the most important details. The Legislature, by adopting measures to correct an evil, revealed clearly and minutely the nature and extent of the evil. The laws enacted for this purpose point out, during a stated period, the various phases of the evil, its increase, its nature and the space of time it covered; whilst the administrative acts in the application of the laws, as a measure of restraint and correction, illustrated the evil in detail. The judicial records indicated the criminals and delinquents, from whence they had come, and the manner in which the crime had been committed. The statistics, civil and criminal, explained, in figures, the amount of criminality, and by a distinct system of legislation, determined the extent of the ills committed; and the above named publications, especially the newspapers, served as a basis for procuring testimony, because in their columns were found documents which could not be otherwise procured, and as giving in detail the circumstances at the times of their occurrence, and expressing the popular feeling on the subject.

These diverse elements have been all applied in various ways by the Commissioners in the course of their labors. The archives of the towns which they visited in their investigation tour furnished the best means of information. The indisputable figures of the statistics; the date of authentic official documents; the nature and result of criminal cases ; the fact that all the circumstantial evidence collected from these archives was, when these documents were filed, never intended to be used as evidence in investigations of this nature, nor even for publicity, are, of themselves overwhelming proofs of the value of the evidence thus obtained, and of its unquestionable strength and validity. For this reason the Commission gave to circumstantial evidence thus procured the first consideration, and, in spite of the obstacles, in the way of political disturbances, and the destruction of property during these affrays, the Commissioners were enabled to obtain an amount of information which enabled them to form judgments principally based on this class of proofs.

The employees in whose charge the archives are placed at first authorized the copying of the documents; but, by degrees, the Commissioners were given to understand that the residents of Texas, whilst using in their defense copies of the municipal archives of the city of Matamoros, added that portions of the originals had been suppressed in the copy.

Although this accusation was wholly without foundation, the Commission was compelled to see that the proofs of this kind brought before them were free from all tinge of suspicion, and to this end, in accordance with the provisions of laws on this subject, they were compelled to produce the archives in many cases, and compare the copies, so as to prove their authenticity, and have them certified to by the secretary.

Besides the official archives of Mexico, the Commissioners considered necessary extracts from the archives of Texas, and, in this connection, they would remark on the activity and intelligence manifested by the Mexican consul in Brownsville, and the vice-consul in San Antonio, in the compilation of this testimony. The partial results obtained have convinced the Commissioners that a detailed examination of these records, particularly those of the tribunals since 1848, which have held jurisdiction in what is known as Western Texas, would manifest data of the most important nature, which are to-day unknown or forgotten, and which could be made of avail in defense of their system of investigation relative to the frontier questions.

In the course of this work the Commissioners heard of a pamphlet published in Washington, under the title of "Report of the U. S. Commissioners to Texas," dated 10th December, 1872, and bearing 'on the questions relative to the frontier. Although the Commissioners had no official knowledge of this document, they have availed themselves of the suggestions therein contained, and made several points in their investigations.

In this manner, and in various other ways, the Commissioners believe they have reached the truth. They threw wide the doors for evidence for or against Mexico, and any who chose could declare as they pleased; they noted the accusations made by both frontiers, and used every method to investigate the truth, concealing nothing; and, when satisfied of the facts, and assured of the degree of fault on either frontier, since 1848, and of the causes of disturbance occurring in those regions, they have endeavored to find the best measures to suppress the evil.

II.

In the examination of the relations between the frontiers since 1848, the first striking point is the system of cattle thieves. During the Texan war and afterwards, in fact up to 1848, horse and cattle stealing increased to so great an extent, in the district north of Rio Bravo to Nueces, as to almost depopulate the country by ridding the inhabitants of their stock.

Bands of Americans, Texans, Mexicans, and Indians, in a few years, exhausted the wealth of that region. The settlers were few in number, and lacked the vigilance of either the Mexican or Texan authorities, so that they not only lost their wealth, but gave scope to a degree of license and immorality of itself dangerous and degrading. The early emigrants to that part of Texas did nothing towards correcting this state of things, but, on the contrary, aggravated the evil, for they were not themselves noted for rectitude or sobriety. It was the refuge for criminals flying from justice in Mexico; adventurers from the United States, who sought a fortune, unscrupulous of the means of procuring it; and vagrants from all parts of the State of Texas, hoping, in the shadow of existing disorganization and lawlessness, to escape punishment for their crimes. Under this head the Commission does not class all the early emigrants to Southwestern Texas since 1848. Far from this ; it acknowledges in many of them the highest moral standard, but, compared with the mass, they constituted but a small proportion, too small to give tone to that class of people, and check the characteristic lawlessness of the district.

The thirst for wealth had become such a strong passion, that any means of procuring it seemed fair and legal. The district from Rio Bravo to Nueces had been cleared of its live stock ; only the land remained; and rapacity knowing no bounds, the lands were seized, by many through force of arms, but generally by persons clothed with feigned legal power. This frontier district, extending along the Rio Bravo, abounded in droves of horses: the horse thieves of Mexico commenced operations here, which assumed from the onset alarming proportions, and the traffic in Texas of horses stolen from Mexico became a matter of commonplace merchandise. The facility which the horse thieves enjoyed, since 1848, of disposing of the stolen animals on the Texan shore of the Rio Bravo, increased the evil to an alarming extent. This pernicious influence has injured the industrial impulses of the Mexican frontier, since the results of horse stealing, and the evil influence of the thieves, have proven more fatal to the country than the revolutions.

Horse stealing in Mexico may be classed under two different heads : one, the appropriation of roving droves, taken a few leagues from the banks of the Rio Bravo, within Mexican territory, transported across the river into Texas, and driven in lots into the interior of the State ; the other is the seizure of horses in the interior of the Mexican frontier wherever horses can be found.

Although testimonial evidence on all these points has been most useful and important, yet circumstantial proofs culled from the archives have in all cases been more conclusive. In those examined by the Commission are a series of regulations framed by the municipal and police authorities for the suppression of horse thieves in the towns lying on the bank of the river. Very few of these measures looked to the prevention of the traffic in stolen cattle from Texas, from which it would seem that this evil did not exist to the same extent ; whilst on the contrary, the laws had in view the damages resulting from horse stealing in Mexico, and the transportation of the horses into Texas, proving that this was the greater traffic, and the one that needed greater legislation. Measures for the prevention of this crime have been issued in every town along the river, from which it may be deduced that like injuries were experienced in every village on the Mexican line ; and as these preventive measures were constant and frequently repeated, it would seem that the injuries were constant and frequently recurring.

It is useless for the Commission to go into a detailed account of the various measures adopted by Mexican authorities to suppress this evil, but, considering these documents of intrinsic value as bearing on the characteristic relations of both frontiers, the Commission took especial care in the selection of extracts from all of these regulations, arranging them in chronological order, and at times copying them entirely, when they offered any particular interest.

The great weight of these proofs cannot be estimated from a few isolated measures of this kind, but must be judged as a whole ; for whilst instituting a repressive system of horse stealing on the Mexican frontier for the Texan market, since 1848, they also indicate the robberies organized on the Texan shore of the Rio Bravo, in injury to Mexican proprietors.

The judicial record is another element for illustrating the frontier question, since 1848, as regards horse stealing in Mexico. In the majority of criminal prosecutions against the cattle thieves, the evidence produced went to show that the stolen animals had been conducted by the thieves to the United States frontier, and then sold to dealers. The Commission has made chronological extracts from all criminal cases relative to cattle thieves tried before the judicial court of each of the towns they visited, and the entire number of these different extracts corroborates the deductions made from the preventive measures adopted by the executive authorities. The number of horses stolen in Mexico for the Texan market may be judged by the following:

1st. From the testimony of those whose horses were stolen, and who had proofs of their having been carried into Texas. The horses, having on several occasions been pursued, were found by their masters, who instituted criminal proceedings against the thieves, the result of which sometimes proved favorable, but generally the costs were so heavy that they often amounted to as much, and at times to more, than the value of the property recovered.

2d. From that of persons who were eye-witnesses to the acts of the robbers, some of them men who had charge of the horses, others who had seen the horses driven across the river to the Texan border, and still others who had aided in the pursuit from the bank of the river into the interior of Texas.

3d. By testimony of members of the police force who, in pursuit of the thieves, noticed that their depredations extended to Jimenez, Marina, and Tamaulipas, sixty leagues south of the Rio Bravo, after the continued robberies had exhausted the horses of the districts of Matamoros and San Fernando, thirty leagues south of the river.

4th. From evidence of those competent to judge of horse-flesh, and familiar with their pasturage since 1848, who have remarked the diminution or total disappearance of them in certain districts where horses had previously abounded, from robberies and entirely independent of their destruction from revolutions.

5th. From that of merchants who, having driven horses into Texas, found difficulty in disposing of them, by reason of the low prices at which stolen horses could be bought, and which was far below their market value. Stolen horses are generally sold in Texas at prices below what the proprietors charge for them in Mexico. Competition is constant when it is remembered that robberies are continued. The nearer you approach the Rio Bravo the greater the competition, and for this reason the dealers in horses honestly procured drive them into the northern part of Texas when possible, so as to secure better sales, and escape the competition with dealers of stolen horses who assemble in the neighborhood of the Rio Bravo.

Notwithstanding all these convincing and varied proofs, which the minutest scrutiny only served to corroborate, and despite the previous testimony given by persons, the majority of whom bear the most unimpeachable reputations, the Commission, in its research for the true facts of the case through the medium of official documents, did not fail to make use of the slightest written proof that could be made of avail.

The repeated measures taken by the administrative authorities doubtless indicate the increase of horse stealing in Mexico for the Texan market, for it is not natural that regulations of such a stringent nature could, through a long series of years, have been enacted by different persons and in different districts, and so tenaciously adhered to, had not the interest at stake been one of great importance; on the contrary, all the data collected from this source point to the general evil, but the Commission needed something still more definite than legal enactments, pointing only to generalities. Statistics are in their infancy in this country, and unable to furnish the Commission with the exact figures, and they were in consequence compelled to be satisfied with the best information they could procure, from scarce and isolated sources.

The robberies at length assumed such proportions that the Town Council of Reynosa, on the 11th of March, 1852, addressed the Mexican consul at Brownsville, informing him of the injuries suffered by the proprietors; and also stating that a band of Americans under Frederick Mathews had established themselves in Las Salinas, and collected a drove of horses amounting to four hundred, stolen from the pasturage on the bank of the river; the corporation also added that this was not the first time that Mathews had engaged in such traffic, and asked the consul to inform the authorities of Brownsville, and request that something be done to stay the evil.

The consul replied that he had conferred with the collector of customs, and that that officer had ordered the horses so introduced by Mathews to be seized as contraband; that the last heard of Mathews he was near Nueces on his way to San Patricio, and that they hoped to overtake him. The consul added that he had induced the collector of customs, to publish a notice threatening the importers of horses with the penalty of the law, if any were found guilty of making contraband importations.

This notice was accordingly published in the " Bandera Americana," a periodical issued in Brownsville, a copy of which dated April 17th, 1853, has been filed with the " *expediente*." In this notice, John S. Rhea, collector of customs at Point Isabel, declares that having received information that a large number of horses had been stolen from Mexican citizens of Reynosa, and had been illegally introduced into the States, and taken to the interior of Texas to be sold, the inhabitants are warned of the penalties of law incured by any who knowingly and willingly take part in these fraudulent proceedings.

They were not successful in recovering all the horses stolen by Mathews; a part only were taken on their way to San Antonio de Bejar, of which seizure the consul gave notice to the authorities of that town; but such was the insecure and disorganized condition of affairs in Texas, that the owners of the stolen animals were attacked by bands of American highwaymen, attempting to regain the stolen property by main force.

Not only do these various documents exhibit the exactness of the judgment formed by the Commission, but they also show how the illicit traffic had increased, mentioning one lot of stolen horses amounting to over four hundred in number. The gravity of the question is revealed by the steps taken by the town council in the appeal to the Mexican consul at Brownsville, and in the prompt measures taken by the custom-house officials, especially those at Point Isabel, who not only took the matter up, but sought through the application of the laws, the remedy of the ills complained of and endured on the Mexican frontier, probably because they were well aware of the extent of the injuries done to the inhabitants along the whole length of the Mexican line.

Horse stealing on so vast a scale from the pastures along the river has greatly diminished in the last few years. The Commission is of opinion that this diminution may be attributed to the scarcity of animals, owing to robberies and revolutions; but although horse stealing lessened in the river pasturage, it continued with some energy in the districts somewhat distant from the river, where the interests of the country were greater.

Laying aside all the corroborative evidence by the various witnesses on this point, there is one document well worthy of special attention. Don Trinidad Garza y Melo, a lawyer, made some notes for the criminal statistics of Nuevo Leon, on the 4th of February, 1870, and these were published long before any one dreamed that they would serve as an index for these investigations. Señor Garza Melo was Judge of the Supreme Court of the State in the years 1868 and 1869, and he affirms that the data from which his work was compiled were selected from " *expedientes* " issued by him. Out of three hundred and eighty-six cases tried before him in those two years, one hundred and thirty-three, that is, the third part, were for horse stealing. He attributes the frequency of this crime to the three following causes: the disorders growing out of a common pasturage; the extent and loneliness of the plains; and finally, the proximity of the Rio Bravo, to the left shore of which the stolen animals could be so easily and quickly transported, with the certainty of disposing of them without delay in foreign territory, and with the still more positive certainty of not being pursued or molested.

By the frequency of the crime the number of animals stolen may be fairly estimated; by the number of cases tried we can judge of the evil; by the condemnation of the delinquents in

2

abode in Texas after becoming citizens, or at all events exercise that right, although abusively.

The emigrants from Mexico to Texas may be subdivided into three categories ; but before naming them it is necessary to explain that the greater portion of Mexican emigrants to Texas are honest, hard-working people, fleeing the revolutions in their own country, and giving their labor, and not unfrequently capital, to the State. These are not the emigrants to whom we allude, but there are others who lend themselves as instruments of the horse thieves, and who may be classed as follows : 1. Criminals escaping from the course of the law and seeking refuge on the Texan shore, or who without having been prosecuted take up their nominal abode there, so as to commit their criminal depredations on the Mexican frontier with impunity ; and it has been observed that the majority of those who are engaged in horse stealing in Mexico reside in Texas. 2. Deserters from the soldiery on guard on the Mexican frontier. 3. Laborers who, on account of the scarcity of hands in Texas and the rate of wages in the States, with great anticipations of acquiring a fortune, and at the same time fleeing from their obligations at home, and who are apt to commit robberies before leaving.

It is absolutely necessary to comprehend these distinctions so as to appreciate the question of the frontier ; but whilst they serve as one of the elements by which to resolve it, they are not the only, and perhaps are the least important features in the case.

It is expedient to investigate where the robberies were organized, where the combinations were formed, that led to the depredations in our country ; it is probable that where these combinations were made, a number of criminals must have been united, perhaps accidently, who resided in Mexico or who as vagabonds were domicile l in Texas.

The question of habitation becomes secondary in this case, and disappears altogether when the place where the crime originated, is fairly located. We must next examine where the stolen goods were transported ; where the traffic in them was established ; for if the crime had reached such an extent as to have a market for the disposal of stolen animals, we have already made an elementary principle, the abode of the delinquents being a matter of little importance as their names. It is very certain that horse stealing would never have reached such an extent had there not been a safe place where the crime could be planned, and after commission, the criminal could feel assured not only of safety but of prompt disposal of the stolen property by advantageous sales.

The principal idea in this question, is to locate the place where the robberies originated, and were encouraged, and made of avail ; the secondary consideration, is the place of abode of those who were employed as instruments for the commission of the crime ; but although this latter is of lesser moment, it does not lack importance, since it shows that the greater number of cattle and horse theives, as well as the most audacious of them, reside principally on the opposite shore, and have crossed from thence to perpetrate depredations in Mexico.

A great many of the documents examined by the Commission enumerate the robbers who have crossed the river to steal horses. From these documents the Commission has made chronological extracts, and sometimes entire copies of the preventive regulations, issued by the bordering towns. In all these series of laws, it may be noticed that great stress was laid by the authorities of the Mexican frontier, on the robbers crossing the river from Texas to Mexico, and on the organized band of theives who arranged their plans on the Texan shore, and crossed over into Mexico to execute them.

These measures plainly indicate that although some of the residents of Mexico have contributed to the number of horse thieves, that the greater danger and damage are experienced by the robbers from Texas. whose only intention was to steal and to return to the United States after accomplishing their object.

The criminal cases confirm the deductions made from these documents. In many of these there are allusions to larcenies perpetrated on the Mexican frontier by persons residing in Texas, and as these are not isolated cases, but on the contrary, are of frequent recurrence, and to be found in all the documents in criminal cases of this nature, and as they do not refer to a certain period of time, but simply to that transpired since 1848, it is to be concluded that the majority of criminals who for years have pillaged our frontier, reside on the Texan line. Conclusive as all these facts appear, the Commission considers the question to have a still more important aspect, and that apart from the nationality or place of residence of the thieves, the point to be determined is the responsibility attaching to the Texan frontier, where the criminal bands are organized, and where the benefit is derived from the depredations of the robbers.

The associations formed in Texas for the purpose of stealing in Mexico have taken various forms. Sometimes the organizations were temporary for a special object or for a stipulated period, and at others the organization of thieves took a permanent form. A great number of documents ascribe the constant, threatening attitude of the population on the shore of the Bravo to be owing to the bands of thieves organized in Texas.

One of the most scandalous occurrences of the period was the alliance of a band of nine thieves in United States territory, who, in April, 1865, went to Burgos, forty miles south of Rio Bravo, and assaulted Manuel and Esteban de la Garza, robbing them of two thousand dollars, and murdering the former; after this they fled across to the left bank of the river for safety and protection. The secret investigations instituted by the Judge of Camargo, in Davis (Rio Grande City), showed the gang to be composed of José Maria Cortés and eight others, whose names also appear in the official documents. The communications which passed between the Judge of Reynosa and the chief of police of the district indicate the complaints made upon this subject, and the decisions arrived at in regard to it, *i. e.*, that the invaders had been organized on the left bank of the Bravo, whither they had immediately returned after the attack.

In former years there had also been transitory organizations, some composed of notorious criminals, whose advent on the Mexican shore was always marked by pillage, although they pretended to have political principles to defend, and who always returned after a short time to the United States with the products of their depredations. To this class belonged the bands organized three times by José Maria Sanchez Uresti, in Texas, in the last three years, and whom he led into Mexico. These gangs were composed of thieves famous in the history of plunder and distinguished for kidnapping and other crimes. They entered Mexico as regularly organized bands, their coming was expected and announced, and was known by every one on the Texan shore. They selected a point on the Bravo river from whence they could most easily and suddenly attack the inoffensive proprietors or secure horses. Some of the stolen animals were recognized in Brownsville. Amongst the companions of Uresti in these expeditions the witnesses recollect Santiago Nunez, Julian Rocha, Zeferino Garcia, Macario Treviño, Santiago Sanchez, Pedro Cortés, Gerónimo Perez, and the two Lugos, Pedro and Longinos, as criminals and accomplices in the robberies of cattle and horses on either shore.

The last time that Sanchez Uresti passed to the Mexican line, he did so with a gang of thieves whom the Lugos had had in reserve in a place called "Trasquilas," Texas, about two leagues east of Brownsville. This will be a subject for examination by the Commission when they come to investigate the question of cattle robberies in Texas ; but for the present, they will limit themselves to saying that the Lugos were notorious robbers, designated as such by the newspapers of Brownsville, which accused them of stealing cattle in Texas. Mention is made of this circumstance so as to give to the Lugos and their accomplices their true position, and to show that because they chose to give to their robberies the semblance of a revolution, it did not alter the fact of theft nor change the actual character of the men.

These temporary confederations of thieves on the Texan shore were doubtless great evils, but although serious enough, they were but fleeting. The crime once committed for which the band had been organized, or a certain period having passed, they disbanded. The gravest question of all, however, and the state of things which has been ruining the Mexican frontier, is not the existence of these fleeting bands, but the organized system developed since 1848, for the protection of horse stealing in Mexico.

The greatest culprits have assuredly not been those who served as instruments, but those who availed themselves of the spoils by purchasing the animals at reduced prices. These dealers may be divided into three classes.

1. Those who dwell in the interior of Texas, buying all the animals they can secure so long as the prices are low, utterly disregarding the manner in which the animals are procured by the venders.

2. Those who come from the interior of Texas to the shore of the river to collect droves of horses, forming contracts with the cattle thieves to go into Mexico and procure them horses at so much a head.

3. Those who reside on the Texan shore, and have in their employ gangs of thieves with a view to horse stealing in Mexico.

These two last are not often seen in person with their employees, but they send them into Mexico with the object of stealing, whilst they dedicate themselves with all security to the criminal traffic.

As regards the first, it is a notorious fact that the purchasers take very little pains to find out how the horses are procured; but, on the contrary, they buy the animals, never inquiring for any document, proving ownership or importation according to law; for generally, when the regular price is charged, the purchaser requires all security possible from future claimants.

Indeed so little scruple is exhibited upon this point, that amongst the various cases examined by the commission, from which its documentary evidence is selected, there appear two cases in which officers of the United States and Texas were implicated in this illegal traffic.

In a case entered on the 22d February, 1850, by the Judge of Camargo, against Cayetano Garza, Dario Juarez, and Nepomuceno Sais as horse thieves, charged with stealing six mules from José Maria Perez, some of which were taken to Rio Grande City, Texas, in which place one of the stolen animals was discovered in the possession of the quarter-master of the United States troops, to whom it had been sold.

In May, 1872, a drove of sixty-six animals, consisting of horses, mares, mules, and colts, was stolen from the rancho "de las Estacas," in the jurisdiction of Matamoros, from Leonides Guerra. Pursued by their owner, a number of these animals were found in the possession of Thomas Marsden, sheriff of the county of Beeville, Texas, who had bought them at the rate of eleven dollars a head.

The price alone is quite sufficient to prove that Marsden had a perfect knowledge of the manner in which the animals were procured ; because, not only in Texas, but in Mexico, horses have always brought a much higher sum when purchased from their legal owners; and the low price at which these were offered was strong presumptive proof that they were stolen. This charge was fully proven against him by the sentence passed by Judge Adkins, who ordered the return of the stolen animals to Guerra.

The dealers of the second class, that is, they who come to the shore of the River Bravo, to organize bands of robbers, are still more culpable. The first lend a tacit alliance to the thieves, affording them a safe market for the stolen animals ; whilst the latter are the direct agents, contracting with the thieves with the understanding that they were to supply them with stolen animals. The habitual periodical visits of these dealers are generally in the months of February or March to October; their arrival is well known, for no sooner do these men arrive, than the horses, mares, and mules begin to disappear from the Mexican coast.

The Commission has not inquired into the manner in which these droves are collected along the Texan frontier, not considering it expedient to do so, but has limited its investigations to the occurrences in the places near Brownsville, because an estimate of the state of affairs in all the counties along the frontier may be easily arrived at, when a decision is formed in regard to the proceedings in more important places, where the population is more dense, and where cultivation and morality are at a higher standard, and the authorities of the law more powerful.

To the surroundings of Brownsville to the Colorado river,

that is to say, about ten or twelve leagues north of Rio Bravo, nature offers wonderful facilities for the concealment of stolen animals. There are dense woods in which are spots easily reached by narrow pathways, and so hedged in by branches as to form secure and perfect enclosures; water is plentiful in the ravines, the pasture is abundant, and everything offers conveniences to the dealers in stolen horses to conceal the fruit of their crime.

The droves of stolen horses collected here never amount to a great number, for as they are often pursued by their owners, the robbers drive them as soon as possible to the interior of the country to avoid their capture. The droves formed on the banks of the Rio Bravo are composed of animals stolen during the night from the breeding farms, enclosures or pastures lying along the banks of the river; these are taken across the same night. The animals that one thief can secure in a single night do not amount to many; the evil consists in the number of thieves and their continued depredations. Thus the drove is increased until the number agreed upon has been procured to fill the dealer's order, and as there are many dealers who carry on this illicit traffic during the course of the year, the horse thieves have almost entirely exhausted the resources of the proprietors along the river margin.

One of the means by which the animals were recognized was the great diversity of marks and brands in a drove, proving beyond a doubt that a great many persons had been robbed. Persons in search of their own property, or by some lucky chance, have had the opportunity of seeing these droves and identifying the animals by their marks and brands. These opportunities have been rare, however, only obtained through superior force or by accident, for as a general rule the drivers of such droves never consent to allow them to be examined.

As horse stealing is generally followed by contraband importations, in Texas, the necessity for concealment becomes imperative, both before and after crossing the river, and first the thieves and afterwards the dealers are compelled to proceed in an underhand manner.

This is one of the forms of robbery organized in Texas since

1848 in injury to the frontier, and although more serious than the first, it is less so than the last case, which embraces the residents on the river bank who have in their employ a gang of thieves which, on some occasions, they have accompanied in person, but who have limited themselves, especially in later years, to direct the proceeding of these bands for their own benefit. These are without doubt the most culpable, because they not only contribute to the development of demoralization, but they are in constant and active conspiracy against the breeders on the Mexican frontier. In the official documents referred to may be found the mention of a great many persons engaged in this commerce, and charges and evidence against them, which the Commission did not care to investigate too deeply, as the work would have been laborious, and the names and number of the instigators of horse stealing in Mexico since 1848 was not so important as the collection of facts. A few special instances have been cited, and even in the selection of these the Commission has been particular so far as persons were concerned, not only because these were unable to defend themselves, but because it is unwilling to expose the names of any save the most notorious, and even this is only resorted to because of the necessity to mention some special cases so as to form a correct idea of the condition of the frontier at this time.

In the years immediately following 1848, there were houses established in Brownsville for the traffic in stolen animals; amongst others was a Spaniard named Ramon Larrosquito, and a guerrilla chief of the war of 1846 who bore the title of Col. Dominguez. Both of these and the others who were dedicated to this traffic had each an enclosure, the walls of which were so high as to impede the view of what was inside; in this were kept the horses or mules until the opportunity offered for conveying them to some of the hiding places in the woods, on the outskirts of Brownsville, where the droves were formed that were to be carried into the interior of Texas.

As regards Dominguez, the documentary evidence is corroborated by the depositions of the witnesses. In a case entered in 1852 against a Spaniard by the name of Pedro Ugarte, various crimes were proved against Dominguez, by whom Ugarte was employed in the capacity of clerk. These two had imported six mules stolen from Eusebio Gomez, of Reynosa. The proof brought by Deputy Collector P. S. Shannon, of the custom house at Brownsville, did not leave the slightest doubt upon this subject.

Besides, Dominguez was not only a dealer in stolen animals. He was chief of a band of robbers who habitually committed depredations in Mexico. Three of these were apprehended in 1854, and executed in Matamoros.

There were other individuals, who although they had no regular commercial house, engaged in the traffic, and went into Mexico to steal. Several Americans and Mexicans are accused of accompanying these expeditions, but it will suffice to mention the names of William D. Thomas, commonly called Red Thomas, and a Spaniard, Juan Lopez Arenas. The former committed horse stealing in this form at first, but of late years he has confined himself to forming the bands and collecting through them droves of horses stolen in Mexico.

As to the latter, traces of his crimes are to be found in some of the criminal cases. The first opens with an accusation against López Arenas, in 1853, for the theft of two droves from the estate Vaqueria: the other followed in 1857, against Porfirio Munguia for having taken Lopez Arenas and some of his gang across the river, from the left bank into Mexican territory, for the purpose of stealing animals.

Of the various persons accused in the documents of actually patronizing the robbers on the other side of the river, and of encouraging theft in Mexico, the Commission will limit itself to the mention of Adolfo Glaevecke, Thadeus Rhodes, and the Estapas, as cases of peculiar notoriety, and because they are so well established by the public voice that the Commission feels confident that the accusations are unbiased by calumny; also because these men hold or have held positions of public trust, and finally because as they live apart from each other, traveling twenty-five leagues from Brownsville to Edinburgh over an extent of land in which is situated three different headquarters of robbers.

The antecedents of Glaevecke and Rhodes are not of recent

date. They are contemporaries, at least, in the robberies committed in 1848, and which have since continued. Adolfo Glaevecke is one of those who have most actively engaged in horse stealing in Mexico, ever since the Rio Bravo has been the dividing line between the two nations.

Persons who have belonged to the police corps, accomplices of Glaevecke, and persons who have appeared in court at various times to reclaim stolen animals, have appeared before the Commission as witnesses against Glaevecke, so that with all the overwhelming testimony before them, the Commission feels confident to express an opinion as to his character. Glaevecke owns a horse pen on the Texas shore of the river, which used to bear the name of Santa Rita, but is now called Lineño. On one side of this enclosure was the ford known as Tia Morales. Here the thieves in the employ of Glaevecke congregate, and to this pen, or enclosure, are the animals stolen in Mexico carried ; driven for the most part across the ford Tia Morales. The evidence of the witnesses on this point is corroborated by documentary testimony. This ford was the object of the most active vigilance on the part of the authorities, and the extracts from the documents in Matamoros show that seizure was here often made of thieves and stolen animals, and that various enactments of law were made to guard the ford of Tia Morales.

Nevertheless, it was not from either Lineño or Santa Rita that the great droves of horses were taken into the interior of the State ; this enclosure was simply used as a temporary resting place, on account of the facilities offered by its proximity to the ford. From here the animals were taken to Palo Alto, and in that district the number necessary to complete the drove was furnished, and from thence driven into Texas.

How vast this speculation was, may be imagined from the fact that Glaevecke had a large farm house in Palo Alto, in which dwelt ten servants who had charge of the animals until they were driven into the State.

Glaevecke did not act entirely on his own account, but was also the agent of other Americans in the interior of Texas, to whom the droves were delivered when completed. The Lineño pen was not only used for illegal purposes by himself, but lent to others for the same purpose; and one of those who made use of the enclosure Santa Rita to conceal stolen horses was Tomas Colorado (William D. Thomas). But apart from these incidental circumstances, in which various other persons were engaged, this spot has been the headquarters of a band of robbers, who at times have made expeditions of one or two months, into the interior of the State of Tamaulipas, from whence they drove large numbers of horses. To this band of robbers belonged Florencio Garza and Juan Vela, who were afterwards hung in Brownsville, Marcos Guerra, a famous horse thief, who is now living, and still under Glaevecke's protection, Tomas Vazquez, not less notorious than Guerra, Cornelio Vazquez, Felipe Treviño Vela, Manuel Rodriguez Vela, and others whose names the witnesses had forgotten.

If the majority of these witnesses are to be believed, and the Commission has had no reason to doubt them, Glaevecke has up to the present continued his illegal traffic in animals stolen from Mexico. He is a juror in the county of Cameron, was elected alderman of the municipal corporation of Brownsville in 1866, and re-elected in 1873.

The second case is that of Thadeus Rhodes, commonly known among Mexicans as "Teodoro." He is a resident of Rosario, in the county of Hidalgo, Texas, and under his authority and protection, especially in former years, a band of robbers dwelt, who pillaged the farms of Reynosa and the villages of Nuevo Leon, which lay near the limits of Reynosa. This band became at last so numerous and so terrifying that in the extracts taken by the Commission, mention is made of depredations committed by them which clearly prove their audacity.

On the 3d of May, 1856, the justice of the peace of Rosario, Mexico, was assaulted, the object being to liberate Leonardo Villasana, accused of robbing, and arrested on the charge. They succeeded in liberating Villasana, and the band of robbers located in Rosario, Texas, were proved to have been the assaulters. From private information received through Martin Washington, a resident of the left bank of the river, who had been an eye-witness of the recurrences related by him

to the military commander of Reynosa, who in turn gave the
details to the judge, it is known that the attacking party consisted of José Maria Zamora, José Maria Mora, Juan de Leon,
Desiderio Perales, Marcelino Ramirez, Francisco Lopez, Ildefonso Cano, and other Indians who came from Rosario, Texas,
to Rosario, Mexico, in the night, passing by Washington's
house for the purpose of liberating Villasana, and returning at
about one o'clock in the morning.

In the investigation which followed, several witnesses who
were present at the attack, testified to having recognized among
the party, José Maria Zamora, Marcelino Ramirez, and some
Indians.

It is also charged that two years previous Zamora had removed to the Texan shore and had since been engaged in robbing, and upon his arrest he stated in his declaration that he
lived in Rosario, Texas, in the house of Teodoro (Thadeus
Rhodes).

The correspondence which upon this point passed between
the Judge of Reynosa and the superior authorities of Matamoros, shows to what condition the question had grown ; the
first declared that the left bank of the Bravo was a harbor for
thieves, and the security which they enjoyed was a constant
inducement to them to ply their illegal trade ; besides which,
the depredations committed by them in Mexican territory had
reached the utmost extent that could be endured. The District
Police Court replied, notifying of the various measures used for
the pursuit " of the criminals residing in the ranche Rosario,
Texas, who boldly came to this shore to commit depredations,
and who had made themselves notorious." The military commander of Matamoros declared that he had spoken to the
Mexican consul in Brownsville on the subject, and asked him
to communicate with the American authorities for " the purpose of devising a measure for suppressing the robbers who
collected on the frontier of the United States, dishonored that
nation, and kept the Mexican authorities in a constant threatening attitude.

In fact, the complaints which reached the authorities involved questions of the utmost gravity. On the 4th May,

1856, the acting judge of Charco Azul, informed the justice of Reynosa that the residents of the ranche of San Lorenzo had manifested how insupportable the depredations committed and damages done their property had become, the same being charged to the bands on the left bank of the river, residents of Rosario, Texas; that these people needed security not only for their property on the field, but also for the animals used in their daily work, such as oxen, horses, mules, milch cows, and even sucking calves from the pens have been transported to the other shore.

Things evidently grew worse instead of better, for, on the 2d May, 1858, the magistrate of Rosario, Mexico, addressing the judge of Reynosa, declared that "the greatest excitement was manifested by the inhabitants on account of the bands of robbers congregated on the opposite shore, and no one felt secure or considered it safe to go a hundred yards from his house unarmed, with the constant dread of being attacked even in his own house, and of seeing his family murdered and his dwelling reduced to ashes."

In seeking the most effectual means for relieving the inhabitants of Rosario from the evils complained of, the authorities of Reynosa commissioned Pedro Villareal, a resident of La Mesa, Mexico, to enlist the robbers located in Rosario, Texas, and to incorporate them with the forces beseiging Tampico. José Maria Zamora was lieutenant of the company. He commenced the march to Tampico, but scarcely had they reached San Fernando, when they mutinied, and deserting fled rapidly back to Rosario, Texas, from whence they continued their depredations on the Mexican shore. Various complaints were laid before Judge J. F. George, by the sufferers. The judge, apparently an honorable, energetic man, took measures to investigate the robberies committed by the band. The stolen horses were found in the enclosure belonging to Rhodes; the robbers resisted the judge, who was compelled to use force, wounding two of their number in the affray. This placed Judge George in great danger.

On the 15th June, 1858, the justice of the peace of Rosario, Mexico, notified the judge of Reynosa of the foregoing occurrences, adding that the judge asked for aid to effect the apprehension of the thieves. At this very time, Judge George himself wrote a note to Dr. Ramon L. Jimenez, stating the situation, and requesting him to ask the assistance of the authorities of Reynosa, and to raise as many Americans and Mexicans as possible to come to his relief. A copy of this letter is on file in the archives of Reynosa. Judge George says, " Bring all you can, and come as speedily as possible; there are thirty robbers in the rancho, and I cannot come out until I have help. Send or go to the judge of Reynosa, and ask him to give you ten or twelve men to assist me. Something must be done quickly, or I will be lost."

Such an occurence proves the audacity of the band, and clearly indicates the crimes and excesses committed by them in Mexico. Judge Cool, of Edinburgh, had a private understanding with the authorities of Reynosa, relative to furnishing the desired aid, and in compliance therewith, fourteen or fifteen men, under command of Capt. Florentino Zamora, left Reynosa for Edinburgh. Judge Cool, on the strength of this force, with the addition of several of the inhabitants, went to Rosario, where six of the robbers were arrested and delivered over to the Mexican authorities. Besides these, Thadeus Rhodes was imprisoned as an accomplice in the depredations committed by the band. The steps taken by the Mexican authorities, in lending aid to Judge Cool, was made the subject of complaint by the commander of Fort Brown, to the Governor of Tamaulipas. The Commission did not find all the documents in relation to this incident; but it is to be supposed that the complainant would withdraw his charges when fully informed as to the facts in the case.

Rhodes is now justice of the peace in the county of Hidalgo, and it appears that he had before acted in that capacity; he has also been collector of customs in Edinburgh, notwithstanding his character has never varied. He has been notorious since the year 1840 for his illegal traffic in stolen animals, and for keeping in his employ men who made a business of robbing in Mexico, and his fame, spite of his position, stays by him to this day. There are cases on file proving that the theft of animals is one of his objects in life, despite his social position.

The third case is that of Leon and José Estapá, the first of whom has been sheriff until last year, and the second a collector in the county of Hidalgo. Both have at their disposal a band of thieves, to which belong the three brothers, Tijerinas. They own the rancho Grangeno, Texas, where the Tijerinas live. In this ranche is an enclosure known by the name of Sabinito, bounded on one side by the river, and on the other by an inlet. To this enclosure the horses stolen in Mexico for the Estapá's are taken, and here the droves are collected and kept until ready to be driven into the interior of the State of Texas.

The examination of these questions gives rise to various conclusions.

1st. A general rule may be established, although admitting of several exceptions, that the originators and instigators of robbery in Mexico are Americans coming from Texas; that the agents and employees are Mexicans naturalized in the United States as residents of Texas, and under the jurisdiction of that State, and others residing in Mexico, or having no fixed place of abode.

2d. A no less general rule may be formed that Texas is the place that receives, and has always received, the benefit of the robberies committed in Mexico; there without the slightest scruple, the dealers in horses receive the stolen goods, purchasing the animals at reduced rates.

IV.

The various cases cited by the Commission as examples, being the most authenticated, and the numerous others filed in the archives, prove by the documentary evidence the existing state of disorganization on the United States frontier; and the inefficacy of the laws and the inability of the authorities to meet the necessities of the case.

It does not require much exertion to understand the reason

of this, when it is recollected that a sheriff like Estapá or a judge like Rhodes charged with the carrying out of the laws and the pursuit of criminals, are themselves the chief instigators, abetting the criminals and enjoying the proceeds of the crime; but the question has a still more general bearing, for when during a long series of years similar acts have been committed in different places, without the proper measures for repressing the criminals having been resorted to, it is not to be presumed that the cause exists in the simply accidental complicity of a public functionary. This might be a motive, as lending facilities and security to criminals, but it is certainly not the only and primary incentive of the robbers.

It has become the common opinion of the proprietors on the Mexican frontier, that it is useless to appeal to the authorities in Texas for justice against the thieves and traders in stolen animals. Their complaints are met with innumerable difficulties, amongst others the cost of prosecution, which often amounts to more than the value of the animals claimed. Besides, there is attributed to several of the Texan authorities, along the line of the Bravo, a spirit of protection to the robbers who commit depredations in Mexico, and to the generality of them the utmost indifference.

In order to characterize this phase of the question, it will be necessary to investigate the deficiencies and defects in the legislation upon this subject, and the course that has been pursued by the authorities of Texas; or in other words, to establish the amount of responsibility to be assumed by the authorities, in default of proper legislation, also the point at which responsibility commences through neglect, toleration or assistance. So combined are these two classes of responsibility, that it will be necessary to analyze them simultaneously.

On the 28th August, 1856, the legislature of Texas passed two very important laws. In the first it was ordered, that if any person committed a crime in a foreign country, State or territory, that if committed in Texas would be classed as robbery, theft or the criminal harboring of stolen goods, and brought said goods into the State, said person should be punished in Texas, as if the crime had been committed in that

State; always provided however, that by the laws of the State or Territory in which the crime had actually been committed, it came under the head of robbery, theft or the receiving of stolen goods (Articles 2438, 2439, Paschall's Digest).

The second provided that any conspiracy formed in Texas, for the purpose of committing crimes in any other State or Territory of the Union, or in foreign territory, should be punished in the same manner as if their object had been to commit the crime in Texas (Articles 2448, to 2453, Paschall's Digest).

These laws are remarkable for the spirit of honor which characterizes them. They were passed at a time when the Mexican frontier was in a high state of excitement, on account of the threatening attitude of the bands of robbers, which had been organized during the first six months of 1856, on the frontier of the United States, crossing the river to commit robberies and assassinations.

The Commission believes that the strict enforcement of both of these laws, would have restrained to a great extent, the depredations committed on the Mexican line; unfortunately, however, it seems that no great effort was made to apply them.

To fully inform themselves as to the facts in relation thereto, the Commission examined the statistics of the criminal court of the county of Cameron, Texas. The facts referring to the period, from 1848 to 1863, relative to criminal cases, are missing, on account of the destruction of a part of the archives during the Confederate war. There remain only those cases which were "Dismissed without trial," and those held open pending the arrest of the culprits, and even of these there is no surety that they are complete. There seemed to be pending three cases of accusations against persons for removing property belonging to the State, and none for conspiracy in Texas for the perpetration of crime in Mexico.

From 1863 to 1866, there was no grand jury called in the county of Cameron. From the spring of 1866 to December, 1872, there have been four criminal cases for exporting property stolen from the State of Texas, and none for conspiracy to commit crimes in Mexico. Of these four cases, one culprit alone was condemned, two found "not guilty," and the fourth "dismissed without trial."

Although the data up to 1863 are very incomplete, the bulk of evidence goes to show that the laws passed by the legislature of Texas in 1856 have proved ineffectual on account of their non-application. There is abundant information that during the past few years—the statistical record of which is complete—the stealing of animals in Mexico for Texas has continued undiminished under all its forms, and it is not reasonable to suppose that, whilst robberies are so frequent, the laws have been properly enforced; nor does the trial of four cases, in three of which the culprits were acquitted, prove the efficacy of the laws.

At certain periods of the year, traders from the interior of Texas come to the river to collect droves of horses stolen from Mexico, and up to the present they have continued their illegal traffic without molestation. The coming of the traders, their arrival and their manner of dealing, as well as the places where the horses are congregated, are facts well known, carrying with them a certain phase of notoriety; so that it is not possible to attribute to the ignorance of the authorities their neglect to enforce the laws and put a bar to these crimes, by restraining the robberies committed on the Texan line, under this guise, to the prejudice of Mexico.

An equally well known and notorious fact is the regular organization of robbers who have existed, and still remain, on the left bank of the Bravo, engaging in robberies in Mexico, without any measures having been employed to restrain them. The only case to the contrary, of which the Commission has cognizance, is the arrest of Thadeus Rhodes, in 1858, and from information given at that trial, it is manifest that the prosecution of Rhodes by the authorities of the county of Hidalgo was not so much for the depredations of which he was convicted, but on account of the threats made by the band against Judge George. After all, these proceedings amounted to nothing in the end; for soon after his arrest Rhodes managed to escape, and since then he has not been disturbed.

In fact, there never has been a single voluntary prosecution on the part of the authorities against the originators of robberies committed in Mexico and planned in ¦United States territory, nor of those who had fled thither with the products of their rapacity, much less against those who shamelessly trade in stolen goods. On the contrary, the instigators and their tools can dedicate themselves with all impunity to their criminal traffic, fearless of any practical intervention on the part of the authorities, unless, indeed, some complainant asks for redress and support, which support, if extended, is generally accompanied by circumstances of unusual difficulty for any action in individual cases.

The Commission does not refer to cases of corrupt functionaries who give aid to criminals; it is evident that in such cases there would be no hope for justice; but the Commission has neither data nor reason to believe this condition of things to be general. The principal difficulty, and the one that has proved the greatest obstacle in the way of redress through the courts, and on which the testimony is especially explicit, is the excessive expense attendant on the intervention of the public authorities in Texas.

This expense commences from the moment that the authorities render aid for the pursuit of the robbers and the recovery of the stolen property. The sheriff or agent of the government, who orders the pursuit, becomes entitled to a fee, the payment of which the complainant is compelled to make. If the stolen property is found, a judgment is necessary, and the employment of a lawyer to present the case naturally follows, on account of the lack of simplicity in the proceedings; besides which, every employee of the court expects and must be paid a fee. From this it will be seen that the expenses necessary to the recovery in Texas of property stolen from Mexico are so enormous that they frequently surpass in amount the value of the property claimed; and consequently, in the majority of cases, the claimants, rather than solicit the action of the public authorities, prefer to lose their property.

Independent of this evidence, there are several documents in which mention is made of this difficulty. In a charge made on 24th June, 1852, against Cosme, Roman and José Maria Cortés, as cattle thieves, one of the witnesses, Manuel Perez, testified to having redeemed two horses on the left bank of the Bravo by payment of four dollars to the Cortés. Another witness, (José Maria Cárdenas), declared that the Cortés had stolen from him two mules, one of which was sold on the left bank of the Bravo by José Maria Cortés, who afterwards stole the animal from the purchaser and brought it to the witness for a given sum; that the Cortés committed a double robbery, carrying the animals first from the Mexican to the Texan shore of the river, disposing of them, and afterwards stealing them from the purchasers for a reward offered by the owner. That in order to obtain their animals the owners were obliged to pay the ransom, it being almost impossible to effect their recovery through legal measures.

In still another document, dated May 4th, 1856, the residents of the San Lorenzo ranche complained through the justice of the peace to the authorities of Reynosa, of the robberies committed by the bands of robbers from Rosario, Texas, adding that they were hopeless of redress, as the authorities of Hidalgo, Texas, apparently wished them to believe that they would carefully attend to their claims, whilst they felt sure from past experience that the authorities were wilfully misleading them so as to effect their ruin.

The two first documents referred to the authorities of the county of Hidalgo, Texas; that is, to the county in which Thadeus Rhodes is justice of the peace, and in which Leon Estapá has just been made sheriff. In these they accuse the above named officers of giving protection to thieves and of preventing the owners of stolen animals from recovering their property. In the conclusion of both documents suspicion is hinted at not only these acts of bad faith, but of a spirit of rapacity, exercised in 'prejudice of the Mexican proprietors who appear before those authorities to reclaim their property.

This aspect of the frontier question called the profound attention of the Commission. It presented the fact that corrupt public functionaries in Texas protected the thieves and abetted stealing in Mexico. But still more worthy of consideration was the combination of circumstances which contributed to the development and existence of the crime. This could not be repressed except by the vigorous and energetic enforcement of the laws by the public officers; and in failure of this, had not ready facilities been afforded and protection secured to the robbers, corruption to such an extent• would not have existed, and the thieves, in place of assistance, would have been met on all sides by insurmountable barriers.

Since 1848 to the present, for the space of twenty-five years, there has existed in Texas the trade in goods stolen in Mexico, without the attempt at interference on the part of the authorities to punish the offenders of law in this illicit traffic. During this same period the collection of droves of animals at certain periods of each year along the whole American line has been permitted, with the knowledge that these animals were stolen from Mexican territory. Finally, there had been tolerated the public organization of bands of robbers, who under the patronage of influential persons have gone to Mexico to steal for the benefit of their patrons.

The neglect of the public authorities is shown by the lack of a police force and other preventive measu es to impede the combinations of the robbers in Texas and the conspiracies entered into for the perpetration of crime in Mexico, and that out of two laws, the upright spirit of which is recognized by the Commission, they have been unable or unwilling to apply them effectually, or to have used some active means for rescuing the property after the committal of the crime.

Without mentioning the denials of justice to Mexican proprietors who appeal to the tribunals of Texas, the fact that the complainants are obliged to pay the officials charged with the pursuit of the robbers and the stolen property, as well as all the costs of the court, amounting very often to a sum equal or greater than the value of the thing reclaimed, is sufficient reason why the aggrieved should prefer to lose his property; and thus the authorities deprive themselves of so certain a means of investigating the crimes of the delinquents as that afforded by the prosecution of private individuals.

The Commission esteems it best to mention two considerations as regards the general character of the responsibility of the authorities on the western shore of the Bravo.

1st. They have not used all the efforts in their power to prevent the schemes projected in Texas for robberies in Mexico, nor taken measures to prevent the stolen objects from being introduced into United States territory, where the thieves find an immediate and easy market.

2d. Not having complied with this duty, they fail to perform another, by collecting fees from Mexican proprietors for coöperating with those who have crossed into Texas to recover their property.

In respect to the last, the Commission recognizes the right of the State of Texas to levy contributions on those who seek the assistance of the public authorities for the recovery of stolen goods, and on those who appeal through the tribunals for justice, whether these charges are in the form of fees paid to employees of the court and police force, or are paid in any other manner. But these expenses ought not, under any circumstances, accrue to foreign owners who would be enabled to remain in the tranquil enjoyment of their property, if the organization of bands of robbers was not permitted in a neighboring country, from whence these marauders come to ravage their properties; or, if there was not in that country a peaceful security for the proceeds of theft, even if these organizations did not exist.

Before the robbery is committed, the goods are beyond the jurisdiction of the authorities of the State of Texas, and the proprietors do not willingly submit them to their control. A criminal act which the authorities were in duty bound to have prevented is what gives them cognizance of the claims advanced by foreign proprietors. The appeal, therefore, of these proprietors to the Texan tribunals is not a voluntary submission to the laws of the State, but an appeal for redress for wrongs which the authorities of the western bank of the Bravo had it in their power to have prevented. If they have been inefficient or neglectful of their duty, and if through their inefficience or neglect foreign proprietors have been made to suffer, and have been compelled to appear before the tribunals and police courts of Texas for redress, and ask of these authorities the aid necessary for righting their wrongs, this aid, the necessity of which having been brought about by their own neglect, should be cordially rendered by the authorities, and every possible means furnished to recover the property stolen from a foreign country, especially under the conditions relating to the protection of the Mexican frontier established since 1848. This second obligation on the part of the authorities is as clear and binding as the first; it is not hampered by any needless conditions, nor is it left to the judgment of the Texan authorities to comply or not with the letter and spirit of the law. They are compelled to perform their duty, and no opening is left them for hedging the law round with such innumerable barriers, under the guise of fees, as to preclude the appeal for justice. This obligation not only proceeds from the right of justice conferred on Mexicans under the laws of Texas, but is made imperative by another obligation, by which the authorities were bound to repress hostile proceedings on the United States frontier against Mexico, and to redress the damages done, when these damages arose through their neglect, and to use all the means in their power to prevent the evil. The appeal therefore made to the Texan authorities against those who are benefiting by property stolen in Mexico, is simply a reparation asked, and such reparation should not be subject to any litigation whatsoever.

V.

The question of robbery in Texas is one of the most complicated in this investigation, embracing as it does, so many details, all of which deserve attention, in order that the case may be fully comprehended.

The Commission, believing it necessary to inquire into the condition of the cattle trade in Texas, having been informed that the cattle of the region lying between the Rio Bravo and the Nueces had augmented considerably during the Confederate war for lack of a market, and that the evidence of the experts shows that the number of cattle have fallen off from one-third to one-fourth what it was in 1866, under the circumstances, too, that there has been no sickness amongst them, nor drought, nor unusual sales, which might explain this diminution.

1st. We notice that this fact is set forth to lead to the inference that this result has been brought about by gangs of thieves organized in Mexico.

2d. If we take into account, as has also been suggested, that the cattle beyond the Nueces, on account of the cold, migrate to the south, crossing the river Nueces, and take refuge in the valley of the Rio Bravo, and,

3d. Then we must conclude that cattle stealing in Texas for the benefit of Mexico has not been confined to a special locality, but has affected the cattle over a great portion of the State.

This result does not only exist in theory, for in the schedule of claims presented for stolen cattle, there appear amongst the claimants the proprietors of the counties of Refugio, San Patricio, Goliad, Lavaca, and Bee, which are on the other side of the Nueces.

The Commission will express its opinion, relative to the counties lying between the Bravo and the Nueces when they treat of the claims presented against Mexico, as regards the disposal of the general question, and from the condition of the cattle trade in that State, the Commission has not antecedents sufficient to enable it to judge whether or not there has been any diminution of cattle in Texas. Witnesses were not examined, for the reason that the solution of the question may be found in the official statistics relating to the payment of duties. Without affirming, therefore, anything relative to this matter, the Commission will limit itself to saying that the cattle in Texas have suffered some reduction, which may be accounted for, independent of any connection with the cattle thieves in Mexico.

The commercial statistics of Texas, copied from the Texas Almanac for 1873, gives the following results :

Horned cattle exported to Galveston and Indianola during the period from

Sept. 1st 1871, to Sept. 1st 1872	58,078
From Saluria, during the same period	24,461
From Corpus	3,180
Transported to Kansas from Caldwell, from May 1st to Nov. 11th 1872	349,275
	434,994

This table does not include the cattle exported from other ports of Texas, nor that taken to the northern portion of the State, not passing through Caldwell.

The statistics show for the same period, $i. e.$ from September 1, 1871, to August 31, 1872, the commerce in raw hides to be, as follows:

Exported from Galveston	407,931
" " Corpus Christi	85,297
" " Rockport	10,240
" " Aranzas	31,720
" " Saluria	330,875
Total	866,063

In this is not included the hides exported from other ports, nor those taken from Shreveport and other points of the Colorado river, nor those employed in manufactures in the State, nor yet the excess lying at the ports, which have not been exported; thus, for example, the number of hides received in Galveston, exceeds the number of those exported during the above named period, by (4,902) four thousand, nine hundred and two; but even if we accept the previously mentioned figures, they will be sufficient to estimate the great number of cattle consumed and exported.

These exportations have not been habitual, nor is there any notice of them previous to 1866, as shown by the statistics.

Taking for example the commerce of the port of Galveston, we arrive at positive conclusions. In the mention made of the traffic of the above named port, published in the Texas Almanac for 1869 (pages 179–180), are contained the two following paragraphs:

"*Cattle.*—In no year previous (1868) has there been so much activity in the exportation of cattle from this port, as at present, owing to large herds collected, the great facility for embarkation, and the urgent necessity of the population, compelling them to use every means possible to avail themselves of the resources within their reach. There have been also exportations from all the other ports, and those transported by land have reached an unprecedented number."

"*Cattle Hides.*—The exportations from this port for the year amount to 205,000 hides, and almost as many have been transported from the other ports of the State, showing an increase of at least fifty per cent. over any previous year."

It is not too much to say that since 1868 the exportation of cattle and hides from Texas has assumed unusual activity, and has continued increasing, as will be seen from the following notice relative to the port of Galveston (Texas Almanac, 1873, page 39):

Hides exported from September 1, 1867, to August
    31, 1868............................205,000
From 1868 to 1869......................294,892
From 1869 to 1870......................332,769
From 1870 to 1871......................371,925
From 1871 to 1872......................407,931

This unparalleled development of the commerce has not been peculiar to Galveston, but general to all the ports of Texas, and is established by the fact that the general exportation of hides which took place from 1867 to 1868 were calculated at four hundred thousand, and considered as an extraordinary number, exceeding that of any previous year. This is less than half the number of hides exported in the period from 1871 to 1872. In other words, the exportation of cattle hides in any year prior to 1867 never exceeded 200,000, so that when, in 1868 and each of the succeeding years, the number increased until it showed the large figure of eight hundred and seventy-six thousand and seventy-three, it produced the plain conviction that since 1868 the sales had been unusual and the numbers constantly increasing.

In proportion to the number of cattle consumed, the production has been alarmingly decreasing, owing to the prolonged droughts suffered for the past three years. A great many witnesses, proprietors of farms in Texas, especially in the region between the Rio Bravo and the Nueces, where it is insisted that no droughts have occurred, laborers working and travelers passing through that portion all testify with singular uniformity upon this point, and give the drought as a cause for the mortality amongst the cattle.

The lack of rain contributes in two different ways to produce this result. The immediate consequence is the drying up of the springs and other watering-places. As soon as the water is exhausted the cattle begin to perish, especially if the herds are large. Although there are places where these springs never dry, and where water is plentiful, the pastures become exhausted, and the cattle fall off in flesh, even though they may not die. The result of this is that during the winter, although it may have rained previously, the cattle are unable to resist the great cold, and quickly perish, so that the lack of pasture is felt by causing other troubles, to which the cattle become a prey.

From year to year the evil has increased, the drought having continued three years, the effects caused by the scarcity of water in one year is again repeated, falling upon cattle not yet recovered from the last year's suffering.

Thus it is that after three years' drought, so great a number of cattle perished during the last winter that some entire herds were swept away, and all are more or less diminished.

The following are extracts from various newspapers of Texas upon this subject :

" This year we have had no rain of any consequence in Santa Gertrudis and Laureles (Nueces) ; the neighborhood of Oakville, is also suffering from the drought."—*The Daily Ranchero*, Brownsville, June 13th, 1872.

" A letter received from a ranche in the county of Nueces declares that the horned cattle, as well as the horses, are dying by the thousands on account of the lack of pasture."—*The Sentinel*, Brownsville, January 14th, 1873.

" It is a fact worthy of notice, and invites reflection, that in reality there is not in the county of Béjar a tenth part of the number of cattle that there was in 1860. Judge Noonan rode to Castroville one day last week, and returned the day following. During the trip he saw but two oxen ; notwithstanding the pasture begins to look green again."—*San Antonio Express*, February 27th, 1873.

"The cattle * * * is beginning to fall off, and has become so scarce that it makes the trade precarious and not very profitable. It is a notorious fact that the native pasturage is disappearing, and without the care and cultivation of art, four of five acres of summer pasturage will be utterly useless."—From the same paper.

"The proprietors of cattle in Western Texas are losing their herds at the rate of twenty per cent., owing to the disastrous results of the past winter."—*Indiana Bulletin.*

"A stranger can form some idea of the cattle which perished during the past winter, when from ten to thirty cargoes of hides leave our city daily for the coast, and the same may be said of twenty other towns, north and south of us."—*San Antonio Weekly Herald*, March 8, 1873.

"In reality there are very few cattle within the radius of a hundred miles of San Antonio; the pasture has been greatly injured by being constantly trodden, and that which remains is being devoured by grasshoppers. It is useless, and worse than useless, it is criminal to attempt to disguise for a longer time the fact that this region of the country is in a transition state; the abundance of nature is fast giving way to the exigences of civilization. The past mode of raising cattle is impossible, with any hope of future profit."—*San Antonio Weekly Express*, March 27, 1873.

The press confirms the evidence of the majority of the witnesses, as will be noticed especially by the conclusion arrived at by the last named paper, and which goes to show that this condition of things has not been sudden, but that the country has been slowly deteriorating through a number of years.

The droughts have entailed a double injury, not only causing the death of the cattle, but impeding their reproduction, by reason of their meagreness and debility, caused by lack of sufficient sustenance. Thus the constant removal of cattle to Kansas and other places for consumption, the mortality among them, and the dearth of reproduction will serve to explain the decrease perceived in the cattle in Texas, if such has really occurred, without recurring to so extraordinary a cause as that of robberies, committed by gangs of thieves organized in Mexico.

VI.

Cattle stealing in Texas has taken divers forms, which will be readily understood by consulting the laws of that State, as said laws constitute one of the necessary elements in order to thoroughly understand the nature of the question relating thereto.

In said laws we can perceive the origin of the mischief, the different forms which it has taken in the course of time, its progress and development.

The Commission could not, therefore, disregard such an invaluable source of information.

On the 5th of September, 1850, the first law of which this Commission has any knowledge was issued.

The object of this law was to regulate the shipping and slaughtering of cattle, and this of itself indicated that at that time cattle stealing was committed either to ship the herds or to dispose of them at the slaughtering houses. Said law adopted easy means to find out the robberies committed, by ordering that all the captains of vessels, as also the owners of slaughtering houses, should keep a registry, wherein entries should be made of the marks and brands of the cattle, giving a general description of the heads, their age, counties, where the same came from, and the names of the sellers.

This registry was to be communicated to the court clerk of the county in which the cattle were to be shipped or slaughtered, and said clerk was to keep another registry, which might be examined by any interested party (Oldham or White's Digest, Art. 1866).

During a long time no order whatever was passed, and this cannot seem strange if we bear in mind that prior to 1848 cattle were not abundant in Texas. Later, when the cattle increased, the crime of cattle stealing began to appear, and thence the necessity of a more extended legislation.

The law of August the 28th, 1856, was passed in order to meet the arising exigences. Said law established a pecuniary punishment against all persons who should brand any herds of cattle, if they are horses, mules, neat cattle, or sheep, without the consent of the owners (Paschall's Digest, Art. 1411). A similar punishment was decreed against all those who should appropriate to themselves the skins of any heads of cattle, or any part thereof, against the will of the owners of the same (Art. 2413). And finally, said law forbade, under a fine, the selling of unbranded calves, either to be shipped or slaughtered (Art. 2419).

We are convinced by this law, that in 1856, cattle stealing had acquired three new forms, viz : the stealing of unbranded cattle ; the stealing of heads by stripping the skins off and abandoning the remains, in order to avail themselves of the said skins ; and by branding cattle belonging to others.

This last form of stealing requires some further explanation.

Up to a certain age stock raisers do not brand their cattle, the ownership being recognized by the young keeping with their mothers.

He who brands such animals, not his own, commits a plain act of robbery. But such an act, can only be committed by cattle owners, who have a brand of their own, and this shows evidently that in 1856, cattle stealing was not only committed by indigent people, but also by those who owned and raised cattle, endeavoring to increase their stock by stamping their brands on young cattle owned by others.

The law passed the 12th February, 1858, indicates that the evil, at that time, far from being extinguished, had been enhanced and was deeply rooted. Said law imposed very severe penalties of imprisonment against cattle thieves, whatever might be the kind of cattle that was stolen (Paschall's Digest, Articles 2409, and 2410,) as also against whosoever might alter or efface the brand of an animal not belonging to him, without the consent of the owner thereof.

So when the Confederate war broke out, cattle stealing was committed in Texas under all its forms.

Demoralization had increased from 1850 to 1858, as an inevitable consequence of the want of preventive laws, such as are customary in all countries dedicated to stock raising.

Disorderly habits had been created during that period,

which in the course of time have been spreading, and the eradication of which will be exceedingly difficult.

The war, by placing the State in an exceptional condition, enlarged the scale of demoralization, the effects of which are felt up to to the present, and will be felt for a long time to come.

The law of March 4th, 1863, shows the principal evils suffered during the confederation.

The purchasers of cattle destined to the use of the confederate army, or to exportation, or to a market, and of the county where the purchase was effected, were obliged to take from the vendor a deed of purchase, wherein the brand, or brands, should appear. This deed was to be recorded by the purchaser with the court clerk of the county, and the record to be accessible to the public for their inspection (Paschall's Digest, Article 2414). Purchasers not complying with above mentioned requirements incurred thereby the penalty of $500 fine (Article 2415). A copy of this deed, certified by the clerk, was *prima facie* evidence against the vendor in any civil or criminal proceeding (Article 2416). The enactments of the law of 1850 were reiterated, augmenting the penalty.

There was some reason for passing this act. The very fact that its penalty was made more severe than the penalties of previous acts, shows that demoralization and robbery had increased.

The requirements of the act in regard to the sale of cattle show that respect for other people's property was by no means the predominant feeling.

And truly, the investigation of the Commission proves clearly the disorders of which Texas was then the stage.

A great number of Texans, some of them officers in the Confederate army, took large droves of cattle to Matamoros as a market, and evidently this was not only in Matamoros, but also in all the towns of Texas, for said act shows this to be the case.

The armed forces of Texas, disorderly and insubordinate, never hesitated to commit any act of plunder. But leaving this aside, the means employed by the beef contractors of the Confederate army deserve a particular explanation.

4

The Commission received some accounts relating to one of these contractors, a Mr. Beecher by name, property owner on San Antonio river, said accounts being given by one who served under him during the war.

Mr. Beecher, with the men under his service, used to go into the pasture grounds, sometimes with and at others without the permission of the owners. He would there make large collections of meat cattle, and select all the fat bullocks of seven years of age and upwards, regardless of their brands. If, perchance, the owner of the bullocks happened to be on the spot, or he came in time, he received the value of the cattle marked with his brand; but if he happened to be absent, this was no objection, and Mr. Beecher would drive off the bullocks without paying for them. Once started on his way, he would incorporate in his drove all the bullocks he came across having the conditions he required.

When he reached Gamstone, a place on the Mississippi river, he delivered all the cattle he had gathered to the agents of the Confederate army. This performance was carried on during the whole Confederate war, and Mr. Beecher was not the only beef contractor.

The act passed in 1863, in no way put a stop to the ever increasing demoralization. When the war ended, there were other causes conspiring to the same object, but as said causes are connected with the stealing of cattle destined for the line of the Rio Bravo, these will be dealt with by the Commission in its proper place.

Nevertheless this will not prevent the Commission from remarking here, that after said war concluded, cattle stealing was not purely local and limited to the Rio Grande valley, but it had a general character, as is shown by the act of November 13th, 1866. According to this act, all sales, whether of horses or meat cattle were to be under bills of sale expressing the number of heads, their brands and marks, and the want of said document in any criminal proceeding, was the *prima facie* evidence of culpability against the person in whose possession the cattle was found.

The bill of sale was to be recorded with the clerk of the

County Court, whenever it referred to cattle taken on the pasture ground. (1st.) To export cattle from the State or any county, it was necessary that the purchaser should file with the court clerk a bill of sale, and a statement of the number of heads, marks, brands, kind of cattle and domicil of the purchaser, said document to be recognized by the vendor, recorded by the clerk, and by this functionary returned to the purchaser, after having certified and sealed it. Whoever was found driving cattle from one place to another, unprovided with said documents, incurred a penalty of double the amount of the value of each animal, and the animals were to be returned to their owners at the expense of the accused. (Sec. 2d.) The owners of slaughtering houses were obliged to present to the Police Court of the county, a sworn statement of the number of heads, color, age, marks, and brands of the animals they had slaughtered, presenting the hides to the chief of the police or to the clerk of the County Court, and these officers were to keep a registry open to the public.

It was required to file with each statement the accounts of the sales made over to the slaughterers, or to express in its case that they were the raisers of the heads that had been slaughtered.

Those who slaughtered or bought unbranded heads of cattle, without a bill of sale, or failed to file the sworn statement, incurred a penalty of from fifty to three hundred dollars (Sec. 3d).

This act endeavored to attack cattle stealing in two of its gravest aspects.

The first was the exporting of cattle by those who drove them out of the State or county, and who while forming their droves, gathered unscrupulously all the heads that might suit them, without discriminating their brands or owners. The second was the facilities the cattle thieves had for selling the animals they had stolen to the slaughtering houses in the towns of Texas, without a vestige being left after a short while, on account of the animals being consumed. As to this last shape of cattle stealing, the act of 1866, when compared with the previous acts, shows that the evil had increased, not only because it made the penalty more severe, but also because it augmented the requirements to which the owners of slaughtering houses were subject.

In February, 1869, Texas constituted the 5th military district. Major General Canby, in chief of said district, by his order No. 17, issued on the 25th of same month, extended to the traffic of hides the enactments of the law of September 5th, 1850, relating to the shipping and slaughtering of branded cattle.

The purchasers of hides were obliged thereafter to file with the Police Court of the county a sworn statement, expressing the number, color, marks and brands of the hides, name and domicil of the vendor and purchaser, or whether the hides had been taken from stock raised by the holder of said hides.

From these statements a record was to be kept open to the inspection of the public ; contraveners were to be punished by fines of from fifty to three hundred dollars. And the purchase of unbranded hides was prohibited, when the marks had been effaced, or removed, under a fine of twenty-five dollars.

The general order No. 108 was issued on June 7th, 1869. In this order it is said that information had been received *from all parts of the State,* showing that cattle stealing had been carried on during that year to an unprecedented extent, and that in many cases the cattle drivers would not allow them to be examined.

The same order established certain rules according to which the inspection was to be made, provided for the appointment of public inspectors, who were to watch that all the laws relating to cattle should be duly fulfilled, establishing also certain rules for the transit of cattle on the Rio Bravo frontier.

The first order gives evidence that hide‧stealing had assumed great dimensions.

This kind of theft, as the Commission has already observed, is committed by flaying the cattle on the pasture grounds, where the remains are abandoned, and the hides carried off. This is easily accomplished on account of the loneliness and extent of the pastures, is full of inducements for the high prices which hides have commanded in late years, and besides this, it is difficult to be discovered and proved.

And now it is readily understood that this kind of theft can only be committed in Texas, by residents of Texas, and to the profit of dealers in hides living in Texas.

The general order No. 17 shows sufficiently that the depredations committed in this way bear no reference whatever to the Mexican frontier.

The second amongst the orders which we have referred to, shows that in 1869, stealing by means of exporting cattle, had assumed considerable proportions, that want of security was general in Texas, and that the stealing of cattle, with a view to drive them to the line of the Rio Bravo, was not by itself the principal question, but one of its incidents only. In the investigation of the causes which have contributed to the increase of the crime, the Commission thinks to have found them in the existing demoralization of a large body of people, composed of merchants and property owners, who evade the fulfillment of the laws, having sufficient influence to carry through their purposes. Besides this, the Commission has noticed a complete subversion of moral principles, which has caused morality to be a practical impossibility.

Witness an Indianola correspondent of the *Texas Almanao* (1870, page 125). After citing the requirements of the laws of Texas in regard to the selling of cattle, and after having explained how the records kept by the clerks of the County Courts are made available to discover when cattle have been sold illegally, by persons who are not their owners, said correspondent adds:

" It often happens too, that different droves become mingled, and it is only by great labor that they can be separated. When this is the case, the general practice is that the owner who finds with his cattle heads bearing marks of other owners unknown to him, may sell them as though they belonged to him, setting down on the bill of sale their marks and brands, in order that the owner who proves his claim may have a right to be paid, according to said bill, the person authorizing the same being held responsible at any time. In the large pastures of the West, where thousands of heads belonging to different owners gather in one drove, it frequently happens that the vendor, while driving his cattle, finds out some heads of unknown brands, and it is less troublesome for him to sell these heads and keep the proceeds, subject to the call of the owner, than to separate the heads from his drove."

Evidently no one could make a mistake by calling this proceeding downright cattle stealing.

As droves of cattle belonging to different owners collect together on account of the pastures being open, and said cattle roam over vast tracts of grazing ground, unquestionably, in the majority of cases, the owners who live in a distant county, and whose heads of cattle have been disposed of in this manner, will never hear of such sale, and the vendor may sell with the absolute certainty that no one will ever claim the proceeds. Nor is it possible that the cattle owners could visit all the places from whence or through which cattle may have been transported, and consequently, the willingness of the vendor to deliver the proceeds to the real owner of the heads he sold, whenever he may present himself, has no importance whatever, and is nothing else but a mark to violate the law and commit crime with perfect impunity.

The remarks made by the correspondent of the *Texas Almanac* explain partly the reasons why, notwithstanding the previous acts, the headquarters of the fifth military district received complaints from all parts of the State of Texas against cattle stealing, whilst droves were being transported, and also show that these depredations were committed by stock owners whilst disposing of cattle, and that the line of the Rio Bravo has had no part in this form of cattle stealing.

The information received by the Commission shows to what extent the abuses concealed under this practice were carried. It not only helps large owners of cattle to take away and sell heads that do not belong to them, but enables individuals of very limited means to sell great numbers of cattle, as if they were rich stock owners.

There is a case in which out of sixty-six heads of cattle

sold, only four bore the brand of the vender, and the balance belonged to other owners.

In another case of eighty heads sold by three persons, there was only one head bearing the brand of one of said persons, and not one with the brand of the other two.

All this information refers especially to American stock raisers of the river Nueces, who complain most bitterly against the Mexican frontier.

The large stock owners complain that these abuses are committed by persons having no capital, but they restrict themselves to sterile complaints, trusting perhaps that they will have more than sufficient compensation in committing like abuses in their turn.

They certainly suffer, but prevent their remedy from being applied, because it would deprive them from committing the very same depredations.

Those who really suffer are Mexican stock owners, against whom the greatest indignation would be manifested, if they dared to act in like manner.

They are really, therefore, the principal victims, and some of them have preferred to abandon Texas.

Some American stock raisers on the Nueces river, have of late fenced larger or smaller tracts of lands, wherein they keep their stock.

No admittance is allowed on the premises, but to their agents or to purchasers, and these have informed the Commission, that said stock raisers hold a large amount of cattle, that does not belong to them, but which they sell as if it did.

Cattle inspection is not and never has been a means of protection; those who commit the abuses we have referred to, alter the marks, and either on account of the swiftness of the cattle, which does not allow any one to approach, especially if he is not on horseback, or because the inspectors cannot distinguish the marks, they are never able to detect the frauds committed by the vendors.

In the majority of cases, said inspectors do not even affect to inspect the cattle, limiting their exertions simply to counting the number of heads, and when it is found to agree with the number on the face of the bill of sale, they set down the marks designated on said bill.

These remarks, referring to small droves, have been made by American stock raisers of the Nueces and Rio Frio, to dealers in Mexico, and they give a good foundation to surmise the enormous frauds committed in those large lots of from five hundred to two thousand heads, which are exported from Texas to the Northern States.

It is very plain therefore, that, even should the owner apply to the registry in order to find out whether some of his heads had been sold, said registry would be of very little use to him, on account of the alteration of the marks.

It is not the perpetration of the crime itself which calls particularly our attention, but its being considered in the category of dire necessity, the origin of which should be accounted for, by the mingling of large numbers of cattle belonging to different owners.

When a large drove of cattle destined for exportation is formed, it is only a certain kind of cattle that is included, which is selected from those large collections called "round ants."

In the mean time, while the picked heads are being exported, it would be very easy to separate the heads having a different mark from the owner's.

Therefore, if amongst the picked lots, heads of cattle with different brands should be found, there has been necessarily a positive act, executed with a deliberate intention and will. This is not, however, the only case in which the Commission has noticed a perversion of the principles of morality.

Further on we shall have an opportunity to show distinctly that cattle stealing, in the shape of branding young heads not belonging to persons so branding them, and the traffic of stolen hides, have found defenders in Texas, invoking reasons of public utility, in which we can only find the crime adorned with phrases that cannot bear analysis.

The military orders issued in 1869 were as ineffectual as the acts previously passed.

It was, perhaps, for this reason, that on the 22d of May,

1871, another act was passed, the most complete of all which had been enacted up to that date, dealing with cattle stealing in all its shapes.

Said act ordered the inspection of hides and animals in each county, with the exception of the counties situated on the west of the Colorado river, and towards the south of the Colorado branch of the same river, in which counties the inspection is confined to certain objects.

A public officer is to inspect all the hides, the sales of which have been notified to him, whenever said hides are to be exported from the county, destined for the market or for shipment, keeping a record of the marks and brands, names of the vendors and purchasers, and this officer is not to allow the exportation of a single animal or hide when the brand is not plain, or when the hide was branded subsequent to the flaying of the animal, and neither to allow unbranded cattle to be killed in the packeries and butcheries of the county, nor that they should be sold or shipped out of the county, unless the ownership be proved (Sec. 4th).

From its sundry provisions it follows that cattle stealing has distinct phases in Texas, which may be reduced to these two, viz: cattle stealing with a view to dispose of the heads out of the limits of the State, and with a view to disposing of them within said limits.

The first is committed in the shape of taking droves of cattle out of the State, either by land or water.

The second has the following forms: I. The appropriating of cattle belonging to other persons, altering their marks either on the animals or on the bills of sale. II. The driving of cattle destined for the butcheries and for consumption. III. The driving in lots to large establishments where enormous numbers of cattle are butchered. IV. The flaying of animals on the pastures to carry off the hides; and V. The stealing of young cattle, branding the heads which still follow their mothers.

The laws of Texas afford very interesting data in regard to cattle depredations committed there in late years. From 1850 to the present, we notice an ever-increasing demoralization, which assumed colossal proportions since the Confederate war.

The evil does not present a local character, but a general one, extending over all the States.

There is not a single shape in which cattle stealing can possibly be committed which has not been tried, and of its six phases, five have been committed by and to the profit of said residents of Texas.

The other phase, namely, when the crime is committed by exporting cattle out of the State, the exportation is made through the ports to Kansas, Missouri, and California, on the northern frontier, and to Mexico, on the southern.

The laws of Texas are, therefore, the first data necessary to understand that cattle stealing on the American frontier, with a view to introduce them into Mexico, is only an accessory to a vast question, and that its causes are not to be looked for on the Mexican frontier, but in the demoralization predominating in some of the masses of the inhabitants of Texas. The testimonial evidence referring to this question presented interesting details for the Commission, and is the commentary on the laws of Texas.

The Commission has already called attention to the vast number of cattle which are being exported to-day from Texas to Kansas.

There has been a case in which an entire drove taken to the last named State was composed of heads stolen by the drivers on several pastures; but this is an exceptional case.

In the majority of cases, when a drove is being formed, heads of cattle the property of other people are mingled with those of a legitimate source; and besides that, the drivers on their way either take deliberately whatever they may come across, or do not take the trouble to separate the heads that get mingled with their droves.

These are formed on the Nueces to be driven to the North, and several persons who have traveled in Texas, have seen occasionally heads of cattle bearing the brands of stock raisers in Cameron county, who never had sold them.

In regard to the droves carried to the ports, the same proceeding is adopted.

The large packeries of Texas are places where stolen cattle

are unscrupulously transported ; when the animal has been butchered, the hides, the fat, the hoofs and the horns are separated ; as to the meat, it is left without any blood and is fed to hogs.

The enormous number of cattle consumed in those establishments can well be appreciated by the exportation of hides, to which trade said establishments contribute to a large amount.

Cattle are rapidly consumed there, without their owners noticing their loss, or without having any means to prove it, in case they should notice it.

Their only protection is the law ordering the inspection of hides, the inefficacy of which is well tested by the very fact that hide stealing is committed daily on a very large scale, and the mischief is increasing instead of decreasing. We herewith annex extracts taken from several newspapers.

" We have heard that on several ranches in the interior of our country, cattle are being killed on the pasture only for the sake of the hides, without any consideration to property. There is a ranche which must be carrying on a very profitable business, as it is said that it can maintain continually traffic with two persons."—*The Sentinel*, Brownsville, Feb. 11, 1873.

" The news received from the northern portion of this county (Cameron) and from the south of the Nueces is very discouraging. The peelers are flaying daily thousands of heads. They don't wait for the animals to die, but shoot at those that have fallen, and their shots can be heard at any hour of the night. They have no respect for the rights of other people, their only object being to make money. They get four dollars on each hide, and as to the purchasers, they have no inclination to be more scrupulous in making the acquisition. * * * *The demoralization caused by the war is yet producing its bad effects.* The people of Texas will yet have to suffer terribly on account of the flayers, the cold and the lack of pasture."— *The Sentinel*, Brownsville, Feb. 14, 1873.

"Many stock raisers of Refugio county have been in our city for several days examining hides by virtue of injunctions, of which they bring their pockets full. They seem to be exasperated from having found the remains of animals killed on the pasture, evidently for the purpose of taking the hides."— *Goliad Guard.*

" A Commission of property owners have arrived in our city (San Antonio) in search of stolen hides taken from dead ani-

mals. We have been advised that a large number of troublesome lawsuits have been instituted against several of our
merchants to whom hides have been consigned for sale."—
San Antonio Weekly Herald, March 8, 1873.

" An organized band of cattle thieves, under the leadership
of the notorious thief Alberto Garza, are scouring Nueces and
Duval counties, said band numbering from twenty to thirty
men.

" The last number of the *Gaceta*, of Corpus Christi, gives an
interesting account of the operations of these banditti, who
killed and flayed in one place two hundred and seventy-five
heads in another three hundred, and in another sixty-six."—
Daily Ranchero, Brownsville, March 1, 1873.

Another newspaper, referring to this same band and to the
ineffectual persecution of it, says :

" We believe that the cattle owners of the Nueces and Rio
Grande ought to do something better than to run after these
robbers. They must direct their attention to the buyers of
hides. A little discipline exercised against these supporters of
thieves will soon put a stop to the trouble. If there were no
buyers the thieves would soon take another course. The merchant who buys from the thieves is worse than the thieves
themselves. He is only one, but he turns twenty into scoun-
drels, trusting in his position to save himself from reproach and
censure."—*The Sentinel*, May 2, 1873.

We are satisfied by these extracts that the act of 1871 was
as ineffectual as the previous acts, probably because demoralization has spread to some of the well-to-do and influential
classes of Texas society.

The last but one of the above mentioned newspapers says :

" We believe the proper time to have ascertained the
ownership of these hides was before they were exported from
the county where the cattle were flayed, and whilst said hides
were still in the possession of the first holders.

" It is somewhat strange to wait for the sale of the hides,
and for these to come in the hands of second or third innocent
parties, and then to waylay them at their place of destination."

The law of Texas contains provisions which, if complied
with, would guarantee all purchasers that the hides and cattle
they bought came from a legitimate source.

If ill-gotten hides are found in their hands, in the majority of cases, it must be attributed to a neglect on their part to fulfill the law, a neglect which has or can have no other causes than a want of scrupulousness in buying stolen property, and the neglect or complicity on the part of the inspectors of hides.

The above article is something more than an alteration of the legal principles guaranteeing to the owner the right to claim his property against whoever may hold it, be it in good or bad faith ; it is the defense of an illicit traffic, of a crime.

The region lying between the Rio Bravo and the Nueces does not constitute an exception as to cattle stealing in Texas ; on the contary, cattle stealing is committed there under all its forms, but its most important characters are twofold.

In the Nueces region, there is certain class of property owners, Americans by birth and nationality, who being influential on account of the wealth they have amassed, are completely unrestrained, because there are no laws or authorities in the county, or in the bordering counties, to restrain them who with absolute impunity commit the greatest depredations, and who unscupulously use their position to increase their wealth.

In the country between the Rio Bravo and the Nueces, the greatest number of property owners are Mexicans, and it is on their property that said depredations are committed.

Amongst the Mexicans it is the custom to mark the young animals every six months, and to brand them every six months afterwards.

The ownership of these young animals is recognized by the brands on the mothers they follow.

The mark is a cut on the ear, and a certain sign of ownership. In case the cow should die, the sign would prove the ownership.

Finally, the brand, which is a mark in the shape of letters, or other characters, which is stamped with a heated iron on the body of the animal, is the evidence of ownership when the animal has been separated from the cow.

Generally the American stock owners of the Nueces have no fixed period for branding their animals. There are some, for instance Richard King, owner of the hacienda Gertrudis

(Nueces), who has ·a large retinue of people in his service. (King's people sometimes number as many as sixty men.) These people visit all the pastures belonging to other owners, where most generally they introduce themselves without asking for the owner's permission, they there mark large collections of cattle, separating all the unbranded heads they find, even if these heads follow cows bearing brands of other owners. If they have marks on the ears, these are disfigured by another cut, then they are branded with the brand of the name of the person for whom they work, and carried off to his pastures.

Very often these heads leave the place and return to. their old pastures, and hence it is that young cattle bearing the brand of Richard King, or some other stock owner, have been seen following cows belonging to different owners.

Referring to this, a Texas newspaper, after mentioning the stealing of hides committed on a ranche adds the following:

" This ranch carries on another speculation, which consists in branding all the young cattle that can be found, regardless of their owners. * * * It is said that some men of the Nueces county not far from here came and collected all the calves they could find and branded .them for the benefit of those whom they serve. If this business continues nothing will be left to our stock raisers but their corrals and wells."—*The Sentinel*, Brownsville, Feb. 11, 1873.

An article published in *The Texas New Yorker*, pp. 110 and 111, " Cattle Raising in Western Texas," contains a paragraph which attracted the attention of the Commission. It says:

"In a large country like this (Texas) where there is so great a number of cattle, it is utterly impossible for the owners to find opportunely the calves to brand them. Before the calves are weaned it is easy to tell to whom they belong by the mark and brand of the cow, and no unauthorized person would touch them, even if their owner should be a hundred miles distant ; but after the calves have been weaned, and when they cease following any particular cow, no one can tell to whom they belong, and it has been the custom for any person having cattle on the pasture to mark these maverick calves with their sign and brand. * * * Our cow hunters divide equally among themselves the maverick calves. Occasionally some young men who have no cattle of their own will take part in these expeditions, or they will give their services by the year to receive a *pro rata* of all the maverick cattle that may be found. I know of several who have begun in this manner, and who are to-day large and respectable stock owners. It is a matter of course that these maverick heads are by no means divided in equal shares. The man who is going rapidly after his cattle brands not only what is his own, but brands also whatever his neighbor leaves unmarked or unbranded.

"*We have had many laws on the subject, but nothing has changed or will be able to change the habit.*

"Should a law be passed making it a crime to mark or brand a calf, the ownership of which has not been identified by the fact of its following a cow, ten years afterwards, these cattle would outnumber the branded cattle, would belong to no one, and would injure the country, bellowing on thousands of hillocks.

"By studying these questions with a sincere wish to discover the truth, any person will immediately understanding why the Texas laws relating to maverick cattle have been ineffectual, and why there is such an interest in preserving the custom that the stock raiser should brand all that kind of cattle he came across.

"Under the shadow of this custom the greatest depredations have been and are still being committed on the property of Mexican stock raisers.

"The laws relating to the inspection of cattle (corridas de ganado), in force in the frontier States of Mexico, and tending to avoid like depredations as are committed in Texas, convince us that there is no foundation in the reason on which said custom is pretended to be based.

"These reasons are substantially the fear that the maverrick calves may turn into wild cattle, and in the lapse of time be so numerous as to frighten the tame cattle, and turn them also into wild cattle.

"This fear *obliges* all the owners who may find such kind of cattle to appropriate them, and under this pretext they appropriate also unbranded calves, notwithstanding that the ownership is well determined by their following cows bearing brands of different owners.

"In said laws it is determined the manner in which the inspection (corrida) is to be made; the conditions necessary to performing the same on pastures belonging to other owners; the notice that is to be given to all the owners in order that they may present themselves and take care of their property;

the persons who have a right to the maverick calves, and the manner in which they are to be distributed.

"All these circumstances are well preconsidered, and to show how well grounded those fears are.

"There are no such laws in Texas to secure cattle owners from the depredations of which they have been the victims up to the present."

The article from which we copied the above paragraphs was written with a view to encourage immigration to Western Texas, by showing how easy it is to make a fortune there by stock raising. To this effect several cases of large fortunes are cited, and amongst others (The Texas New Yorker, p. 111) the case of an inhabitant of the Nueces, who began to work in 1865. His compensation was a share in the maverick calves at first; he afterwards received a certain number of cattle on the third part of the profits. From others he received a dollar a a head to collect cattle for them, and fifty cents for branding their calves. In this way he had obtained in the beginning of 1872 a fortune in lands, and seven thousand heads of meat cattle.

Now, no matter how favorable the circumstances of Texas might be supposed to be, it is impossible to acquire such a large capital in so short a time, and by such means. Wealth made so rapidly must generally be attributed to other causes than honest work. Right alongside of some large stock owners, to whom neither droughts nor any *other* calamity of that kind is a hindrance to the progressing of their cattle, there are others whose cattle are in a state of decadence, or are stationary. The lands are the same; the conditions of labor equal, and the influences of nature also equal; and still one cattle improves and augments whilst the other is diminished and perishes. The depredations committed by the first on the property of the last stock raisers explain this contradictory situation in the same locality.

And this is by no means the only grievance suffered by the Mexican owners in their cattle. During the cold weather, when the cattle of the Nueces take refuge in the most southern parts, or when, on account of the drought, they have gone in late years to other pastures, the American stock owners of the

Nueces, in collecting their cattle, have carried away with them large numbers of heads belonging to Mexican owners, even though they were marked, and there is no relief from these depredations, as there is none from the others. To the ignorance of the language, of the laws and of their rights, is added all that the prejudice of race can imagine to constitute these Mexicans into an oppressed class. They do not enjoy the full protection of the laws, and justice is in the hands or is controlled by their adversaries. There are some who dare not use their property with absolute liberty; for instance, in several counties, they do not brand their cattle by themselves, fearing that some imaginary crimes may be invented to injure them, but they bargain with the foreman of some American party to brand them, paying them fifty cents for each calf branded.

The Commission has heretofore examined cattle stealing in Texas in its general forms, inferring that the commission of the crime, with a view to carry the stolen cattle to the bank of the Rio Bravo does not present the aspect of the principal question, much less, of the exclusive one; but that is one of the many details of the vast demoralization under which Texas is laboring. But as this phase of the question affects the friendly relations of the two frontiers, the Commission studied it in a very prolix manner.

VII.

The robberies committed from the interior of Texas to the line of the river, have been carried to the American and to the Mexican banks. Both are so confounded that it may be said that they recognize the same cause and were perpetrated by the same parties, there being no other difference between one bank and the other than the places of consumption, and of the dealers who brought to the market the meat of cattle stolen in Texas.

The direct causes of the ruling demoralization on the American bank of the Rio Bravo are four, viz: the practice of cattle stealing, dating as far back as 1848, on Mexican soil for

Texas, under the protection and connivance of citizens and residents of the United States; the organizing of armed forces on both frontiers during the Confederate war by agents of the United States government to combat the Texan forces; the driving of large droves of stolen cattle, collected on the pastures, during the Confederate war, by Americans, who took into their service a large body of men with a view to commit those depredations; the appointing of commissions by the commanders of the United States forces, on both occasions of the occupation of Brownsville, in order that said commissions should go to the pastures on the Bravo and the Nueces to take the cattle which was said to be confiscated to the Confederates.

The first cause was anterior to the civil war in the United States, and gave rise to the existence of a mass of immoral people who would not lose the opportunity to commit in Texas the crimes of which Mexico had been the victim up to that date. The other causes require greater explanation.

When the civil war broke out in the United States, efforts were made to force the Mexicans living in Texas, whether or not they had American citizenship, to take a part in favor of the Confederates. Either on account of their dislike to the Confederate cause, or on account of their living amongst its defenders, those very persons from whom they had received so many vexations, the fact is the great majority of the Mexicans presented an absolute resistance, and it was only a small number who joined the Confederates. The rest found themselves persecuted and more oppressed than ordinary, the most remarkable event being the raid by the Confederates on Rancho Clareño, Zapata county (Texas), in April, 1861, in which raid several inoffensive inhabitants were assassinated.

By cause of these persecutions the Mexican inhabitants of Texas took refuge on the Mexican frontier, abandoning their interests and property. The agents of the United States Government conceived that a powerful ally could be found in those inhabitants, on account of the past oppressions and the hatred of the present, and they tried to utilize it. It was at this time that the organizing of bodies of men on Mexican soil took place, at the expense and in the service of the United States, for the purpose of crossing into Texas to give hostilities to the Confederates. It is easy to conceive the bitter discussions carried on for this reason, between the authorities of the Confederation and Mexico. The Commission has collected all the data it had within its reach relating to these difficulties, which they will fully discuss further on, limiting itself now to characterize those facts in their general aspect.

On September 27th, 1862, the Confederate commandant of Ringgold Barracks, wrote to the authorities of Camargo, as follows:

"During the last twenty-four hours, the band of marauders under the command of Vela, * * * * after having raised the *Yankee* flag, the flag of our enemies, on Mexican territory, which pretends to be neutral, threatened to invade Texas, with the manifest purpose of assassinating, robbing and destroying the peaceful citizens of this State, whenever and wherever they might be found; and carrying into execution their threat, they crossed the Rio Bravo, at the distance of eighteen miles from here, intercepted four wagons loaded with provisions belonging to the Confederate States, assassinated three of the drivers, and captured and destroyed said property. This same band captured a Mr. Kifles, private in the company of Captain R. Benavides, in the service of the Confederation, and said individual is believed to have been assassinated. Moreover, another band under the command of the notorious thief and assassin, Octaviano Zapata, crossed at a distance of forty miles from here, at the Clareño Ranch, took away the horses belonging to the company of Benavides, whilst they were grazing, and hung a boy citizen of the Confederate States, called Juan Vela."

On the 20th of January, 1863, the same military commander wrote:

" I am duly informed that these bands are continuing to be organized, on the western bank of the river; their intentions are not only hostile to my government, but they boast of being the allies of *Yankee despotism.*"

About 1862, Octaviano Zapata, who was one of the refugees of Cariño Ranche, entered into the service of the United States. He organized in Mexico a party of from sixty to eighty men, paid by the agents of the United States Government at the rate of two hundred dollars for the enlistment of each man. Said force was maintained in Mexico, avoiding the persecution of the Confederates, and whenever a favorable chance presented itself, they would cross over to the American side of the river and carry hostilities to the Confederates.

On January 6th, 1863, the Confederate officer in command at Carrizo, wrote to the president of the town council of Mier, as follows :

" I have the pleasure to advise you that within the surroundings of this place some parties of men are being organized for the purpose of carrying hostilities into Texas, *under pretext of the government of the North*, and the commander of said parties is Octaviano Zapata. * * * There is no doubt that said parties do exist, as they have robbed me of thirty-two horses at Carrizo, and I expect of you, that you will catch the robbers, as otherwise I will be obliged to cross over to that side with my force and persecute them until I chastise them."

Zapata continued in this manner until he was killed on Mexican territory by a Confederate force who invaded our soil with that purpose.

The enlistment and organizing of men on Mexican territory continued. One of the cases known by the Commission was that of Regino Ramon, who was enlisted in Camargo, Mexico, in 1864, by agents of the United States Government. The object of the enlistment was for Ramon to organize a force of Mexican volunteers on both sides of the river to carry hostilities to the Confederates. He was to receive a third part of all the prizes captured from the Confederate forces, or from all those who, although they did not actually belong to said forces, they had manifestly taken part in the rebellion. Ramon, in the capacity of first lieutenant in the United States army, organized a force composed of Mexicans of both sides of the river, and went to the war. He attacked and captured a train of wagons. He subsequently, and after a skirmish, captured a party of Confederate lawyers in Rome, Texas, and also bought and captured seventeen wagons at Prieto. In all these instances he followed the instructions of the United States agents, to whom he delivered the captured persons and property.

The Commission possesses no data to judge if these guerrillas caused any harm to cattle in Texas. It is an unquestionable fact that in the latter part of 1862 or the beginning of 1863, stolen cattle were transported to the bank of the Rio Grande, and though the Confederate officers endeavored to hold in their correspondence with the Mexican authorities that the mischief was committed by said guerillas, there is no evidence to show that this was the case. The only well defined case is that of Guillermo Vinas, who belonged to Zapata's force, and who, in 1862, stole some cattle in Texas and crossed to Mexico, from whence a difficulty arose between the two frontiers.

But it is easily perceived that the violation of neutrality of the Mexican territory, the organizing of armed forces initiated or accomplished thereon, the fact of constituting said territory into a basis of operations hostile to Texas, and the authorizing by the agents of the United States government undisciplined forces to cross over to the American territory and carry hostilities to the Confederates, would necessarily give rise to loose habits amongst the inhabitants of the two frontiers, from which nothing but evil could result. On the other hand, even granting that said forces should do harm to the cattle, it was very likely that under their shadow, and pretending to have a political character, bands of robbers should be organized, who under the pretext of hostilities should commit robberies in Texas, taking refuge in Mexico, there to reorganize and return to Texas. Amongst other charges against the Mexican frontier, it is said that even previous to 1866 armed bands organized on Mexican soil used to cross over to the United States and make hostile incursions on American soil. By studying the question we are convinced that neither Mexico nor her authorities or people authorized said incursions, nor are they blamable for the subsequent difficulties connected with cattle stealing in Texas.

The Commission has collected innumerable and sundry documents, taken from several archives, referring to the relations of the two frontiers during the Confederate war, in all of which documents the foresight of the Mexican authorities is remarkable. They made repeated efforts to put a stop to the invasions organized in Mexico against Texas. Possessing a thorough knowledge of the frontier, the authorities perceived that the policy adopted by the United States agents could not produce any benefit whatever to them, but in lieu grave difficulties would then arise for Mexico, preparing evils for the future, and creating new elements of immorality (Report of the U. S. Commissioners to Texas, page 6), which would give vigor to those already existing.

During the Confederate war a large number of cattle were abandoned. The Mexicans left their property and took refuge on this side of the river, some enlisting in the army. Many persons availed themselves of this opportunity to brand all the young cattle they could secure, and at the close of the war found themselves in possession of great wealth in stock, when it was a notorious fact that they had not a single head of neat cattle or horse when the war began, or their stock was very reduced. But said circumstances were utilized besides in another manner. In the state of abandonment in which cattle were left, several individuals, some of whom are proprietors to-day, or were so at that time, took into their service great numbers of people. These entered the pastures, made large collections of cattle, separating all the heads that suited them, regardless of their brands, and formed droves which they transported to the Rio Bravo, where they sold them on both banks. Amongst others who acted in this manner were the Wrights, of Banquete Ranche, Texas, Billy Mann and Patrick Quinn.

At the conclusion of the Confederate war the evil increased ; during said war the Texas forces had committed many depredations ; several of their officers transported cattle to Matamoros for sale, amongst whom was William D. Thomas (known as Thomas Colorado). When the war was over and the forces were disbanded, a large number of people were left without any occupation, and the bands who used to bring stolen cattle to the banks of the river increased. The Wrights had the largest force under them. Sometimes William D. Thomas, Billy Mann, Patrick Quinn, and others, would combine with them, and others, each would act on his own account. The Wrights were dedicated to this trade up to 1866, this at least being the last year that one of them made sale of cattle in Matamoros, according to the knowledge of this Commission.

But it is not difficult to perceive tracks of demoralization which these and other similar organizations left behind them. There were regular bands of banditti, paid by the leaders who formed them, and who received the benefit of their plunder. The leader might disappear, but he had shown them the way and had trained them in the career of robbery.

Brownsville, and a portion of the American frontier of the Rio Bravo, were for the first time occupied by the forces of the United States, at the latter part of 1863; they were again occupied near the downfall of the Confederation, and, during the intervening time, the United States maintained a detachment of troops at Brazo de Santiago. On both occasions, the military commander appointed commissioners to examine the pastures, to collect all the cattle belonging to Confederates, and to transport the same to the bank of the river, subject to the orders of said forces. This proceeding was adopted under the principle that the Confederates had forfeited all their property.

All the Commissioners had a certain number of men under their orders, through whom they carried on their orders, through whom they carried on their expeditions. Without detailing the abuses they may have committed in the fulfillment of their trust, we may form an idea of the consequences originating from such a situation, by noticing that some of these agents and their companions were afterwards very busily employed in cattle stealing. The best authenticated of this class of cases are those of Joseph Paschall and José Maria Martinez, the latter a Mexican by birth, and citizen of Bexar, Texas, captain in the irregular army of the United States, and who afterwards formed a band of robbers on the Mexican frontier, and was killed by a Mexican posse.

Bearing in mind these antecedents, it will not seem strange that cattle stealing should be practiced. There were many criminals, who had always found refuge on the American frontier; to these people, from whom Mexico had suffered so many wrongs, a new field was opened, where they might exercise their inclinations to crime. The behavior of the residents of

Texas, who tried to amass wealth at the expense of others, the policy followed by the United States agents, who organized hostilities on the Mexican frontier against Texas, and the subsequent confiscations, augmented the number of criminals, created new habits of crime, added new strength to those already in existence, gave a new direction to the movement of crime on the line of the Rio Bravo, and the demoralization thus produced, was superadded to the general demoralization prevailing in the State of Texas.

The war was the general cause, but in each locality, special causes were added. The Commission has enunciated those that exist on the banks of the Bravo. They convince us that our frontier had no participation in creating that situation. But the reverse has notwithstanding been maintained. A local character has been assigned to the demoralization, limiting it to the line of the Bravo, so as to make it appear, that the Mexican people, especially those living on our soil, are the cause and the instrument of the crimes committed in Texas. Reference has been made to the criminal statistics of Cameron county, and by comparing former times to present, an excessive increase of criminality has been detailed, the explanation of which has been sought for in the tendencies of our people to disorder and crime.

VIII.

Two are the questions involved in these appreciations : First, the general question as to the State of Texas ; and second, the special one relating to the robberies committed on the line of the Bravo.

Demoralization is not peculiar to the Rio Bravo valley, and neither is it a question of race or nationality. Between this river and the Nueces, the majority of the inhabitants are of Mexican origin, from whence it necessarily follows that the generality of robbers there must belong to that race. But as these practice cattle stealing under one form, the American proprietors of the Nueces practice it under another. Extreme demoralization prevails in this region, but by no means greater than in all the rest of Texas. Some extracts from the newspapers convince of this.

" There is not a single prisoner in the prison of this county (Hidalgo), not for lack of criminals, but because none bring their complaints to the judges. The disorganized condition of the county ever since the war broke out ; the impossibility of investigating and punishing crime ; the danger to which the witnesses are exposed by giving their depositions, are undoubtedly the causes of this abnormal state of affairs."—*Daily Ranchero*, Brownsville, July 6th, 1871.

" There are yet some disorders on account of the lynchers in the counties of Comanche and Erath. A short time ago fifteen horse thieves were hung, and the perpetrators of the deed were arrested and tried by the Courts. * * * State police is a *desideratum* in some parts of Texas."—*Galveston Standard*, February 7th, 1873.

" Amongst other proceedings of the legislature on the 14th, we hear that the special committee appointed to visit Madison county, to investigate the disturbances that have so much alarmed the governor, has returned and reported as the result of their investigation, that ten or fifteen desperadoes were the cause of the alarms and disorders in the county. Said committee censured severely the district judge, the sheriff, and the judicial functionaries ;° some, because they sympathized with the criminals, and all because of their incompetency."—*San Antonio Weekly Herald*, February 22, 1873.

" We have seen of late several attempts at horse stealing in this city, which shows the presence of a band of robbers among us, who must be watched, and should the opportunity occur, be entertained with a small quantity of lead. We are satisfied that this band is managed by the notorious thief, Lem Murray, whom, it seems, no efforts are made by our officers to arrest, notwithstanding it is well known that he comes to the city every night."—*Indiana Bulletin*.

" *The Courier of Sherman* relates a thorough slaughter in those places. The existence of a band of robbers, organized some time ago is reported, having their headquarters near Collinsville. Several nights ago an officer called Keltner, backed by a *posse*, went to the place where this band was, killed some of them and dispersed the rest ; one of the *posse*, called Stakes, was killed in the attack. Jim Campbell, Rob Broyles, Bill

Brewster, and two others of the gang were killed, and still the work has hardly begun. There are some twenty more implicated, and it is feared that their lives will be sacrificed before the tumult may be quelled."—*San Antonio Weekly Express*, March 20th, 1873.

"The Governor (of Texas) sent yesterday (March 26th) to both houses the report of Adjutant General Britton, in regard to the firing at the police in Lampazos. Said report shows that a reign of terror and crime are prevailing in that county, which the authorities and inhabitants are unable to counteract. A panic prevailed after the assassination of the public men, the inhabitants shut their places of business, barred their doors, and waited with anxiety the arrival of General Britton and his men, for him to disperse the half hundred of banditti who controlled the city."

"Four of the party who assassinated Captain Williams and his men were arrested by the Adjutant General. The assassins were only fifteen, but they were reinforced afterwards by their friends and numbered fifty. These, after the arrival of General Britton and his police force, dispersed."

The report says:

"These men bear the worst character, and they are so dreadful to the residents of the county in which they live, that a simple outcry of theirs, uttering *hide*, is sufficient for all to shut their doors as soon as they hear it. Up to the present they have been amusing themselves by unloading their six shooters on the knobs of the doors of those persons who have incurred their displeasure by helping the sheriff or other officers of the county to bring to justice the transgressors of the law." —*Galveston Standard*, April 3d, 1873.

All the Texas newspapers perused by this Commission published continual accounts of such disturbances, that by far surpass those occurring on the banks of the Bravo. In order to form a just idea of this question, it is proper to make an abstract of the message addressed by the Governor of Texas to the House of Representatives, on the 19th of last April, vetoing a bill to repeal the act creating the police force of the State.

The Governor, referring to his annual message in regard to the police, said that he had expressed the opinion that their services were still needed, basing his opinion on the information he had received in regard to the condition of the State; that having been advised that a majority of the two houses were of

adverse opinions, he required the Adjutant General to furnish
a report of homicides and attempts to commit homicide perpetrated in each county from the 15th of January of this year;
that according to the official information received from twenty-
nine counties, and that received from private sources in twenty-
five others, seventy-eight homicides and seventy-two attempts
at homicide had been committed during that period; that very
likely the number of such crimes committed in the counties
from which he had received private information was greater
than that mentioned in the report; that in the balance of the
one hundred and thirty-five counties into which the whole
State was divided, in all probability the average number of
homicides was greater than that of the fifty-four counties he had
heard from; but even taking this as an average, it would appear that during the first three months of the year (195) one
hundred and ninety-five homicides had been committed in the
State, and following this average for the rest of the year it
would give the result of (780) seven hundred and eighty homicides during the whole year; that notwithstanding, and as a
consequence of the repressive acts of 1870 and 1871, this condition was better than in 1867, as could be shown by comparing
the criminal statistics collected by the military authorities of
that time; but still there was much yet to do in order to civilize
the State, and instead of abolishing the means of punishing the
criminals, it was imperative to enlarge and give vitality to the
same; that in order to show the disorderly condition of the
State and the extraordinary insecurity of life, the preceding
facts could be compared to the criminal statistics of New York,
which State, although it contained a city of over a million of
inhabitants, and notwithstanding that in large cities crimes are
always greater, there were only thirty-seven homicides in 1860,
its population being then composed of three millions, eight
hundred and eighty thousand, seven hundred and thirty-seven
inhabitants, (3,880,737), when Texas, according to the census
of 1870, contained eight hundred and eighteen thousand, five
hundred and seventy-nine inhabitants (818,579). Moreover,
and apart from the special crime of homicide, fourteen counties
had, through commissions composed either of citizens or officers,

applied to the State authorities for help for the purpose of controlling certain criminal combinations too strong for the local
authorities; that the public records had been taken by force
and destroyed in two counties; in two other counties the criminal dockets and records had likewise been destroyed, and in a
fifth the cattle registry had disappeared; that there was a
desire to conceal this situation from all those who were invited
to settle in Texas, but it did not behoove a government to over-
look them. Said Governor goes on examining the sundry
means proposed to put a stop to the evil, and concludes that
the police force is the best. He mentions that the police have
arrested (581) five hundred and eighty-one persons accused of
assassinating, and some *thousands* of other classes of criminals;
that many hundreds of assassins, cattle stealers and other criminals had fled from the State to avoid arrest; that fourteen
policemen had been killed and many more had been wounded
by the criminals; that the measures proposed to repeal the
police laws were contemporary with the increase of the criminals, and that if the police system was defective, on account of
which some bad men were employed in the police force, the
government was disposed to adopt such modifications that
should give greater efficacy to said force.

This document shows the grossest immorality in a considerable portion of the inhabitants of Texas. By the newspaper
extracts we have inserted above, it may be observed that those
crimes have been committed in such counties where there are
no Mexican residents, and where forty or fifty criminals combine to control whole cities, placing themselves above the authorities. Notwithstanding our revolutions, the Mexican frontier has never arrived at such a condition, nor are the crimes
committed between the Rio Bravo and the Nueces attended
with such circumstances as those committed in the remaining
portion of Texas. When the moral condition of our frontier is
far superior to that of Texas, it does not seem proper that the
causes of the existing criminality of the counties situated alongside of the Bravo should be looked for on the Mexican border.
There are great centers of corruption and unprecedented immorality in Texas, and it is more reasonable to suppose that its

pernicious influence spreads to the region of the Bravo and
the Nueces, for the general motives from which that corruption
had sprung would be necessarily felt there, and even reach our
border. To look on the Mexican border, which is less vicious,
for the cause of the depravity prevailing in Texas is tantamount
to reverse entirely the rules of nature.

The Commission examined also the criminal statistics of
Cameron county, through the authentic data which came to
their hands, and they did not find anything that could change
their views.

" In the statement of indictments drawn from the criminal
records of the District Courts of Cameron county, Texas, down
to the spring term of 1866," there appears (39) thirty-nine indictments, eight of which were dismissed, and (31) thirty-one
are still pending for the arrest of the accused. The functionary
who certifies the statement adds the following note :

" During the rebellion the records of the District Court of
Cameron county, Texas, from the organization of the county,
in 1848 to the spring term in 1866, were mutilated to a great
extent. The above statement comprises those cases in which
no judgment was passed before the rebellion, as far as any
certainty can be acquired, and were collected from the best data
obtained in the spring of 1866, and the subsequent terms. The
cases adjudicated or otherwise decided before 1866 are not included in this statement, and there are no data in my office to
determine their number."

Consequently, according to this statement it is not known
who were the persons condemned and who the persons acquitted. The principal data are wanting, and this must have constituted a greater number of indictments. This, notwithstanding we have compared this very incomplete statement with the
statistical *resume* of 1866 to 1872. This *resume* gives the following result : (382) three hundred and eighty-two indictments.
Of these (145) one hundred and forty-five ended in condemna-
tory judgments; in (50) fifty the accused were absolved, (102)
one hundred and two cases were dismissed on *nolle prosequi*,
and (85) eighty-five are yet pending for arrest of the accused.

A special comparison has been made as to the indictments
for assassinations. According to the first statement (8) eight
occurred in the space of thirteen years, and (40) forty according

to the second in the space of six years. This increase seems rather excessive at first sight, but by examining these data we find that the first eight cases are still pending for arrest of the accused, and the number of those that have been either acquitted or condemned is not known ; whilst in the last statement, in (13) thirteen cases the criminals were condemned, in (8) they were acquitted, (6) six cases ended by dismissal on *nolle prosequi*, and (13) thirteen are still pending for arrest of the criminals. It is therefore impossible to come to any conclusion derived from a comparison between the two statements, and even more, to state that in the towns on the Mexican border a tendency is developing to assassinate American citizens.

Criminality has certainly been increasing in the region lying between the Bravo and the Nueces rivers, but not on such a scale as has been maintained, and this increase is due to the *augmenting demoralization, the want of good* (Report of the U. S. Commissioners, page 34) police system, and to the interest of many influential persons in keeping up that state of disorganization. But we can easily perceive by the message of the Governor of Texas, which we have just cited, that these conditions are not peculiar to that region of the country. A Texas newspaper says :

"In 1862 Texas had only (22) twenty-two convicts in her penitentiary ; in 1872 she had (944) nine hundred and forty-four."—*San Antonio Weekly Herald*, March 22, 1873.

By comparing the two figures it will be obvious that in point of increasing criminality Cameron has fared as all the rest of Texas, and that the Mexican frontier has had no influence whatever in that condition. Causes which are general to all the State have necessarily produced consequences equally general.

Circumscribing our attention to cattle stealing especially, in order to precise the influence that our frontier may have exercised in regard to the increase of criminalty in Texas, it is necessary that we should determine who have been the cattle stealers.

The Commission reserving for another place the discussion of the charges made against General Cortina's troops, and to express their opinion on the subject, will, for the present, direct their attention to the other individuals who have been accused. They can be classified in the four following groups:

The 1st group comprises residents of both frontiers, who began to commit depredations in Texas since armed forces were organized on Mexican territory by the United States, for the purpose of carrying hostilities to the Confederates. This group is formed of Mexicans, many of whom are either naturalized or reside in the United States, a fact proved by the several criminal proceedings consulted by the Commission. As to race, therefore, they may be called Mexicans, but they were under the jurisdiction of the State of Texas when committing the crime.

As to Mexicans residing in Mexico, there is no doubt that several of them committed robbery in Texas.

On the 16th of January, 1864, the local judicial authority of Las Cuevas communicated to the alcalde of Reynosa that, "considering it private duty of every citizen to preserve public order, which was being violated by several individuals whose occupation was to bring stolen cattle from the left bank of the river to the Mexican border, he advised him of this fact, in order that he might communicate the same to the chief of the rural police if he deemed it advisable." On the 19th of May, 1869, the custom house officers of Reynosa captured a drove of cattle stolen in Texas, which had been smuggled into Mexico by Dionisio Menduola, a resident of Las Cuevas.

On the 10th of May, 1871, the Mexican commander of the post on the line of the Bravo, Mexico, advised the alcalde of Reynosa that according to public rumors in Brownsville, a party of men were being formed in the ranche of "Las Cuevas," with the sole object of invading the ranches of Texas. In response the alcalde reported that having sent a secret commission to said ranche, he had learned that the residents of "Las Cuevas" held property on the left bank of the Bravo, and for this reason they crossed the river every day in larger or smaller groups, but the places where such a band did exist, as it was of public notoriety, were the ranches called Valadeses,

Villarsales, Potrero de Los Longorias, Laja, Tepeguage and San Francisco. The Commission based their opinion on these and other less important documents. The Commission presumes, although possessing no clear data by which to be guided, that some of the criminals classified in the first group have been living also on some other ranches belonging to the Mexican border, acting in connivance with robbers living on the Texas line. To this and to no other cause, in the judgment of the Commission, is to be attributed that the bands of robbers should have been able to support themselves during the last years, notwithstanding the persecution carried against them on both sides of the river.

2d. The second group of cattle thieves are the American Texans, who, during and after the Confederate war, formed droves of cattle and transported them to the banks of the river. The Commission designate as comprised in this category the Wrights, owners of Banquete, William D. Thomas (alias Thomas Colorado), Billy Mann, Patrick Quinn and Charles Karr.

In regard to these three last named, the Commission obtained certified copies of five indictments by the grand jury of Cameron county, on the 1st of March, 1868, against them and against Peter Marnill. These indictments express that said individuals stole cattle belonging to Henry A. Gilpin, Y. H. Clark, R. King & Co., which firm was composed of Richard King and Mifflin Kennedy. Patrick Quinn was not only accused of being an accomplice in the robbery, but also of having incited and enticed Peter Marnill into it. These four indicted individuals are American citizens, and they have been and are now residents of Texas. Several persons were witnesses in these indictments, and amongst others, Mifflin Kennedy and Richard King stood witnesses in five of the indictments, Adolphus Glaevecke in three, and Dominick Lively in two of them. The five indictments were dismissed.

This documentary evidence corroborates the depositions of several witnesses in regard to the existence of bands of thieves under the leadership of the aforementioned individuals. The stolen cattle, to which said indictments referred, belonged to persons who afterwards filed claims against Mexico, alleging that the robberies of cattle in Texas were perpetrated since 1866 by bands of Mexicans organized on the Mexican frontier. But our attention is specially called to the fact that Mifflin Kennedy, Richard King, Adolphus Glaevecke and Dominick Lively, on whose testimony the indictments of the grand jury were based, should notwithstanding complain of having received injuries in their property, which they impute exclusively to robbers living and organized on Mexican soil—injuries which Kennedy and King, in what concerns them alone, raise to millions of dollars. Patrick Quinn and his accomplices had stolen the cattle of these complainants, and they well knew it, since they could stand as witnesses against them ; and this, notwithstanding they intentionally omitted to mention these circum-· stances in their complaints, trying to prove that it was only by the hands of Mexicans residing in Mexico and organizing under the protection of our authorities, that they had received injuries in their cattle. They therefore affirmed under oath facts, the incorrectness of which they were perfectly convinced in the intimacy of their conscience.

Nor were these the only Americans residing in Texas who dedicated themselves to cattle stealing to carry their plunder into Mexico. In 1871, Nathaniel White took over to Matamoros a flock of sheep, and was extradited upon a petition of the courts of Texas, who condemned him to several years confinement in the penitentiary. Besides these individuals there were others whose names were not known or remembered by the witnesses.

3d. The third category of cattle thieves who committed robbery in Texas and carried their plunder to the banks of the Rio Bravo, comprises those who organized and committed robbery in consequence of the commissions given to confiscate cattle belonging to the confederates. When these commissions ended, some of the commissioners continued in committing depredations, acting on their own account. Others, who never held such commissions, availed themselves of the reigning disorder, and organized regular gangs of robbers. Amongst the

6

first we have already mentioned Joe Paschall and José Maria Martinez.

The name of one Fernando Lopez, a native of Bexar, and domiciled in Texas, appears also on the records of the Com- mission in the capacity of agent for the confiscation of cattle. The Commission has no means in their power to ascertain the truth of this imputation ; but they discovered that at the time Lopez was believed to hold that position he transported to this side of the river cattle stolen in Texas.

Joe Paschall was in partnership with Peter Mainiel, and both, aided by several others, formed large collections of cattle on the pastures, separating such heads as they saw fit to form a drove. The Commission was never able to ascertain the length of time Paschall followed this sort of life.

Martinez was a captain in the United States forces. After being discharged, and after his commission to confiscate con- federate cattle had expired, he continued to bring cattle to the banks of the river, a large portion of which he crossed over into Mexico. At first he made believe that said cattle were legitimately acquired, and to this effect he showed bills of sale, which were found afterwards to be false; but after a certain length of time he was persecuted in Texas on account of his depredations, and towards 1868 he took refuge on our frontier with his band.

His band was increased by other robbers from Texas join- ing them. He established a ranche at Mezquitito, near the sea, in a lonesome place, and had there about three hundred cows, stolen from Texas. But this was of small consequence.

At the time Martinez and his second, Andres Flores, estab- lished themselves with their band of highway robbers in Mexico, there were other cattle thieves in Texas, whose most prominent leaders were Ricardo Flores, member at present of the police force of the State of Texas, and Pedro Lucio. Among these were also Pedro Cortina, Justo Lopez, Marcos Sanchez, Severiano Hi- nojosa, Angel Aguirre, Rodolfo Aguirre, Apolinar Rios, Apo- linar and Rafael Herevia, Juan Sanchez, Juan Saenz, and Angel Vazquez. These and other individuals were not precisely or- ganized in a regular band. They lived, and are still living, in the ranches of Texas, distant from each other. At times some of them would assemble to collect a drove of cattle, and occasionally would accompany Tomas Vazquez, a resident of Brownsville, or some other individuals for the same purpose. They acted also in accord with the band of José Maria Martinez and Andres Flores, who carried to them horses they had stolen in Mexico, and the former in exchange would turn over to said Martinez and Flores heads of neat cattle which they probably had stolen on the ranches where they lived.

The exchange of stolen horses in Mexico for cattle stolen in Texas, does not seem to have been exclusively practiced by these two organizations of robbers; nor does it appear that the persons employed on the ranches were accomplices in these robberies. There are some other similar data in the *expedientes* formed by this Commission, but we only mention them in a general manner, not deeming them to be sufficiently precise as to enable us to give with conscientiousness the names of the culprits.

We quote the following extracts from a correspondence dated at Rome, Star County, and published in a Texan newspaper :

"In Guerrero, Mexico," says the correspondent, " I was informed by the city authorities that there was an organized band of robbers, whose constant occupation was to steal horses in Mexico and carry them to Texas, where they in return stole horses and cattle to bring back to Mexico. The three principal leaders are, Atilano Alvarado, Procopio Gutierrez, and Landin, the former being the foreman of Captain R. King, on whose ranche he has lived for a number of years, and is well known to the stock-raisers of that section of the country ; our informer says also, I am sure they have many accomplices and co-operators on the ranches of Texas on this side of the river and all along the coast. Procopio Gutierrez resides a part of. the time in Texas, on San Bartolo ranche, Zapote county, with his adoptive father. * * * I crossed afterwards to the American side and investigated the matter in the most secret manner possible, and found all these things to be perfectly correct. * * * I asked several persons of the city whether they were doing anything to put a stop to the robbery. What can we do? they replied. Our sheriff lives on a ranch twenty-two miles from here, and has not come within the county

for several months, and even he himself has aided in transporting the stolen animals through his ranche over into Mexico on
the 10th or 12th of November. No one knows or can swear with
any certainty that said cattle had been stolen, but it is presumed
that the whole or a part of them were stolen, as the drivers
kept away from the collector of customs and from the inspect-
or of hides and cattle; and when an authority of the county
connives in the robbery, instead of preventing it, there is nothing to be done against such powerful bands of robbers."—*Daily
Ranchero*, Brownsville, January 12th, 1873.

4th. Under the fourth class of cattle thieves the Commission
place all the vagabonds living on the whole frontier, who are
always in readiness to commit any crime. It is certain some
of them accompanied the robbers of the three preceding classes,
but they did not act a principal part, and were rather co-operators, although now and then they would act on their own account, and in all probability they are the ones who had a
greater influence in cattle stealing during the last three years.
Auxiliaries and secondary accomplices at the beginning, they
got into a habit of stealing, and afterwards continued in the
path they had been shown by others under whose orders they
served.

The band appertaining to this class which had a more permanent character was that led by Pedro and Longinos, who
acquired notoriety, not so much for their participation in cattle
stealing, as for their being supposed to be in communication
and under the protection of General Cortina. The robberies
committed by the Lugos were those that afforded more grounds
to the newspapers to bring charges against the authorities of
our frontier, and for this reason the Commission made the
minutest investigations possible in regard to these individuals.

Further on the Commission will express their judgment in
regard to General Cortina ; here they will limit themselves to
the proceedings of the Lugos.

They were born in San Carlos, Tamaulipas. Being yet
quite young they committed a murder and fled to the interior
of Texas, where they lived for a long time. The Commission
does not know the precise time when they returned to the banks

of the river. The first notice we have of one of them (Pedro), is that he served as private in the 7th regiment of cavalry from February 13th to August 27th, 1871, when he deserted, mounted and armed.

It appears that Longinos Lugo was living by plunder when his brother met him. They formed an organization with other robbers to steal on both sides of the river. They both lived in Texas, two leagues distant from Brownsville, at a place called Las Trasquilas. Many witnesses saw them there with their families. They saw them when they had stolen cattle on the bank, and saw them likewise when they were transporting said cattle to the Mexican bank. It is understood that they fixed their residence on the bank of the river both to facilitate the transporting of their plunder, and to fly easily in case they should be persecuted.

To this band belonged Manuel Garcia Lugo, Lino Reyes, Macario Treviño, Cecilio Jaime, Margarito Garcia, Gerónimo Perez, Secundino Castro and others whose names have not been perfectly identified. They lived in Texas on ranches alongside the banks of the river, and they used to meet whenever an opportunity presented itself to commit robbery on either side of the river.

Some individuals of this band, amongst others the Lugos, accompanied José Maria Sanches Uresti the last time he crossed from Texas to Mexico with a view of stealing, although under pretext of political purposes. They were persecuted and the majority of them killed by the Mexican *posses* at the beginning of 1872. Some of those who escaped came from time to time to commit depredations, others were killed, and ever since then the depredations ceased on both frontiers in the places where the band of the Lugos had their quarters.

It is worthy of notice that these men and their bands of thieves should constitute one of the principal grounds of the attacks of the Brownsville press against our frontier, assuming the organization and existence of the outlaws was to be found there, under the protection of the authorities, when said outlaws lived and organized their bands on Texas land belonging to Alexander Wierbisky, the present Mayor of Cameron county. The reports collected by the Commission in regard to Wierbisky confirm that he is a person of irreproachable character, and incapable of giving any protection to criminals. It is therefore to be believed that he found himself in the same position as the land proprietors of those regions very often are placed, having to tolerate notorious criminals on their estates against their will, for fear of greater evils, and for want of sufficient protection on the part of the authorities. The only thing remarkable in the eyes of the Commission in regard to Wierbisky, is his having presented claims against Mexico for large sums of money, attributing the injuries that he and others alleged to have suffered in their cattle, to the depredations of robbers organized in Mexico, when he could not help having a thorough knowledge of the place where the Lugos lived ; that said place was the headquarters of a gang of outlaws, and therefore affirmed under oath a statement which was not exactly correct.

By examining through the general character of the circumstances of the individuals who have been stealing cattle to transport them to the bank of the Rio Bravo, we come to the conclusion that our frontier not only has not had the *unique* influence in this aspect of the robbery, nor in the increase of criminality in Texas, but its influence has been very secondary.

Leaving aside the course which gave rise to this crime, and taking only into consideration the persons who have committed the same, it is noticed that it originated in Texas, and that there was an increase of demoralization, which was not to stop at the banks of the Rio Bravo. Quite the contrary, it overflowed into our frontier, giving vitality to the natural elements of disorder that have always existed there, and sowing in it new grounds of corruption, that necessarily would fructify in due time.

The depredations committed by the Wrights, Patrick Quinn, Joe Paschall, and others, was the school in which many were taught stealing in Texas, carrying their plunder to the line of the Bravo. The band of José Maria Martinez and Andres Flores was composed of individuals from Texas, as was also a part of the band of the Lugos; the band which is said to exist in Guerrero is under the leadership of Atilano Alvarado, a resident of Texas, and a number of individuals living in the United States are comprised in said band, and finally it was through individuals living in Texas that droves of stolen cattle were delivered to the robbers.

The traffic in stolen cattle on our frontier was the result of those robberies committed in Texas. It is evident in many cases the purchasers were innocent, especially at the beginning; but when in years subsequent to 1866 cattle stealing in Texas was made a notorious fact, the purchasers were in duty bound to investigate the origin of the cattle, and thoroughly ascertain that they were not constituting themselves accomplices of an illicit trade.

The conduct observed by Dionisio Cardenas and Nicolas Solis was the object of an investigation. They have been bitterly denounced by the Brownsville newspapers, and the circumstance that said individuals have been employed in the city council of Matamoros, requires minute investigation.

In regard to the former, the Commission is perfectly convinced that he was connected in the shameful traffic of stolen cattle in Texas, which he was in the habit of buying for his packery. It appears that in 1869, when a drove of stolen cattle being driven by Patrick Quinn was pursued by the police, they were found in the corral of Dionisio Cardenas. He, in explanation, said that he had no reason to distrust Quinn; but in the opinion of the Commission, he ought to investigate whom he purchased from, considering the antecedents then existing. It would have been easy for him to find it out, as in the neighboring town of Brownsville he could have acquired all the necessary data, and learned that Patrick Quinn was under pending indictments for cattle stealing.

On the other hand, this was not the only case investigated by the Commission. There are foundations to believe that Pedro Mainiel delivered to Cardenas several droves of Texan cattle, which were consumed in the butchery of Cardenas. He could not but know that Mainiel was not the owner of the cattle, nor was it possible for him not to surmise the origin of said cattle. This cause, leaving aside the first one, is sufficient for the Commission to form their opinion.

A grave reason for suspecting the conduct of Nicolas Solis presents itself to the candid mind. On the 30th of June, 1871, the commander of the rural force of the eastern section of Reynosa informed the judge that eleven heads of cattle had been transported in a clandestine manner through the ranche of La Bolsa, proceeding from the Texas bank. From the communications written on this subject it is apparent that said commander made minute investigations relating thereto, seized two heads, and that Nicolas Solis carried to Matamoros four of them.

Some explanations are necessary in order to understand the true import of this fact. When the treaty of Guadalupe was signed, the ranche of " La Bolsa " was separated from Texas by the river, and consequently formed a part of Mexican territory. After the great inundation the river changed its course, leaving on its left side said ranche, which since that time has been only separated from Texas by a branch of the river, which, most of the year, is perfectly dry, so that without any difficulty, and by only walking a few paces, any one can go from Mexican territory to the United States, and *vice versa*.

Such circumstances have been very favorable to criminals. Opposite the " Bolsa," on the ranche of San Pedro, Texas, belonging to an American called Green Malstaed, a pack of outlaws fixed their quarters. To this party belonged Cipriano Flores, Desiderio Villareal, Julian Villareal, *alias* Garibay, Francisco Perez, *alias* Chicon, Victor Gonzalez, *alias* el Coyote, Francisco Gonzalez, *alias* el Chineno, and several others who are mentioned on the record. Whenever the Texas *posses* came near the place where these banditti lived, they got out of the difficulty just by walking a few yards and taking *refuge on Mexican* soil. If any crossed the river, the robbers had ample time to run to Texas.

The facilities which the situation of " La Bolsa" offered in the way of security to the robbers, were not less for the transit of cattle stolen in Texas. They could be brought from one territory to the other without crossing the river, as this was done when the cattle were already on Mexican soil. Thus one of the dangers to which the robbers are exposed, from the length of time it takes them to transport the cattle across the river, was avoided.

Hence it is that San Pedro ranche in Texas, and La Bolsa in Mexico, were places of transit for stolen cattle. Therefore it is a legal presumption that all cattle passing *via* those places were ill-gotten. This presumption holds good as to the four heads that Nicolas Solis took from there into Matamoros.

The Commission knew of this fact through a document found in the archives of Reynosa, but they were unable to investigate the matter for the want of witnesses, and therefore limited themselves to state the presumption which is drawn from it against the conduct of Nicolas Solis.

Both Dionicio Cardenas and Nicolas Solis appeared before the Commission to defend themselves from the charges brought against them by the complainants of Texas, producing evidence, which it is true showed that some of those charges were false.

Nicolas Solis was accused, for instance, of having enclosed stolen cattle in the corrals of " Saliseño," [*] and he proves that this was utterly impossible, as there are no corrals in the " Saliseño. "

Cardenas was accused of having bought one hundred stolen heads of cattle in Texas, by way of the " Horcones," on the ranche called " Los Mogotes,"[†] and it is proved that there is no such ranche alongside of the river. There was a decided interest to prove that Cardenas was alcalde in 1869, [‡] the object being to show that he had taken the lead in certain complaints made in that year, by the city council of Matamoros, against certain measures taken by the judge of the first instance in regard to cattle stealing. The falsity of these investigations was shown by the electoral votes produced before the Commission, from which it is seen that Cardenas had not been returned to the city council in 1869.

---

[*] Report of the U. S. Commissioners, p. 17, Gregorio Villareal.
[†] Report of the U. S. Commissioners, p. 17, Apolinario Hernandez.
[‡] Report of the U. S. Commissioners, p. 28, Alexander Wierbisky.

There was still a greater interest in stating that in the transcripts of some of the documents relating to the proceedings of the municipal corporation, in their complaints against the judge of the first instance, and which were given to the complainants of Texas, under certificate, the name of Cardenas was failed to be mentioned, * supposing that his name was mentioned in the originals, as being under indictments. This was enunciated to bring a charge against the Mexican functionaries who issued copies of said documents, and as if to signify that their intention was to conceal the unlawful acts of Cardenas. The documents obtained by this Commission show that the copies were correct in relation to this matter.

The Commission investigated these and other points, but it is well established from the whole of their investigation, not the innocence of the accused, but the unscrupulousness of the Texas accusers in committing the grossest perjuries. Their accusations are grounded on divers facts, which are certainly difficult to investigate, but of undoubted truth so far as Cardenas is concerned, and giving place to well founded suspicions as to Solis.

The cattle which are brought from Texas into Mexico have been consumed in the slaughtering houses, and it is safe to state that a large number of persons dedicated to this branch of industry must have participated in the trade of stolen cattle. The Commission limited, however, their investigations to the two persons aforementioned, because they have held public offices in the municipality of Matamoros.

Dionisio Cardenas was third alcalde in 1870, and president of the city council in 1872. Nicolas Solis was alderman of the same corporation in the same year, and justice of the peace of Saliseño in 1866.

The influence our frontier has had in the robberies committed in Texas, so far as the criminals are concerned, is evidently of a secondary importance. It is of more importance in regard to the purchasers of stolen cattle, as it is unquestionable that if there were no purchasers on the Mexican line, none would

---

* Report of the U. S. Commissioners, p. 29.   J. S. Parker, p. 30, Doc. 19.

have been brought to it. As to this last phase of the question, there are two persons implicated who have held public trusts in Mexico, but the Commission must add that amongst the authorities of the frontier of Tamaulipas they constitute an exception.

IX.

But secondary as this influence might have been, it has existed, however, giving rise to consequences, the extension of which must be defined, *i. e.*, it is indispensable that we should fix the amount of injuries caused in Texas by robberies committed there to be disposed of on Mexican soil. But before we proceed let us state that not all of the cattle stolen in Texas and brought to the bank of the river were transported to Mexican territory. A considerable portion were consumed on the American bank, and there are sufficient data to affirm that Adolphus Glaevecke, the same individual in whose service there was a band of robbers stealing horses in Mexico, and who has been and is now alderman in Brownsville, is one of those who received stolen cattle.

The Commission, in their investigation, believed that what had occurred in Matamoros afforded a safe criterion for the whole question. The most bitter complaints have been directed against Matamoros. This city was supposed to be the center of the robberies; that a considerable portion of the stolen cattle were carried there; that her authorities were either accomplices or connivers at the robberies. That the inhabitants fed on the products of the depredations committed in Texas, and finally that her merchants lacked decorum to such an extent, that they speculated knowingly in stolen hides.

On the other hand, it was only in Matamoros where it was possible to collect the most complete statistical data taken from the archives of both frontiers. It was therefore in Matamoros where the most minute investigations could be carried on, which would enable us to form our judgment of the whole question.

In late years a commercial phenomenon has occurred on

both frontiers, which is perfectly surprising at first sight, and which needs some study in order to be understood. We refer to the low price of cattle and the high price of hides. It is not unusual that the hide should be sold for the very same price at which the animal was bought. Heads of cattle are worth on an average, say five dollars. But, however, it has fluctuated according to kind and condition, rising sometimes to seven dollars a head, and going at others as low as three dollars.

Although this phenomenon is common to both frontiers, attention has only been paid to the low price of cattle on our frontier, the explanation of which has been sought in the numerous robberies of cattle.* Even some of the witnesses who appeared before the Commission have viewed the facts in the same light.

If the low prices of cattle were really a true sign of robbery it would go so far as to prove that the crime had been committed on a very large scale for the benefit of the Texas line, as the price of cattle has had the same fluctuations on both sides of the river.

A majority of proprietors in the counties of Texas bordering on the Bravo, are Mexicans, who generally bring the produce of their cattle to the towns of both lines for market. A number of these proprietors appeared before the Commission, and they all testified that they had sold on both lines at the very same prices, as low on one as on the other.

The firm of Woodhouse & Co. established a packery in Texas, where they bought cattle from the Texan proprietors at the rate of four dollars a head. So the representative of that firm deposed before the Commission.

But the statement that low prices of cattle are the consequence of robbery is not correct. This has been the general case in Texas.

"In several portions of the State," says the *Texas Almanac* for 1867, p. 197, "droves of cattle can be bought at from three to five dollars a head." "Cattle (*Texas Almanac*, 1871, p. 165, quoting the *Columbus Times*) can be bought in Western Texas at from two to six dollars a head, and in late years of scarcity,·

---

* Report of the U. S. Commissioners to Texas, Note.

opportunities have been offered to buy splendid droves of cattle even at lower prices. By cattle we understand cows, heifers, and bullocks two years old. By purchasing at so much a head, they can even be had cheaper."

Some of the proprietors in the State of Nuevo Leon, Mexico, have gone to Texas to buy cattle for their farms. In Mexico they had to pay five dollars a head, and being advised they could get them at less price in Texas, they went there and made their purchases. The circumstances showing their legal acquisition are well defined. The price they paid was from three dollars and a half to four and five dollars for grown cattle, the vendors undertaking in some cases to deliver the same in Mexico.

We are convinced by these statements that the sales of cattle or sheep at low prices have no connection with cattle stealing; that said sales were not caused for fear of the bands of Mexican robbers, as has been defended sometimes, and moreover, that the low prices of cattle were not peculiar to the Rio Bravo region, but were general to all the State of Texas.

The true cause of this abatement is to be found in the excess of cattle and the want of consumers proportionate to the existence on hand. Hence, large establishments were started in Texas in which great numbers of cattle were slaughtered to gain the hides, the fat, the horns and the hoofs, throwing away the meat or feeding hogs on it. The want of exportation allowed such speculations, in which a profit was obtained on the price which cattle usually commanded.

It was not in the power of every one to start such an establishment, as it required a heavy outlay, which even on a a very economical basis could never have been less than ten thousand dollars. The small proprietors especially were unable to establish such packeries, even on a small scale, and on the other hand they were obliged to sell, and therefore, although through such establishments they could realize greater profits, still they had to dispose of their products at a reduced price.

In said packeries the waste of the meat was possible on account of the hides and fat being made of avail; the high prices of the hides was the cause also that meat for the consumption of the towns, should command a very low price. The compensation to this loss was sought for in the hides, and this explains why the raw hides on both frontiers as well as in the interior of Texas should command high prices, while the cattle were at a low price. In other words, the scarcity of consumers of meat, preserved the low price of cattle, and as they was principally killed on account of the hides, the compensation was looked for in these.

It was the natural laws of trade, therefore, that produced this situation, which in no way was connected with cattle stealing. Consequently it is not from the reduced price of cattle on the Mexican frontier, from whence it is possible to derive a general rule which would enable us to appreciate the amount of robbery committed, since we have explained that it was the excess of cattle which cause the reduced price, varying from one dollar and a half to seven dollars per head. *

Nor can we take as a starting point the excessive increase of the hide trade in Matamoros to solve the question. † It is not the profits realized from capital employed in speculating in stolen hides, which has given rise to that trade, but causes of an entirely different nature.

By examining the current prices in New York from 1862 to 1872, and taking into consideration the fluctuations of currency, it is observed that raw hides are worth at present in the United States double the amount they were ten years ago. This increased demand must be ascribed to the progress of manufacture, which demand has been from year to year on the increase, as is shown by the fact that from year to year the price of hides has been increasing.

This increasing demand naturally causes the price of hides to go up in the places where cattle were more numerous. Hence a traffic arose on the Mexican border in the States of the Mexican frontier heretofore unknown, and Matamoros became the center of this traffic, on account of the facilities it afforded

---

* Report of the U. S. Commissioners, page 18, Note.
† Ibid., page 19, Importations of hides.

for exportation. The Commission caused the registry to be produced, and in view of the books in which it is contained, they formed a *" statement of hides introduced into Matamoros from September* 15*th*, 1870, *up to December* 31*st*, 1872."

We would not be able to find positive data in this statement if we were to look for the exact amount of hides introduced, because, on account of smuggling, the total amounts to much less than what really has been introduced into the city. But if we want to direct our inquiries as to the places from whence the hides have been sent to Matamoros, the statement is then complete. According to the same, the towns of the north and center of Tamaulipas, those of Nuevo Leon, Saltillo, Chihuahua, and others in the interior all have contributed to the trade of hides exported from Matamoros. Before proceeding any further, let us remark that in speaking of hides we refer only to those of neat cattle. The Commission has refrained intentionally from using the large testimonial evidence in their possession relating to this point, thinking that those statistical data were sufficient to show that the hides proceeding from the bordering States of the west, as also from some of the interior, concentrate in Matamoros. The commercial as well as the statistical data convince us that the great traffic in the exportation of hides from Matamoros affords no grounds to calculate the amount of cattle stolen from Texas for the Mexican frontier.

The Commission has formed an opinion on this point which is based on the judicial proceedings and the registry of cattle on both frontiers. On the 20th of September, 1869, fifteen proprietors of Cameron county applied to the judge of the first instance of Matamoros complaining of the robberies they had suffered. The judge ordered a search to be made in the hide stores and butcheries they designated, to enable them to examine all the hides and animals found there. The owner or person in charge of one of the hide stores refused to allow the inspection, alleging that the warrant was against the law, as it had the character of a general search, stating, nevertheless, to the agents of the proprietors that they could examine his establishment, but in a private manner, and not by virtue of the

judicial mandate. Said agents refused, and this was the only
establishment of all those they mentioned which was not
searched. All the rest, as well as the butcheries, were inspected. One hundred and thirty-three (133) hides marked
with brands of American stock raisers were found, but not one
single animal so branded.

When the lamentations on account of the robbery were so
frequent against our frontier, when at that time it was supposed
that all the people of Matamoros were feeding on cattle stolen in
Texas, and that the speculators traded with the hides of those
animals, the judicial proceedings promoted by the Texan proprietors, proceedings not only witnessed but executed by their agents,
clearly demonstrated the exaggeration of those complaints.

The statistics in regard to hides in Matamoros give a more
approximate idea. The Commission investigated whether on
the ranches and pastures within the jurisdiction of Matamoros
there were any cattle from Texas. A large number of persons
of different localities who go about the pastures, witness the
inspection of cattle and their collection, and who consequently
have a perfect knowledge of the number of cattle, deposed
unanimously that in said pastures there were not and never
had been any cattle from Texas.

Other witnesses deposed that the heads of cattle stolen in
Texas, as a general rule, had been consumed in the butcheries
of the city, and they certainly could not have had any other
destination, as they are not to be found in any other place. It
would have been easy to prove the reverse, had this been the
case. The pastures on which the cattle graze are open, and
they offer no hindrance, even to a person unprovided with a
judicial order, to examine the cattle existing thereon. If
amongst said cattle there should be any from Texas, it would
be easy to point out by eye-witnesses the ranches on which
they were, and to designate the names of the persons who held
them. The want of such a proof confirms the truth of the
investigations made by the Commission.

In the municipal treasury of Matamoros a registry of
brands is kept. It was established to protect the stock raisers
and prevent cattle stealing, or give an easier means of investi-

gating it. Of every head of cattle that is slaughtered in the city
or within its jurisdiction an entry is made on the registry,
specifying the date on which it is taken to the butchery, the
name of the owner or sender, place from whence it came, number of heads, brand or mark traced on each animal. By these
entries on the books the proprietors are enabled to investigate
whether any of their animals have been slaughtered, and to
know from whom to claim them.

The Commission ordered this registry to be presented, and
in due compliance therewith the municipal treasurer presented
the books corresponding to the period from September 15th,
1870, to December 31st, 1872. The books corresponding to
previous years were not lodged with him, as the treasurer was
not in charge of the registry of hides before that date. Even
those corresponding to 1870 and 1871 are incomplete, not being
therefore reliable, though we have formed an abstract of them
in the *espedientes* of this Commission. The only reliable basis
is the registry kept in 1872.

This registry was submitted to experts, who were persons
having a practical and thorough knowledge of the marks of
Texas and Mexico, in order that by examining all the brands,
and fixing the amount of cattle consumed in Matamoros and
its jurisdiction, they might declare what number of heads bore
Texan brands and what number Mexican.

The examination of these experts gave the following
result: In 1872 seventeen thousand two hundred and eighty-
three heads were consumed (17,283). Of these thirteen
thousand nine hundred and twenty-one (13,921) bore Mexican
brands, one thousand one hundred and fifty-seven (1,157)
Texan brands, and two thousand two hundred and five (2,205)
were registered without annotating the brands, or as maverick
cattle, or having the brands effaced.

These conclusions show what importance cattle stealing
has had in Texas during 1872, and how groundless it is to
state that the revolutions have destroyed the cattle in Mexico,
wherefore the consumption of meat in Matamoros would not
have been possible but for Texas cattle, and considering the
low price which it commands on the Mexican line, said cattle

7

must be ill-gotten. Although it is true that public convulsions have injured the stock raisers, the injuries are never tantamount to the complete destruction of the cattle; they consist ordinarily in the fact that the contending forces take all the number of heads they need without paying for them, and with great waste.

Although said injuries really do exist, however considerable we may suppose them to be, it could never be held that there were not sufficient cattle in the North and center of the State to supply such a small city as Matamoros. The Commission investigated from what places of the State of Tamaulipas the cattle consumed in Matamoros were brought, and the testimonial evidence showing that it was from the estates in the north and center of Tamaulipas corroborates the correctness of that statistical datum. The elements of this evidence are the proprietors who made the sales and eye-witnesses who saw the droves of cattle.

But the most important proof on this question is that taken from the archives of Brownsville. According to the Texas law, inspection is to be made of all hides introduced into the State from Mexico, by the inspector of hides and animals, who is to register the brands. The Commission endeavored to obtain the result of the inspection made in the hides taken from Matamoros to Brownsville.

Through the Mexican Consul the Commission obtained complete data, but in one of the documents certified by the inspector this officer added a note to the effect that said document did not express the number of hides stolen and carried into Mexico, some of which were sent to the interior of said Republic for manufacturing purposes, and others exported directly by Boca del Rio. Really, that officer affirmed a thing not verified in the archives under his charge; but let us analyze this remark. As the hides of cattle used in Matamoros are considered as national products, their introduction into the interior requires a document from the collector of the revenue (*agente fiscal*) of said city issued by the collector of customs. They must be afterwards carried to the gate (*garita*) leading to the road, and as no duties are collected on their importation into the interior, there can be no possible interest in eluding these formalities. With this understanding, the Commission applied to the respective officers for information as to the introduction of hides, and received the depositions of the officers whose duty it is to issue those documents, the depositions of the watchmen of the gates who necessarily must have seen the exit of the hides, and also the depositions of the watchmen of the custom house who watch the road; and this evidence, diversified and complete as it is, gave the Commission a positive knowledge that hides have never been carried into the interior of Mexico.

And it is to be presumed so, when we consider that hides command a high price in foreign markets, which is one of the greatest inducements for robbery; that instead of the hides being sent to the interior of Mexico the reverse occurs. Hides are sent from the interior to Matamoros in order to obtain those high prices and a ready market. It would be very strange that robberies should be committed in order to send the stolen property to places where it is not in demand, overlooking others where sales are easy and profitable. The idea is also inadmissible because the inspection of hides in Brownsville renders their exportation difficult. Boca del Rio presents an easy exit to all who want to dedicate themselves to such an immoral and indecorous traffic.

If to the inferences derived from the evidence produced we add the circumstance that there are no industrial establishments in Matamoros where hides are manufactured, we must unavoidably arrive to the conclusion that all the raw hides there are destined to exportation, and they are actually exported.

The Commission also investigated the amount of hides exported by the Boca d. Rio. The custom house data gives a total of (1,477) one thous. four hundred and seventy-seven hides in 1871, (798) seven hundred and ninety-eight in 1872, and not one hide in previous years. There never has been through said place the fabulous exportations that some have imagined * in order to exaggerate their claims; but this, not-

---

* The report of the U. S. Commission, p. 20—this documentary—where the entry.

withstanding, the Commission candidly admit that there are grounds to presume that all hides exported by Boca del Rio come from cattle stolen in Texas. This presumption is founded on the fact that before the inspection of hides was established in Brownsville there was not a single hide exported by Boca del Rio, and besides, on the fact that exportation by United States territory requires less time and affords easier means of transportation, two circumstances from which it follows that there must be an unlawful interest to deviate exportation from its natural channel.

Being, as it is, a well established fact that no hides are introduced from Matamoros into the interior of Mexico, and that neither are they destined to manufacturing purposes, having also fixed the amount exported by Boca del Rio, it is unquestionable that the remainder must have been exported by Brownsville and consequently must have been submitted to the inspection of the Texas officers.

The inspection went into effect on the 12th of August, 1871. The result from said month up to January 31st, 1873, are as follows :   Out of (39,450) thirty-nine thousand four hundred and fifty hides inspected by Charles Murphy, (38,790) thirty-eight thousand seven hundred and ninety bore Mexican brands, (660) six hundred and sixty had American brands, and out of these (32) were claimed as having been stolen. The report states also that besides these (7,000) seven thousand hides were imported from Matamoros which were not inspected.

Out of (36,625) thirty-six thousand six hundred and twenty-five on the registry of Facundo Cortez, they were all Mexican except (373) three hundred and seventy-three of American brand, (195) one hundred and ninety-five of which were claimed to have been robbed. A notice added, saying that in (800) eight hundred hides introduced from Camargo, about half that number bore American brands, but of these only (202) two hundred and two were claimed, no one appearing to claim the others.

Out of (27,366) twenty-seven thousand three hundred and sixty-six hides on the books of Robert Kingsbury, only (457) four hundred and fifty-seven bore American brands, and the rest Mexican brands. Fifteen of the former were claimed as having been stolen.

The following is a *résumé* of the above data, viz:

Hides exported from Brownsville and submitted to inspection, total number	110,441	
Imported from Camargo	800	
Hides with Mexican brands, including four hundred, half of the amount imported from Camargo		102,351
Hides of American brands unclaimed, including one hundred and ninety-eight, as per last item		1,436
Hides of American cattle claimed as having been stolen, including two hundred and two imported from Camargo		454
Hides not inspected		7,000
	111,241	111,241

It can easily be perceived by this statement, that in the exportation of hides from Mexico to the United States, American hides bear a ratio of less than two per cent. It is certain that not all were stolen hides, as is shown by the fact that only twenty-five per cent. were claimed; but even admitting they were so, and adding the number of hides exported by Boca del Rio, we would have a total of (4,156) four thousand one hundred and fifty-six hides proceeding from Texas, i. e., one-fourth per cent. on the general exportation of eighteen months; during the first twelve of which, such bitter complaints were advanced against our frontier, on account of cattle stealing, which is made to amount to some millions. In Texas the assessed value of each head of cattle, is five dollars; but even allowing its value to be ten dollars, as is stated by claimants against Mexico, we have a loss amounting to ($41,560) forty-one thousand five hundred and sixty dollars, during the whole period of eighteen months.

In this exportation it is not only hides proceeding from Matamoros which are included. In the statistical data on the origin of these, we can perceive that the towns alongside of the Bravo, as well as those situated in the interior of the frontier, have made remittances of hides to Matamoros; thus admitting the whole amount to be stolen hides, said amount represents not only the robbery committed in Texas for one locality, but for several localities of the frontier of Mexico during a period of eighteen months. And as Matamoros is the place to which the largest number of hides are sent, that figure represents the largest number of cattle stolen in Texas and brought into Mexican territory. Moreover, our frontier is not liable for the whole amount of that sum; we are left to ascertain what part of the robbery was committed by robbers living on our frontier, and which by those living on territory of the United States.

The documents on which the Commission based their judgment are authenticated, the first by Charles Murphy, inspector of hides, extending from August, 1871, to June, 1872; the second by Henry Klahn, and the third by H. S. Rock, the two latter deputy-inspectors. It has, therefore, been almost incomprehensible for this Commission, that from these registers it should be inferred that twenty-five per cent. of the hides imported from Mexico to Brownsville were of American brand, and at least twenty-five per cent. had the brands effaced or altered.*

The Commission consulted also the judgment of experts and persons of practical knowledge, all of whom calculated that in 1872 the proportion of American hides in the general exportation did not reach five per cent., that in 1871 it averaged from five to ten per cent., and in previous years it never went over ten per cent. It cannot be stated that all the hides in the afore-mentioned years were stolen hides, as it is well proved that in the same years the American stock-raisers in Texas made considerable sales to Mexico, and they have been selling hides even of late to Monterey; but in the opinion of the Commission it is beyond doubt that cattle stealing was conducted on a larger scale prior to 1870 on account of the bands

---

* Report of U. S. Commissioners, p. 20.   Where the entry ?

led by the Wrights up to 1866, Paschall, Patrick Quinn, and others up to 1869 and 1870 ; and also because no persecution was organized against cattle stealers in Texas until 1870, and they were enabled to commit their robberies with absolute impunity.

The statistical data prove to what extent they were committed, carrying to Mexican soil the stolen cattle. The observations of the Commission in regard to Matamoros which was considered as the center place of robberies and of the traffic of stolen hides and animals, may serve as a rule to judge as to the rest of the frontier, which was never judged so severely as that city by those who complained in Texas of their cattle being stolen.

The antecedents of these affairs, all the complaints, the newspaper articles of late years, and the findings of the juries have been limited to the stealing of neat cattle. As to horse stealing, the utmost that has been said is that the robbers used to change their horses, taking fresh ones on the pastures. The Commission was therefore surprised, as they noticed that when the claims were presented in a formal manner an enormous number of horses were added, supposed to have been stolen by Mexican robbers.

The Commission investigated the matter, and it resulted from their investigation that stolen horses had been brought sometimes to Mexican soil, but horse stealing on a large scale would have no object whatever, as the horses could not be disposed of ; that as a general rule horse stealing is practiced in Texas, as well as on our frontiers, with a view to carrying the horses to the interior of Texas, where there is a great traffic in horses and mules, and large herds are formed destined to other places in the United States.

Some proprietors of Cameron county, Texas, appeared before the Commission and gave their depositions as to the horses they had lost through the robbers. In every case in which the robbers were persecuted, it was invariably shown that the horses were carried to the interior of Texas.

In one of these cases which occurred in June, 1869, there were strong grounds tending to show the culpability of an

American by the name of Brown, residing in *Auras* ranche, Nueces county, who it seems came to Cameron with a number of men in his service to steal horses and mules which he sold in San Antonio, Texas.

In another case there were strong suspicions against Emmil Rutledge, a resident of Hondo Creek, Karnes county, as a speculator at least in stolen animals.

The Commission, as the result of their study, have come to the conclusion that the Mexican frontier has had no direct or in any way important influence in cattle stealing in Texas, either considering who have been the criminals or what has been the amount of the injuries caused.

X.

The residents of Texas have complained constantly that the Mexican authorities have not taken all the necessary precautions to prevent the stealing of cattle on our borders; that the State of Texas has, to the contrary, done all in its power by way of keeping the laws.* Now an investigation has become indispensable in order to ascertain what has occurred on both frontiers in this particular.

The question relative to Texas presents four aspects—her legislation, her public administration, her police, and her administration of justice.

The Texas legislation is imperfect. It contains no efficacious, energetic means to prevent the robberies which take place in the branding pens, and which contribute to maintain a state of perfect disorder, in the prolongation of which the proprietors who give themselves up to these depredations are interested. To commit these depredations they require accomplices—men destitute of conscience, who rob for others without any other consideration than the pay which they receive; and

---

* Report of U. S. Commission to Texas, p. 7. ✶ While the United States.

it is certain that these men, accustomed not to respect property, rob on their own account whenever it is possible.

One of the proprietors who has distinguished himself most in these depredations is Ricardo King, owner of the estate Santa Gertrudis, county of Nueces. He has had as chief Tomas Vazquez, accomplice in robberies of Mexican horses, and in the robberies of cattle committed in Texas, and Fernando Lopez, accomplice in the last. He has kept in his rancho this Atilano Alvarado, who is thought to be chief of a party of robbers stationed in Guerrero. They appear also in the dispatches drawn up before the Commission, the dates of which are not very accurate with regard to the robberies in which the individuals have participated who have been in his service. Ricardo King had a large band who ran constantly in all directions of the country marking calves, though they did not belong to him. It is impossible to admit that the people forming that party possessed any sentiments of morality. The laws of Texas offer no energetic remedies for this evil, and are insufficient.

The inspection of animal skins has been established, but this is equivalent to a wish to correct the evil in its effects, and not in one of its most important causes. And even this law has proven ineffectual in practice.

Those in Texas who complain of the grievances received from our frontier, finding probably that the result of the statistical data taken from the registers of inspection in Brownsville, destroys entirely all their pretensions, look to the corruption of the public employees for a reason to assert that the number of American skins exported from Matamoros were many more.* The Commission has no data to calculate the exactness of these decisions; they believe them to be unfounded, without any other motive than that of having a place like the mouth of a river where exportations can be made with less sacrifice than that required to corrupt an employee; but in case of this admission it is proper to say that in the opinion of the complainants the laws of Texas against robbery have failed to

---

* Report of the U. S. Commission, page 22.

produce effect, because the officials of the administration protect the seizures and robberies.

Notwithstanding, on other reasons the Commission founds the belief that the laws of Texas are not to be blamed. The robbery of skins there has attained extraordinary proportions, and continues on the ascending scale. With these skins they trade, they are taken to the towns where they are bought, and this would not be possible without the complicity of the inspectors of skins. With regard to the cattle, the Commission has already explained the causes of the inefficacy of the laws of inspection; the owners are persuaded that some of them have united together and named inspectors in the port nearest them where cattle are exported.

On the 1st of July, 1870, a law was made organizing the police of the State. To form an idea of what this police has been, the Commission has limited itself to copy an extract of one of the discussions held in the House of Representatives of Texas.

"HOUSE OF REPRESENTATIVES.—An interesting discussion on the resolution presented by Sayers, to the end that no assignment be made for the pay and support of the police of the State. Ford favored the resolution, as he did not think the State was in condition to pay the police, and at the same time to reimburse those whom they robbed. Powers believed the police force ought to be paid up to the date of their past services; but Prendergast thought it was not commendable to pay ruffians for killing, maiming, and assassinating peaceable citizens. Denton said that the actual police of the State, was a disgrace to Texas. Washington diffused in the radical style, in favor of the State police. Smith of Colorado, thought the sum already spent in paying truants and criminals was sufficiently large. The resolution was approved."—*Galveston Three Weekly News*, April 12th, 1873.

The admistration of justice leaves also much to be wished for. The statistics of crime in the county of Cameron, from the end of the summer of 1866, to the close of December, 1872, in point of robberies, give the following result:

"The grand jury made (97) ninety-seven indictments, in (25) twenty-five of which the accused were condemned, and in ten acquitted ; in the cases of (34) thirty-four judgment was not rendered on account of a change in place of residence, death, or *nolle prosequi*, and twenty-eight are still pending on account of what is feared by the accused. When the crime of cattle stealing is so extended in Texas, it calls attention to the fact, that in the county referred to, the best organized of all those which are between the Bravo and the Nueces, there have been four condemnations yearly, partly on account of cattle stealing."

And this attention increases when on the list of the pardoned are found Patricio Quinn, Billy Mann, Charles Karh, and Pedro Mainiel, notorious and famed on the frontier for their depredations. These individuals were accused on the 1st of March, 1868, and the cases were pending till the 1st of March, 1870—that is to say two years—and eventually they were dismissed without judgment. It is to be seen at once that the real intention is to retard this business, and afterwards to avoid the judgment of the criminal where, probably, according to the class and number of the witnesses, a sentence of condemnation awaited him.

The Commission desires to explain the irregularity of the cry against the cattle thieves, and that altogether they not only miss a good opportunity for the chastisement of the great criminals, but the authorities favor a bill commending the liberation of the accused, thus eluding judgment. It is not difficult to find the solution.

The class of agents which Ricardo King has under his command, for committing depredations on the cattle of others, has already been mentioned. He is not the only one, nor are the deeds committed all of the same kind. In the ranchos of Francisco Iturria, one of which is called Punta del Monte, are employed and live, or have lived, Pedro Lucio, corporal of the rancho, Pedro Cortina, Marcos Sanchez, Severiano Hinojosa, and others already mentioned in the dispatches. They have been participators in the cattle stealing, and in connivance with a band of robbers commanded by José Maria Martinez for exchanging cattle robbed in Texas for horses robbed in Mexico. In this manner, under the protection of persons of influential positions, there are in Texas certain bands of immoral men

who aid these persons in these unlawful proceedings, and at the
same time receive protection. If any of them fall in the hands
of justice, this influential power is called into play to save
them, and only those who have not this protection would be
condemned. A minute examination, kept in the judicial
archives of the counties between the Bravo and the Nueces,
would be a satisfactory illustration of this question.

A Texas newspaper, referring to the same thing, says this:

"There are many persons on this side (Texas), who maintain themselves by cattle stealing. The peculiar character of
our Mexican population, combined with the advantages of a
very scattered population and the dense thickets, makes this
cattle stealing a very profitable business. Where there is fire
there is smoke. This old proverb occurs to us when we hear
said 'such or such a person has made his living by cattle stealing.' We know they cannot be reached by our tribunals. They
have many able friends. * * * The public opinion
certainly accuses many among us of being implicated in cattle
stealing."—*Daily Ranchero*, Brownsville, February 10th,
1872.

"Two men by the name of Pancho Blanco and Cipriano
Guerrero, were caught and hanged from a mezquite tree by the
rancheros (ignored up to the present time), on one day of last
week. The thieves were known by the rancheros for a long
time as robbers of great notoriety. Latterly they had engaged
in the robbery of horses. We approve of the former way of
disposing of all suspicious characters the whole length of the
frontier, for the following reasons: If they are taken they remain imprisoned at the expense of the county for three or five
months, which up to the present has occurred, and they have
no difficulty in being cleared by means of chicanery or by the
cunning of their lawyers. During the last seven years * *
many of them have been tried more than once, but they have
always easily escaped, and this resulted in their thinking that
they might continue their business with perfect impunity, in
proof of which see the numbers of this paper in the last few
months."—*Daily Ranchero*, Brownsville.

In these years the robberies have been common on both
frontiers. Various documents prove it, the most notable being
a manifestation made before the first prosecuting judge in
Matamoros by the owners of fifteen properties in the county of

Cameron, to which allusion has before been made. In judicial writ of 14th of September, 1869, they described the cattle stealing as being notorious, from one side of the river to the other ; that is to say from Texas to Mexico, and from Mexico to Texas.

And notwithstanding its being so, there is no assurance that the authorities on the Texas side have taken measures in their sphere of action to prevent Texas from becoming the market for property stolen in Mexican territory, or that the theft should end there. It is not possible that they should have ignored the fact of the probability that those who robbed in Mexico would do the same in Texas, and the necessity that both frontiers should prosecute the crime in whatever place it might be committed, not so much for the protection of the frontier as for self-preservation, and to guard against similar evils. Not only have they done nothing to remedy a situation so demoralized, but the indifference of some and complicity of others, as that of Judge Thadeus Rhodes and the sheriff Leon Estapá, fomented the general demoralization, the consequences of which have fallen on them on account of their own proceedings.

The complaints made by the residents of Texas against Mexico, and the form and manner in which they have been made, and the extent to which they have been made, has a triple signification.

Before 1870 there were hardly any measures taken in Texas to stop the robberies, making the responsibility fall on our frontier entirely, pretending that Mexico was responsible for the omissions of the Texan authorities.

After 1870, there were established inspectors of skins and agents of police, who have been called by Texas itself corrupt and immoral men. To wish that our border should be responsible for all, is to say that the ill effects of the corruption and immorality of the Texan public officers should fall upon her.

In all these years they have continued to organize in Texan territory the business of cattle stealing, that they might continue it in Mexico ; and there they have had a public and ready

market for the stolen property. The authorities of that State
have taken no means to prevent it, notwithstanding that these
crimes spread on the frontier a great demoralization, the consequences of which are perceived in that of the United States by
the stealing of cattle. To attribute this demoralization to Mexico is equivalent to saying that the Mexican Republic is culpable of the increase of the disorder which it has, in its
toleration, received from the borders of Texas; and even
protection has, in some cases, been given to cattle stealing
committed on our territory.

XI.

The Commission has also examined into the conduct of the
Mexican authorities, and in some cases found them inefficient,
and in others guilty ; but in general conforming to their duties.
At this increasing demoralization which, from Texas, runs over
to our frontier, considerably augmenting the disorder already
there, and which was shown by the cattle stealing, the authorities of Mexico were obliged to raise a dike. It was of no
consequence whether the stolen property was of small amount,
because the question was not a matter of amount but one of
duty. The question has three phases, one of which refers to
the direction part, another relates to the execution or policy,
and the third is in regard to the suppression or judicial part.

The difficulty with regard to the United States frontier, as
regards cattle stealing, commenced in 1862. From that time
it has been noted that the Mexican administrative authorities,
military and civil, superiors and inferiors, political and municipal, were executing orders to put an end to the robberies committed in Texas for Mexico. Copies or extracts have been
added to the dispatches of all those depositions which make
known a constant system of watchfulness.

In some towns it has been exacted from the importers of
Texas cattle that they prove their ownership by a bill of sale,
and in cases where it has not been exhibited, the killing of the

cattle has not been consented to, except under security, and with obligation to present at a certain time that document.

In reality the persecution of those who robbed in Texas was a measure of self-protection, because the thefts took place on both frontiers, and with experience acquired since 1848, the necessity of being able to control the deprivation which threatened our proprietors with ruin was understood.

There was, besides, a great personal interest. A great number of the inhabitants of Mexican lineage are proprietors in Texas. In Mier alone there are over three hundred persons who own cattle between the Bravo and Nueces. These persons are influential in the places where they live, and in general exercise authority. As for instance in the past year the president of the corporation in Camargo was Eligio Garcia, and to-day it is Trinidad Aldrete, both owners of cattle in Texas. Their own convenience advises them to prevent the thefts which are made on the left border for Mexico, and hence it is a great amount of personal interest which forms a safeguard against this kind of stealing.

One of the measures of the administration, which always produced the best results on the frontier, was the registering of hides, and of animals to be killed, by this measure making public what was consumed in this line, and so putting an end to cattle stealing.

The administrative authorities, who had in former times perceived the beneficial effects of the register, made an effort to establish it there effectually, and have been carrying into effect the necessary arrangements, which they have reformed according to their experience, and have shown the greatest interest in obtaining a happy result.

Notwithstanding there has been an exceptional case, in which all has not been obtained which was necessary to regulate this branch, and in which omissions have been made, which the Commission could not pass over without notice.

The archives of the register of hides in Matamoros before the 15th of September, 1870, have been lost, and the same has happened to the archives of the register of animals killed previous to 1872.

The reason for this is, that every year a new recorder has been appointed in charge of the registers, of which properly speaking no books were kept, and that the appointed one, on leaving his business, took no care of the notes which he or his agents had made.

These irregularities continued up to September, 1870, when this business was transferred to the municipal treasury ; some months after, wardens were appointed at the toll gates for the purpose of inspecting imported hides ; there was besides a special commissioner of butcheries, belonging to the treasury already mentioned, and every one of the employees has kept a book, the collection of which was shown before the Commission.

In this there is nothing to oppose the law regulations, and we believe to the contrary, that if strictly complied with, it will be a complete guaranty against theft ; but the same cannot be said with regard to the application of them. The register ought to embrace the slaughtered cattle consumed in Matamoros, and the hides of the cattle consumed in the jurisdiction ; the first are inspected on entering the slaughter pen ; the second, on passing the toll gate to be sold in the city. It does not appear that either has been strictly complied with.

The missing register of cattle killed in the city of Matamoros, before 1872, that is to say, from the 15th of September, 1870, to the 31st of December, 1871, destroys the principal guaranty of the proprietors in the investigation of the theft. Not to make the inspections, not to take care of the books in which they are kept, and not to find them when they are required to be examined, are one and the same thing.

To this another irregularity is added ; in the year 1872, appear (2,205) two thousand two hundred and five hides not registered, the largest number of which were introduced through the Guadalupe toll gate ; they came from the ranchos of the jurisdiction of Matamoros, and consequently the necessity of a branding register was felt. Some of these, though the smallest number, were registered as maverick, or their marks could not be identified ; but almost the whole lot had no entry whatever on the register ; and there was a month, as for instance the month of May, in which were discovered (535) five hundred and thirty-five skins that had not been registered.

The series of orders issued in Matamoros since 1866, on this subject, indicates the desire to establish the register of hides in terms adequate to its object, but in its practice there has not been the interest necessary to realize the views contained in the precautions.

Notwithstanding this want of solicitude, the general character of the administrative authorities has had a tendency to look for some remedy against the evils, and not only they, but also the judicial functionaries had the same inclination. At the same time that the former attended with its regulations to that situation, the latter procured the punishment of the guilty and the restoration of the stolen property to their owners with the least possible difficulty.

Amongst the various cases which came to the notice of the Commission, there are some which were initiated for the prosecution by the Mexican authorities, as soon as they had received the slightest notice that there was passing or had passed a herd of cattle robbed in Texas. Once in a while the guilty were discovered and chastised, and in many other instances, now by the watchfulness of the custom house officers and the police, now through the strength of the residents, herds of stolen cattle were captured, and in all cases were returned to their owners if they were claimed either by themselves or through their attorneys, and those not claimed were sold and the proceeds deposited. And it is to be understood that in the generality of these cases they proceeded with such rapidity that sometimes between the capture and delivery to their owners they did not take twenty-five hours, and in many cases this was done on the same day, and sometimes within an hour. The only proofs exacted were the attestation of personality, if the owners claimed through their attorneys, and the identification of the brand. Not even a power of attorney was exacted in form when it occurred that the agents were creditable persons. No cost was required because the judges themselves simplified the proceeding, and placing it in the reach of all, made unnecessary the help of lawyers.

8

The extracts of the criminal cases and the declaration of some who have been judges, and of various agents of property holders in Texas, show that this has been the general spirit of the tribunals on the frontier of Tamaulipas.

Notwithstanding, they have managed to create a contrary impression, for instance, a judge of Camargo has been accused of having refused to return a herd of stolen cattle to some agents of the Texas police who presented themselves laying claim to it.* One of the newspapers which availed itself of this incident to accuse the Mexican authorities of being implicated in the theft, gave itself the answer shortly afterwards :

" It is just to observe," it says, " that the judge of Camargo was disposed to do it; he is ready to give up any property to an American provided that he can prove his right to it."—*The Sentinel*, Brownsville, January 27, 1871.

In the judgment of the Commission the judge of Camargo complied with his duty. Two unknown persons presented themselves, without proving a right, with the character of Texas police, but who were not accredited by our authorities. These proceeded discreetly in not acknowledging their pretensions to receive the property stolen in Texas and seized in Camargo. Sometime before Patricio Quinn, feigning to be agent of proprietors in Texas, came to the Mexican authorities and asked for the delivery of some cattle stolen on United States territory, brought by him to Mexico, and captured by the police from Quinn's accomplices.

The Commission has been detained in this case because it is one which characterizes the nature of the accusations directed against our authorities. The spirit of justice has, however, been so general in the tribunals that there have been no exceptions.

On the 19th of March, 1872, were captured Gabriel Treviño and six others with twenty-three cattle of Texas brands, and a suit was brought against them for cattle stealing. On the 1st of April, 1872, were seized Andrés Y. Hermenegildo Holguin, on the plains of Santa Fé, with a herd of cattle stolen

---

* Report of the U. S. Commissioners to Texas, page 12. William Burke.

in Texas, and criminal proceedings were also instituted against them. There was this in particular, in the first of these cases, that it resisted the police force.

The cattle were returned to their owners in the way shown by the Commission, but they did not proceed with equal justice in the chastisement of the criminals. The first prosecuting judge of the Northern District, lawyer Trinidad Gonzalez Doria, not only liberated them, but what is worthy of especial attention, he proceeded to dispose of the case without the slightest kind of judicial decree, leaving the *expediente* unfinished. It is not necessary that the Commission should enter into the particulars of all the immorality in such conduct. It is sufficiently plain even for those not familiar with criminal proceedings, and this procedure is even more condemnable when coming from the judge whose jurisdiction embraced the most important civil and criminal business of the Northern District of Tamaulipas. If, in his judgment, the Mexican tribunals were not competent to chastise the crime, the laws had provided a mode of proceeding which the Commission could not have reproved, even if the judge so thought, however it might have been dissatisfied with them. What the Commission censures is the violation of the criminal proceedings by liberating the accused whose trials were pending, without passing judgment on them, and postponing them indefinitely.

But just as the Commission has thought it to be its duty to condemn the judge in the former case, they consider themselves also obliged to give judgment favorable to the Mexican authorities, in an act which took place in Matamoros at the close of 1869, to which the complainants in Texas give exceptional importance.*

On the 24th of September, 1869, fifteen proprietors of the county of Cameron came to the first prosecuting judge of the northern district of Tamaulipas, lawyer Agustin Menchaca, complaining of the robberies from which their interests were suffering. Afterwards the agents of these proprietors were

---

* Report of the U. S. Commissioners to Texas, page 24.

Henry Klahn and L. Shedd, and since then it has become
known that these were not only their representatives but that
they derived their nominations from the Texas authorities ; subsequent revelations have shown that the judge of Brownsville
had nominated them that they might live in Matamoros, and
to act as inspectors of animals* and hides with a view of suppressing the theft. There would have been nothing especial in
this if they had limited themselves to private agencies, but
they pretended that our authorities had upheld them, and the
resistance which they met has furnished material for subsequent accusations. It is sufficient to announce the act to be
able to appreciate the excessive pretensions of the Brownsville
authorities.

The first step taken was to ask for an examination of the
packeries and butcheries, with a view to find out if there were any
stolen skins or cattle. The order was solicited from the first
prosecuting judge, who ordered Klahn and Shedd, assisted by the
police, to identify the skins and cattle enclosed in those establishments. Being prohibited by the law from making general
inquiries with regard to crimes and delinquencies, there is no
doubt that the judge already mentioned did more than was
permitted.

All the places mentioned were examined by Henry Klahn
and L. Shedd with the exception of one, whose owner opposed
the carrying out, on his property, of the order of the judge ;
alleging, for a reason, that it was unconstitutional, and that
general inquiries were against all law ; that if any one
thought he had stolen hides they should formalize their
accusation, so that in case of the result proving this to be false,
he might claim damages and injury against the accuser ; that
he would not consent to his establishment being searched without their first showing an order to this effect, in conformity
with article 16 of the constitution. In this proceeding the
Commission found nothing to be reproached. The law gives
the right to proclaim these errors before the authorities that
they may amend them.

---

* Report of the U. S. Commissioners, page 29. Henry Klahn.

But the same individual who made this opposition, went further. He was alderman (Regidor) of the council of Matamoros, and called an extra session, which was held on the 25th of October, 1869. After putting forward the complaints against the first prosecuting judge, and among them that relative to the general inquiry which the latter had ordered, founded on the 14th article of the laws of the council, he asked that a Commission might be formed, composed of the aldermen, to assist the first judge in the investigation which would be raised with regard to the truth of the acts which were known, and also upon others which might have been committed by the said judge, and if these acts were justified by the result, the information would be conveyed to the State Government. In these proceedings of the council, there was an excess; the municipal coporation had the right to accuse the judge if they believed him responsible, but it was not lawful to raise information similar to that introduced.

And so there was an excess in the Brownsville authorities naming agents, with the purpose of being upheld by ours, that they might establish in Matamoros, officers to inspect hides; it was on account of the co-operation of the first prosecuting judge that they decided that Klahn and Shedd, assisted by the police, should inspect all the packeries and butcheries, resolving in the council to raise information on the proceedings of the judge, to be conveyed to the State Government.

In the conflict which ensued between the first prosecuting judge and the council of Matamoros there was an object. The complainants of Texas have endeavored to show this, seeking in it a reason against our authorities, supposing there is in them a desire to resist what would procure the suppression of cattle stealing. They have been given to understand that the resistance to the examination of the hides already mentioned, arises from the desire to conceal hides illy acquired, saying that the citizens of Matamoros showed themselves so indignant against Judge Menchaca, owing to his efforts to comply with the laws and chastise the crime, that the city council adopted resolutions addressed to the supreme government of the State of Tamaulipas, asking the removal or impeachment of Judge Menchaca, which obliged him to resign and take refuge in Europe; and that Judge Menchaca was succeeded by Pedro Hinojosa, who privately made known to Klahn that he could not uphold him, by reason of which the latter found himself obliged to abandon his mission and return to Texas. To arrive at these conclusions the complainants on the banks of the Bravo have related the facts, omitting important details and using incomplete documents, withholding all that would have characterized the affair in its true light.

The owner of the hides on opposing the judicial order told the agents, Klahn and Shedd, that his resistance was not made with the object of concealing stolen property; that they might on this or any other occasion examine the establishment and skins found in it, but that this should be in a private character, and in no case in compliance with a judicial order contrary to the laws. The agents Klahn and Shedd refused the offer.

The owner of the hide establishment, not satisfied with having made the offer, when these orders were being executed and whilst his establishment was closely watched by police that no skins should be extracted therefrom, reiterated his offer in the presence of several persons, and among them the United States Vice Consul at Matamoros. All these persons appeared before the Commission and deposed that it was so. Mr. Lucas Avery, Vice Consul in 1869, said that "All met together at the house of Klahn and Shedd, and that the witness heard Mr. Manauton (owner of the establishment) say to them that he was disposed to have them visit it and inspect it to their entire satisfaction with the hides contained in it, with the understanding that this offer was merely voluntary and friendly, and not as the result of the judicial order, not recognizing in the authority that dictated it the right to do so; it was sufficient that the said order was contrary to the Mexican laws." The witness heard Mr. Klahn answer that he was much obliged for the offer, but that in accordance with his duties he could not accept it, because he and his partner, Mr. Shedd, desired above all things to establish as a precedent for similar cases the one then pending, that the American cattle breeders might, with the intervention of the authorities, practice general searches in quest of such hides as had American brands. To this Manauton replied, that in no case would he allow a search into his establishment unless the law so determined it, and unless, too, the warrant ordering the search should be based on the legal grounds provided by the law.

All these circumstances have been carefully concealed by Henry Klahn when, to corroborate the complaints of the residents of Texas, he undertook to explain the action of the Mexican authorities in 1869.* He, without any doubt, withheld said circumstances because it would have been apparent from them that there was no purpose at all to conceal the stolen hides, and no obstacle to prevent him from carrying into effect the inspection ; but there certainly was a refusal to allow, under the pretext of said inspection, a violation of individual rights, an undue intervention on the part of the Brownsville authorities and of the proprietors in Texas, and that our judicial functionaries should become accomplices to both irregularities. Mr. Klahn, in keeping silent upon all these circumstances, which would have cleared their conduct, and in acting so as to show their conduct in a different light, has, under oath, affirmed that which was not strictly true.

The proceedings of the council of Matamoros were not arrested by anything which had before been said by the Commission. On the 8th day of November was begun a session which was interrupted but resumed on the 18th day of the same month. In this the first judge declared that he believed himself without the power to execute the judicial process agreed on by the council on the conduct of Judge Menchaca, and for this reason he had done nothing. The council revoked their first judgment of the 25th of October, in which they had been willing to receive this information, with which the conflict was terminated.

All these documents relating to the first action of the council have been used by the complainants of Texas to find a reason for accusation against Mexican authorities ; † but they

---

* Report of the U. S. Commissioners, page 29. Henry Klahn.
† Report of the U. S. Commissioners to Texas, page 30. Document 19.

have not mentioned the last, that is, those which show that the judge charged to execute the judicial process refused to comply with the agreement of the council, and that he, seeing his error, retraced his steps.

The mass of the documents show that the council of Matamoros never asked for the removal of Judge Menchaca; that its object was to collect the proofs with regard to the actions on which said functionary was accused by one of the aldermen, with a view of making them known to the State government; that this was never executed, and that soon after the former decision was revoked; in all this was acquired the certain knowledge that this incident never had the slightest importance.

And this judgment is so correct that Judge Menchaca continued afterwards tranquilly executing his functions during several months, notwithstanding that the complainants in Texas asserted that, as a consequence of those persecutions, the aforementioned judge found it necessary to resign and take refuge in Europe. •

It does not seem necessary to have sought protection at such a distance, unless he believed his persecutors to feel a most persistent hatred against him, and did not think it sufficient to go to the borders of the United States, putting the river Bravo between himself and his enemies, but considered it indispensable that the ocean should separate them.

But these dramatic proceedings are not sustained by the documents. The judge Menchaca resigned with a view to go to Europe for the restoration of his health, and the court of justice of the State refused to accept his resignation. At his request they gave him a leave of absence of three months, which began the 22d of January, 1870. Up to the present date, that is, until long after the occurrence of the incidents narrated, he continued to exercise his judicial functions. Being in Washington, he received a telegram from the convened court recalling him to take charge of the court, but he answered it was necessary for him to go to Europe, and in case they could not wait on him they might consider his resignation made. He returned in 1871, and was nominated adviser of the constitutional judges of Matamoros; he was unanimously elected con-

stitutional judge for the year 1872 ; during all of which time
he discharged the duties of the court, and was commissioned in
his judicial character to receive the information on the claims
pending in the joint commission in Washington ; he is at present district attorney of the federal court in Matamoros.

It is seen that the action of the Matamoros council has not
been an impediment in the way of attorney Augustine Menchaca in the exercise of his judicial functions before and after
his absence from the country. It is seen that there is no correctness in saying that the public indignation was manifested
against him on account of his efforts to suppress cattle stealing,
because on his return in 1871 the town of Matamoros unanimously elected him constitutional judge for 1872. It is seen
even in this trivial affair that he resumed his important
character.

The council was not guided by ignoble views, though they
erred in their course. That same council, against which those
reproaches were made, discussed in the session of the 18th of
September, 1869, the question of cattle stealing. The act relative to this, says :

" Mr. Campuzano called the attention of the municipal
body in regard to the clandestine traffic of herds of cattle which
are passed from the other side of the river, and asked that the
R. Corporation should take such preventive measures as they
deemed expedient. The president replied that he had previously instructed the municipal justices to carry out the different
rulings on this subject, which had been communicated to them
with a view of putting an end to the illegal traffic of
cattle. Mr. Mainero remarked that the complaint set
forth by Mr. Campuzano was a notorious truth with
regard to the illegal traffic carried on on both sides
of the river, in the transportation of cattle from the left
bank into Mexico, as well as the transportation of horses and
mules from this bank to the opposite shore of the Bravo, regardless of the measures taken by the president of the council
to enforce the ruling on this subject, and the repeated notices
issued relative to this abuse, and which had been sent to the
judges of the district for their instruction. That notwithstanding all these regulations the evil has not been remedied, and in
spite of all the measures taken, and of all the circulars issued to
all the justices, as well as to the chiefs of the country police,

instructing both not to permit the transportation of animals, either in the case of importation or exportation, unless those interested first present a permit from the custom house, which is required by the general laws. Sufficiently discussed, it was unanimously approved."

At the time the conflict alluded to took place, the municipal corporation of Matamoros realized the evil in all its extent, and spontaneously, without its having been exacted, they sought remedies in the best faith. And not only does the former act justify the authorities, who exercised their functions in Matamoros in 1869 ; the circular issued on the 28th of September, of the same year, to the principal justices of the peace, demonstrated that the council of that year endeavored to prosecute the thefts. In it was admitted that the greater part of the cattle passed from one bank to another was stolen ; the former orders to prosecute them were reiterated ; the justices of the peace were threatened with the responsibility which they incurred if they did not take precautions to prevent the clandestine passing of cattle from one bank to another.

The orders dictated by the Mexican authorities, and the proceedings of those in Texas, characterized the propensities of both. The first recognized the evil in its fullest extent ; they saw that not only was our frontier robbed, but also that of Texas ; their measures take steps to remedy these robberies ; their just views show that in nothing have they attempted dissimulation. The second, to the contrary, are only affected by the damages they sustain, and they take no notice of the organized robbery of horses, on their own frontier, to the detriment of Mexico ; they keep silent on the latter, and not only do they remain quiet, but even the grand jury of the county of Cameron, in its reports of the 22d of April, 1872, says that only occasionally were horses stolen in Mexico and taken to Texas ; that the guilty parties have been Mexicans, and it has been impossible to find a single American involved in these transactions. They do not recognize the truth in regard to Mexico, and they arrive at the most unreliable statements in reference to Texas. There is an absolute indifference in the

Texas authorities to suppress the theft committed on our frontier for the United States; but they are very pressing with regard to those committed in Texas for Mexico. The Mexican proprietors who claim their stolen property before the Texas authorities had difficulties placed in their way to such a degree that pay was exacted for the sheriff or agent who pursued the robbers; but the judicial pressure as regards Mexico has been carried to the extreme, by pretending that inspectors whose nomination originated with the Texas authorities should perform their duties in Mexican territory, and that our authorities should give them support, in violation of the laws of the republic.

In the unlawful interference which the officers on the left border of the Bravo pretend to exercise should be sought the cause of the conflict begun by the Matamoros council in 1869. It was not in truth the desire to protect the theft which moved them, because from their own wish they had formerly adopted means to punish it. The Commission recognizes in the municipal corporation the right to oppose that intervention. That which condemns it is the form which the resistance assumed. If in place of the measures which they took and afterwards found necessary to revoke, they had complained before the court of justice of the State, demanding that it should make the judge responsible for having exceeded the powers invested in him, the Commission would have recognized that the council, in its proceedings and the spirit of its tendencies, had complied with its duties. With regard to the judge, his very error is the greatest proof of his honorable intentions and of his earnest desires to discover the crimes of the guilty.

Nor is there less foundation to the reproach made against Judge Hinojosa, who succeeded Augustin Menchaca. Henry Klahn, in private conversation and not officially, pretended to have received from him an order to search all the pastures in search of stolen cattle. It did not designate any place nor necessitate any act. The judge refused to become an instrument to any such deception, and answered that the pastures should first be searched, and when he could say there was anything stolen he would lend necessary assistance for its recovery.

In putting forth these acts in the complaints made against Mexico all the circumstances are omitted, and it is only shown that the judge, Pedro Hinojosa, refused his assistance and made it known privately to Klahn, making it appear that the judge found himself under such a pressure that only privately could he treat of this subject.

It was indispensable that the Commission should carefully discuss this incident, because it has been the one used to sustain that the corruption of the Mexican employees reaches the extreme, not only in protecting the theft but also in preventing faithful officials from complying with their duties. When, to prove this, are presented acts and incomplete documents, they cannot but presume that there is a want of better reasons; thus the accusation becomes the most complete defense.

A cause has existed by which, notwithstanding the interest generally taken by the administrative authorities and the Mexican judicials, these orders have failed to produce all the effects which might have been expected. The reason of this has been the want of a police force sufficient to pursue the robbers. The agents of justice on the ranchos did not count on any official help, and their lives would have been endangered if they had attempted to enforce the compliance with all the necessary orders which they had received.

The country police of Tamaulipas is a force made up of the proprietors and their servants; it was established for the care and security of the country—this vigilance commending itself to those most interested—but the organization became an office of trust, but assumed no permanent character. When they had any work on hand, some of the residents united at the order of their chief to do the work commended to their care and then return to their labors. This has been one of the principal elements for the persecution of the theft, and it can be seen that this could not be sufficient.

Later the authorities on our frontier saw the necessity of organizing a system of persecution of the evil doers, and this ought not only to be done when they carry stolen goods, but at any time. On conceiving this idea they immediately commenced to put it into execution.

The gang of thieves which were most notable was that of José Maria Martinez and Andres Flores. The first prosecuting judge of Matamoros ordered the country police in the east to pursue that gang of robbers. The chief of that expedition, Juan Treviño Conales, made an agreement with Colonel Ford, of the left side of the Bravo, that they might simultaneously pursue the robbers on both sides, thus preventing the fugitives from this side from uniting and organizing on the other ; the result was the death of both of the chiefs in September, 1870, and the taking of Baltasar Flores and Magdaleno Carrillo ; the rest of the gang dispersed themselves, and flying, took refuge in the interior of Texas, where many of them have been seen.

At the beginning of 1871, the chief of the country police of the south received orders to go in search of the robbers, and of these were killed the robbers Ildefónse Rodriguez, Manuel Garcia, and Candido Garcia.

In January, 1872, General Cortina organized a force for the purpose of pursuing thieves ; they went after the Lugas gang, who had united themselves in the interior of Texas to José Maria Sanchez Uresti, and passed over to Mexico to commit depredations. Both the Lugas' were killed, Pedro and Longinos, Agapito Galvan and Santiago Sanchez, all famous robbers.

The country police, at the beginning of the same year dispersed another gang organized in Texas, and to which belonged Antonia Sardineta, Antonia Garcia, Benito Alaniz and Agapito Yanez. The last was taken and executed according to the laws.

The Commission has already mentioned the situation of the Bolsa, and the facilities which it presents to criminals for hiding themselves on both banks. The Mexican authorities, in August, 1872, ordered the pursuit of the robbers who were hiding themselves there, but that this might porduce the best results, there was a previous agreement made with the United States consul at Matamoros that a force should be in pursuit on American territory at the same time it was being done on the Mexican side. The combination had a good exit, leaving the gang destroyed, and having killed Cipriana Flores, Victor Gonzales (alias) the Coyte, Francisco Gonzales (alias) the Chineño and Rafel Hinojosa (alias) the Cucho.

On the course east of Matamoros it had continued its pursuit of the robbers, the rest of the Lugas gang, and who were commanded by Manuel Garcia Luga. In this new pursuit were killed Margarito Garcia, Geronimo Perez, and Severo Acoña.

The Commission has only referred to the organization of thieves, the suppression of which has been sought for since the year 1870. But apart from this they have been in pursuit of other thieves, many of whom were executed, and others were killed through the resistance which they made. Among these are counted Santiago Nuñes and another called Monterey, and others whose names are not known.

The consequence of this systematic persecution has been that the frontier of Tamaulipas is no longer a rendezvous for the thieves, or a point of refuge for the runaways who habitually reside in Texas. The largest number of those of whom these bands were composed came from the interior of Texas. Those who were not killed returned to the places from which they came, and a small number went to the interior of Tamaulipas. With them considerably disappeared the crimes which were being perpetrated on both frontiers, which fact corroborates that it is not with the inhabitants of the Mexican frontier that the origin of the disorder can be looked for, nor were they its principal agents. It is certain that on our frontier there must have been accomplices, but these, according to the proofs, did not take the principal part. It is also beyond doubt true that on the Mexican side there must have been co-laborers to assist them, but the robbing enterprises were organized on the Texas " ranchos," whose residents stole cattle to make over to others, to be carried to the banks of the Bravo.

The pursuit which was made after the gang of José Maria Martinez and that of Cipriana Flores, are examples which ought not to be forgotten. It is shown by these that a happy termination in such cases, can only be effected by the combined action of the authorities on both sides.

With rare exceptions, the Mexicans have been extremely solicitous to correct the disordered state complained of by both borders. Their repeated orders, show that they proceeded with perseverance in a system for this purpose, and that on convincing themselves that the ordinary means were not sufficient they sought more effectual remedies.

Our frontier is tranquil, while in that of Texas exists increasing disorder, and the cattle stealing, under the form of skinning cattle, has assumed extraordinary proportions. The comparison of what is taking place in both countries would convince the most incredulous that the corruption so extended in Texas had its beginning there, being there propagated and there perfected. It is not confined to any particular class; all take part in it, who steal one animal and skin it; and the merchants who without scruple buy the skins, and the proprietor who marks calves that do not belong to him, and the herder who sells cattle not belonging to him, on the pretext that he will return it, if the owner claims it, are all engaged in it. These are the causes of the demoralization on our frontier; there are the traders of horses stolen in Mexico, and from them is received the impulse by the cattle stealers to fall on the Mexican frontier.

General Juan N. Cortina's conduct has been made the subject of most special inquiry. He has been made the object of the severest criticism along the whole length of the Mexican line; his forces have been termed organized hordes, and it was said that they penetrated into Texas for the purpose of committing the greatest depredations. In order that the full extent of the charges made may be understood, the Commission have annexed to the *expediente* copies of the Brownsville papers containing them, and the reports of several of the grand juries of Cameron and Starr counties. The consideration of the question relating to the frontier under this aspect convinced the Commission that the recent complaints are so intimately connected with General Cortina's previous life, that it would be impossible to estimate the former without a full examination of the latter. These considerations induced the Commission to make a lengthened investigation with regard to General Cortina, and the influence exercised by him upon both sides of the Bravo since 1859.

On the 26th of April of this year, the grand jury of Cameron county found three bills of indictment against Juan N. Cortina for "cattle stealing." The number of such indictments was subsequently increased in Cameron county to eleven, and in Starr county to four. The crimes of which he was accused were homicide, attempt at homicide, and treason. These latter are subsequent to his revolt in 1859, and were, no doubt, consequently influenced by that occurrence. But with regard to the three former, that is, those for cattle stealing, as these were prior to that occurrence, it is presumable that no other influences were exerted, except those usually present in such cases.

His revolt was brought about by the following circumstances. He saw the sheriff at Brownsville dragging a Mexican along by the collar; Cortina remonstrated with him; the sheriff made use of insulting language in his reply; Cortina then shot at and wounded him, and carried off the prisoner. This occured on the 13th of July, 1859. On the 28th of September of the same year, he again appeared at Brownsville with some fifty men, and took possession of the town. Several of those who, it was alleged, had been guilty of outrage toward the " Texan Mexicans," were killed, and all the prisoners who joined him were released. At the request of various persons he left the city and retired to his ranch; he was disposed to lay down his arms and leave Texas ; several parties saw him for this purpose, and he agreed to it, requiring only from four to six days to transfer to the Mexican side some cattle which some of his companions had, and divide his people into small parties of three or four each, to avoid their being pursued by the Mexican authorities at the time of their crossing the river. He did so, but shortly after he was told that one of his followers had been hung at Brownsville, upon which he went into Texas and began gathering people together, giving his movement a more definite character.

It is worthy of notice that when the revolt assumed this aspect it was highly popular among the " Texan Mexicans," that is, among all the Mexican population which had settled in Texas before or after the treaty of Guadaloupe. The fact that Cortina was joined by a large number of these, some of whom were land owners, can be attributed to no other reason. One of these was Theodore Zamora, who at the time he joined Cortina was one of the authorities of Hidalgo county, and several witnesses have deposed that he was the mayor of the county at the time.

The Commission has already referred to the condition of the Mexicans in Texas subsequent to the treaty of Guadalupe. Their lands were especially coveted. Their title deeds presented the same confusion as did all the grants of land made by the Spanish government, and this became the fruitful source of litigation by which many families were ruined. The legislation, instead of being guided by a spirit of equity, on the contrary tended toward the same end ; attempts were made to deprive the Mexicans of their lands, the slightest occurrence was made use of for this purpose, and the supposition is not a remote one, that the cause of such procedure may have been a well settled political principle, leading as far as possible to exclude from an ownership in the soil the Mexicans, whom they regarded as enemies and an inferior race.

At the commencement, and during the disorganization which was prolonged after the Treaty of Guadalupe, robberies and spoliations of lands were perpetrated by parties of armed Americans. It is not extraordinary to find some of them whose only titles consist in having taken possession of and settled upon lands belonging to Mexicans. After these spoliations there came the spoliations in legal forms, and all the resources of a co plicated legislation.*

---

* At the time the Commission made its report it had not then received various documents to which reference will be made in their proper places by notes. Some of these show the insecurity under which the Mexican population in Texas had labored, and refer to the difficulties known as the cart question.

The residents of Uvalde county, Texas, in September, 1857, passed several resolutions, prohibiting all Mexicans from traveling through the country except under a passport granted by some American authority. At Goliad several Mexicans were killed because it was supposed that they had driven their carts on the public road.

On the 14th and 19th of October the Mexican Legation at Washington addressed the United States Government a statement of these facts, adding that it had been informed that in the vicinity of San Antonio, Bexar, Texas, parties of

9

The Texan Mexicans enjoyed no greater personal security than did their property, and what is remarkable, is that they

---

armed men had been organized for the exclusive purpose of pursuing the Mexicans upon the public roads, killing them and robbing their property, and that the number of victims was stated to have been seventy-five. That it was also informed that Mexican citizens by birth, residing peaceably at San Antonio, under the protection of the laws, had been expelled from the place, and finally that some of the families of the victims of these extraordinary persecutions had begun to arrive in Mexico on foot and without means, having been obliged to abandon all their property in order to save their lives.

The Secretary of State on the 24th of the same month addressed a communication to Mr. E. M. Pease, the Governor of the State of Texas, in which he says:

" These reports are not exclusively Mexican. The least among the outrages appear to be the violation of rights guaranteed by law, and under treaties, and I have no doubt that you will have already adopted speedy and energetic measures to ascertain the truth and punish the aggressors."

Governor Pease on the 11th of November, 1857, sent a message to the Texas Legislature. In it he stated that during the month of September previous, the Executive had received authentic information that a train of carts had been attacked a short distance from Ellana, Carnes county, while peaceably traveling on the public highway, by a party of armed and masked men, who fired upon the cartmen, killing one and wounding three others. That at the same time he had also received notice of another attack which took place the latter part of July, upon a train in Goliad county. That the attack was made at night, and three of the cartmen were wounded. That the killed and wounded in both instances were Mexicans, with the exception of one who was an American. That with these same reports proofs had also been received that a combination had been formed in several counties for the purpose of committing these same acts of violence against citizens of Mexican origin, so long as they continued to transport goods by those roads.

The Governor continues by stating the measures adopted by him for suppressing and punishing such outrages. He states that he proceeded to San Antonio for the purpose of ascertaining whether measures had been taken for the arrest of the aggressors and to prevent the repetition of such occurrences, to which end he had conferences with several citizens of Bexar. The result of these conferences convinced him that no measures had been taken or probably would be taken for the arrest of the guilty parties, or prevention of similar attacks. That in fact combinations of the kind mentioned did exist, and that they had been the origin of repeated assaults upon the persons and property of Mexicans who traveled over those roads. That in several of the border counties there prevailed a deep feeling of animosity towards the Mexicans, and that there was imminent danger of attacks and of retaliation being made by them, which if once begun would inevitably bring about a war of races.

The following paragraph of the same message shows how inexcusable these outrages were :

were wronged and outraged with impunity, because as far as they were concerned, justice and oppression were synonymous. Here is what a Brownsville newspaper says upon the subject:

"We have had occasion frequently to deplore that want of the administration of the law in such manner as to render to all parties the justice to which they were entitled. According to our ideas, when an officer enters upon the discharge of his duties, he should mark out for himself such a line of conduct as would insure the impartial exercise of his duties, laying aside all distinctions of race and persons, and remove from his proceedings everything which would tend to give them the appearance of a farce. Our population is, as is well known, divided into two classes, Americans and Mexicans; the latter are unquestionably more exposed to wrong than the former; their natural timidity makes them inoffensive, and by reason of the difference of language they cannot well understand our laws, or fully enjoy their rights. We have heard one of our highest officers state that it would be difficult to find a class of people more obedient to the laws. It is true that among them there are bad characters, and these should be severely punished,

---

"We have a large Mexican population in our western counties, among which are very many who have been carefully educated, and who have rendered important services to the country in the days of her tribulation. There is no doubt but that there are some bad characters amongst this class of citizens, but the great mass of them are as orderly and law-abiding as any class in the State. They cheerfully perform the duties imposed upon them, and they are entitled to the protection of the laws in any honest calling which they may choose to select."

The condition of the Mexican population residing in Texas has changed but little since 1857. Governor Pease's message to the Texas Legislature that year exposes and explains the reason of revolts such as the one which occurred on the banks of the Rio Bravo under Cortina in 1859.

A large portion of the disturbances which occurred between the Bravo and Nueces rivers is attributable to the persecutions suffered by the Mexicans residing there ; persecutions which have engendered the most profound hatred between the races.

Governor Pease, in the message referred to in the forgoing note, gives it to be understood that the Mexicans did not enjoy the protection of the courts and the authorities. He says our laws are adequate to the protection of life and property, but when the citizens and authorities of a county become indifferent to their execution, they are useless. Some remedy must be found for this condition of things, and the only means which suggests itself to me, is that jurisdiction be given to the grand jury, the officers and courts in any adjoining county where an impartial trial may be obtained, to arrest and try the offenders.

This passage shows that there was no justice for the Mexicans in Texas, and with regard to which the complaint has frequently been made.

but this fact at times gives rise to their all being classed in the
same category, and ill-used. We do not address any one in
particular, our remarks are general. Americans have at times
committed offenses which in them have been overlooked, but
which, if committed by Mexicans would have been severely
punished. But when election time comes, it is wonderful to
behold the friendship existing for the Mexican voters, and the
protection extended to them, the sympathy which until then
had remained latent or concealed, suddenly reveals itself in all
its plentitude, and many are astonished not to have found until
then the amount of kindly feeling professed towards them by
their whilom friends. Promises of all kinds are made to them,
but scarcely are the promises made, when they are broken.
An hour before the election they are fast friends, 'Mexicans,
my very good friends'—an hour after the election they are a
'crowd of greasers.' The magistrates are not Pachas or absolute rulers ; a certain respect is due to their position, and the
consciousness of the responsibility resting upon them should
make them feel their duties."—*American Flag*, Brownsville,
August 20th, 1856.

The Mexicans, whether they be Texans or whether they preserve their original nationality, have been the victims both in
their persons and property, and they have not been fully protected by the laws. Upon such antecedents, the cause of the
popularity of the Cortina movement among the Mexican population in Texas is easily understood. He issued several procla-
mations, in the first of which, dated the 30th September, 1859,
he said :

"Our purpose has been as you have seen, and your testimony to the fact you cannot withhold, to punish the infamous
villainy of our enemies. These have banded together, and as
it were, form a treacherous inquisition to pursue and rob us, for
no other reason and for no other offense upon our part, except
being by birth Mexicans, and because they suppose us to be
destitute of those very qualities which they themselves do not
possess. * * * The board having been organized and
being presided over by me, thanks to the confidence which I
inspire as being one of the most greatly wronged, we have
searched the streets of the city for our antagonists, to punish
them, since the law is inoperative for them, and justice as administered by them is unfortunately a dead letter. They, as
we have already said, with a multitude of lawyers, form a band

in concert, to dispossess the Mexicans of their lands, and afterwards usurp them. Adolpho Glaevecke's conduct proves it. Invested with the character of a member of the Legislature, and in combination with the lawyers, he has disseminated terror among the unthinking, by making them believe that they were about to hang the Mexicans upon any pretext, that they would burn their ranches, to thus compel them to leave the country, and so attain their ends."

In another proclamation, of the 23d of November, 1859, various resolutions were published, of which the 1st and 3d stated :

" An organized society in the State of Texas will untiringly devote itself, until its philanthropical purpose of bettering the condition of the unfortunate Mexicans who reside there shall have been attained, to the extermination of their tyrants, and to this end those composing it are ready to shed their blood or die the death of martyrs.

" ARTICLE 3D. The Mexicans in Texas place their future under the protection of the kindly feelings of General Houston, the Governor elect of the State, and confide that upon his elevation to power he will inaugurate such measures within the sphere of his powers as will give them the protection of the laws."

The popularity of that movement among the Texan Mexicans is disclosed by another document. A report of the grand jury of Cameron county said :

" Owing to its extended ramifications, or his (Cortina's) influence, the secrecy which he imposes, and the general sympathy toward him on the part of the lower classes of the Mexicans, there is little room to doubt that he could get together a large force under his orders.

" Whether it be fear or sympathy with the marauders," says the same document, " which prevents them from appearing, the Mexican residents of the county generally fail to appear, and when they do, they dislike to give information with regard to the numerous robberies and murders which are committed."—*Report of the Grand Jury, Cameron county, November*, 1859.

The higher authorities of Texas believed that there was more in the revolt of Cortina and his followers than an inten-

tion of murder and robbery. Governor Houston, in a proclamation on the 28th of December, 1859, said:

"If any parties have been injured, there is no necessity for
them, under a free government such as ours, to have recourse
to acts of violence to redress their grievances, because they
may rely for protection upon the guaranty which the Constitution and laws furnish. * * * The laws will be equally
executed towards all of our fellow-citizens, and none need fear
persecution. It is necessary to make an investigation, and it
will be made; if any persons have been injured their complaints
will be heard. Their continuance in rebellion against the laws
can only weaken their claim to justice. If, as they state, they
confide in the present executive, to see that legal protection is
extended to them within the sphere of his powers, he assures
them, that he will omit no constitutional means to protect the
rights of all good citizens; and those who return to their duty
may be assured of the protection of the law."

The Commission have made every effort to define the nature
of these occurrences, according to the documents of the time,
because at a later period it has been attempted to deny that
these events were questions between Texans, and throw the
responsibility on the frontier and the Mexican authorities.
The foregoing remarks refer to the nature of the movement,
but there are others which relate to those who participated in
it, and which further remove any doubts which might arise.

In his proclamation of the 30th of September, 1859, Juan
N. Cortina said:

"Laborious and thirsting for the enjoyment of the blessings
of liberty in the classic land of its origin, we were induced to
become naturalized in it. * * * Casually separated from
the inhabitants of the city on account of being outside of it,
but not relinquishing our rights *as citizens of the United
States.*"

This character which Cortina and those who had revolted
with him assumed, was recognized before and after their rising.
Before, because they were allowed to vote at the elections in
Texas. After, because on the 12th of May, 1860, the grand
jury of Cameron county indicted Cortina for treason, which indictment would have been impossible if he had not been a
citizen.

The Brownsville press when explaining the elements of which Cortina's forces were composed, says :

" On the morning of Wednesday (September 28th, 1859), he (Cortina), with a force estimated at from sixty to one hundred men, armed and mounted, all Mexicans by birth, but the greater part of them criminals from Mexico, *to whom an asylum has been stupidly furnished on the American side*, arrived in our city. * * * And to make the condition of things worse, the greater part of these men have committed crimes in Mexico, on account of which perhaps there is as little or less safety for them in Mexico ; in the meantime, many among them pretend to be citizens of the United States, and are determined to keep on this side of the river."—*American Flag*, Brownsville, October 8th, 1859.

There were in fact among the people who had revolted with Cortina some criminals ; the Texas side was suffering the consequences of the protection which it had afforded the marauders who sallied out from thence to perpetrate their crimes in Mexico, but at the same time the remarks made by the journal referred to, show that the movement had its origin in Texas, and was promoted by persons residing there, and that our frontier had nothing to do with these occurrences.

The officers of the United States were of the same opinion. The same journal copied from the New York *Herald*, the following paragraph :

" The war department has received a letter from Captain Rickets, which states, 'The origin of the difficulty is owing to a quarrel among people mixed up in private matters, and is so complicated in its character, that it is difficult to ascertain the truth.' "—*American Flag*, Brownsville, January 26th, 1860.

General Winfield Scott, in his report of the 19th of March, 1860, expressed himself as follows :

" The recent disturbances on our side of the lower Rio Grande were commenced by Texans, and carried out by and among them ; Cortina himself and the greater part of his bandits are natives of Texas. * * * But few Mexicans from the other side of the river, if any, took part in those disturbances."

The same opinion prevailed on the Mexican frontier. A paper at Matamoros said :

"The proclamation issued by John N. Cortina, a citizen of the United States, was printed at the city of Brownsville, and has been circulated in both cities."—*El Jayne,* October 12th, 1859.

In a communication of the 1st of November, 1859, addressed by the Mexican consul at Brownsville to the Mexican legation in the United States, relating the occurrences, and stating that he had been called upon, together with other persons, to see Cortina, he says:

"I informed them that I could not do so in my official capacity, because in addition to the fact that Cortina was not the representative of any legal authority, he and the parties who were with him, were naturalized citizens of the United States."

In a communication of the 30th of January, 1860, addressed by the gefatura politica of the district of the north, to the municipality of Reynosa, it stated:

"That it had been informed with regard to the late occurrences concerning the North American faction headed by Cortina."

In nearly all the communications of that time he is styled the same. The quotations would be lengthy, and the Commission refers to the documents taken from the divers archives, which appear in the *"expedientes."* In all of them it is seen that the Mexican authorities always held an unvarying opinion with regard to the character of Cortina and his forces, whether he was marauding on this or the other margin of the river.

At the commencement, and when the occurrences took place, the truth was not denied, the press of Brownsville and Matamoros, the grand jury who indicted Cortina as a traitor against the State of Texas, the United States authorities, and those on the Mexican frontier, admitted that the difficulties had their origin in Texas and among Texans, and that neither Mexico or the Mexicans had any interest or participation in the question. Nevertheless, a short time after, when the most imminent risk was passed, attempts were commenced to be made to distort the facts. The first was made in a report, of the grand jury of Cameron county.

When Cortina made his first revolt and took possession of Brownsville, on the morning of the 28th of September, 1859, several residents of the place represented to the Mexican consul that it was desirable to ask aid from the authorities at Matamoros. The consul agreed to grant their request, upon the condition that the authorities at Brownsville should make the request, and authorize the coming of the force. At nine o'clock on that day, the sheriff of the city made an official communication asking aid from the military commander at Matamoros; this was immediately granted, he replying that, "not only the regular troops, but the people of the city were ready and willing to aid the inhabitants of Brownsville, and that for this purpose they would cross the river, if necessary, whenever requested to do so by the authorities of the latter city."

Cortina again revolted in October of the same year, and threatened Brownsville; the authorities there requested aid from the Mexican authorities, which was promptly granted, and not only were troops sent, but arms were furnished for the arming of the people. On both occasions Brownsville was garrisoned by Mexican troops, and these preserved the city and its inhabitants from all attacks or threats. Further, the last time the Mexican forces made an expedition against Cortina and were defeated.

The proceedings of the authorities at Matamoros received the full approbation of the government of the State of Tamaulipas and of the Federal Government. The former, in a communication of the 10th of October, addressed to the military commander of the line of the Bravo, after expressing its approval of all that had been done, added:

"The government confides in you, that you, with your usual activity will continue taking all the measures in your power to insure the public tranquility within the bounds of your command, and aid the authorities of Brownsville for this same purpose whenever they request it. You will please to make a similar manifestation (of approval) to the authorities and residents of your city, who with such kindly feelings resolved to give that aid which humanity and our friendly relations with the American people demanded."

The Federal Government, in a communication of the 3d of December of the same year, addressed to the government of the State of Tamaulipas, and by it transcribed on the 30th of the same month to the military commandant of the line, after referring to the occurrences, directed:

" Orders will be issued to the forces on the frontier of the State, to prevent the crossing to the right bank of the Rio Bravo, of the bandits who attacked Brownsville, and that they, together and in concert with the officers in command of the American forces, pursue these bandits until they are brought to order, or exemplarily punished."

The action referred to by the authorities of the republic, both superior and inferior, and that of the people of Matamoros were uniform as to the course to be pursued. This the authorities at Brownsville were unable to deny at the time. The mayor of the city in a communication of the 29th of November, 1859, addressed to the Mexican consul, says:

" I am the organ for expressing the general feelings of my fellow-citizens, when I assure you of the great satisfaction which I have experienced upon learning of the action of your government in this respect (it referred to the government of Tamaulipas). This is another of the many proofs given by the present government of Mexico, of its desire to maintain the principles of good friendship towards the United States as a nation, and towards the inhabitants of a sister city."

The good offices of our authorities were recognized at that time, because it was impossible to conceal them, but at the same time they affected to entertain an opinion, which in the course of years, was to suffer various transformations, until it arrived at the one, that Mexico was alone culpable.

The grand jury of Cameron county, which commenced its sessions on the second Monday of November, 1859, submitted a report with regard to the disturbances which had taken place. They related the origin of the revolt, and that Cortina subsequently crossed the Rio Grande into Mexico, where it is said that he was recruiting soldiers for the Mexican army under a captain's commission, the truth of which the jurors added, they did not know. That he afterwards crossed the river with many persons residents of Mexico, and was joined by other Mexican citizens of the left bank of the river. Of the fact that all Cortina's companions were Mexicans, that he was a fugitive from justice, and had taken refuge in Mexico for three months, that he made use of the Mexican flag, to the cry of " Hurrah for the Mexican Republic ! " The jurors conclude, that there had been an invasion by armed Mexicans, under the Mexican flag, with hostile intentions towards the authorities of the State and the nation. ‑ That in view of the activity and zeal with which the authorities, both civil and military, of the State of Tamaulipas, and especially of Matamoros, endeavored to relieve the city of Brownsville from the dangers with which it was surrounded, they were unwilling to believe that the latter had sustained or aided this piratical invasion.

The report continues by endeavoring to create the impression, that Cortina's revolt was an act of invasion supported by the Mexican frontier. It states, that at least three-fourths of Cortina's companions had until then resided in Mexico, that he had received a reinforcement of fifty men, who arrived from Monterey under the command of an officer ; that not long since, he had received the reinforcement of another corps of from thirty to sixty men, from Victoria, in the State of Tamaulipas, that his force was under the military management of men who had acquired their knowledge in the wars of Mexico, and that he, on his expeditions made use of the Mexican flag. That for these reasons the jury were convinced that the Mexican population in Texas were united in a secret society, whose purpose was to expel the Americans from the Rio Grande, and that for this object they were in secret combination with some of the contending parties in Mexico, from whom they received arms and ammunition for their ulterior designs, the immediate discovery of which was not possible.

It concluded by expressing the hope that the authorities of the State would make use of their influence with the Federal Government to make a treaty or obtain other guaranties from the Mexican Government in such manner that in future the soil of Texas should not be sullied by the foot of the invader, nor the blood of her sons spilled by the hands of these.

The truth is ignored in this report, and those who affected to ignore it did so with a perfect knowledge of their wrong doing.

According to it those who revolted were not Texans by naturalization or domicile, but Mexican citizens residing in Mexico. It was not a local question, but a war of invasion supported by our frontier, and it was supported by one of the contending parties in the republic during the war of the reform. Its origin was not questions of private interest but something unknown, ulterior designs on the part of Mexico.

Some criminals broke jail at the city of Victoria, in Tamaulipas, and fled towards the Bravo river, in search of that protection which the residents of the left bank always gave to those who were guilty of crime in Mexico, and this fact is distorted into a confirmation that Tamaulipas lent its support to the movement which took place in Texas. Our people were openly reproached, our authorities, though not so, were suspected, when doubts were expressed whether a captain's commission had been issued to Cortina under which he was organizing soldiers with which to invade Texas. They were unwilling to believe that our authorities, after their zeal and activity in protecting Brownsville, had supported Cortina, but they did not assert a contrary belief, and appeared to be vacillating. They spoke of Cortina's having taken refuge in our territory when he was a fugitive from Texas, and although not even they themselves said, except in concealed terms, that Cortina violated the neutrality laws of Mexico, they reproached our public officers with not molesting him. The grand jury who did this placed itself in contradiction with the one who, months after, acknowledged Cortina's citizenship by indicting him for treason.

It placed itself in contradiction with the documents in its own archives where were recorded the votes of many of Cortina's companions ; it placed itself in opposition to what its own press asserted in the beginning concerning the criminals guilty of crimes committed in Mexico, whom they had stupidly protected on the left bank of the river, and who were Cortina's companions ; they placed themselves in contradiction with the agents of the United States, who characterized the movement as one which had its origin in Texas and was supported by Texans.

All this was done for a purpose, and that the United States, exacting guaranties from the Mexican Republic, difficulties might be created between the two countries. It was then that the "motto" which since that time has been in use by the residents on the Texas side as against Mexico had its origin—" *Compensation for the past, guaranties for the future.*"

Such proceedings appear ungenerous on the part of the people of Brownsville when but a few days had elapsed since the protection of the Mexican forces had saved them from greater misfortunes. It appears ungenerous that so short a time after this occurrence reproaches and accusations should have been brought against our country, but this was only the beginning. The time was to arrive when not only the inhabitants of the Mexican side of the river, but all its authorities, were to be openly accused of being the accomplices of Cortina, and when our frontier was to be constantly menaced and frequently invaded. Cortina's revolt now formed one of the accusations made against the republic. It is now asserted that Mexican forces accompanied Cortina. (No. 1.) (Report of the United States Commissioners to Texas, page 29.) Among the accusers are Mifflin Kennedy, Adolpho Glaevecke and several others who were residents of Brownsville at that time, and who owed their personal safety to the action of the authorities on this side. The latter especially was one of the persons against whom the rebels entertained the deepest hatred. If to-day those parties recollect those occurrences it is not to show their gratitude to the Mexican frontier, but to present heavy claims against Mexico for losses which they allege they suffered during Cortina's raid. Cortina continued within the territory of the United States until shortly after his defeat, which occurred on the 29th of December, 1859. The Mexican authorities from the commencement foresaw the possibility that parties belonging to Cortina might cross into Mexico, and had been giving their orders in anticipation of this occurrence.

On the 3d of October, 1859, the gefatura politica of the

northern district, fearing that the dispersed belonging to the band of Juan N. Cortina in the neighborhood of Brownsville might pass over to this side, directed the formation of patrols to patrol the pastures and arrest all unknown persons or those whom they had reason to believe ought to be tried and sentenced as vagrants. At the same time the municipality of Matamoros gave its orders to have the directions of the gefatura carried out. On the fourth of the same month the chief of police of the East answered that he had taken his measures for the purpose mentioned in the foregoing communication, notwithstanding the greater part of that force had crossed by way of the " Sabinito."

On the twenty-fourth of the same month, the military commandant at Matamoros, fearful that Cortina might again pass over to this side by way of the Sabinito ranche, placed a detachment there, with orders to watch the fords of the river, and prevent the passage of any of the armed forces which were with Juan N. Cortina, to arrest the fugitives from the prison at Victoria, Tamaulipas, who it was said had marched in the direction of the Bravo river, and had been seen at a ranche to the north of the jurisdiction of San Fernando.

In the month of December, Juan N. Cortina with his force went up the river to Rio Grande City, Star county. The Mexican authorities then displayed the greatest vigilance along the bank of the river, the strictest watch was kept on Cortina's movements, and none of them failed to be reported. At the time of his defeat, and when it appeared imminent that he would cross into Mexico, the vigilance was increased, and orders multiplied to prevent if possible his crossing.

The Mexican authorities considered Cortina's continuance on the Texas side as a menace to the people and property in Mexico ; his crossing as an act of invasion ; his permanence on our frontier as an act of hostility which demanded sacrifice on the part of the government to remedy, and which kept that part of the republic in a state of constant alarm. This alarm was so much the greater inasmuch as the nation was then fighting for its liberties in the war of reform. The frontier forces were participating in this struggle in the interior of the country, and the menaces towards the population increased in proportion with the scarcity of their elements for defending hemselves.

Nevertheless the Mexican authorities fulfilled their duties. They dispatched forces to quell these disturbances, and confided the undertaking to General Guadalupe Garcia. The character of this campaign was exceptional. Extensive wastes and thick forests on the frontier permitted an easy escape and a safe refuge to a band, which the smaller its numbers the greater would be its faculties for escaping pursuit. The campaign was not one in which there was even skirmishing, Cortina's party, too weak to resist any attack, cónstantly fled, and the pursuit had to be as tenacious as the flight to prevent him from reorganizing. It was so, but it is easily understood that its consummation could not be the work of a moment, that only by continual pursuit and after a certain length of time, could a result be reached.

Not only the superior authorities contributed to carry out this end, but the towns also. Forces were organized in them which aided these operations. In their archives are found constant notices concerning the movements of Cortina and his men, they facilitated everything because the support was general. General Garcia was taken sick, the geffe politico of the district took command of the force, and in June of 1860, succeeded in driving Juan N. Cortina from the bank of the river; he took refuge in the Burgos Mountains, and was not heard of for a long time. The military authorities even exceeded their powers. At the end of April, 1860, they made an arrangement with the officer commanding the United States forces to cross a cavalry force into Mexico, which in company with that under the command of Major José Maria Zuñiga was to pursue Cortina; Major Zuñiga did not go upon the expedition, but Major Cecilio Salazar did, and was directed to place himself in concert with the officer commanding the American forces, for the better execution of his commission, if it had already crossed the river. This force which was to visit Mexico, by virtue of the agreement of April, 1860, did not finally cross, but by these arrangements, which were beyond the attributes of the military authority on the frontier, and which the Commission is compelled to condemn, is shown the desire on the part of those officers to obtain the destruction of Cortina's band. The Mexican authorities not only engaged in the pursuit of it but also in its suppression. A large number of the individuals who accompanied Cortina, and whose names appear in the " espedientes," were arrested and tried by court martial. By the instructions given on the 25th of May, 1860, by the commander of the Bravo line to Major Cecilio Salazar, engaged in the pursuit of Cortina, he was ordered to shoot all of those belonging to the band whom he might arrest or apprehend. In compliance with this order, Florencio Hernandez was shot. On the 5th of July, 1860, in addition to those who had been already imprisoned, the military judge ordered the imprisonment of fifteen individuals who, it was said, had accompanied the North American Juan N. Cortina on his invasion into Mexico, and who had taken refuge at some of the ranchos. The arrest of the greater part of these was effected, and they were tried ; the result of which trial the Commission is not informed of, as the archives have been lost.

The documents relating to the occurrences of that time show that, while the zeal of the Mexican authorities increased, Texas became more exacting. She could not prevent Cortina and his forces from invading our frontier, and Mexico had just ground of complaint because the State of Texas showed itself unable or unwilling to carry out its laws on the banks of the Rio Bravo, and also because disturbances were there created which, during several months, were a menace to our lines, a menace which afterwards resulted in an invasion. Mexico had to defend herself against this, because she had already sufficient elements of anarchy within her own limits, and she could not allow those emanating from Texas to be added to them. Mexico, for the space of six months, was under the necessity of keeping an army in the field, and suffered from the natural consequences of such a situation. But, notwithstanding all this, the tables were turned. Complaint was made against Mexico because she did not speedily exterminate Cortina's band ; she was criminated and accused of having given him support and protection on our soil. A volunteer force of Texans was organized (the rangers), men without discipline, who made a series of invasions on the Mexican frontier and there committed the greatest excesses.

The condition of our towns on the frontier was then most difficult. It was necessary for them to be organized to protect themselves against the menace of the Texan force, and at the same time protect themselves against Cortina's band. Documents in the archives and the orders issued show this situation, and the effort made to save it. The necessity of being on the watch against the Texas volunteers prevented a more efficacious pursuit against Cortina.

These aggressions and the menaces made at that time against the Mexican line by the Texans, show the desire to involve both frontiers in a conflict in which the two nations would subsequently become involved. They could not have believed that Cortina would find sympathy with our authorities, because they must have had the recollection of the proceedings of these in previous months. In October of 1859, Brownsville had no forces of any kind whatever. Indifference at this time on the part of the Mexican authorities would have been sufficient to have allowed this city to have become the victim of its enemy. They lent the aid of their forces, and when they so conducted themselves at the time when Cortina's revolt was in force, and only required inaction on their part, it is unreasonable to suppose that they would await the moment when Cortina should be routed, a fugitive, and without men to aid him, and then give him their sympathy. It was certainly unreasonable, but nevertheless they pretended to believe it in order to decide the United States to take hostile measures against Mexico.

Colonel Lockridge said, in a correspondence of the 28th of December, 1859 :

"It is reserved for the future to decide, whether the government will require from the Mexican government the delivery of Cortina, and in the event of the latter's refusal, whether this will not be a sufficient cause for the immediate occupation of the northern part of Mexico by our troops, until they 'indemnify us for the past and give us guaranties for the future.'

10

You may be assured that this is the opinion of every American now serving in the army. It is undeniable that Cortina has received assistance and reinforcement from Mexico, and even that he has crossed the river, and that they have publicly received him at Matamoros, Reynosa, and other points on the Rio Grande."—*American Flag*, Brownsville, Jan'y 5th, 1860.

It appears that these intentions were not overlooked by the American Government. This is revealed in a proclamation addressed to the people of Texas by Governor Samuel Houston, on March 24th, 1860. In the part of it relating to the disturbances on the Rio Bravo, he stated that he considered it to be his duty to communicate to his fellow citizens the efforts made by him to obtain the assistance of the Federal Government on behalf of the frontier which had been outraged by robbers organized in Mexico:

"I believed it to be my duty," he said, "to defer to the authority of the United States with regard to the invasion of our soil by Mexico. * * * With a barbarous and cunning enemy at our doors, there was sufficient reason for my addressing the Federal authorities. Fearing that the thousand rumors with regard to my intentions concerning Mexico might operate adversely to the employment of our volunteers and the sending of arms, and desirous of insisting upon the necessity that the Federal authorities should protect Texas, on the 12th instant (March, 1860), I addressed the Secretary of War the following communication."

In this communication Governor Houston refers to a telegram from Washington of the 3d of March, published in a New Orleans paper, which telegram said:

"The President has disapproved of Governor Houston's conduct in calling out the Texas volunteers for the defense of the frontier."

He States, that it is not true that he had sent troops to the Rio Bravo; that far from this, when he assumed the government, that he discharged four companies who were on the Rio Grande, and that two were subsequently organized by the advice of the Texas commissioners, who conferred upon the subject with Major Heintzleman of the United States army, and that these were under his orders.

"*If I had consulted*," says the communication, "*the wishes and desires of my fellow-citizens, I would have called into the service all the disposable forces of Texas, 1 would have crossed the Rio Grande, and never have recrossed it without having obtained 'guaranties for the future.*'

"The government of the United States, perhaps crediting rumors and newspaper articles, supposes that I entertained some covert design of invading Mexico. * * * It is true, that since 1857, I have been written to from various places in the United States, urging me to invade Mexico with a view to establishing a protectorate, and assuring me, that men, money and arms would be placed at my disposal if I took part in the undertaking. To these suggestions I have replied unfavorably, although as an individual I might have co-operated by placing myself without the jurisdiction of the United States. Nor was the security wanting that a large portion of the Mexican population would receive and co-operate with me, towards the establishment of order in their country. Nevertheless I have remained quiet and silent, *under the hope that the government of the United States will consummate a policy which must be, and which will be carried out, if the wretched inhabitants of this beautiful region are to be exposed to destruction in a conflict with robbers.*"

The intention thus of producing a conflict with Mexico came not only from the civil and military authorities which Texas had on its borders, but from its high officers. For this purpose the facts were first distorted, and afterwards followed a series of aggressions for which Cortina was the pretext. It was well known that Cortina, subsequent to his defeat, was a fugitive and a wanderer, with but few of his companions, and that not only was it impossible for him to undertake any attack upon the left bank of the river, but not even to defend himself against his pursuers. Nevertheless importance was pretended to be attached to him to maintain the excitement among the people of the United States, and drag their government into projects of invasion under the semblance of "guaranties for the future." There were not wanting in General Houston's proclamation the inducements which filibustering always present to deceive the incautious by supposing a mass of the people anxious for the invasion of the republic, and ready to aid the invasion. All means were brought into play to deceive the people and the government of the United States. The question between the North and the South was then being agitated, and Governor Houston endeavored to find a solution of it by a war with Mexico on the Cortina question. A political resort was sought in it for the internal questions existing in the United States.

After the volunteers were removed from the banks of the Bravo the government of Texas became convinced that their intentions were not supported by the government of the United States, and the difficulties on the Rio Grande subsided, and thus, notwithstanding Cortina was not driven from those places until the month of June, and yet from April to June no difficulties of any kind occurred. This conclusively shows that an artificial life had been given to him in Texas, and that when it ceased to serve as a political means for more extended purposes, that he resumed his natural proportions.

XIII.

After Juan N. Cortina took refuge in the mountains of Búrgos, nothing was heard of him till the following year, and after the Confederate war had broken out. The Clareño ranche in Texas had been attacked by the Confederates and several Mexicans killed. Cortina then came down to the edge of the river, and aided by the refugees and some Mexicans from Guerrero, he invaded Texas by way of the Carrizo, in May of 1861. On the twenty-third of this same month, he was defeated, and this was his last attempt on Texas.

He continued a wandering life in Tamaulipas. At the end of 1861, Jesus de la Serna was declared Governor of this State; a revolution ensued against him, in which Matamoros and Tampico refused to recognize him. Tamaulipas was for some time the theater of a civil war, and Cortina endeavored to participate in it on behalf of Governor Serna. He made his first approaches to the authorities at Reynosa, but these refused to accept his co-operation, to avoid complications with the Confed-

erates. His second attempt was with the forces who were besieging Matamoros, but the officers in command of these decided
that Cortina ought not to be employed except in the interior of
the State, and at a distance from the river. He then retired,
and placed himself under the orders of General Martin Zayas,
who was operating about Victoria, Tamaulipas, and with whom
he remained during that local war.

The republic at this time was menaced by the European
intervention. The Federal government, in order to terminate
the conflict in Tamaulipas, at the end of December, 1861, declared it to be in a state of siege, and appointed Santiago Vidaurri, the governor of Nuevo Leon, the governor and military
commandant; he transferred his powers to General Ignacio
Comonfort. The contending forces were ordered to place themselves under the orders of this latter; some obeyed and others
disbanded—Juan N. Cortina was among the former. By these
means, he succeeded in confirming his position in Mexico, and
entering the army against the European intervention. He
passed through the campaign at Puebla and other places in the
interior, until August or September of 1863, when he was sent
to Matamoros in command of a force of cavalry, General Manuel Ruiz being at this time governor and military commandant
of Tamaulipas. At the time of Cortina's arrival at Matamoros
he held the rank of lieutenant-colonel of cavalry in the militia.
The Commission is not informed of the reasons or how he
reached this position.

The situation of the republic at this time was most critical
and deplorable; the Mexican armies of the center and the east,
at San Lorenzo and Puebla, had been defeated by the invading
forces; the city of Mexico abandoned by the Federal government, and it ready to leave San Luis for refuge on the northern
frontier, with the doubtful co-operation of Santiago Vidaurri,
the governor of Nuevo Leon, without resources and surrounded
by enemies, its position could not have been more discouraging.

During these moments Lieutenant-colonel Juan N. Cortina
commenced a series of revolutions at Matamoros, all with a
view to improving his position. He formed a league with José
Maria Cobos, a Spaniard by birth, and a reactionary general of

Mexico, who had taken refuge at Brownsville. This person gathered together a certain number of French, Spaniards, and Mexicans, with whom he crossed to Matamoros, on the night of the 5th of October, 1863. Lieutenant-colonel Cortina, who was the officer of the day, pronounced with his corps, and made such others pronounce with whose subaltern officers he was in connivance. Some officers succeeded in escaping, and others, among them Governor Ruiz, were thrown into prison. The rebellion assumed a reactionary character; Cobos refused to recognize the constitution of 1857, and proclaimed himself in command of the forces. It was clearly a movement in behalf of the intervention. The views of Cobos were to organize his elements in such a manner as to make them dependent upon himself, doubtless for the purpose of getting rid of Cortina; but he had no time to realize his intentions. On the night of the 6th, Cortina threw Cobos and his second in command, Romulo Villa, a Spaniard, into prison, and, on the morning of the 2d, shot them both.

On that same day Cortina again recognized Governor Ruiz, and he conferred upon him the rank of colonel; but, at the same time that he did this, he endeavored to get the national guard of Matamoros together, and place himself in a condition to control Cortina. Cortina, a few hours later, again revolted; but, still keeping his rank of colonel, issued a proclamation raising the state of seige, and calling upon Jesus de la Serna to take charge of the government of the State. The latter was apparently in command, the former was in reality so.

Governor Ruiz had succeeded in escaping, the federal government placed a force, which was marching on Matamoros, under his command. Arrangements were entered into between Ruiz and Cortina, the result of which was that, on the first of January, Ruiz took possession of Matamoros, and the latter was to leave to join the campaign at Tampico. Cortina delayed his departure; another conflict ensued on the 12th of January, in which Ruiz's forces were defeated. Cortina thereupon proclaimed himself governor and military commandant of the State of Tamaulipas, and protested his obedience to the supreme government.

The situation of the country could not have been more arduous.

After the President abandoned San Luis Potosi, it was occupied by the forces of the intervention, and General Negrete who attacked the place was defeated. Vidaurri, the governor of Nuevo Leon, had refused to recognize the federal government, which remained at Saltillo without the means of action, and it was in these moments that the occurrences which we just mentioned took place. They were more serious than they appeared to be upon a first view. Matamoros, in consequence of the blockade of the ports of Texas, had become a great commercial center for the exploration of cotton and the trade with Texas ; its resources amounted to a considerable sum, and they were the only ones at the disposal of the government. It, under these most difficult circumstances, accepted the condition of things which had been consummated at Matamoros, and shortly after conferred the rank of general on Cortina. While General Cortina was governor, about the middle of 1864, he entered into double negotiations with the Confederates and the agents of the United States. The result of the former was a species of convention partly commercial and partly political, in which Colonel John S. Ford represented the Confederates. The convention was circulated among the Mexican towns on the banks of the river on the 7th of June, 1864. One of its most important stipulations was, that it obliged the authorities on both sides of the river to permit the goods belonging to both governments to cross to either side at the necessary points. It is clear that a convention of such a nature could only be of value to the Confederates. But while Cortina by these means was endeavoring to eradicate the want of confidence towards himself on the part of the Confederates, he was engaged in more important negotiations with Pierce, the United States consul at Matamoros, and with the officer in command of the forces of the same nation, stationed at Brazos Santiago. The Commission has been unable to precisely ascertain the tenor of those negotiations, but they may be presumed from their results. The French had landed at Bagdad (the mouth of the river) ; General Cortina went out to attack them. Notice was spread among his forces that he had a safe retreat in the event of experiencing a reverse, because he had made arrangements with the officers of the United States to cross with his force into Texas in the event of this occurring. He advanced on Bagdad the beginning of September, 1864 ; he fought the French on the 6th at night; he retired to Burrita, at which place he directed part of his forces to cross to the American side, where they were met by a company of United States dragoons. The Confederates, who doubtless had notice of what was occurring, left Brownsville and made two attacks upon the American and Mexican forces, one at Tulito and the other at Casa Blanca, in both of which they were repulsed.

General Cortina, with the remainder of his forces, returned to Matamoros, and this fact as well as the fact that the Mexican force was met by a company of United States dragoons, shows that the attack on Bagdad, and the retreat to the United States in the event of a reverse, were a pretext for placing his forces, or part of them, at the disposal of the commanding officer of the United States against the Confederates. There are grounds for presuming that Cortina, a long time before, had been offered the command of a regiment of Mexicans in Texas, as the person best adapted to carry on the war on the banks of the Rio Grande on account of his old antipathies against those who subsequently became Confederates. There are also slight indications that, for the purpose of preventing Cortina from joining the forces of the North, General Magruder issued a commission as a confederate general, and gave instructions to have it offered to him, together with four hundred bales of cotton. It appears that the negotiation was not initiated with Cortina. He was now serving the Mexican republic ; its situation was compromised, because all the frontier was in the possession of the Imperialists. After having placed a portion of his forces at the disposal of the commanding officer of the United States at Brazos, he, with the remainder, in September, 1865, submitted to the empire. The commencement of the following year, when General Negrete was approaching Matamoros, General Cortina revolted against the empire. From that time he has continued in the service of the republic, on the frontier up to the beginning of 1867, and in the interior, or the State of Tamaulipas, up to 1870, at which time he returned to the line of the Bravo.

XIV.

Two kinds of feelings have predominated against General Cortina on the Texas frontier, or rather a single feeling under two aspects, a personal hatred due to his revolt in 1859, and a political hatred arising from his league with the northern forces in 1864. He was also considered a source of disquietude. That hatred and this disquietude gave rise to two different opinions upon General Cortina's return to the frontier in 1870 ; some thought it desirable that the authorities of Texas should pardon Cortina ; they deemed that by confirming his position in the United States that all grounds of fear would be removed ; others tenaciously opposed the pardon. Cortina, at the beginning of 1871, addressed a petition to the government of Texas asking for a pardon ; it was submitted to the legislature of the State, inasmuch as it involved the making of a law or the passing of an act, as he had never been sentenced upon the indictments pending against him. This petition was urged by various residents of Cameron County, and, among them, Mifflin Kennedy, as there were also indictments pending against Cortina in Star County, a certain number of the inhabitants there were also in favor of the pardon. One of the reasons by which they supported it was the important protection given by Cortina during the years 1864 and 1865 to American citizens belonging to the Union party during the late civil war.

These petitions were favorably received by the legislature of the State of Texas, but the rest of the inhabitants of the United States frontier, particularly at Brownsville, where they opposed all idea of a compromise with Cortina, succeeded in dissipating the favorable impressions which had been created.

Simultaneously with these petitions for pardon, the accusation was originated against General Cortina that he protected cattle stealing in Texas. Previously they talked about bands organized in Mexico, of the protection given by the authorities, but never had any direct charge been brought against General Cortina until the question of his pardon was agitated. It is incredible that when this matter presented so favorable an aspect, that General Cortina would have jeopardized the result by taking an active part in cattle stealing. The antecedents make it presumable that these accusations were the machinations of his enemies to defeat the pardon, because it was impossible that this would be granted to a person who, at the moment of soliciting it, was rendering himself guilty of new crimes. Of those who had previously supported the pardon the greater number retracted, to follow the stronger current. That which at its commencement was an intrigue, subsequently became converted into a system. The former was merely personal in its purposes; the latter was more extended in its views, because it arrived at the conclusion that it was necessary to demand from Mexico " compensation for past injuries, and guaranties for the future."

This system was continuous. No crime was committed on the Texas side in which General Cortina's influence was not seen ; his desire was to make war upon the Americans. Not a cow was stolen in Texas, but General Cortina's hand was discovered in it. When a fact really occurred, it was disguised under the darkest colors, and when there were no facts, these were invented.

But before commencing the analysis of these, the Commission should refer to a circumstance which has most singularly favored those accusations. The revolution at Monterey was threatening when, on the first of October, 1871, General Cortina commenced the organization of a cavalry corps called " *Fieles de Cortina*," composed in its greater part of adventurers from both frontiers. The Commission have ascertained in its investigation, that many people of the worst reputation joined it. Later, he organized another corps called " *Exploradores*," consisting in part of the same characters.

Before this occurred, the charges were made with special

reference to General Cortina. No other officer or soldier of the army was mentioned, because in reality there was none other to accuse, and consequently the reproaches were confined to general statements as to robbers organized in Mexico under the protection of General Cortina. At most the Lugos, or some other notorious robber, of those who were marauding on both frontiers, was named, and of these it was said they were Cortina's accomplices.

But from the moment of the organization of the corps of "Fieles de Cortina" there was something definite. Men were seen in the service who had been in prison for robbery, or whom the public considered guilty of these crimes; several of them were known to have been accomplices in the cattle stealing which had been committed in Texas, and therefore the accusations had a greater appearance of truth.

Other circumstances occurred which might well have caused the best disposed to doubt. That force consisted principally of men undisciplined and immoral, and who remained but a short time in the service. They frequently deserted, stealing both the horse they rode and their arms ; several of them did so within a few days, and others after two or three months of service. In order to avoid the pursuit to which they were exposed on account of their desertion, they took refuge in Texas, where, in all probability, they returned to their previous life of crime and robbery.

It was natural that anybody who might have seen these individuals among General Cortina's forces the day before, and on the following one should see them in Texas, although not admitting the accusations made against this latter, would vacillate with regard to his conduct, especially if the former were found complicated in any robbery.

In the complaints brought against Mexico, these circumstances have been made use of. The guilty have been sought among those who served in the corps of " Fieles de Cortina," or " Exploradores," but as the people of Texas were ignorant of the length of time during which the parties they accused were in the service, the result has been that when they have fixed a date for the occurrences stated by them, the latter appear to have been prior or subsequent to the time when the accused parties served under the orders of General Cortina, and while that person was a private individual. There is but a single exception, and that is of Captain Sabas Garcia, who is accused of having crossed from Texas into Mexico with a herd of stolen cattle at the end of 1871 (1).

The Commission, in its investigations, have acquired proof that Garcia was guilty of cattle stealing in Texas, but they believe that there is no ground for charging him with the commission of this crime during the time that he was in service. In order to make an estimate of the aggregate value of the proofs in support of the complaints, it is proper to make some remarks.

In order to show that soldiers of the Mexican army committed robberies in Texas, it has been stated, and some assert that they saw it, that, in March, 1872, seventy or eighty armed and uniformed Mexicans had five or six hundred head of cattle on the Mexican side, in front of the Florida ranche, Texas (2).

The incorrectness of this is shown when we consider that the force consisting of adventurers, and among which the complainants in Texas have sought the guilty, because only thus would the complaint made by them be plausible, had no uniforms.

José Maria Martinez, R. Echazarreta, and F. Milan, or Millan, are accused of a robbery committed in Texas in May of 1872, and it has been asserted that they were then in the service of Mexico under General Cortina's orders (3). Neither of the three individuals mentioned have served on the frontier since 1870, at least, and with regard to the first he was a captain of the United States forces, commissioned to confiscate cattle, afterwards a robber and a captain of robbers in Texas, from whence he crossed into Mexico, where he continued committing robberies on both frontiers, until he was pursued and killed by the Mexican military commissioners.

It is said of Pedro Jurado, Pedro Lugo, and R. Echazarreta, supposing them to be Cortina's officers, that they were at the Calabozo ranch, in March, 1872, on a cattle stealing enter-

prise (4). The truth of this charge with regard to Pedro Jurado is doubtful, because he was killed on the fifth of that same
month in an encounter with the revolutionists. With regard
to Lugo it is absolutely impossible that what is stated of him
can be true, because he was killed on the 2d of February in a
fight with a force which overtook his band of robbers at the
Albercas.

Of General Cortina it is stated that, in August of 1871, he
was counter-branding cattle at Santa Fé (5). These cattle belonged to the heirs of Pedro Bouchard, were sold to General
Cortina by Rafael Garcia, of Texas, and received by him at
the Laguna of Santa Fé, where the purchaser branded it with
his own brand.

While acknowledging the integrity of Colonel Arocha, it
was, nevertheless, said of him, that, during his residence at
Mier, he had in his corrales a hundred head of Texan cattle ;
it was not stated that these were stolen, but it was so intimated.
(6.) These cattle belonged to George Petit Grew, the owner of
the Arroyo of Alamo, Texas, and who resided at Corpus. He
imported them into Mexico, with the intention of carrying
them into Nuevo Leon. This was during a time of revolution,
and all traffic with that State had been prohibited ; the cattle
were seized and inclosed by General Arocha, at Mier, until
General Cortina was informed of the fact, when he directed the
release of the cattle, because Petit Grew showed that the authorities at Guerrero had given him a permit. Petit Grew sold
these same cattle in Mier to Ramon Guerra.

A robbery of horses, stolen from Albert Champion at the
Torrana, Texas, in February of 1871, is mentioned, and accusing Ildefonso Salinas, who is styled a captain, under Cortina's
orders, of it. Champion states a conversation which he says
that he had with General Cortina, in which Cortina stated that
Salinas, on the night of the robbery, was in camp, and added,
" Champion, you are mad with Salinas for something." (7.)
The Commission, without assuming to defend Salinas's credit,
which is not the best, and without defending him from the
charge brought against him, because it is not in possession of
the necessary data to do so, nevertheless thinks that the state-

ment is incorrect, because Salinas was not a captain in General Cortina's forces at the time the robbery was committed. He enlisted as lieutenant of the first company of the corps " Fieles de Cortina " on the first of October, 1871, and served as such until the 30th of November of the same year. He again enlisted on the 31st of December, 1871, as captain of the fourth company of " Exploradores," and was discharged on the 21st of May, 1872. No error in the date is to be supposed, because the Brownsville papers of the month of February, 1871, speak of the robbery of Champion. It is consequently impossible that General Cortina could have expressed himself in the terms attributed to him, giving Salinas a position which he did not hold, and calling him an officer in his force. To subsequent accusations made against General Cortina by the Brownsville press concerning this matter, he answered by a communication, stating that Albert Champion wrote to him on the 13th of February, 1871, informing him of the robbery, and requesting him to pursue the robbers; that he did so, and of the nine horses which were stolen, seven were found on the lands belonging to the hacienda of the Vaqueria, and returned to Champion.

In August of 1871, a band of robbers were driving a herd of stolen cattle in Texas. While crossing it, they were attacked on the United States side of the river and fled, after having succeeded in passing eighteen head into Mexico, which they also abandoned. On the following day, these cattle were recovered by Macario Cruz, the justice of the peace at Pedernal, and placed at the disposal of the authorities.

In alluding to this fact it was stated that more than a hundred head of cattle were recovered; that the justice of the peace in his first notice to the authorities at Matamoros, did not state the number; that shortly after General Cortina arrived, and upon being informed of the occurrence, directed the justice to make a second report stating the number of cattle to be eighteen, and that after the lean ones were separated from the others, the remainder were sold by Cortina to his agents.

This statement is a tissue of falsehoods. The Commission investigated the number of reports made by the justice of the peace, and there was but one, in which the facts and the number of head of cattle was stated. Upon an investigation of the facts, it was ascertained that the residents of that part of the country, on account of the drought, had driven more than a hundred head of cattle to pasture on the farm of Angel Benavides ; that the attempt was made to drive the stolen cattle through this same farm, and some of the stolen cattle had remained there ; that notice of this was given to the justice of the peace, and he took up all the cattle, in order that each party might point out that which belonged to him, and thus show exactly that which belonged to other people ; that eighteen had remained unclaimed, and of these he made report to the authorities at Matamoros ; that General Cortina was not there, and probably never heard of the occurrence.

It is useless to pursue further this series of remarks. From the "espedientes" formed by the Commission various others are derived, but the foregoing are sufficient to show how unscrupulous were, first the papers of Brownsville, and subsequently the persons who have testified under oath with regard to the facts, either by distorting the circumstances, or stating palpable falsehoods. The Commission cannot but fix its attention on the grounds upon which the complainants of Texas rest the charges brought against General Cortina. These grounds consist of Apolinar Hernandez and Gregorio Villareal, (1) who served under the command of General Cortina. Hernandez served a month and a half in the "exploradores" corps, and Villareal about four in the "fieles." With regard to this person, the testimony produced by the complainants show, that Villareal was to some extent an accomplice in the cattle stealing (2). With regards to the first named, he is a fugitive from Mexico, by reason of orders issued by General Cortina to pursue him for horse stealing, he was also caught "infraganti" at the Encenada, by Mexican forces, while driving stolen horses toward the bank of the river, and fled.

The Commission by its own experience is convinced, that although to a certain extent the testimony of parties accomplices in the robberies is admissible, it is not the less proper to receive it with suspicion. It is impossible to believe them as though they were honorable people, and still less to give their statements the weight of an unquestionable truth, upon which to condemn the authorities of another country.

The Commission has remarked that the parties most complicated in the robberies have been the most extravagant in their charges against Mexico. Adolpho Glaevecke, who had a band of robbers on his ranche for the purpose of stealing horses from Mexico, and who subsequently speculated in cattle stolen in Texas; Thadeus Rhodes, who was the accomplice and instigator of a band of robbers who were for a long time a terror in the vicinity of Reynosa; William D. Thomas (alias Red Tom), a horse thief in Mexico, and a cattle thief in Texas; Tomas Vazquez, of the same stripe; Marcos Sanchez, Severiano Hinojosa, Justo Lopez, and various others who in Texas acted in concert with a band of robbers commanded by Jose Martinez to deliver them stolen cattle, and Cecilio Vela, a criminal and fugitive from Mexico, are among those who have shown most zeal in criminating our frontier.

The base of the proofs in questions such as the present is to be found in the criminal statistics. An examination of the archives of the courts of Texas show the great number of parties who have participated in cattle stealing. Although the delinquents may succeed in evading the law; although they may be acquitted, criminal cases always leave their traces after them, and they must always be the principal source of information in questions of this nature. Crime has its ramifications, and especially cattle stealing, which to a certain extent can only be carried on by bands. Those who to-day gather together for the purpose of committing a robbery, separate the following day, to again connect themselves with others, and in this manner, at the end of a certain length of time, the traces of their crimes are found among a multitude of criminals. When the law overtakes a criminal, the investigation of his crime is the examination of facts in which other parties are complicated. They may not be imprisoned, no sentence may be pronounced against them, but on the records of the court is registered a record of their deeds. If Mexican soldiers had been guilty of depredations in Texas, if these depredations had been of a systematic character, extending over a number of years, there cannot fail to be data establishing this fact in the criminal cases in Texas. There is where the grounds of accusation against the armed force of Mexico should be looked for. General Cortina's conduct on the frontier presents itself to the Commission-stripped of the character with which it has been sought to clothe it. Far from this, when his military duties permitted him, during the agitated period that he remained on the banks of the Bravo, he pursued and punished criminals. His enemies acknowledged this before General Cortina applied for pardon, or his petition was made public. One of the Brownsville papers (*The Sentinel*, January 27th, 1871), recognized General Cortina's disposition to aid in suppressing robbery. A conversation is mentioned, held with him upon this subject, in which the General suggested various ideas, expressing the necessity which existed for the co-operation of the authorities of Texas. So persuaded was this paper of the loyalty of General Cortina's intentions, that its article concluded by saying:

"A better opportunity perhaps may not present itself again in many years to free this frontier from the criminals who have been following their raids on society, devastating and even murdering. Not to take advantage of the circumstance is to neglect the interests and happiness of the residents of this valley."

When this was written, General Cortina had been several months on the frontier.

There was ground enough for this confidence. The same paper furnished the notice that on the Texas bank, there was a meeting of robbers for the purpose of crossing into Mexico and cutting down a criminal who had been hung by General Cortina.

But all this changed with the question of the pardon. His present faults were not in fact the cause which gave rise to the change, but the personal hatreds growing out of his revolt in 1859, and the political ones, which originated from his participation in 1864 against the Texans at Brownsville. Nevertheless, now and then some of the most excited yielded to the

11

evidence of truth, and their acknowledgments are General
Cortina's acquittal.

At the beginning of 1872, a police force was organized under General Cortina's direction for the pursuit of robbers.
The organization was formed by voluntary contributions made
by the land owners, and he was one of those contributors.
The first act of this force was the rout of the Lugos' band,
which accompanied Sanchos Uresti. Here is what a Brownsville paper said upon the subject:

"The recent fight between Captain Amador and Colonel
Uresti, has given us much food for reflection. We find among
the names of the killed, wounded and prisoners, those of well
known cattle thieves, for example, the Lugos, who certainly
did not belong to Cortina's forces. This person may perhaps
have been made the scapegoat for the sins of others."—*Daily
Ranchero*, Brownsville, February 7th, 1872.

A newspaper stated this, which nevertheless before had
constantly made use of the name of the Lugos to reproach
General Cortina. All the charges, more or less, were about as
follows: "Pedro Lugos and other captains of cattle stealing
bands, report to Cortina and receive orders from him."

The most singular is, that months after, when the complaints were brought against Mexico, the Lugos were again
spoken of as General Cortina's accomplices, and still more singular is it, that Pedro Lugo, who was killed on the 2d of February, 1872, was declared to be alive in the March following,
and one of Cortina's officers; it was asserted that in this month
he was engaged in a robbery (1).

It is comprehensible how there might have been an error
of date, but in this case, to the anachronism is added the want
of correctness in the facts, and such want is inexcusable,
because events of public notoriety and within the knowledge of all, show the contrary. The Commission, although
holding this opinion, believe that the occurrences with which
General Cortina has been mixed up on the frontier since
1859, show the propriety of his not holding any public office
whatever there. The events of 1863 and 1864, relating to interior politics, must also cause him to be always viewed as a

cause of alarm, and although this may be unfounded, the want of tranquility will always prevail in the minds of men with regard to our interior peace.

His presence on the line of the Bravo in an official capacity will thus always be a difficulty for the interior, and the cause of complications between both frontiers. Some parties will zealously spread the most absurd rumors, and the more absurd they are the more readily will they be credited by the timid, on account of their predisposition to believe them. If these rumors are examined, their groundlessness will be apparent; yet they are brought forth with such remarkable tenacity that the time may come when the impartial will believe, or at least doubt. This course of conduct, which, with regard to another individual, would be treated with contempt, plays upon feelings created by previous occurrences, with which all are prejudiced and ready to believe without discussion. The person, then, against whom these feelings are entertained, is a constant menace, and after the lapse of a certain length of time so great would be the prejudice engendered that no human power could destroy it. This is what has occurred with regard to General Cortina, and both the requirements of our interior policy and our foreign policy on the frontier require that he should hold no public office in that part of the country.

The Commission also deem it indispensable to fix its attention upon the organization of irregular troops on the frontier, such as those raised at the end of 1871.

Not only the experience of our own frontier, but also that of Texas, confirms the inexpediency of this kind of forces. Further on, the Commission will refer to the serious disorders committed by the irregular forces of the United States, or by Texas volunteers (rangers). These occurrences, and the difficulties to which the troops before mentioned gave rise on our frontier, show conclusively the necessity that none but fully disciplined forces should ever be used on either side of the frontier.

XV.

The Commission has previously shown that, at the commencement, the accusations made against General Cortina were a personal intrigue, and that they were subsequently continued for the purpose of strengthening the vague accusations which up to that time were directed against our authorities. For several months facts were invented, or those which really occurred were distorted, and when it was deemed that the public mind had been sufficiently prepared, it was proclaimed that it was necessary to exact from Mexico "*compensation for the past and guaranties for the future.*" The first part of this motto is synonymous with claims against the republic; the latter part, to a war of conquest on the part of the United States against Mexico. From the moment that this vast horizon was perceptible, complaints increased in their intensity; they were bitter, and accompanied by all that interest or passion could add to them. The Commission also considers it as its duty to examine the value of that motto in connection with the facts proven, and for this purpose will express its opinion with regard to the complaints and the complainants.

The property of several of these is found in Bee, Refugio, Goliad, and San Patricio counties, which are situated on the other side of the Nueces river. They state that on account of the "Northers" their cattle wandered to the South, where the robberies are committed, and that then they suffered losses. By the investigation made by the Commission it is ascertained that this is impossible. Cattle which pasture on the other side of the Nueces, never cross this river either by reason of the Northers or the storms vulgarly called "snow-rains." The shelter which on these occasions the cattle seek, is found in a strip of woods running along the whole length of the Nueces river; this, moreover, is marshy, and its fords well determined. Even to bring cattle there, hard driving is necessary, because they will not come voluntarily. That the cattle do not cross to the south of the Nueces is proved by the fact that the

herders of the North, in general, do not cross that part of the
country for the purpose of herding there, which they would
not fail to do in a contrary case.

It is imposible for the cattle stealing done on the margin
of the Rio Grande to reach those counties, nor can it reach
the Nueces, as they try to maintain. When a robbery is
contemplated, the easiest mode is preferred, and it is not
necessary to go a distance from the banks of the Bravo
to steal cattle; herds enough are to be found within twenty
leagues of its margin. The greater the distance to be traveled, the greater are the dangers; and hence it is not presumable that the cattle stealer would unnecessarily expose
himself to these, when with a great deal less risk he might
carry out his intentions. One of the complainants is Henry
Scott, a resident of Refugio county, commonly called, on
the banks of the Bravo river, *Higinio Scott.* On the thirty-
first of May, 1853, the Court of First Instance, at Matamoros,
tried Eugenio Leal, Felipe Rodriguez, and Susano Cisneros:
the first a runaway servant, and the two last residents of
Nacogdoches and Corpus Christi, for the robbery of four
horses. From the evidence in the case it appeared that there
was an American at Brownsville, named H. Scott, who purchased stolen animals, and sent somebody here to receive them
and cross them. Rodriguez did this on that occasion, and he
and his accomplices confessed that they supported themselves
by this traffic.

In order to judge what each one of the land owners between
the Bravo and the Nueces may really have lost, one of the
points for making the calculation is the statements made by
them for the payment of their taxes. If any of them have not
paid their taxes, this implies either that they have cheated the
State, or committed perjury by complaining of the loss of
property which they never owned, which is most probable.
If some, in later years, have paid taxes upon an equal or a
greater number than they did during the previous ones, it is
beyond doubt that they experienced no losses; or if they did,
they were so trifling as not to have affected the bulk of their
property. If a year later they paid taxes upon an amount less

than they did the year before, it would be necessary yet to ascertain that there was no fraud in this proceeding, that the cattle had really diminished in numbers, and that the origin of the difference was not the drought or the stealing among the cattle owners themselves, but that owing to Mexican robbers.

The fiscal statistics of Texas must necessarily be an indispensable aid in this aspect of the question, in order to estimate the correctness of the complaints; and when the departments furnish the best proofs, the statements of witnesses become unimportant, especially if they contradict each other in their evidence. The Commission regrets that, at the time of making up this report, it had not received the various and numerous reports which it solicited, concerning the cattle and cattle owners in Texas generally, since 1860, and with regard to each one of the complainants individually, since the year in which they state they commenced experiencing losses; this information is one of the means to form a history of the fortune which they possess in cattle. The Commission thus confines itself to estimates, not very precise, but which show what there really is of truth in the complaints. The people of Texas, in order to create an impression with regard to their losses, set forth that the cattle in the region between the Bravo and the Nueces, had diminished from one-third to one-fourth, between the years 1866 and the middle of 1872 (1). The Commission previously examined this statement with regard to the State of Texas, and without maintaining that there was or not such a diminution, and still less determining the amount of the depreciation, it confined itself to showing that in the event of its having been so, reasons for it were not wanting, and further postponed until now the examination of this same question in its special connection with the complainants. Taking Cameron and Nueces counties as an example, where the complaints have been greatest, by reason of the number of persons and the amounts, the fiscal statistics for the payment of taxes published in the Texas Almanac for the years 1869, 1870 and 1872, furnish the following result:

No. 1.

| | 1867. | | | | 1869. | | | | 1870. | | | |
	Horses.	Value.	Cattle.	Value.	Horses.	Value.	Cattle.	Value.	Horses.	Value.	Cattle.	Value.
Cameron	6,253	$66,045	27,179	$142,218	7,988	$76,749	32,709	$149,867	8,968	$97,718	58,088	$167,183
Starr	15,568	243,525	188,688	679,177	19,176	208,584	158,208	567,249	26,187	304,177	183,068	594,994

The foregoing statement proves that in these counties, far from a loss of two-thirds being announced, from 1867 to 1870, on the contrary, cattle and horses had been on the increase. The fiscal statistics should also furnish some indication of this diminution, in case there was any, either on account of the fact that the heavy robberies are dated as commencing in 1866, or because the commencement of the depreciation of the cattle is assigned to that year. This further corroborates that the losses must have been really of very little importance, since they exerted no influence upon the fiscal statistics for the payment of taxes. In these counties, cattle have been sold, exported, shipped to Kansas, consumed, stolen, and destroyed for their hides, and nevertheless, cattle upon which taxes were paid were on the increase up to 1870.

In order to estimate the complaints at their just value, the Commission submit a statement of the total, which a very small number of persons, residing in Cameron and Nueces counties, allege they lost by robberies committed by bands of armed Mexicans:

No. 2.

	CATTLE.				HORSES.				
No. of Claimants.	Number of Cattle alleged to have been stolen.	Value.	Natural Increase.	Value of Increase.	No. of Claimants.	Number of Horses alleged to have been stolen.	Value.	Natural Increase.	Value of Increase.
Cameron......... 20	143,776	$1,437,766	82,742	$824,720	11	5,712	$179,640	1,425	$45,750
Nueces.......... 33	328,643	3,286,430	680,397	6,803,970	18	7,008	348,6(5	10,108	484,540

A comparison of both these statements show that twenty owners in Cameron county complain of losses of cattle equal to five times the total number upon which taxes were paid in all the county for the year 1867 ; to more than four times the number on which taxes were paid in 1868, and nearly four times that of 1870. In Nueces county, thirty-three persons state that they have experienced losses amounting to double, on the average, of the number of cattle upon which taxes were paid in the county during the same years. With regard to horses, the incorrectness and exaggeration is noticeable, although not to so great an extent. Taking into consideration all the complaints for cattle stolen of which the Commission is informed, it is found that eighty-two persons show a loss of more than twenty-five millions, that is, three-fourths of the total value of all the horses and cattle in Texas in 1870.

In view of the unanswerable objections which the statistics would show, not with regard to the indirect losses, but the direct losses, it has been attempted to explain, that inasmuch as the pastures are open the herds spread themselves over a vast extent of country, and that the true total is greater than the number designated for the payment of taxes ; that as this does not occur with regard to the horses, because they are more careful, a more exact statement of their number can be given.*

Such observations with regard to the cattle is equivalent to the owners saying that they do not exactly know the amount of their property for the payment of taxes, and state it approximately ; but if this is so, their want of knowledge with regard to their property should be an obstacle to their designating their losses. Nevertheless, some have done it with such precision that they have not overlooked the most trifling fraction. For example, Richard King & Co. make their direct losses between 1866 and 1869 amount to one hundred and eight thousand three hundred and thirty-six head ; Henderson Williams to four thousand four hundred and thirty-six ; Dimas Tores Velasquez to seven thousand eight hundred and ninety-three. Now, neither of these three parties have forgotten the trifling fraction of six, five and three, which shows that they have a most exact knowledge of their property. With regard to horses, the remark states that it does not apply to them, yet eighteen breeders of Nueces county, and eleven in Cameron, state that they lost a number which, compared with the total number in these counties, would have produced the annihilation of the breed of horses ; nevertheless, the statistics show that there was a considerable increase in this line. *

---

* After having extended this report, the Vice Consul at San Antonio furnished the statistical reports taken from the archives at Austin with regard to the property existing in the counties between the Bravo and Nueces. These reports commence with the year 1860, those relevant begin with 1866. These counties are Cameron, Hidalgo, Starr, Webb, La Salle, Eucinal, Duval, Zapata, Live Oak, Mc-

Apart from these general considerations, which suggest the strongest doubts against the claims made, there are certain mo-

---

Mullen, and Nueces, and it is asserted that these are the ones which have suffered most from the depredations committed by bands of robbers organized in Mexico, being the counties most adjacent to the river bank.

The last report shows that the number of cattle in the eleven counties referred to, so far from having diminished a third or a fourth part in 1872 compared with what it was in 1856, as the complainants in Texas assert, had, on the contrary, doubled (Report of the United States Commissioners to Texas, page 6, at the close).

It is also shown that the business of stock raising has been in these same counties on the increase up to 1871. The body of the report contains an explanation of the probable causes which gave rise to the decrease in the year referred to, so much so that the tax lists for 1872 showed a falling off in the amount. The stealing on the banks of the Rio Grande could not have been one of such causes, because in assigning this cause a commencement long prior, it would have caused the diminution of the cattle in years previous to 1871, if stealing had been the cause of such diminution in the number of the cattle in the last of the years referred to. The great exportation of cattle and hides and the drought, explain the reasons why cattle began to diminish in 1871.

In the complaints submitted for depredations committed in Texas against Mexico up to the end of 1872 (Report of United States Commissioners, page 43), there appear only sixty-five owners from the eleven counties lying between the Bravo and the Nueces. These sixty-five persons state that they lost five hundred and nineteen thousand five hundred and four head, which, at the rate of ten dollars per head, amounts to more than five millions of dollars for direct damages. They further state, that they lost nine hundred and fifty one thousand four hundred and twenty-nine head (951,429) as consequential damage, or nine and a half millions of dollars.

Rejecting this latter species of damage, and considering simply the direct damage, and comparing this with the statistical information as to the number of owners, the total number of cattle, and the total amount of property in these eleven counties, the following conclusions are arrived at :

In the year 1872 there were (2,367) two thousand three hundred and sixty-seven cattle owners in these eleven counties, and they owned among the whole of them a total of (368,352) three hundred and sixty-eight thousand three hundred and fifty-two head of cattle. Now, then, (65) sixty-five of these cattle owners assert that they have been robbed of a number of cattle vastly in excess of all that was owned by the (2,637) two thousand six hundred and thirty-seven owners, including, among these, the claimants themselves.

The value of the cattle in these same counties, in 1872, was ($1,361,217) one million three hundred and sixty-one thousand two hundred and seventeen dollars, distributed among the 2,637 owners referred to. Nevertheless, sixty-five of these assert that bands of Mexicans have, robbed them alone to the amount of more

tives peculiar to the Texans, motives partially connected with their interests and, to a certain extent, to their character. A

---

than ($5,000,000) five millions, that is to say, more than three times the value of all the cattle existing in that locality.

The total amount of property in these same counties, in the year 1872, amounted to a little more than six millions of dollars ($6,000,000).

This amount belonged to a multitude of persons, both merchants and the owners of real estate, and yet, (65) sixty-five persons composing part of this number, assert that they lost five-sixths of the total value of all the property existing between the Bravo and the Nueces !

This comparative examination may be extended to each one of the years from 1866 up to 1872. It may also be made by comparing with each other the statistics of all the years, to estimate the change between one year and another in the number of the owners, the number of cattle, and the value of the property; but in whatever light it be examined, it is incomprehensible how sixty-five persons could have been robbed of a number of cattle greater than the total belonging to all the owners, in each of the years from 1866, including the complainants themselves. If the consequential damages are taken into consideration, the amount of the losses is nearly ($15,000,000) fifteen millions of dollars ; now, if this loss is estimated only with regard to sixty-five owners, the loss by (2,367) two thousand three hundred and sixty-seven cattle owners in these counties becomes almost incalculable. It being, then, also incomprehensible how the loss by cattle stealing could reach this amount, inasmuch as, according to the statistics, the total value of the cattle existing in the counties before referred to is less than a million and a half of dollars; the absurdity of the complaints made against the Mexican frontier become palpably apparent.

The aggregated statistical reports showing that from year to year there has been a visible increase in stock raising, show the correctness of the views of the Commission founded upon information of other kinds, and which are stated in the body of this report, as to the unimportance of the cattle stealing into Mexico.

(1) Among the documents received by the Commission after the extending of this report, are found statements of the number of horses and cattle owned by each one of the complainants, and the value of this property according to the lists made out for the collection of taxes in Texas, during each of the years from the time they state they commenced experiencing losses. This document is attested by the respective comptroller, and throws a great deal of light upon the claims made.

Antonio J. Iznaga alleges that he lost, from 1859 to 1872, (10,913) ten thousand nine hundred and thirteen heads (Report of the United States Commissioners, page 45, No. 16).

According to the list, in 1859 Iznaga paid taxes on (147) one hundred and forty-seven heads; in the subsequent years up to 1867, at times, he paid on (250) two hundred and fifty heads, and at others on (300) three hundred; during the following years up to 1872 it was constantly augmenting, and in this latter he paid taxes on (1,216) one thousand two hundred and sixteen heads. It is incom-

study as to the history of their fortune would show whether they have experienced losses, the extent and cause of these.

---

prehensible how so large a number could have been lost by a person who always had so small an amount of property in cattle. There are many others in the same predicament, such as Adolpho Glaevecke, Cornelius Stillman, Dimas Torres, Henry Scott, and Luis Renaud, the latter of which claims for the loss of (8,334) eight thousand three hundred and thirty-four heads from 1855, when it appears that in 1857 for the first time he commenced paying taxes on eighty heads, and in the years subsequent up to 1872 his statements show from (250) two hundred and fifty to (300) three hundred heads.

It is useless to enumerate the parties who have presented claims for robberies which they attribute to bands of Mexicans, and in whose statements for the payment of taxes there is found the most palpable proof of their unworthy intentions; there are some, such as George Krausse, who states that he lost cattle in 1854, in which year, nor in any of the subsequent ones, does it appear that he ever had any such cattle; but the most remarkable cases in the series of claims are those of the three brothers Champion, who make their losses amount to nearly a million of dollars.

Albert Champion for the first time had cattle in 1857 to the number of (140) one hundred and forty head, which number was increased by successive purchases to (700) seven hundred in 1859. During the subsequent years he paid taxes on a much less number, so much so that in 1866 he only paid on (25) twenty-five head, and the number after this date, although increasing, did not exceed (100) one hundred in 1872. The same remarks apply with regard to the other two brothers, each of whom at most have stated (300) three hundred head, while in some of the years the statements did not reach (100) one hundred head, and in others not (50) fifty. A loss of more than ($900,000) nine hundred thousand dollars is scarcely compatible with such limited means.

The examination of all the documents with regard to the means of the Texan claimants, show the degree of importance which should be attached to the complaints made against the Mexican frontier, the meaning of these complaints, and the purposes which they had in view when they made them. They also corroborate the views of the Commission with regard to the value of the cattle stolen and carried to the Mexican frontier. Finally, they show that if since 1871 the number of cattle has diminished between the Bravo and the Nueces, either from natural causes or by reason of the robbery, a great number of the claimants have rapidly recuperated their losses, and in view of the customs in Texas, as a general thing the losses have not been recuperated by the purchase of cattle from their owners.

	OWNERS.
In 1866	1,202
1867	1,373
1868	1,445
1869	1,298
1870	1,505
1871	2,303
1872	2,367

The examination of their personal characteristics would show whether they have good grounds for regretting the existing disorganization. With regard to the former, the Commission is only in possession of vague indications, because the point of departure is to be found in the statistics (1). With respect to the latter, charges have been brought against several of the complainants, from which it appears that some of them have contributed directly and indirectly to the demoralization. Francisco Iturria, a Mexican by birth, became naturalized and resided in the United States ; while such, and living at Browns-ville, he took a most active part in the civil war at Tamaulipas at the end of 1861. The party to which he belonged triumphed in Matamoros, and the compensation received for his services was the commencement of his fortune. When the frontier was occupied by the forces of the empire he joined them. When Matamoros was besieged, in October of 1865, by General

---

The total value of the real and personal property in the same counties, and during the same years, was—

In 1866.	$4,022,725
1867	5,394,400
1868	5,249,772
1869	4,342,287
1870	5,746,517
1871	6,913,702
1872	6,171,814

The total value of the cattle, and the number of the same, in these same counties, and during the same years, was :

YEARS.	NUMBER OF CATTLE.	VALUE.
1866	192,497	$977,105
1867	327,264	1,493,161
1868	372,448	1,464,002
1869, except Live Oak county, which is not included in the aggregate of this year	227,843	880,418
1870	415,105	1,442,815
1871	467,109	1,872,869
1872	368,352	1,361,217

Escobedo, Iturria was so closely allied with the empire that he was appointed commander of the inner or second line. While in this position he maltreated several citizens who refused to take up arms against the republic. Mejia, the Imperialists' general, prohibited the transit of people and goods from one side to the other except under special permit. Such permits with regard to goods were granted by Iturria, or through his influence, with which a monopoly was established in his favor. But apart from this, which shows a propensity to speculate upon our misfortunes, there are other proceedings more relevant to the present questions.

The Commission has already, for other reasons, stated that Iturria has two ranches in Texas in which he has sheltered, and shelters, parties engaged in cattle stealing; and not only this, but one of these he employs Pedro Lucio as a herder. In addition to him there are also Pedro Cortina, Justo Lopez, Marcos Sanchez, and Severiano Hinojosa, all of whom have not only been guilty of cattle stealing in Texas, but, according to what has been stated before the Commission, belong to those who were in connivance with the band of José Maria Martinez and Andres Flores. One of these ranches is called "Punta del Monte," and within its corrales have been found calves belonging to other people, which had been carried there for the purpose of branding them with Iturria's brand; outside of the corral, cows bearing other brands were lowing, which is a sure sign that their calves were shut up inside. The calves were let out, when they immediately followed the cows, an equally unmistakable proof that they belong to other people.

The complainants against Mexico state, that in December of 1871, (370) three hundred and seventy hides were exported at Matamoros, from "Boca del Rio" for Liverpool, on board the Sarah Douglass; the statement is correct, except in some minor particulars; the vessel was called the Mary Douglass, and the exportation took place in November. It is said that these hides were branded with the brands of Americans, and were stolen. The Commission thinks that this statement is correct, and upon investigating who was the exporter, discovered that they were exported by the house of Francisco Iturria, at Matamoros. Furthermore, this house was the only one which was expo*rting hides at "Boca del Rio" in 1871, and their exportation reached the number of (1,477) fourteen hundred and seventy-seven hides. Nevertheless, Francisco Iturria is one of the parties who complain of the robberies, and it will appear strange, that in order to throw the blame upon the Mexican frontier, he has endeavored to support the charges made against Mexico, or his own complaints, by those same robbers which are sheltered at his ranche, and that these charge the bands of robbers organized in Mexico with the cattle stealing.

Adolpho Glaevecke and William D. Thomas (alias Red Tom), also complain of the robberies and the losses they have suffered. In the course of this report, the conduct of both of these has been shown as to horse stealing in Mexico, and cattle stealing in Texas.

The Wrights were among those who initiated cattle stealing on the Mexican frontier. Availing themselves of the disturbances, they went on to the pasture lands under the pretence of looking for their own cattle, and then gathered herds together belonging to other people, which they subsequently sold in Mexico. They committed these depredations at the head of a large band whom they paid, and had for accomplices Patrick Quinn and Billy Mann, and are consequently of the number who have contributed towards the demoralization. They even now continue their depredations on cattle, by selling that belonging to other people, or branding other people's calves, and these men have also raised their voices to assert that they have been robbed by Mexicans, and that their losses amount to many thousands of dollars.

It is said of Martin S. Culver, in an article published in the Texas New Yorker, page 111, and who is held up as an example showing the facility of acquiring a fortune in Texas, that he commenced in 1856 by receiving a *pro rata* compensation of the "orejano" calves, and had succeeded in amassing a property of which his share was (7,000) seven thousand head of cattle. It may be doubted how, in so short a time, he has reached this position, if it is remembered to what, in the demoralized language reigning among the stock raisers on the Nueces, the name of orejano is given.

He also presents himself as one of the victims of robbery.

Richard King has in his service a large band ; he makes use of it for depredating upon other people's cattle, by seizing all of the unbranded calves, which are then branded with King's brand, notwithstanding the ownership of the calves is shown by their following cows bearing other people's brands. These depredations are continuous, because King's band is almost always uninterruptedly in movement. He thus develops and maintains demoralization among a great number of people, because only men without principle could accept the position of instruments for the commission of such crimes. He has had among his herders the accomplices in robberies committed in Texas or Mexico, as, for example, Fernando Lopez and Tomas Vazquez ; nevertheless, he states that his injuries amount to millions.

These instances show the nature of the complaints ; but it is not less important to inquire how they are organized by the complainants. A hundred individuals meet and render each other a mutual support. Each one asserts that some one of the number has suffered great losses, and he in his turn receives a similar service from all the others. There would be nothing remarkable in this, if the press of a portion of Texas had not been urging the formation of complaints for the purpose of demanding reparation, showing a personal interest in the matter, and the possibility of obtaining a fortune by this means. This association of a hundred individuals have each the same cause, the same purposes, the same pecuniary interest, and each of them, to the success of his interest, is supported by all the others. In fact, the tendencies of these hundred individuals is the same as that of a single person.

To support their pretensions, they call upon their relatives and employees, who form a second element in the composition of their claims. Then, as a third one, there enters a considerable number of thieves residing in Texas, who have co-operated in the cattle stealing, and who doubtless are considered honorable men, because they are produced to show that the Mexican authorities were corrupt. This element was the most bitter in its statements against Mexico.

Some of those who supported the complaints of the Texas people appeared before this Commission to depose, and there stated the contrary to what they appear to have before stated in support of those complaints. With regard to one of these witnesses, his perjury is evidently shown. With regard to another, the Commission had not within its reach the means to ascertain whether his deposition was correct, and the causes which he assigned in explanation of the discrepancy true.

The number of impartial persons was small. And as stolen cattle had been really carried into Mexico, the statement of those with regard to some of the facts served to give an aspect of probability to the perjurers, several of which the Commission have noted in this report. The complainants did not mention the true condition of Texas with regard to the way in which the robberies were committed, the origin of these, and the great state of demoralization there existing, because this would have been their own condemnation. They either invented or distorted the facts, either by attaching circumstances to them which did not occur, or suppressing the real aspect of those they presented. They ignored the fact that between the Bravo and the Nueces there is a large Mexican population, and that much of this is American. They confuse the question of race with that of nationality and residence, in order that speaking in general terms of Mexicans as engaged in stealing, the reproach might fall upon Mexico.

The means employed show the want of stronger grounds, and the weakness of the foundation upon which the charges made against Mexico by the complaining Texans rest. The depth of these charges only show the concerted action of a small number of persons moved by personal motives. The statistics, the influence exercised with regard to the demoralization and the development of crime, which several of the complainants have had, the means which they have made use of to systematize the injuries with a hope of a compensation, demonstrate without the necessity of further explanation, what is the real signification of " *compensation for the past*," the first part of the motto adopted against Mexico.

12

XVI.

Combinations have been made upon the frontier of the United States, for evils of a very different nature from horse stealing in Mexico, and the means for carrying them into execution have there also been furnished.

When the institution of slavery existed in the United States, some of the slaves succeeded in escaping into Mexico. Occasionally the old masters made attempts to recover their slaves, and for this purpose organized a party with which they came into our territory. The Commission learned of three such occurrences, in one of which the aggressors were assisted by Mexicans on this side. There was a case in which the carrying off of a family of five persons was effected. Of these acts, one occurred at Matamoros, another near Reynosa, and the last at Laredo. It is just, nevertheless, to remark that Mexico made similar attempts to recover their fugitive servants from Texas. The Commission cannot state the means employed, nor the mode of procedure, because it has not learned the details of any case, still the general fact is proved by documents taken from the public archives. The kidnapping of free men of color has also been among the crimes planned on the Texas side, to be executed in Mexico. The Commission were informed of two cases. In the first, some Americans and Mexicans crossed to this side, and carried off, upon the pretext of his being a slave and a thief, one Aunastasio Aguado or Elua, whom they whipped and kept in prison for three days. The crime was committed near Matamoros, but, doubtless owing to the measures of the Mexican authorities, the aggressors found themselves compelled to set Aguado at liberty, of whom it is probable they intended to make a slave.

The second case, which occurred near Mier, was less successful. A Captain Jack made use of the services of a colored man named Melchor Valenzuela, a resident of Mexico, to steal a skiff from this side. When Valenzuela was arrested by our authorities he confessed the fact, and he was released on bail.

Pending the trial, Captain Jack and another American, Dixon, crossed to this side, and threatening Valenzuela with a pistol, they carried him off.

The illegal attempts against individual safety not only assumed this form, but others more serious. One of the most infamous crimes ever committed on the frontier was the murder of Juan Chapa Guerra, a resident at Ranchito. In January of 1850, some goods were stolen from Charles Stillman, residing at Brownsville. He got together a force of Americans, with which he left the American side in search of the stolen goods. He arrived at the Palmito ranche, and ordered that all the people there should be tied up and whipped until they confessed who where the thieves. It appears that he made no discovery by this means. He was informed that Juan Chapa Guerra, a resident of Mexico, was the guilty party, he then sent his party to Ranchito, in Mexico, where the accused lived. They seized him and brought him into Texas, when Stillman told his party to do what they pleased with him, Chapa was whipped and then killed. It was afterwards found out that there had been a mistake in the name; that the guilty party was not Juan Chapa Guerra, but one Juan Chapa Garcia. The judicial proceedings had at that time, disclosed the horrible details of the murder. Charles Stillman was a person of wealth, and who exercised a controlling influence in Brownsville. The relatives of the victim tried to find a lawyer, but none of those in the city would act for them against Stillman. Upon the solicitation of other persons, one consented privately to give advice. This simple proceeding is enough to show the condition of things on the Texas frontier. This murder was never punished.   •

In addition to these attacks upon the safety of private individuals, others were organized against the public employees. In the years immediately subsequent to 1848, smuggling across the frontier of the United States into Mexico increased immeasurably. There were then a party of smugglers, consisting of Americans and Mexicans, who defied all pursuit and committed the most outrageous aggressions. Two most serious occurrences took place, which show the then condition of things.

In November of 1849, a contraband was seized by the custom house guards at Camargo. While these were escorting it they were attacked at the Guardado ranche, in the jurisdiction of Mier, by a party of Americans, who surprised the guards, recaptured the cargo and crossed it into Texas.

In August of 1852, the custom house guard of Matamoros seized a cargo at Olmos, in the jurisdiction of Reynosa. While on the road the guards were attacked by a party of six Americans and sixteen Texas Mexicans; among the former were the owners of the goods. These were carried to the Capote ford, where boats had been prepared in which the cargo was crossed to the United States side.

In addition to these occurrences, which were fully consummated, in January of 1850, a party of forty Americans, which had been organized at Rome, in Texas, put themselves in motion for the purpose of recapturing a cargo which had been seized by the custom house guards, and which was in transit at the said Guardado ranche. The authorities received timely notice, and were enabled to send a force sufficient to protect the cargo.

In all these occurrences it does not appear that the Texan authorities took any measures to prevent the aggressions, or to punish them after they had been committed. In the second of the occurrences just related, Santiago Enriches (the name is probably badly spelled in the documents from which this information was obtained), who was one of the owners of the goods, quietly returned to Edinburg, in Hidalgo county, after having consummated his illegal proceeding.

The discharge of fire-arms from the United States side upon the Mexican side has also been the origin of accidents, and at times of conflicts. Such attacks have been made both by private individuals and by the United States forces, and the attacks were made upon persons on this side and upon troops stationed there.

The Commission received information with regard to ten cases of this nature, which it will proceed briefly to state. In April of 1851, the military commandant at Mier prohibited crossing from one side to the other after seven o'clock at night by way of the Arroyo ford. Later than this hour, four Americans of Rome, Starr county, attempted to pass, and having been prevented, shots were exchanged between several of the residents at Rome and the Mexican guard. It is not clearly stated in the documents examined by the Commission how the attack began, and even in these there is a difference in the explanation. The military commandant at Mier went to Davis' Camp (Ringgold Barracks), and the latter offered to make the necessary investigations.

On the 14th September, 1855, at nine o'clock at night, three Americans approached the Piedras Negras ford from the Texas side, and requested to have a skiff sent to them. The boats were on the Mexican side, and passing had been prohibited that late at night on account of the threatened filibustering invasion. The guard answered and stated the prohibition, upon which the three individuals referred to opened fire upon the Mexican force and the adjoining houses, which firing lasted for an hour and a half. The officer in command of the Mexican forces went the following day to see Captain Burbank, the commander of Fort Duncan, who replied to him that the guilty parties were civilians, over whom the military had no authority, but nevertheless he would endeavor to avoid such outrages, and in case there was sufficient proof, the civil authorities might imprison and punish the guilty ones. The same Mexican commanding officer, in making his report to the government of Nuevo Leon, stated that he had given orders not to answer the fire unless the force should reach the middle of the river, in order not to offend the United States. This conduct was approved.

What is remarkable in this occurrence is, that the firing having lasted an hour and a half, that neither the civil authorities of Texas nor the military authorities of the United States should have taken any steps to ascertain what was going on, and the consequence of which would have been the arrest of the guilty parties. This shows an absolute indifference in the fulfilment of a duty.

At the time of Cortina's revolt, at the end of 1859, the greatest persecution was displayed against all those who it was suspected might be in connivance with him. The family of

Teodosio Zamora lived at the Reices ranche, on the Texas side. An American force went there; the family, being informed of their coming, abandoned their house and property to cross to this side. They arrived on the Mexican side at the same time the force reached the ranche, when these commenced firing upon the refugees acro-s the river.

About 9 o'clock on the night of the 31st of December, 1859, firing was commenced from the Texas side upon the Garita of Santa Cruz in Mexico. This Garita is in front of Brownsville. The attacking party hid themselves behind some trees, and from there discharged their arms. Some of the balls penetrated the house at the Garita. The firing lasted an hour and a half.

A similar occurrence took place on the night of February 2d, 1860, only at a different place. The one selected for this attack was another of the Garitas, on the river at Matamoros, called Freeport, or Parades. The firing continued long enough for the alcalde of the city to get a force of police together, go to the place where the occurrence was transpiring, and witness the last discharge from the Texas side.

In both cases the darkness of the night prevented the recognition of the attacking party, but it is undeniable that the length of time the firing lasted afforded sufficient opportunity to the military and civil authorities of Texas to inquire into the occurrence and suppress the outrage. Their negligence in this respect furnishes a just ground of complaint.

After Juan N. Cortina was defeated in Texas, and took refuge on our frontier, a force of Texan volunteers took up a position in front of Reynosa. This same force had previously invaded the town; but the people, who had received timely notice of what was going on, armed themselves, and compelled the invaders to recross the river. After the volunteers had reached the Texan line, they fired upon the Mexican side, and particularly upon the people of the town when they came to the river for water. Antonio Loera and Juan Barrera were wounded. The authorities at Reynosa made complaint to John S. Ford, the captain of the volunteers; his reply has been lost, but by the answer of the municipality of Reynosa, thanking the captain, it would appear that the latter offered to make an investigation upon the subject. The authorities at Reynosa and Ford's forces mutually reproached each other for the commencement of these aggressions. The presumption, however, is against the latter, not only because the Mexican authorities, understanding the weakness of our frontier, avoided a conflict, but also the pressure under which the volunteers were compelled to abandon Reynosa, would be likely to create feelings of revenge in them.

After this occurrence, one Saturday in Holy Week, the people of Reynosa discharged their arms, and some of the balls fell in the camp of the volunteers. This act cannot but be presumed to have been intentional, although in the explanations given by the authorities at Reynosa to Captain Brackett and Lieutenant Owens, who were commissioned by Colonel Lee to investigate the matter, it was said that the occurrence was accidental, and they appeared to be satisfied. Colonel Lee offered the authorities to withdraw the volunteers in a few days, which, in fact, he did; and thus the difficulties which for several months had so frequently occurred between both frontiers were terminated.

At the time of the attack on the Clareño ranche, Zapata county, in April of 1871, by the confederate troops, a party of these located themselves at the Carrizo, and from there fired upon this side. The municipality of Guerrero complained to the commander of the force, and he replied that, so far as his company were concerned, they would do no injury to the people of Mexico; but at the same time he said this, some of his soldiers fired upon some persons who were in charge of some boats on this side, and drove them away, while others belonging to the force swam across the river and carried them off. The authorities at Guerrero sent a force to occupy the point; it hardly reached the bank of the river when the confederates made a discharge upon it, and killed Antonio Ochoa.

On the 2d April, 1862, some Americans crossed from Texas into Mexico at Piedras Negras; there was a quarrel between them and some Mexicans, when they hastily returned to the United States side and fired some shots at the Garita, which were replied to by two of the custom house guards. During the time of the Confederacy, in August of 1863, while a boy named Nicanor Gongora was on the edge of the river at the Parades ford, he was wounded by a shot fired from the American side by a person who came out of a tent. The aggressor was a soldier, who, it appears, proceeded deliberately, because he approached the river, drew his pistol, appeared to examine it, and then fired. The boy Gongora died the following day, and the guilty party was only kept in prison a few days.

In December of 1868, some United States soldiers, who, it is believed, were in pursuit of robbers, approached the river in front of the Burita ranche ; they saw a boat approaching the Mexican side, and fired two shots at it. In this boat there were two ladies and some children. One of the former, Mrs. Francisca Hínojosa, was dangerously wounded.

If all the facts related by the Commission up to the present time be considered ; if the illegal attempts against life, personal liberty, or the free exercise of their duties by the employees and public officers, are considered, and that they have not been single acts, but have been repeated at different times over a vast extent on the bank of the river, the propensity which has existed, upon the part of the United States frontier, to depreciate the rights of Mexico, will be apparent, as also the tolerance of the Texan authorities, a tolerance which, in certain cases, has amounted to complicity. Nevertheless, however serious these facts may be, they do not show to its full extent the invading spirit which has reigned upon the left bank of the Bravo river.

XVII.

The Mexican frontier has been the constant victim of invasions organized in or departing from the United States. They may be classified under four heads : first, those the purpose of which has been simply robbery ; second, those which, under the pretense of political principles, were aggressive against the nation; third, those which proclaimed open hostility against Mexico; and fourth, those which involved a certain intervention on the part of the United States forces in the internal questions of Mexico.

Those under the first head commenced in 1848. A force of American volunteers left Matamoros; it is believed that they were discharged, although it is not certain. They went to the city of Guerrero, and from thence to Nuevo Leon, in the interior. On the 16th of July in the same year, they arrived at Villa Aldama, stating that they were on their way to Monterey, for the purpose of joining the forces which were going to California. During that day and night there was nothing in their conduct calculated to discover their intentions. On the following day, they dispersed in groups of six or eight, and took up position at the principal houses. The officer in command then applied to the alcalde, for the purpose of calling the municipality and the curate together, with a view to inform them of a communication from General Wolf; this was done, when the officer immediately ordered the doors to be closed, and he and three soldiers cocked their pistols, and he then notified the alcalde, that if, within fifteen minutes, ($60,000) sixty thousand dollars were not paid, that he would fire a shot, and this would be the signal for the pillage. The impossibility of delivering so large a sum was notorious; each one offered to give what they had, and he accepted the proposition. They commenced visiting the several houses in company with the officer in command of the volunteers, for the purpose of his receiving the money; he thought they were deceiving him, gave the signal, and the pillaging began. The town was robbed, several persons were killed, the alcalde was tortured and hung in his own house, to make him confess where he had his money.

On the same day, this same party of volunteers left for Sabinas; they arrived there at half past one o'clock. Part of them surrounded the town, and the remainder divided themselves up into parties of ten or a dozen; upon a signal of four shots, the pillaging commenced, and the same acts of robbery were repeated which had been committed at Villaldama. A force of volunteers were at this time quietly passing through

Laredo, when the American commandant was informed of the horrors being committed by this party. He replied that it was his duty to arrest the guilty, but that he had not sufficient force to do so.

On the night of the 12th of December, 1848, the Pando ranche was attacked, the witnesses say, by United States soldiers; but the Commission doubts whether they may not have been volunteers belonging to the company which, at different times, the State of Texas had in its service on the banks of the Rio Grande. The soldiers belonged to an encampment which was opposite Pando, a few leagues to the east of Brownsville. They crossed to this side, fired upon the houses, and killed Encarnacion Garza. On the 14th, they returned, and robbed the ranche, which had been abandoned by its inhabitants on account of these outrages; it was completely plundered, and the horses and cattle stolen.

In October of 1859, the Arroyo Saco ranche, situated eight leagues to the east of Matamoros, was attacked by a party of soldiers, who were encamped opposite the ranche. Although the witnesses call them United States soldiers, the Commission is in doubt whether they were such, or whether they belonged to the Texas volunteers.

Six soldiers entered the house at the ranche, threatened the people with death in case of resistance, tied them up, stole everything there was there, and afterwards returned to the Texas side.

About the middle of May, 1864, a cotton train, which was on the road between Reynosa and Matamoros, was attacked. The cartmen, upon being surprised, abandoned it, when a force of the people of Reynosa came to their assistance, and pursued the assailants, who were a lieutenant and two soldiers, Mexicans by birth, then in the United States service, and forming part of the garrison at Edimburg, in Texas. The lieutenant's name was Hinojosa; the names of the soldiers were Sabas Garcia and Severo Resendez; the two latter were arrested. The former of these is the captain Garcia who recently served under General Cortina's orders, and is accused as being an accomplice in the cattle stealing.

On the night of the 14th of January, 1856, the force of the imperial garrison at the town of Bagdad (Boca del Rio) was surprised by an American force which was on the opposite side in the camp at Clarksville. The imperial forces were dispersed, and the Americans took possession of the place; the soldiers of the latter were colored, and under command of white officers. A plundering of the place was organized. The person who had been alcalde was murdered, because he refused to give up his watch, as was a little girl, in order to take from her a trifling sum which she was carrying in her hand, with which to buy meat. The pillaging lasted twenty-two days. A party took up his quarters at the " San Carlos Hotel," and placed a sign on his door saying, " *United States Quartermaster.*" When a group of the plunderers had loaded themselves with booty, and crossed it to the other side, another party came to carry on the same operation. Night and day they were at this work, and carried off the goods from the stores and shops. They took the steamer " Prince of Wales " and other boats, loaded them, crossed them over to the other side, discharged them there, and then brought them back again to this side and loaded them again. The officers paid the laborers, who were working in transferring the stolen property from the houses and stores to the bank of the river, five dollars. A few days after it began, a force of dragoons arrived, upon the pretext of suppressing the disorder, and then they joined in it also. The plundering ceased at the end of twenty-two days, the town was destroyed, and its inhabitants ruined. A letter from the collector of the custom house at Clarksville, said : " I had resided three weeks at that point (Clarksville), when the colored troops belonging to the 118th regiment seized the vessels which were in my care, crossed the river and took Bagdad. They there plundered houses and killed people—the scene was indescribable. The soldiers murdered people in the streets, because they refused to give up their purses ; and they threatened to shoot me because I made them pay importation duties."

The invasions to which a political character have been ascribed were, in part, acts of plundering ; and some of these were accompanied by circumstances which were really disgraceful.

At the beginning of September, 1851, José Maria J. Carbajal, subsequently a general of the republic, seconded by a great number of the inhabitants on the Mexican frontier, made a revolutionary proclamation at the "Lobar," Mexico, in which he set forth, as a political measure, the expulsion of the army from the frontier, and, as a commercial measure, the reduction of duties and the removal of prohibitions.

These ideas were extraordinarily popular in that part of the country. The old army had behaved in an oppressive manner towards the towns on the frontier, and this had rendered it exceedingly distasteful to them. The commercial restrictions had reduced the towns on the line of the Bravo to a state of misery, and the people were daily seen leaving with their means for the United States.

General Carbajal, after having proclaimed these principles, established himself at Rio Grande city, in Texas, where he commenced gathering together and organizing his elements for the purpose of crossing into Mexico and combating the there existing authorities. The Mexicans who accompanied him knew nothing of his plans; they commenced understanding them about the middle of September, 1851, when the force which had been gathered together at Rio Grande City crossed from Texas into Mexico. Among this force there were some thirty Americans, which greatly displeased the inhabitants of the frontier who had joined Carbajal; but all this was settled by his promise that they should be the only ones who he would receive in aid of the enterprise.

The result of the first action was unfavorable to the government; the town of Camargo was attacked, taken, and its garrison capitulated. A few days afterwards they advanced on Matamoros. From the day after their arrival in front of the town, parties of Americans, to the number of three or four hundred men, who publicly crossed the river at the Parades Garita and other points, commenced joining Carbajal's forces.

This produced a disagreeable impression upon those who participated in Carabjal's views. The people of Matamoros,

among whom the plan of the " Loba " had been popular, decided to oppose the movement, seeing in it not a revolution,
but an invasion. They considered that the governing spirit
was filibustering, and that nothing but evil could result to the
frontier by giving the question such a direction. The subsequent occurrence justified these fears. The Americans who
crossed into Texas consisted of some companies of Texan volunteers (Rangers), who had been serving on the banks of the
Bravo, and had just been discharged. General Carbajal enlisted them for six months. In his proclamation of the 25th of
September, 1851, he explained the reasons which had decided
him to take this step. The commander of these companies,
and the second in command of the whole of the expedition, was
Captain John S. Ford, whose conduct during the whole course
of his life has ever been absolutely hostile to Mexico.

The movement counted upon the support of Charles Stillman, a merchant of wealth residing at Brownsville, who furnished it with considerable resources. The Americans residing
in that city also supported it; several of them crossed in the
afternoon, participated in the fighting, which took place during
the night, and returned to Brownsville on the morning of the
following day to attend to their business. Night and day they
were crossing from that city into Mexico, by the public fords,
both ammunition and provisions. Some houses were intentionally burned, and the combustibles were obtained from the
house of Charles Stillman. The siege lasted nine days, during
which all these horrors were committed. About the end of
October, the assailants were repulsed and compelled to retire.
Everything showed that the movement had been perverted.
From a political point of view, the prevailing spirit in the occurrences which had taken place, was a hostility on the part of
the Texas frontier against that of Mexico. In its fiscal character, the movement degenerated into smuggling operations,
in which the people of Brownsville were interested. For the
inhabitants of the Texas side, it was a means of prosecuting the
attempts began in 1848, and leading to the ruin of our towns on
the Bravo, for the purpose of aiding the progress of their own.
This latter, and the prejudices which had been created between

both frontiers, explained the popularity of that movement on the Texas side, and the animosity displayed by the inhabitants of Matamoros in resisting the attack. The result of this was, that General Carabajal, after his retreat, was little by little abandoned by the Mexicans who had accompanied him. He took refuge with his force in Texas, and established his camp at the " Sal," in Hidalgo county.

Monterey—Lerado was menaced, during several months, by a party of the same adventurers under the command of James Willreison and E. Alt Evans, who crossed several times during the first half of 1852, and carried arms in the name of General Carabajal. Complaint was made to the commander at Fort McIntosh, and he replied that the acts in question were those of pillage, against which he could do nothing as a military officer. These adventurers were at Lerado, in Texas; they were supported there, and crossed to this side with impunity to commit these outrages.

In September of 1861, General Carabajal with his forces crossed a second time; they went to Cerralvo, and were there defeated. In February of 1852, he made a third attempt near Camargo, was again defeated, and thereupon took refuge with his followers in Texas.

In these cases the enlistment, the gathering of the people, the camping, all was done publicly. The authorities of Starr county, which was the base for the organization, took a most active part. N. P. Norton, the district judge of the county, headed the last expedition of this kind in March, 1853. At this time no political principles were invoked; it was purely and simply acts of vandalism and robbery.

On the twenty-fifth of March, 1853, N. P. Norton crossed from the Texas side into Mexico, at Reynosa Biejo. He was accompanied by forty Americans and ten Texan Mexicans. He reached Reynosa on the 26th, where he arrested the alcalde and Francisco Garcia Treviño, whom he threatened to shoot if within two hours they did not deliver ($30,000) thirty thousand dollars. The former he shut up and kept a prisoner; his force disseminated itself through the town, plundered various houses, stole all the horses, mules and arms which they could find. The people were only able to get together two thousand dollars, which were delivered to Norton. He abandoned Reynosa at five o'clock on the afternoon of the 26th, pursued by a force which had left Camargo; a slight skirmish took place, and in the night Norton crossed the river at the Capote ford. The only purpose of his expedition was robbery, and this was done by the first authority of the county. He and two of his accomplices were indicted at Brownsville for a violation of the United States neutrality laws; in June of 1855, that is two years after the indictment, a "*nolle prosequi*" was entered in the case.

The third class of aggressions comprises the cases in which open hostility was manifested against the Mexican nation. The first of these was the invasion of Piedras Negras, in 1855.

This expedition was organized at San Antonio, Texas; several men of means took part in the enterprise, and two hundred men who had served in the Rangers, constituted the force. The pretext was the pursuit of the tribe of Lipan Indians of whom the Texans complained, accusing them of being the authors of much of the injury suffered by them. It is probable, nevertheless, that one of the incentives was the capture of fugitive slaves, a great number of which had taken refuge on the frontier of Coahuila; the negotiations previously initiated with several persons at San Antonio makes this to be suspected. If successful, they would not stop there; a more extended field of operations would present itself to the adventurers, even the occupation of the country. Under the pretext then of the Lipans, there were necessarily concealed more extensive plans.

On the 25th of August, 1855, some Americans, residing at San Antonio, Texas, addressed Colonel Lanberg, who was in command of the frontier at Coahuila, inquiring from him upon what conditions he would deliver up the negroes who had taken refuge in Mexico, how many could be recovered, how much would have to be paid for each delivered on the banks of the river, and the mode of payment. The finale of the letter contains a covert threat; it says: "Our future measures and proceedings will wholly depend upon the report made by you ; in the mean time we are preparing to act promptly. "

Colonel Lanberg gave a favorable reply, and suggested the idea of an arrangement by which the runaway negroes should be exchanged for the Mexican " peones " who had taken refuge in Texas ; he also supported the project with the government of Nuevo Leon. The Commission, in passing, are compelled to condemn this attempt on the part of a government officer to make an exchange of human flesh, and this, at the same time, shows the necessity that Mexico should be represented on the frontier by men of high tone, and who, by their character, will command respect and consideration.

The government of Nuevo Leon, on the 11th of September, replied that, in fact, it was convinced of the injuries suffered by both frontiers, but that, in matters of this nature, it could not enter into arrangements with private individuals ; that the proper party to initiate these was the Governor of Texas, with whom it was ready to come to an arrangement, by making a provisional agreement, until the government in Mexico should be organized. The communication concluded in the following terms : " If, notwithstanding the foregoing, the people of ' Bejar,' who have addressed you (Colonel Lanberg), decide to invade our frontier with a view of recovering their runaway negroes and stolen horses, in this case you will be compelled to repel force with force."

The communication of the government of Nuevo Leon requiring an impossible condition, was a refusal, and it was fully understood by both sides that an aggression was to follow. All these antecedents give reason to believe that the question of the Lipans was but a pretext.

The expedition arrived at the bank of the river on the first of October, 1855 ; this same day twelve Americans opposite Piedras Negras seized two skiffs, and carried them to the place on the river where the filibusters were encamped, a league from Fort Duncan. The party crossed the river without being molested, notwithstanding the publicity which had been given to the expedition. On the 3d of October they were defeated by the Mexican troops, at the place called the " Maroma ; "

after their defeat they retreated, and arrived at Piedras Negras, which town they pillaged and burned. The Mexican forces, which had been detained awaiting ammunition, arrived near Piedras Negras on the 6th, and there stopped, without attacking the filibusters, because the commander of Fort Duncan had made demonstrations to protect them. These demonstrations consisted in placing four pieces of cannon pointing upon Piedras Negras, while the invaders quietly crossed without molestation, carrying with them what they had stolen from the place, and in full view of the civil authorities of Texas and of the military authorities of the United States. After reaching the other side, the filibusters made a breastwork of bags of flour, corn, and sugar, which they had stolen at Piedras Negras, and from thence fired upon the town, without the military authority at Fort Duncan interposing any obstacle. The people at Piedras Negras informed the Mexican officer commanding that during the continuance of the invaders in the town, two companies from Fort Duncan crossed over every night to protect the filibusters, and retired again on the morning of the following day. Complaint was made to the commander of the said fort concerning these hostile proceedings, and his reply is far from being satisfactory. The defeat of the filibusters created a feeling of great indignation at San Antonio, Texas, because a very different result had been expected. A meeting was held, at which it was resolved to invite the people of Texas to join in a campaign against the Mexican Indians, to request the government to furnish arms, and that it should take the necessary measures for the purpose in view. C. Jones, J. H. Callaghan, S. A. Willcox, T. Sutherland, Asa Mitchell, and J. A. Maverick published the call, and appointed the 15th of November for the meeting of the volunteers at the confluence of the Santa Clara and Cibolo rivers. A committee was appointed to receive contributions, and the officers of the expedition were appointed.

Under the pretext of the Lipan Indians, a more extensive filibustering expedition was organized than the previous one had been. Capitalists took part in it, and in reality the question assumed that character which the difficulties between the

13

frontiers have always assumed, when the greater influence is exercised by the Texans on the bank of the Rio Bravo. It was a war of invasion openly proclaimed, and the most remarkable feature was the publicity given to those acts, and the aid demanded from the government of Texas. If there existed but this fact, it would be sufficient to decide as to what is the cause of all the questions on the frontier, and what is the prevailing opinion among the inhabitants of Texas in the vicinity of the Rio Bravo. A short time after this call was made, the circumstances attending the defeat of the filibusters began to be known, and it was understood that the undertaking presented more difficulties than had at first been anticipated. The capitalists withdrew their names, while the attitude assumed by the government of the United States was sufficient to put an end to further attempts.

Cortina's revolt in 1859, and his taking refuge in México in 1860, were also made the pretext of invasion by the volunteers in the service of Texas. They were headed by John S. Ford, captain of one of the companies, and who had been in command of the filibusters, and the second in command of the expedition which attacked Matamoros.

The trouble began to be felt in January of 1860. At the end of this month, a party of Americans appeared in front of the Soledad ranche and fired upon families residing there, and, almost at the same time, eight of them were seen on our side in the direction of the same ranche. On the fourth of February, the Bolsa ranche was attacked and burned, and the occupants killed. An explanation of these disgraceful occurrences has been attempted in a supposititious attack on the steamer Ranchero by Cortina, a supposition which was sufficient for Mifflin Kennedy, the owner of that steamer, to swear that he suffered great losses.

General Scott, in his report to the war department at Washington, on the 19th of May, 1860, states that there was no such attack, and his statement is perfectly true. Cortina arrived at this ranche from up the river, remained there several days, and was about leaving the place because he was suspicious of it ; during the night the Ranchero arrived with a force on board,

and anchored in front of the Bolsa. The people on board fired
several shots at the ranche which were replied to. The force
then landed, concealing its movements, and surrounded the
ranche. After sharp firing, Cortina retreated to a place in the
neighborhood, where he remained until the following day, when
American cavalry crossed over. So, far from the Ranchero
having been attacked, she served as the means of an aggression
against our frontier, an aggression which had been previously
organized, and in the execution of which the steamer approached the Bolsa, and those who where on board of her
opened hostilities against the Mexican lines.

There occurred then what took place on all the following
invasions, an unoffending man was accidentally killed, another,
Cleto Garcia, was arrested and hung by the volunteers as one of
Cortina's friends, although he was a peaceable and inoffensive
man; after the murdering, robbing, and burning the ranche,
the volunteers stole horses, killed cattle, and then crossed the
river at the Santa Maria ford.

Cortina's revolt was a critical period for the Mexican
population on the left bank. All who were suspected of
sympathizing with him, were murdered without pity, their
families compelled to fly, and their property stolen. The
conduct initiated by the volunteers at the Bolsa was followed
up on the occasion of the second invasion.

The military authorities at Matamoros received notice that
Cortina was at the "Mesa" ranche, and sent a force in pursuit
of him. They notified Major Heintzleman, of the United
States Army, to be on the alert on the left bank, and the
Major communicated the notice to the troops who were at
Brownsville and Edinburg. The Mexican forces arrived at
the Mesa without having heard anything of Cortina, and
departed again leaving a picket force of twenty-six men there.
Ford, the captain of the volunteers, crossed at Rosario on the
night of the 16th of March, and attacked the picket which had
been left at the Mesa; some of the soldiers were killed, others
dispersed, and the rest made prisoners. Captain Ford then
discovered that they were Mexican forces, and explained by
saying that it had been an error, as his scouts had informed

him that Cortina was at the "Mesa." A youth at the ranche was wounded, several houses were pillaged, the money destined for the payment of the force stolen, but few articles were ever restored.

The disrespect towards our soil had inordinately increased with these people. The volunteers, instead of returning to Texas, went several leagues inward, and made incursions upon our frontier. They visited several ranches, made prisoners of the people, and pursued those who fled to the woods. They searched for Cortina's friends to hang them, and at the "Magueyes ranche" killed Elijio Tagle, stole horses, and several days after returned to Texas.

Ever seeking the friends of Cortina, or rather making use of this as a pretext, Captain Ford again crossed into Mexico at Reynosa Vieja, on the 4th of April, 1860, and shut the people up in some sheds, to prevent them from giving notice to the authorities at San Antonio de Reynosa, but these had had timely notice that an invasion was on foot, and soon learned what was going on, and that the Texan volunteers, to the number of sixty men, were within two leagues. The people were armed and ready ; Ford penetrated the town to the principal square, and when he arrived there, the people showed themselves on the roofs of the houses, and at the heads of the streets, and gave Ford to understand that he was surrounded, and that they would not permit the slightest disorder; Ford stated that he had crossed upon the authority of General Guadalupe Garcia, and produced an order signed by him, authorizing him, Ford, to cross to the Bolsa ranche, and arrest Cortina, whom he was informed was there ; he also demanded the delivery to him of such friends of Cortina as were at Reynosa. They answered him that their town was not the Bolsa, and that they had no friends of Cortina there. Ford found himself compelled to abandon the town and depart by the public ford, because they would not permit him to cross elsewhere, being suspicious of his intentions towards the ranches. After he had crossed, a conflict ensued by the firing across the river, as previously stated by the Commission.

The Commission had diligently sought to ascertain whether

the Mexican authorities ever gave the volunteer force permission to cross. With regard to the invasion of the "Mesa," the raids subsequently made on several ranches, and their appearance at Reynosa, the documents which were exchanged concerning these acts, show that not only had they no permission, but that the proceedings of the authorities at Reynosa in resisting their incursion met with full approval. With regard to the attack at the Bolsa, the reason for doubting whether or not such permission was granted, is the deposition of two witnesses, who state that they saw the permission granted by General Garcia to Captain Ford, permitting him to cross at that place. The Commission has not found any documents confirming these depositions, although this is not strange, on account of the losses which the archives have experienced. But in any event, such a permit is not a permission to rob, murder and burn as they did at the Bolsa. What is fully ascertained is, that in April, 1860, an arrangement was made with the American commanding officer, to cross a force to pursue Cortina, in company with the Mexican force ; but this force never crossed. The latest acts communicated by the authorities at Matamoros concerning these aggressions, state that a force of Americans were encamped opposite the Puerta ranche, which force in July of 1860, opened fire upon the latter place, to drive the inhabitants away, and they then subsequently crossed several times, and stole everything that they found there.

These invasions have two phases. For the party directing them, they were a means of keeping alive a feeling of alarm in the United States, by making it appear that Cortina was in force, and that the Mexican authorities were in connivance with him, so much so, that it appeared necessary to invade Mexico with stronger forces. For the subalterns, they were a means of gratifying their propensities for plunder. These aggressions were stimulated, and even defended in Texas. Governor Houston, in his communication to the war department of the 12th of March, 1860, sustained the necessity of the attack on the Bolsa ranche ; thus it had a character eminently political. Even tolerance with regard to robbery might contribute toward the same end ; there was a hope that the exasperation on the Mexican frontier would reach its limit, and produce a conflict attended with the most serious consequences. With the exception of the Bolsa, Cortina was nowhere met with, nor was it possible that he should be, and hence this is not the place to inquire into the purpose which carried the volunteers over the Mexican frontier. They crossed at the Mesa where they thought to find him, and attacked a picket of Mexican soldiers; after they were undeceived, or made it appear that they were undeceived, instead of returning to Texas, they visited several ranches and there committed the greatest excesses. They subsequently undertook more extensive enterprises; hitherto they had only invaded ranches, they now attempted to invade towns. Upon their first attempt, the energetic attitude assumed by the people of Reynosa, who were resolved to punish them if they did not keep themselves within the bounds of the greatest moderation, restrained them.

If in fact permission was given to the volunteers to cross the Bravo at the Bolsa, the Commission must strongly condemn such a proceeding. The matter in question was a most serious one, which by the constitution was reserved to the Federal authority alone, and could not be submitted to the judgment of an inferior. It must have acted as a stimulus to the aggressors to continue the same course of conduct afterwards without any such permission, thereby throwing the greatest obstacles in the way of harmony on the frontier.

The Confederate war was the cause of great difficulties. The Commission has previously explained the organizations which were made on this side to harass the Confederates in Texas, and the threats which these made to cross the river. The war against the European intervention had compelled the concentration of all the elements of resistance in the interior of the republic, the frontier was defenseless, and menaces were the consequence. The Commission have before related the occurrences which took place at the Claraño ranche, and the robbery of a skiff from this side by the volunteers; these immediately crossed to our side and committed several robberies. Shortly after, a Mexican force sent by the municipality of Guerrero arrived, and while upon the spot, fifteen volunteers again attempted to cross into the republic, when they were fired upon and compelled to return. The object of these invasions was robbery; the object of the following ones was more serious. In December of 1862, a troop of Mexican Confederates under the command of Captain Refugio Benavides, crossed from the Texas to this side, pursued Octaviano Zapata, defeated him at the place called Mezquital Lealeño, and then burnt the farm of Jesus Vidal; but in addition to all this, there was a constant state of alarm upon the Mexican side of the river, on account of the continual demonstrations made by various parties of Confederates to invade our territory.

The authorities at Tamaulipas endeavored to remedy the situation, but it is easily understood that every means would be inefficacious without the necessary physical force. In February of 1863, the "jefe politico" of the northern district entered into an arrangement with the Confederate authorities. The principal stipulation with regard to this point, referred to mutual assistance to be given by the Mexican forces to those of Texas, for the pursuit of those who, from the Mexican territory, might attempt to cross and harass on the Texas side, and *vice versa*. If the forces of one State were found to be insufficient, it might call upon the other State for assistance. It was also further arranged, that cattle imported from Texas to Tamaulipas should be accompanied by a permit issued by the Confederate authorities, that in the absence of this permit it should be detained until it was ascertained where it came from, and in the event of its being found that it had been stolen, it should be returned to the Confederate authorities. The Mexicans took all proper measures to carry out this part of the arrangement in good faith.

With regard to the first clause, its intention is perfectly clear; apparently, an alliance had been entered into, but in reality it was a means made use of to prevent attacks from their frontier, fixing by agreement the relations between the two lines. The Confederates would not permit any Mexican forces to cross into Texas, because they were suspicious of them. They could not cross into Mexico without being called upon by our authorities for assistance, which they certainly would not do, because they were endeavoring to prevent those aggressions; at first sight it appears as though great concessions were made, when in reality there were none.

The Confederates soon became convinced of the inefficiency of these arrangements, because they continued their hostilities. Under the pressure which was being brought to bear on the Mexican frontier, which was defenseless against the menaces, without means of resistance on account of the war against the French in which the country was involved, the government of Tamaulipas endeavored to give some tranquility to the population, and for this purpose, on the 4th of March, 1863, consented that the Texan forces might cross into Mexico, and the Mexican forces into Texas, in pursuit of robbers or Indians, without further requisite than notifying the nearest authority. It was hoped that by this means the feeling of insecurity which was felt upon the right bank of the Rio Bravo would be terminated, but experience soon showed that no concession would satisfy that disorderly people, and that in fact force was necessary to repel their aggressions. It is probably due to this, that some time afterwards a force of regular Mexican troops were sent to the line, to give greater security to its inhabitants, but before this was done there had been a series of invasions.

On the 10th of March, 1863, Encarnacion Garcia, a Confederate soldier belonging to the company under the command of Captain Santos Benavides, together with a sergeant, crossed to Monterey Larado drunk; he attacked the Mexican guard and threatened him with his pistol, in consequence of which he was killed. Immediately thereupon Santos Benavides crossed the river, invaded Larado with fifty or sixty men, and peremptorily demanded that the alcalde should arrest the individuals who had killed Encarnacion Garcia and immediately try them. The Texan soldiers were in the court room, grossly insulting the authorities and threatening them with their pistols. After a length of time the invaders returned to Texas.

At four o'clock on the morning of 15th March, 1863, a force of Confederates under the command of Colonel Chilton, and which left Brownsville, crossed from Clarksville to Bagdad. Colonel Davis, now Governor of the State of Texas,

Captain Montgomery and several Union Americans, who were to sail on that day with those officers in a United States steamer for New Orleans, were at the last named town. The Confederates surprised Bagdad. Colonel Davis who was lodged at the custom house, was the first one made prisoner, and immediately crossed into Texas; Captain Montgomery arrived shortly after in search of the Colonel, he was pursued by a group of the Confederates and fired upon in the middle of the town. The rest of the party were in pursuit of the Union Americans who were going to New Orleans, and arrested several of them. Some of the invaders, unable to resist their natural instincts for stealing, robbed several houses in the town; Captain Montgomery was hung upon a tree on the other side. These acts produced a profound indignation in Mexico, and threatened a rupture.

The commanding officer at Brownsville ashamed, perhaps, of such proceedings, or perhaps from the appearance of an imminent rupture of the relations existing between the two sides of the river—a rupture which would have been of great injury to the Confederates on account of Matamoros being the point of transit for the goods with which Texas was supplied —to the complaints made by the government of the State of Tamaulipas replied by setting Colonel Davis and the other parties arrested at liberty.

On the 23d of June, 1863, some Confederate soldiers crossed from Texas to the "Adjuntas ranche," at Guerrero, in Mexico. They concealed themselves behind the fence of a cattle pen, and when José Maria Salinas, who was accused of belonging to Zapata's band, passed by there, they fired upon him and killed him. Octaviano Zapata, for account of the United States, had carried on hostilities against Texas, and when he found himself pressed he took refuge on our frontier. Some soldiers of the garrison at Mier revolted, killed their officer and joined Zapata. Another force which was in pursuit of them had a skirmish with this latter. The officer returned to Mier for the purpose of obtaining reinforcements, but in the mean time, on the 2d of September, 1863, Santos Benavides, the Confederate captain, crossed into Mexico at Salinillas, and defeated Zapata, and killed him and eight of his companions. This Confederate force did not cross the river in accordance even with the agreement made in March previous, it failed even to notify the nearest authority which was at Mier.

The last species of invasions comprises those whose purposes have been to exercise an intervention in the internal questions of the country. A case of this kind presented itself on the frontier of Tamaulipas. In August of 1866, the garrison at Matamoros pronounced and proclaimed Colonel Servando Canales governor and military commandant of Tamaulipas. He accepted the revolt and the position which it conferred. The Supreme Government had appointed General Santiago Tapia to the command of that State, and sent forces to Matamoros, whereupon the siege was begun. Shortly after General Escobedo, who was the general in command of all, arrived with others. On the 23d of November, of the same year, General Thomas D. Sedgwick, the officer in command of the district of Rio Grande, Texas, addressed a communication to Colonel Canales, in which he stated that he had been informed that he had notified his forces that it would be impossible for him to pay them, and that they must provide for themselves, and that inasmuch as the neutrality laws of the United States had been frequently violated of late by Canales, that he demanded the surrender of the city of Matamoros for the purpose of assuring protection to life and property, and that Colonel J. G. Perkins was commissioned to arrange the preliminaries. On the following day, the 24th, Colonel Perkins and Colonel Canales stipulated that the life of this latter, his liberty and property, and also of his forces should be guaranteed, as also that of the people residing in the city, without distinction of nationality ; that no forces except those of the United States should enter the town, and that Colonel Canales should hold his positions. On the same day a pontoon bridge was constructed across the river ; a United States force crossed to Matamoros, the United States flag was raised on the parish church, and Colonel J. G. Perkins issued his general order No. 1, taking the command of the city in the name of the United States, and designating the persons who were to compose his staff. The result of this arrangement and the subsequent measures was that the United States forces obliged themselves to prevent General Escobedo's entrance into the city. On the same day General Sedgwick addressed a communication to General Escobedo informing him of what had occurred, and that he would hold the city of Matamoros until both he and Colonel Canales had had a conference, for which he appointed the following day.

At the conference, General Escobedo informed General Sedgwick that it would be impossible for him to enter into any arrangement, the base of which was not a full submission of the rebels. The American officer then promised to allow the former full liberty of action; but on the 26th, he addressed him a communication stating that he considered it to be his duty to hold possession of the city until receiving further instructions from General Sheridan, inasmuch as no peaceable solution had been arrived at, adding that he wished matters to be continued in the same condition they were.

On the same day, General Escobedo demanded the evacuation of the city by General Sedgwick, when the latter replied, that his views were for the protection of the life and property of the people, and he desired that a peaceable arrangement should be made. It was then agreed, that during the combat a force of fifty Americans should remain in the center of the town for the purpose of preventing robberies and disturbances, and the remainder withdraw, leaving a picket at the Garita of Santa Cruz to protect the families crossing to Brownsville.

The city was attacked on the twenty-seventh. The moment the fortifications were attacked, a United States officer appeared with a flag for parley, notifying General Escobedo, in the name of the United States officer commanding at Matamoros, that in the event of his taking any of the fortifications, that he was not to enter into the interior of the city, and that he was to notify the latter of each point as he took possession of it. Fearing a conflict, General Escobedo retired within his positions.

New explanations were entered into, when General Sedgwick stated that there had been mistakes and misunderstandings. But on the 30th of November, he addressed a communication to Colonel Canales, directing him to surrender, imposing as conditions that the forts and redoubts should be delivered up to the United States troops, to be held by them, that Colonel Canales' troops should concentrate on the public square for the surrender and delivering up of their arms, and that Colonel Canales with his officers and troops should be held as prisoners of war, until the receipt of further orders from the United States authorities. He further required an answer by nine o'clock on the morning of the following day.

Colonel Canales preferred to surrender to General Escobedo, and did so on the night of the 30th of November, when the city was occupied by the government forces. On the first of December, General Sedgwick was informed of what had occurred, when he replied that he had given orders for the evacuation of the city by his troops, which was done.

Although it does not appear by the records, it is well known that the government of the United States disapproved of General Sedgwick's conduct, and relieved him from his command. It is not improbable that General Sedgwick's intentions were to favor the troops of the republic, by bringing a pressure to bear upon those in the town, with a view of compelling them to surrender without bloodshed. If this was so, he unquestionably did not select the best course.

The Commission in the course of this report have examined proceedings, some of which, either from their nature or by reason of the parties committing them, do not render the government of the country where they originated responsible. With regard to others, even though they may have created such responsibility, it cannot be asserted in the present condition of the arrangements made between both governments, as to claims. However, the Commission stated at the commencement that it was not its intention to present charges against the United States. Its principal purpose has been the study of the relations existing between both frontiers since 1848, in order that the spirit of these being understood, the political importance of the question of cattle stealing, and the diversion which the people of Texas have sought to give it, being also understood, the remedy for the abnormal condition of that part of the country, may in good faith be sought.

If the occurrences which have just been related, are considered in connection with the time when they happened, it will be remarked that from 1848 until the present time, all possible difficulties have been marring the relations of the two lines.

For greater clearness, four epochs should be designated. That which elapsed up to 1858; that which covers the time of Cortina's revolt; the period of the Confederate war, up to 1866; and that embraced from this latter year up to the present time. Subsequent to 1848 the republic was exceedingly feeble, its debility was not only physical, but also moral, from the continued reverses which it had experienced in the war with the United States. This awoke in Texas the ambition of adventurous spirits, who hoped to find on the Mexican frontier a field for the exercise of their activity. It was then that the idea of the Republic of the Sierra Madre sprung into existence. This was the first step for extending the sovereignty of the United States over all the Mexican territory embraced between the Rio Bravo and the passes of the Sierra. The spirit of filibustering seized the idea, and the successive invasions, up to the last at Piedras Negras, in 1855, were so many attempts upon divers pretexts to obtain this end. As late as 1858, attempts were made to organize expeditions against the Mexican frontier, but these attempts were frustrated, because probably they had become convinced that private enterprise could not successfully contend against the republic, and the population on the Mexican line were opposed to it. The tactics were now changed, and the attempt was made to involve the United States in a war of conquest against Mexico; Cortina's revolt, in 1859 and 1860, afforded the first opportunity for obtaining it. The Commission has stated the result of their study and consideration of these facts. It is there shown, that the people residing on the left bank of the Bravo, and the Texas forces in the field, did their best to bring about a conflict between the two lines, and to maintain a constant state of excitement among the people of the United States. It is there shown that this course of conduct was sustained by the government of Texas, and that upon the theory of preventing the organization of parties in Mexico for robbing the Texas line, and obtaining guaranties against such aggressions, a war for the acquisition of territory was in fact intended ; the government of the United States understood what was meant, and their labor was lost. Governor Houston, in March of 1860, was already convinced of the impossibility of obtaining his purpose, to which, and the withdrawal of the Texan volunteers from the margin of the Bravo, is to be attributed that, in the following April, the conflicts on the frontier were brought to a close. The Cortina question had finished some months before, and if they gave it an existence in Texas, it was for the purpose of carrying out political plans of greater magnitude.

In 1861 the Confederate war broke out, and then the extent of the ill-feeling entertained on the Texas frontier towards Mexico became manifest. The Texans upon the left bank were convinced of the good faith which governed the proceedings of the Mexican authorities, and nevertheless they lost no opportunity of promoting broils and bitter discussions. Their situation did not permit them to undertake any formal enterprises against the Mexican frontier, but they had no hesitation in committing the greatest outrages. The invasion of Bagdad, for the purpose of arresting officers and Union soldiers, who were under the protection of neutral territory, carry them off to Texas, and thereupon hang Captain Montgomery to a tree, is an act which merits the severest criticism.

At that time the Texans went as far as they could under their circumstances ; these did not permit them to take possession of the country, but they proceeded as though the country in question was not a foreign one. The spirit prevailing in the first filibustering invasions, and the one which guided the policy of the Texas frontier during Cortina's revolt, inspired them with an utter disregard of the rights and sovereignty of the Mexican Republic. Subsequent to the year 1866, the question of the Free Zone was first brought forward. It was stated that it was the cause of immense smuggling into the United States, and that her revenues were defrauded thereby of millions; the necessity of taking possession of the Mexican territory up to the Sierra Madre was defended as the only means of preventing contraband. It is not within the province of this Commission to examine the question of the " Free Zone," but it having been presented as an injury, and a ground of demoralization, on account of the smuggling to which it gives room, and the indirect influence which it exerts in the increase of crime, it is impossible to pass it over without a few words of remark.

During the years immediately following 1848, smuggling became one of the most serious questions in connection with the frontier. The Commission has already referred to two cases, in which, after the seizure of the cargo for violation of the revenue laws, large parties of armed men crossed from the American to the Mexican side, attacked the custom house guards, recaptured the cargo, and again crossed it to the Texas frontier, where the parties committing these illegal acts enjoyed every immunity. These facts furnish us with the measure of the situation; the fact that such parties could be gathered together at a moment's notice, shows to what extent smuggling to the injury of Mexico was organized, to what extent it was protected and encouraged, and to what degree demoralization prevailed.

The rising of 1851 had for its object a commercial reform, but in this, as in its political aspect, it was completely perverted. The commercial reforms driveled away into smuggling operations, which were commenced on an immense scale, and which resulted in the " Avalos " tariff, issued by the commanding officer at Matamoros. By it prohibitions were removed, and the duties reduced. This measure was most efficacious in counteracting the political movement, because it separated from it numerous Mexicans whose national sensibilities had been wounded by the participation in the revolt of Texans, whose intentions could not be relied upon by the people of Mexico. That revolution was thus reduced to a war, supported and

realizing in a short time an immense fortune by defrauding Mexico and spreading demoralization. All these interests which had been destroyed considered that they had been injured when a bar was placed to their further disorderly proceedings. Hereupon they endeavored to secure the support of the government of the United States for their immoral purposes by asserting that the Free Zone was an act of hostile legislation against it and the direct cause of a great contraband across our frontier into Texas. The Commission acknowledges that this contraband has existed, but of how little importance is shown by an examination of the scanty population which could consume it, and the not less significant fact that most of the goods consumed on the American frontier are of American production. If the origin of this smuggling is considered, it will be found that its cause must be sought for elsewhere, and not in the " Free Zone," and a proof of this fact is, that although the traffic is constant, smuggling at certain times has not existed at all, or at least has been confined to liquors or tobacco, which expert swimmers cross during the night.

The " Free Zone," thus is neither by its origin nor present condition, a measure by which the United States receives any injury. Nevertheless the people on the Texas bank zealously maintained the contrary, and for this purpose distorted the facts and circumstances, and arrived at the conclusion that the only adequate remedy to prevent the United States from suffering on account of the contraband which was carried on from Mexico into Texas, was to take possession of the Mexican territory lying between the Bravo and the Sierra. Thus did the people of Texas continue what they had previously commenced in the Cortina question, and what they subsequently did in the question of cattle stealing. A real fact, simple in its character and circumstances, was distorted to create an artificial question between Mexico and the United States for the purpose of bringing about difficulties, the solution of which was to be found in a war of conquest.

When the Texas frontier became satisfied that the question of the " Free Zone " would not produce the desired effect, they

14

brought to life the question of cattle stealing. This explains the reason why since 1870 they resorted to complaints upon this point, notwithstanding that cattle stealing has existed since 1862, and that previous to 1870 it was committed to a much greater extent.

The petition to the legislature of Texas, in 1871, for General Cortina's pardon excited passions of another kind, and these passions were an auxiliary for those purposes. From an offense of a common nature, such as is simple cattle stealing, which only demands the ordinary action of the tribunals, a question of great political importance was made. It was not an interest to suppress robbery and demoralization that guided the people of Texas, because they have shown the contrary by the tolerance and, in certain cases, protection, afforded by them to cattle stealing committed in Mexico, although this maintains a state of disorganization in which they have to bear their share. A concerted and harmonious action between the authorities on both banks to pursue the crime, independent of the frontier where it may have been committed, would have been quite sufficient; but this concert was avoided in order that a conflict and an uproar might be produced.

The question of cattle stealing under a political aspect is merely artificial, and is of no importance except as a pretext. In the same manner as in the Cortina question in 1860 and that of the " Free Zone," in 1868 and 1869, it has served to sustain the necessity of the United States taking possession of the territory embraced between the Bravo and the Nueces rivers. The political theory upon which this necessity is made to rest is that the Bravo river is not a boundary which protects the United States against marauding Mexicans and Indians, and hence that it is indispensable that the boundary be extended to the Sierra Madre. This is the reason why there has been so much interest in maintaining that the robberies and all kinds of crime in Texas are committed by bands organized in Mexico. Hence it is that the urgency of " guaranties for the future " is proclaimed, and hence it is also that these guaranties seek an acquisition of territory.

The Commission have obtained various Texas newspapers,

in which are contained articles showing the political character stamped upon the question of cattle stealing. An extract from one of them is sufficient.—*The Brownsville Sentinel*, November 3d, 1872, Our Boundary.

The article commences by copying the resolutions submitted in the United States Senate, on the 28th of February, 1848, by General Samuel Houston, as an amendment to the treaty of Guadalupe:

"That the dividing line should start one league south of Tampico, in a straight line to the south of San Luis Potosi, thence to the Sierra Madre, and following the 25th parallel to the east coast of lower California, this and the islands in the Pacific to be embraced within the limits of the United States."

It adds, that General Taylor during the war recommended the Sierra Madre as the most desirable for the dividing line between the two countries. It also explains the causes which probably influenced the selection of the Rio Grande as the dividing line. Alluding to General Houston and his action in the Senate to change the dividing line, it says:

"He supported the resolutions presented by him for this purpose, by many reasons full of force and worthy of a statesman. He had witnessed the inefficiency of the Rio Grande; the difficulty of defending it; the facility with which it could be crossed in spite of all precautions, and the consequent insecurity which would result to ourselves, if Mexico reached the state of demoralization which he predicted. His efforts for the passage of an act establishing a protectorate in Mexico, which was his ardent desire, the result of his profound foresight, his solicitude for the welfare of Texas, and the protection of the inhabitants on the frontier—"

This same paper referring to the causes which gave rise to its article, states:

"Cortina's invasion of 1859 and 1860; the continuance of this war of depredation which with some short intervals has lasted for thirteen years; the great loss of life and property experienced by the people of Texas; the operations organized in Mexico by the Kickapoos and other tribes of Indians, and those by Mexican citizens, and the officers and soldiers of the Mexican army, show the feeling of insecurity which has prevailed among the inhabitants of the Rio Grande and the Nueces, as well as those living upon the banks of the tributaries of this latter river, a feeling which has retarded the settlement of the country, the development of its resources and much other important business, thus tending to draw attention to the line of the Rio Grande, and create the opinion that it is an unsafe line between the United States and Mexico."

It continues by saying that this demands a change. That both governments have sent Commissioners to inquire into the difficulties on the frontier. That the United States Commission have gathered together a mass of undeniable proofs, which show a criminal neglect of its duty on the part of the Mexican Government, and connivance, on the part of its agents or employees, in the piratical acts upon the people of the United States. That the weakness of the Mexican Government renders it impossible for it to guarantee the future, however good its intentions may be. That two plans had been proposed as a remedy for the situation, the first of which was a treaty permitting the troops of either government to cross the Rio Grande in pursuit of the guilty persons or parties. That this plan was unacceptable because it might give rise to serious conflicts. The following explanation was given with regard to the second plan :

" Make the Sierra Madre the dividing line, and thus protect the settlers in Western Texas ; *accept compensation for the past, and give certain fixed and irrevocable security for the future.*"

The question of cattle stealing presents two aspects. In the one which may be called its personal aspect, there is an attempt made by a greater or less body of people for the purpose of committing an act of expoiliation, to the injury of the Mexican Republic, and to obtain the support of the government of the United States, toward those improper designs. This is called " *compensation for the past.*" In its political aspect, it is an effort to carry out the projects which were conceived in 1848, and the realization of which was at first attempted by means of filibustering undertakings, and subsequently, when these failed, by endeavoring to involve Mexico in a war with the United States. This is called " *Guaranties for the future.*"

From the moment in which cattle stealing ceases to be the question, and becomes the pretext, as other previous acts have been, the supposition is not improbable that, for some time to come, and until there is an increase in the population and strong ties of material interests between the two frontiers, difficulties of a more or less serious nature, incited and exaggerated by the present residents upon the left bank of the Bravo river, will be brought to notice.

Both frontiers are thus, for both nations, places of the greatest importance. The difficulties arising there are generally artificial, due to trifling causes for the settlement of which, in a majority of cases, it would be sufficient that the military command of the frontier should be in charge of persons of sound judgment. With regard to Mexico, the Commission is of opinion that the military command of the frontier of the Eastern States is a position of great responsibility, and to which should be attached all the importance to which it is entitled, because in all probability, if serious complications should at any time arise with the United States, their origin will be here.

XVIII.

It is impossible to deny that since 1848 the stealing of horses has been carried on in Mexico, for the purpose of carrying them into Texas and selling them there. It must also be admitted, that since 1862 cattle have been stolen in Texas, taken into Mexico, and sold there, but it is not true that this has been carried on to the extent alleged by the complainants in Texas ; there is no doubt, however, about the fact. This is not a political question within the meaning given to it; it has no such character as the complainants have endeavored to invest it with ; nevertheless, both governments are certainly interested in regulating the condition of their respective frontiers. With regard to the cattle stealing, the remedy is with the police and the courts, and consequently it is to the interests of both governments that these should produce their proper fruits.

The Commission have had an opportunity of observing the

inefficiency of the local authorities on both frontiers. The Mexican authorities do not possess sufficient means of action, while the disorganization of those of the United States is notorious. The evil is greater between the Bravo and Nueces rivers, by reason of the want of large towns. Furthermore, upon both lines the authorities are elective ; at times honest men may be elected, but at others, corrupt ones may be. These reasons show the necessity of extending the action of the federal authorities as far as possible, or the laws will consent.

As a consequence of these facts, and without prejudice to the action of the local authorities, it is desirable that a federal force should be detailed, sufficient to watch all the frontier from Matamoros to Piedras Negras ; but in order that this force should answer its purpose, it ought to be composed of two elements, men of the regular army, and a federal police, auxiliary to and under the command of the former.

The regular army by itself is insufficient, because it is impossible to exercise due vigilance, and efficiently pursue the criminals without possessing a full topographical knowledge of the country, of the places where robbery is most easily committed, of the fords of the river most frequented by cattle stealers, and of the parties engaged in such crime. Criminals driving stolen cattle do not travel on the highways ; it is not there they are to be sought for, or pursued, and hence the propriety of a federal police composed of honest men belonging to the place, and who would be an auxiliary to the regular troops.

It is unnecessary to call attention to the great care which should be used by the officers commissioned to organize this police, in the selection of the elements of which it is to be composed, as otherwise it would produce a contrary effect. This force does not require to be numerous if it be well organized ; its results should be anticipated rather from the nature of its elements than from its numbers. As a regulation of great importance, the Commission would suggest that this police use no distinctive uniform whatever, as this would serve as a notice to the criminals whom they are to persecute.

The regular force and the police should render their services in such manner as to be a means of real protection to all citi-

zens against the robbers. When the proprietors upon the
frontier become satisfied that they are sufficiently protected,
they will become powerful auxiliaries in the persecution of
the robbers. If at present they show indifference, it is
owing to the fact that they have no protection on either frontier ; they are compelled to tolerate the criminals and be silent
as to their offenses, because the authorities furnish them no
means of defense. The nature and organization of the service
are matters with which the Commission are not acquainted, and
belong to the military. Nevertheless it is impossible to leave
unremarked that upon both banks of the Bravo river there are
ranches, several of which have become noted as the hiding
places of robbers, and that it is certain that those upon one
bank are in connivance with those upon the other. In order
that the service be efficient, it is necessary to make a special
investigation as to the ranches on either side at or near which
detachments should be placed. Harmonious action upon
the part of the military authorities would produce the happiest
results in this connection. It is unnecessary to remark that
it is not desirable that a force should remain too great a length
of time at one place ; on the contrary, it should be frequently
moved as a means of preserving discipline. A second train
of measures necessary for the suppression of cattle stealing,
is one which would lead to an expeditious action on the
part of the courts. Although the Commission deems it very
advantageous to carry this class of cases before the federal
courts on both frontiers, as being more independent in their
action and freer from the local influences arising out of elections, it has to confess that, with regard to Mexico, it has found
no means to this end compatible with the Constitution ; it does
not know whether there may be any such means in the United
States.

The suppression of all kinds of expenses, in the form of
fees to the public employees or any others, is a matter of necessity. The legislation of the frontier States of both nations
should tend to facilitate the persecution of cattle stealers and
cattle stealing, without regard to the place where the offense
may have been committed. Measures of this nature are for

their own protection. For this purpose, and with a view of converting individual action into an auxiliary of the authorities, every possible facility should be offered to such action. With regard to Mexico, no charge is made, all is gratuitous ; but in Texas the necessity exists of abolishing the fees paid to the sheriff and the courts. The propriety of a simple proof is indicated, in order to avoid as far as possible the assistance of a lawyer. In Mexico it has been the practice to require the proof of presenting the brand, because it establishes a presumption of ownership. This throws upon the possessor of it the necessity of proving that it was lawfully acquired. These provisions are substantially the same as those contained in the first section of the laws of Texas, passed on the 13th November, 1866, but there is this difference, that this latter confines itself to Texas cattle. It is not extended to cattle stolen in Mexico and carried into the United States, while the courts in Mexico have applied the principle to cattle brought from Texas.

In Texas the proof by the brand, with regard to horses stolen in Mexico, is not sufficient, further proofs are required. The Commission suggests the propriety of the first section of the law of Texas of 1866, being made to extend to both frontiers, for animals stolen on either side. If this was done, the proof of the brand upon the part of the plaintiff, and the want of a bill of a sale in the possession of the defendant, would amount to a presumption, or as called in law, a "*prima facie*" proof of an unlawful possession of the animals. Some measure of this kind is indispensable, both for the purpose of facilitating the recovery of the stolen property by its owners, as well as to place within the reach of the courts the same means of investigation used by private parties.

The Commission has elsewhere remarked that cattle stealing is generally accompanied by smuggling, so that there are two offenses coming under different jurisdictions, and very different in their results. There can be no doubt that the original offense is stealing, and that the smuggling can work no prejudice to the owner of the property, who is innocent, and that hence it is simply a matter of robbery, and should be so tried for the

purpose of returning the property stolen to its owner. The
Mexican authorities have taken this view of the matter, and
the custom-house employees have placed the cattle thus smuggled at the disposal of the local judges. In only one single
case of those which came under the observation of the Commission, was the matter referred to the federal judge.

In the United States, smuggling always determines the
nature of the suit. A case has occurred, for instance, of the
owner pursuing horses and mules which had been stolen from
him, and after having found and recovered them, in a suit before the courts of Texas, he has been compelled to defend
another suit on account of the contraband committed by the
thieves. The owner certainly cannot be prevented from appearing and claiming his property, and although, notwithstanding the smuggling, it is returned to him if he proves his property, this result is only reached after unnecessary annoyance.

With regard to Mexico, the question is easily decided.
Cattle pay no importation duties, so that if they are clandestinely
imported, there are grounds to presume that theft and not
smuggling is the cause of the secrecy. This presumption should
be held as the basis of the legislation to be made upon the
subject.

With regard to the United States, the subject presents more
difficulties. Horses, mares and mules are subject to importation duties. The clandestine importation thus may be by reason of robbery, or for the purpose of defrauding the government of the duties. These two presumptions then are present,
but as the Commission is not sufficiently acquainted with the
laws of the United States to give an opinion, as to the means
adequate for the protection of the owners on this side against
the vexations of a suit, it confines itself to stating that that
legislation is imperfect, because it does not keep in view the
peculiar circumstances of the frontier.

These various measures are intended to protect the rights
of the owners, by removing all the obstacles in the way of the
recovery of their property at the least possible cost. Not only
morally speaking, but as a matter for their own benefit, the
Federal and State authorities should make such laws as would

establish easy and simple means for the protection of the rights of the owner and the punishment of the crime. The laws of Texas which punish the crime of stealing, when committed outside of its territory and the stolen property is carried within its limits, as also conspiracies for crime to be committed outside of its limits, are worthy of special mention, and leave nothing to be desired with regard to the matter. If, in Mexico, the laws are properly applied, no others are necessary. The party committing a robbery in Texas, and bringing the stolen property into Mexico for the purpose of sale, is guilty of a crime continued (*de tracto succesivo*), and subject to punishment. Also those who conspire to commit crimes, although not to be committed on our frontier, are from the simple act guilty. The Mexican courts have applied these principles, without the necessity of a special legislation, to such cases as have occurred, and at times have even gone farther. On the eighth of May, 1863, while the town of Mier was temporarily annexed to the State of Nuevo Leon, the government of that State ordered, that when the residents of that town were guilty of crime or disorderly conduct in the United States, and did not demur to the jurisdiction of Mexico, upon complaint being made against them, that they should be tried by the State authorities.

This latter practice has never come into general use, and its propriety may be doubted, on account of the risk incurred by the accused party, in being tried at a different place from where the occurrences took place, and where it would be easier for him to establish his innocence. With regard to the former, there is no doubt as to its necessity, and, in the judgment of the Commission, it is expedient that such laws be made the subject of special legislation. The reasons which govern this judgment are, that doubts have been expressed as to the application of those legal principles to crimes committed in Texas, although such doubts are groundless; because in one case the crime is initiated, and in the other consummated in Mexico. Nevertheless, it is desirable to remove all doubt, in order that there may never be any difficulty, when there is an object in making one, for the punishment of criminals. The extent of the penalty attached to cattle stealing in the State of Texas, leaves nothing to be desired in this respect. Horse stealing, although it may be only of a single one, is punished by five to fifteen years in the penitentiary, and cattle by two to five years. A reform is required in this particular in the laws of the frontier States. The law of the 5th of January, which is in operation in those States, affixes the penalty in proportion to the amount of the theft, the result of which is, that the penalty for cattle stealing is very slight. It frequently occurs that cattle stealers are only punished by four or six months in the chain gang, upon the conclusion of which they are set at liberty to again continue their career of robbery; the impropriety of this has been already remarked by other persons. Lawyer Trinidad Garza Melo, in his notes for the criminal statistics of Nuevo Leon, in referring to this same question stated:

" The same cannot be said with regard to the penalty attached to cattle stealing, by the said law of the 5th of January. The penalty attached to cattle stealing is not sufficient to suppress this crime in the State according to that law; that which might be proper and sufficient in the States of the interior, is not so in Nuevo Leon, nor do I believe it can be so in any frontier State."

He continues by explaining the causes of the frequency of cattle stealing, and which have been enumerated elsewhere by the Commission, and continues by saying:

" Since the causes which make cattle stealing profitable, or render its commission easy, cannot be removed or directly influenced, it is necessary that the cattle stealers should be more severely punished. Cattle stealing, which in itself is serious on account of the abuse of the public confidence, in whose custody the cattle in the fields are, is also so by reason of the serious losses inflicted by them upon the stock raisers; those who require them for their business, and especially to the wagon trains on the road, the theft of some of whose mules makes it a matter of impossibility for them to continue their journey, and this naturally becomes the source of great losses to the merchants, consignees of the goods which they are transporting. It does not thus appear that the parties committing a crime, attended with such serious consequences, are properly punished by the same penalty affixed to a simple larceny, even though this penalty be doubled as to the time in the chain gang, as directed by the law of the 5th of February. The penalty of the larceny being made by this law commensurate with the value of the property stolen, it rarely occurs that at the time of conviction in cases of cattle stealing, the penalty can exceed one year, because the law does not sanction it, which, as I said before, was given in 1857 for all the republic. Though this law with regard to cattle stealing may be proper and sufficient in the interior States, it is not so in Nuevo Leon, which by its topographical position is, as are the other frontier States, under very different circumstances, and offer greater facilities and more certain profits to cattle thieves.

"Hence it is necessary that, in such cases, the State should make a law attaching heavier penalties than those which are now imposed, according to the law of the 5th of January, 1857, referred to."

The punishment of the purchasers of animals stolen on either frontier should be made the object of a law. At times there have been applied in Mexico, to parties purchasing cattle stolen in the United States, the provisions with regard to the receivers of stolen property, but this, neither by reason of the time or place, has been the general practice. Nevertheless, it is from this class of dealers that the crime receives the most encouragement, and in the judgment of the Commission they should be most severely punished. It will be impossible radically to remedy this, so long as there may be persons, in any of the frontier States of Mexico or the United States, who purchase with impunity the proceeds of the raid made upon the other nation.

As a preventive, and in order to facilitate the action of the courts, the Commission deem it desirable that the extradition treaty should be amended in various points. This treaty is, and has been wholly inefficacious, because it is not adapted to the circumstances of the frontier. In the opinion of the Commission, it requires the following amendments and additions.

First. Extradition should be applicable to the crime of cattle stealing, whatever may be the amount stolen, and even though it did not amount to twenty-five dollars, repealing the last part of the third article of the treaty. The facility of committing this crime, and the difficulty of discovering it, show the propriety of allowing no opportunity to pass of punishing it, and for this purpose every means should be facilitated which leads to this end. Furthermore, in the frontier States the extent of this crime should not be measured by the value of the stolen property, either with regard to extradition or its punishment. Cattle stealing is governed by special and easily perceptible considerations, if the recent difficulties are remembered.

Second. The extradition of deserters in active service belonging to the garrisons on the frontier, within, for example, say twenty leagues of the dividing line, appears also to be a necessity. The deserters from the Mexican army take refuge in Texas, where, not finding means of employment, they embark in crime, and increase that floating mass of criminals so prejudicial to both frontiers. Such an emigration cannot be desirable to Texas; on the contrary it contributes to her insecurity.

Third. The Commission consider the principle worthy of consideration that the citizens of either of the two nations who, within the jurisdiction of the other, exercise some political rights, and thereby commit an offense, are subject to extradition. The latter part of the sixth article of the treaty provides that neither of the two contracting parties shall be compelled to extradite their own citizens. It has frequently occurred that Mexicans by birth and nationality have participated in the elections in Texas, and have thus perpetrated an offense there, and then sought refuge in Mexico. The fact of voting at elections does not deprive them of their Mexican citizenship according to our laws, nor does it confer upon them a United States citizenship according to the laws of that country, hence there are no grounds to resist extradition according to the terms of the treaty. Nevertheless the generality of these parties commit offenses on both sides of the Bravo, and remain unpunished. Their punishment at the place where it could be proved they had committed their crimes would be very advantageous.

Fourth. The great distance from Matamoros to Monterey Laredo and the intermediate towns, following the Mexican frontier, and from Brownsville to Laredo and the intermediate towns, by way of the United States frontier, suggests the propriety of appointing an extradition commissioner according to the fourth article of the treaty, at each one of these places, in order that the proceedings may be efficient. In view of the facility which both frontiers furnish for the escape and concealment of criminals, the greatest possible facilities should be provided for their arrest.

These measures have suggested themselves to the Commission, but it must confess that, until the State of Texas adopts a better legislation, and endeavors to have it strictly enforced, doing away with the abuses which, under the name of custom, are so many means for cattle stealing, there must be on the United States frontier a constant cause of demoralization which, under certain conditions, will show itself in the stealing of cattle and carrying them to our side, in spite of all the measures which may be taken. The Commission is aware of the difficulties surrounding the undertaking, on account of the great number of persons who have made and are endeavoring to increase their fortunes through such disturbances, while as many more would like to do so by the same means.

XIX.

The Commission in the course of its labors has taken special care to investigate the truth, has omitted no means to attain this end, and it now seeks to present it in this report.

In the history of the relations between the two frontiers, the question of cattle stealing is only an incidental one, and is doomed to disappear so soon as it shall have answered its political purposes.

What merits particular attention is, that series of crises which have periodically occurred in their intercourse since 1848, and the invariable solution of which has been sought for in the expansion of territory. This is in substance the meaning of the question of cattle stealing.

Until the spirit prevailing on the left bank of the river is modified, a similar condition of things must continue to exist, and, certainly, neither laws nor treaties will prove a remedy, although they may perhaps contribute thereto.

The most powerful preventive will be found in the development of a class of interests, different from that at present existing on the frontier, and especially an increase in real property, to the end that, instead of as now, seeking to bring about a rupture for the profits expected to be derived from it, their exertions might then be directed towards maintaining friendly relations, for the benefits to be obtained through them and the necessity of their preservation.

MONTEREY, May 15th, 1873.

EMILIO VELASCO,
YGNACIO GALINDO,
ANTONIO GARCIA CARRILLO.

AUGUSTIN SILICIO,
Secretary.

LATE REPORTS.

COMMISSION OF INVESTIGATION

ON THE

NORTHERN FRONTIER.

COMMISSION OF INVESTIGATION

ON THE

NORTHERN FRONTIER.

CITIZEN MINISTER:

In the communication which I have the honor to forward you, in compliance with the decree of 2d October, 1872, which provided for the scrupulous investigation of the injuries suffered by the inhabitants on the Northern frontier of Mexico, you will see these injuries specified in detail, setting forth their origin and characteristics, and showing the evil in all its various phases.

It was not possible to give to this work less magnitude than that which it has assumed, for the reason that the simple narrative of the facts, and the quotations from various documents necessitated quite a volume. It also includes the opinion of the Commission on the best remedies to be applied to each of the obstacles which retards the progress of that part of the country, and it has been deemed expedient to compile these suggestions in such form as will facilitate their presentation by you to the president, for his consideration.

In the first place, it is shown that the establishment of a military post on the frontier is indispensable to maintain order, and form the basis of a regular footing for the relations between this republic and that of the United States. The officer to be placed in command of these troops should be of high rank, and possessed of qualities to render him respected.

2. It is of the utmost importance that the upper portion of the Rio Grande be guarded by detachments of from 250 to 300 men, to be posted at San Vicente, el Burro and las Vacas, by which measure the incursions of the savages can be restrained, and a stop put to the raids made by the Texan populace from this quarter, and the injuries received by Mexicans.

3. To advance the interests of the inhabitants of the vast wilderness lying between Chihuahua, Coahuila and Durango, and to give encouragement and protection to Mexicans who will settle there; keeping in mind that the settlement of this tract can only be effected by first guarding the frontier, and thereby giving security to the settlers; the government lands should be surveyed and distributed to applicants, or to emigrants from the central States of the republic, as was done by the Spanish Government.

4. To encourage the settlement of towns under the principles indicated, employing the resources conceded to the frontier States, under the name of "assistance," and protecting the capital so invested, that it may not be diverted from its object.

5. To form a new territory of all the new towns, so that the General Government may be more active and energetic towards the advancement of the settlers, provided, always, that they are Mexicans.

6. To regulate the intercourse between the innumerable ranchos lying on the border of the Rio Grande, in such manner as will not injure nor compromise the international relations, nor affect the revenues of the public treasury, by permitting the introduction of contraband goods by the inhabitants thereof, or by their protection to contrabandists.

7. To promulgate such laws as are considered best for the suppression of the cattle thieves, including such measures as may be necessary to prevent the flight of servants, who carry off from the country vast capital, and who, by their crimes on either shore of the Rio Grande, compromise the international relations.

8. To try and better the condition of Mexicans residing in Texas who are owners of property in that State. This is made essential from the feeling against them, shown by the unprecedented injuries to which they are daily subjected. Besides the action of the diplomatic bureau, the establishment of a consulate in Corpus Christi would contribute greatly towards effecting a beneficial change in this particular.

9. To so reform the regulations governing the trade of the Zona Libre, that no articles of merchandise can be consumed by the inhabitants of the region without the payment of taxes, however moderate; and that the new tariff should embrace some of the articles now included in the present tariff rates; and that this change be effected upon the basis indicated in a separate memorial addressed to the Secretary of the Treasury.

10. That without departing from the rules laid down in the Circular of 10th September, 1850, such others may be applied as have been proved by experience to be best for the solution of Indian questions, thereby inaugurating a simple policy, straightforward and just towards these tribes, whenever they present themselves in our territory.

11. Appoint a council, whose duty it shall be to inform itself on all questions relating to Indian depredations, taking exact evidence relative to the injuries sustained by Mexican citizens, and upon all other subjects bearing upon the question, so as to avoid responsibility and secure the rights of such Mexican citizens as have been injured; in all cases the council must take cognizance of the tribe of Indians committing the depredation, their place of residence, the amount of the damages done by them, and the responsibility incurred by authorities or citizens of the United States; also the action taken by United States officers for their punishment, and that used by Mexicans for their repression. The council to be specially charged to open relations with Texas or such portion of the State as is inhabited by Indians, in order to investigate fully the conduct pursued by American authorities towards native tribes, and that maintained upon the government reservations, and towards those who lead a nomadic life, using meantime every measure

to inform itself as to the ultimate destination of the stolen property.

12. To inaugurate reforms in the laws of justice, by reorganizing the federal tribunals in such manner as that the courts may be administered by persons of known ability, having for their assistants in all cases men no less worthy than themselves. Their jurisdiction should include all such crimes as compromise the international relations.

13. That the penal code, relating to contrabandists, is likewise in want of thorough reform ; frauds against the treasury by smuggling are not considered dishonorable, and demand the severe treatment of corporal punishment, such as imprisonment of the merchant who commits the crime, and the closing of his place of business should he be a Mexican citizen, and banishment from the republic should he be a foreigner.

After enumerating all the troubles which afflict the Mexican frontier, in the report made by the Commission, they considered their work incomplete, and proceeded to express their judgment as to the proper means of remedying the evil. They do not presume to say that they have discovered the best means, and perhaps no measures could be applied which would correct such inveterate wrong doing, which, by reason of its long duration, is rendered the more difficult to deal with ; but it is certain that the measures and regulations which they propose have all been deliberately and carefully studied by them ; and should they even prove not equal to extirpating the evils on the frontier, which have taken such root, at least they will undoubtedly conduce to an amelioration thereof, and admit of a choice by such persons as are well posted in regard to the general situation of the country, the character of the people, and in fact the true condition of affairs.

In presenting to you this compendium of the result of the labors confided to us, we must not conceal that the inhabitants of Northern Mexico, wearied by their sufferings which number half a century, desire even more than the reparation of losses and damages sustained, a regular system of protection which will secure them from future annoyances. They wish to live in security from the injuries, which, up to the present, they receive almost daily from the authorities and citizens of the United States, and which they are compelled to endure through their weakness and inability to resent them.

If some of their objects have been accomplished, the Commission will feel perfectly satisfied, and if the results desired have not been so successful as intended, they will still enjoy the consciousness of knowing that their efforts were solely engaged to this end.

Independence and Liberty.

Mexico, March 13, 1874.

(Signed.)   IGNACIO GALINDO.

(Signed.)   FRANCISCO VALDEZ GOMEZ.
Secretary,
To the Minister of Foreign Relations.
(Copy.)

Mexico, March 13, 1874.

FRANCISCO VALDEZ GOMEZ,
Secretary.

COMMISSION OF INVESTIGATION

NORTHERN FRONTIER.

THE Commission charged with the investigation of the affairs on the northern frontier of the republic, in the States of Coahuila, Nuevo Leon, and Tamaulipas, have made a detailed report of the result of their labors to the Minister of Foreign Affairs. Besides showing the evils existing, the Commission have pointed out such remedies which, in their opinion, they consider as best adapted to elevate that important portion of the country from the prostration to which it has been reduced.

As some of these remedies suggested belong to the military branch, it has been determined to forward a minute of them to you, that through you they may be brought to the notice of the President for his consideration and resolve.

In the above-named report the Commission showed the urgent necessity of guarding the line of the Rio Grande by a regiment of infantry, to give dignity to the republic, and restrain by their presence the disorders which so frequently occur whether by the incursions of Indians or the invasions of filibusters. This measure recommends itself; and it is a fact that Mexico has always endeavored to maintain a respectable guard on her frontier. If, in 1855, she was compelled to withdraw these forces, it was not because she did not recognize their utility and, in fact, necessity, but on account of the demoralization existing, which had extended to the army. Now that discipline has made this branch of the public service distinguished, the frontier claims its co-operation in the public welfare, and hopes that a guard may be sent who will contribute to the bettering of their towns.

The same necessity exists, and, in fact, there is greater urgency for the garrisoning of the old Fort of San Vicente, of el Burro, and of las Vacas, each by a detachment of from two to three hundred men. These points are situated on the margin of the Rio Grande, and it is the opinion of old officers of the disbanded garrisons of these forts, with whom conference has been had upon the subject, that these points command the best strategical positions for covering the whole line, and defending Coahuila, Durango, Zacatecas, San Luis Potosi, Nuevo Leon, and Tamaulipas from the incursions of savages.

Without possessing any military knowledge, the Commission, nevertheless, takes the liberty to recommend the garrisoning of the above-named points, not only because this is suggested by superior officers of the old companies of those forts, but because they had been selected for this object ever since the days of the Colonial Government, which left so many proofs of its skill in these matters.

In order to influence the government to adopt these or other similar measures, plans of the country have been made, in which the rivers, mountains and valleys are laid down with the object of their being considered by officers of the army, amongst whom there must be many well versed in this branch who can study such points and classify the opinions collected upon the subject, as already stated.

The defense of the frontier is of the greatest importance, and should be decided upon, and organized without delay, since an exact report of the sufferings of the inhabitants has been made. Never before has the country been able to dispose of so well disciplined an army which does credit to the country it serves, and never before has there been known to exist such an immensity of wrong with such easy facility for curing it.

The system of defense will lack completeness if forces are not stationed at the entrance of Bolson de Mapimi, or, what is the same thing, at the Lagoon of Tahualilo ; and it is the general belief that these guards, properly stationed, will encourage emigration to that part of the country, which is inviting with its wealth and abundance.

There is a law relating to the establishment of military colonies on the frontier, and although this is of itself sufficient to better the condition of things, yet, on account of its great costliness, the benefit to be derived will have to be postponed.

It is better to state here that, without such enormous expenses, equal benefit may be obtained, and would already have been reached, had the appropriation of five thousand dollars monthly, accorded to the frontier States, been applied to this object as judiciously as it should have been by the Governors of the frontier; but this amount, expended without any special or settled plan, makes the sacrifices of the nation useless, and retards the progress of the country, whilst dangers threaten from the incursions of the Indians on one hand, and international complications on the other, arising from the abandonment of our line, and giving rise to the complaints made by our neighbors.

The ten thousand dollars apportioned to Coahuila and Nuevo Leon, employed as intended, which, up to the present has not been done on account of the shortsightedness of those charged with the distribution of the funds, would have settled a town one year, and another the next year, and by the payment of guards to give security and protection during the first few years of their establishment, astonishing results might have been attained, particularly if the emigrants had been drafted from such places where numbers of families live in abject poverty and misery. It was by this means that all these regions of country were peopled, after their discovery. Besides, it is mere illusion to believe that other emigrants will settle there, nor is it patriotic to people the frontier with other than Mexicans in heart and nationality.

The ideas here expressed, it is not necessary to say, are the result of careful observations on the part of the Commission, and of a minute and detailed examination of the present and former situations. For this reason they are recommended to you, and we pray you to present them to the President for his consideration, and for the adoption of those which, in his opinion, will produce any public benefit. You will undoubtedly succeed with your exquisite tact and that experience and knowledge of men and things which your years of labor in the administration of affairs of the republic have gained for you.

Independence and liberty.

MEXICO, March 10, 1874,

IGNACIO GALINDO.

FRANCISCO VALDEZ GOMEZ,
Secretary.

To the Minister of War.

(Copy.)

March 10, 1874.

FRANCISCO VALDEZ GOMEZ,
Secretary.

COMMISSION OF INVESTIGATION

ON THE

NORTHERN FRONTIER.

AMONGST the many inconveniences which thwart the progress of the frontier, the principal one is the sparsity of the population; in that region there are large tracts of waste lands which no one cares to appropriate, on account of the immense expenditures necessary to acquire property, and the delay attendant on the information which must be given to the Governor of the State in which the land lies, the securing of the approbation of the minister, apart from cost of surveying, which very often no one dares to make on account of the perils incurred in the wilderness from the attacks of Indians. All these are barriers to the settlement of the country.

If this state of things continue, the frontier will never be peopled, and the wealth of the land will remain unproductive. It is easy to infer what class of people are likely to settle this region; by changing the tariff, making the acquisition of the lands more easy by apportioning the lots from surveys previously made, and numbering them in order to make the transfer easy, and by thus disposing of all the Government waste lands, the country will soon be fully populated.

In order to realize these ideas, the Commission took the first step by addressing a surveyor in Monterey, who has agreed to make the measurements on the basis of the accompanying note. As you will observe, his propositions do not appear exaggerated, and contain all the necessary qualifications for giving impetus to the development of the country without great expense to the republic. He suggests an easy method for populating a desert, the existence of which is not unfrequently a cause for charges against Mexico.

Although this same project has been proposed through the

Minister of Foreign Relations, under general principles, it specially pertains to the office under your charge, and it has therefore been considered advisable to make these explanations, accompanied by a draft of the measures proposed, in order that you may bring it to the notice of the President, and with his advice, determine the course to be pursued.

Independence and liberty.

Monterey, February 1, 1874.

IGNACIO GALINDO.

Francisco Valdez Gomez,
Secretary.

To the Minister of *Fomento.*
(Copy.)

Mexico, March 10, 1874.

Francisco Valdez Gomez,
Secretary.

———

In reply to yours of the 6th instant, asking me for the conditions under which I would be willing to make a plan of the lands in the northern part of the States of Nuevo Leon and Coahuila, and to give some of the details in relation to the proposed measurement, in order that the proposal may be made to the national government, I address to you the following :

1st. The plan or map of these lands, which are almost unknown, covers an area extending from about the 27° to the 30° of north latitude, and from 0° to 3° of longitude west of the meridian of Mexico, including besides points which, although outside of these limits, deserve, in my opinion, to be better known to the national government.

2d. The plan will contain, besides the mountains, rivers, and general features of the country, a minute description of the geographical situation of that region, its elevation above the sea, the settlements now in existence, as well as those places sparsely or totally uninhabited which deserve particular attention on account of their fertility, pasturage, and mines, which make them especially adapted to the maintenance of a population more or less numerous.

3d. The above named map will be accompanied by special plans of the towns and places mentioned in the second proposition, showing the topography of the place.

4th. As a road is contemplated from Piedras Negras to Chihuahua, its track will be laid down on the map, and a note made of such places on its route as are best adapted for settlements, marking the water, and their distance from it, and giving the quantity of water found in such places as are considered to have the best facilities of every kind, keeping in mind that the road is a public highway.

5th. The general and special plans will be accompanied by a diary of the expedition, which will contain a detailed description of everything that will lead to a thorough knowledge of the face of the country, and of its properties and qualifications, as well as all the proceedings employed in making the survey, in order that confidence may be felt in the reliability of the work. A copy of these documents will be presented to the government and another to the society of "Geografía y Estadística."

6th. That I shall be paid the sum of $300 monthly, whilst in the performance of this work, which will probably not exceed two years, and besides this salary I shall receive $1,000, to be paid with $600 advance salary, two months before commencing the work, in case these conditions are accepted, in order to buy the instruments and make the preparations necessary.

7th. That the employment of six men during the whole time the work lasts, will be at the expense of the government.

8th. As the district to be surveyed is frequently overrun by hordes of savages who cross from the left bank of the Rio Bravo, an escort of forty men is indispensable, in order to repulse or attack tribes who molest or interrupt the work, and that the escort be paid by the government and placed under my control.

9th. If it is decided to undertake the work spoken of, the government will please forward the orders which I am to follow immediately, and advise me as to whom I am to address myself during the time I am engaged in the work.

These are my propositions; if you consider them acceptable, they may be presented to the national government for its determination. I do not think that any others more satisfactory or economical could be made.

In regard to the loyal and conscientious fulfillment of these proposals on my part, I leave you to be the judge; you ought to know me well enough.

I will add, that as both you and I know somewhat of the signs and situation of the mineralogical districts from persons who have gone over many of these points, if the government should decide to have me accompanied by a scientific mineralogist, I believe that interesting results may be obtained. I would suggest, therefore, that when you propose the surveying expedition, you also urge that it be accompanied by a mineralogist.

MONTEREY, December 10th, 1873.

(Signed),   FRANCISCO L. MIER.

SR. LIC. D. IGNACIO GALINDO.

(Copy).

MEXICO, March 10th, 1874.

FRANCISCO VALDEZ GOMEZ,

Secretary.

INVESTIGATING COMMISSION

OF THE

NORTHERN FRONTIER.

CIT. MINISTER:

Animated by the sentiments heretofore expressed in this report, and prompted by the same spirit with which they had organized the work in Matamoros, confided to the Commission by decree of 2d October, 1872, they left that city on the first of last June in order to visit the towns on the banks of the Rio Grande, from Ciudad Guerrero to Resurreccion, and also those of Nuevo Leon and Coahuila, for the purpose of hearing the complaints of the inhabitants and of studying the diverse questions of the frontier in its relations with the United States.

With the consciousness of never having omitted a single opportunity of arriving at the truth, which they have invariably sought with the spirit of rectitude and impartiality which their responsible position demanded of them, the Commission are enabled to present at this time the result of their labors together with the second part of their report, which, on account of its voluminousness, was not ready for presentation at the appointed time. It includes a complete opinion relative to the depredations committed by Indians living in Mexico and by those living in the United States, and of the damages sustained by both countries.

Following the same system initiated in Matamoros, the Commission continued the examination of the question of horse and cattle stealing along the line of the Rio Grande in the three States to Piedras Negras, which is as far as is settled by Mexicans and Americans, and on this subject which they have already discussed and presented under all its phases, the Commission will only add a few new observations as to other points presented by the unsettled regions, and give another cause for the origin of this evil, from which Mexico has suffered since her towns and settlements became in such close contact with those of the neighboring republic.

The knowledge which the majority of the Commission has of the principal towns on the frontier, as well as of many of the less important localities, has greatly aided it in the accomplishment of its labors, and enabled it to reach the object desired—the truth. The well established integrity of the greater number of witnesses and the plan followed in the investigation leaves no doubt of the desired result, as is proved by the unanimity of the witnesses examined and the evidence obtained from the archives, setting forth clearly the number of incursions which occurred during twenty-five years, the tribes by whom they were committed and the amount of damages done.

The Commission did not limit itself to these points. It traced the Indians to their camping grounds, to which it proceeded through the guidance of those who had pursued the savages thither and by directions from ransomed prisoners, by those taken in war or rescued by the United States troops on their own territory. It was determined that all of these witnesses should testify as to what they had actually seen, and thus obtain facts and details which could not easily be obtained elsewhere. The importance of this testimony was highly estimated by the confirmation it received from the opinions of the military occupied in making war on the Indians, but who were unable in later pursuits to follow the savages to their camping grounds as had hitherto been done.

After having collected all the evidence possible from old captives, whose declarations went as far back as the colonial government, as well as from those who have been made captive in later years, it became necessary, in order to substantiate the proofs and explain the origin of the evil, to inquire by every possible means into the policy which has been pursued towards the different tribes of Indians who have been hostile to Mexico since 1848, and who live in United States territory. Besides,

16

it was necessary to discover, even though in a general way, the hostile attitude of those tribes towards the United States, and to this end the Commission directed its energies, collecting all the data furnished by Texan newspapers of late dates, and using efforts to procure all information on the subject published in former years.

The application of these published notices was of the utmost importance, and to secure them the Commission employed every means at its command, for it well understood that they alone were all-sufficient to destroy the value of the charges brought against Mexico by persons who, blinded through prejudice, would never see but one phase of the question.

This labor showed the fallacy of the judgment of the American Commission, who attributed, in its report of the 1st December of the past year, the depredations committed on the Rio Grande to the Kickapoos, Lipans, Seminoles, Carrizos and other Indians, who, having haunts in Mexico, Chihuahua and Coahuila, came on the American frontier to molest the settlements.

In addition to this general investigation, special care has been given to obtain all the information possible relative to the above named tribes, and the result of this investigation has shown the incorrectness of the report. With the exception of the Kickapoos, none of the tribes mentioned live in Mexico; many of them only existing in name, the tribe having entirely died out.

A long list of invasions and injuries committed on the banks of the Rio Grande in Mexican territory by American citizens was also discovered; and although the spirit which prompted or characterized these abuses was extensively discussed in the first part of this report, it must again be touched upon in order to present the question under all its phases, one of these especially being a determined tendency to disturb and annoy, under one pretext or another, the tranquility of the frontier towns of Mexico.

Another distinct cause has presented itself to the Commission at every step, showing a great difficulty to exist in all these towns through fugitive servants. On account of the close connection which this evil maintains with natural difficulties, which it has contributed to increase, to the injury of Mexican settlements and Texan proprietors, as well as the participation by these fugitives in horse and cattle robberies, it was thought indispensable to collect all data which would give a clearer idea of the situation than could possibly be arrived at without such information, and which would likewise demonstrate the origin of serious social evils, which should be as promptly dealt with as the gravity of the case seems to demand, whether the question to be considered be the loss of men to the republic, or the complications which their naturally bad conduct causes on either frontier.

In the development of a mercantile spirit, noticeable in the populace with which Texas is being filled, there have been found points worthy of study, and it may also be considered that the results of this enterprise have given rise to many of the existing complications.

In treating these questions, more or less closely connected, care will be taken to point out in each the cause of the general evil resulting to the frontier of both countries. To do this, all data possible have been accumulated, the archives of more than one hundred and fifty leagues of the line of the Rio Grande having contributed largely to the fund of information. The dates of these proofs and their conformity with other evidence carry with them such evidence of proof, that they may be implicitly trusted and the deductions made from them relied upon.

Fully appreciating testimonial evidence, the Commission determined not to omit securing it, although, for the investigation of Indian depredations, it was not absolutely indispensable, on account of the old custom of the authorities of the States inserting, in the official papers, the incursions and depredations of Indians, furnishing thereby a rich fund of information, from which has been made a general estimate of the damages done by the savages. This has also been used as corroborative testimony, in order to test the veracity of witnesses, their correctness, their judgment, and the knowledge which they possessed about the matter upon which they testified. In the narration of this long series of events, many of which were cruel and bloody, the witnesses were often moved to tears, although the occurrences had taken place many years before. Nor could anything else be expected from men who had passed the greater part of their lives in combats with Indians, and number their fights by the number of their wounds. Memory cannot play them false in that which concerns the Indians,—when the witness, through the murder of a father, a son, or a brother, has good cause to pursue the savages and to avail himself of every opportunity to avenge the injuries done him. Not unfrequently this leads to a still greater loss of life, and punishment and vengeance have to be left to the charge of strangers. Such is the history of the frontier towns.

From sources as direct and positive, the Commission has collected the material from which the judgment to be expressed in its report was formed ; nor will the Commission hesitate to affirm that all the circumstances set forth are true, because it has examined the evidence with diligent research, and because it is corroborated by the history of these towns, by the experience and remembrances of men, by the old landmarks and monuments, and by the stories of young men just escaped from captivity.

HISTORICAL SKETCH OF INDIAN WARS ON THE FRONTIER BEFORE 1848.

When the limits of Mexico reached to the rivers Sabine and Arkansas, the eastern and northern boundaries of Texas, this immense territory was inhabited in a very few settlements, which were constantly molested by several tribes of Indians. The northern line of outposts was rapidly settled about the close of the last century, in consequence of the establishment of military colonies by the Spanish Government. Don Juan de Ugalde, the first commander-in-chief of these colonies in Tamaulipas, Nuevo Leon and Coahuila (then including Texas), still lives in the memory of this region, on account of his exploits against the Indians in the campaign of 1796 ; a town and a county in Texas bear his name, the latter having been the theater of some of his battles.

Eight companies, full and well equipped, were distributed along this line—four in Coahuila, three in Tamaulipas and one in Nuevo Leon—and were found sufficient to repress the incursions of the Indians, who, for a long series of years, never penetrated to the second tier of settlements towards the south. During the war of Independence the Indians were kept at bay, although a part of the frontier troops was drawn off to the center of Mexico, to operate against the insurgents.

After the Independence the new government maintained the colonial companies, and in 1826 introduced in them several reforms found necessary by experience. Peace reigned in all this region, which became highly prosperous, increasing rapidly in cattle raising, the chief pursuit of the settlers on the right bank of the Rio Grande.

The district between the Nueces and the Rio Grande, now a part of Texas, but then owned by the inhabitants of Reynosa, Camargo, Mier, Guerrero and Laredo, was very soon filled with flocks and herds, and was fully protected by the companies stationed at Bahia, Alamo and Espiritu Santo. Through lack of population, no settlements were made farther north, and the security thus obtained was enjoyed by the foreign colonists who accompanied Austin and located near San Antonio de Béjar.

When, a few years later, the Texans revolted against the government, a new era began, which is still well remembered ; for the incursions of the Comanches, Lipans, Mescaleros, Caiguas, and other allied tribes date from 1836. The frontier companies were no longer able to repel the invaders, who penetrated in numerous hordes into the villages, spreading death and desolation. It was said then, and it has been again alleged recently before this Commission, that this aggression of the savages was stimulated by the Texans, who sought thereby an auxiliary in their movement for independence. The Comanches and other allied tribes had previously lived near the Colorado and on the prairies ; they now established themselves on the left bank of the Rio Grande. At this time the districts of Monclova, Villaldama and Matamoros were first invaded, and the coincidence of these depredations with the Texan war, along with the peace existing between those tribes and the insurgents, was, in default of more positive proof, a sufficient foundation for believing these hostilities to be encouraged by the Texans.

Further invasions were soon made in the districts of Salinas, Monterey, Saltillo, Párras, Viesca, Lináres, Matehuala, Catorce, and the frontier of Zacatecas. As was natural, the remnants of the frontier garrisons, of those companies who, for so many years, had formed a wall against the Indians, resumed their task, though now superior to their ability ; but by the aid of the citizen militia, then first called out, they drove back the invaders and pursued them into the interior of Texas. The campaigns then made at San Sába and Rio Puerco proved that the rebellion had not extended to the west of Texas, and that the insurgents, protected by deserts, forests and an unhealthy climate, were reduced to their own proper limits. ·

The hordes which invaded Mexico were now settled upon the rivers Brazos and Colorado, and scattered throughout the immense plains lying between Texas, New Mexico and the frontier of the United States. It was there, according to the expression of an American traveler who traded in 1834 in Santa Fé and Chihuahua, that the savage tribes of the great western prairies lived. The Comanches, the wandering Arabs of this hemisphere, were the largest known tribe, considering themselves as the only lords of those plains, where they hunted the elk in summer, spending the winter upon the banks of the tributaries of the Brazos and Colorado rivers in Texas.

From these regions they moved southward to undertake their career of hostilities along the present Mexican frontier from Chihuahua to the Gulf of Mexico, robbing cattle and mules, killing men and taking captives women and children.

These Indians of the prairies and of Texas amounted to 47,620 in 1842, according to a census taken by the American Commissioners for Indian Affairs. The Comanches appear in this census as owners of the prairies, and with the Kiowas,

Apaches, Arapahoes and Cheyennes, amounted to 16,100, or about half the number of the remaining small tribes which were generally subject to them, and with which they sometimes had bloody wars.

The Commission would note here that the Indian agents formed a census of the Comanches and the allied tribes which purported to be complete and accurate. If these Indians lived in Mexico, the census could not have been taken, nor would there have been any occasion for it. The Indian Commissioners undoubtedly formed it when the Comanches and the other tribes came to the settlements to trade, or perhaps when they all lived on the banks of the river Platte, which has always belonged to the United States.

The inclination of these Indians to plunder, and their bad faith in the observance of treaties, which they respect or break arbitrarily without the least scruple, involved them in hostilities with the Texans, and in 1840 they penetrated into the capital, marking their path with bloodshed as far as the bay of Matagorda. In their invasions of Mexico they had proved their strength, of which they now gave the Texans a specimen, but afterwards made peace with them.

For the better understanding of the mode and conditions of this warfare, it must be noted that the United States had gradually driven the Indians of Florida and the other Southern States to the frontier, and placed them between the Arkansas, the Red river, and the False Wachita, then the boundary with Mexico. According to the census of the Commissioner of Indian Affairs, there were in 1843, 81,541 inhabitants in the above territory, Cherokees, Choctaws, Chickasaws, Creeks, Seminoles, Kickapoos, Potawattomies and others. Near these tribes, in the Wachita mountains of Texas, lived the Wacoes, Wachitas, Towakanoes, Caddos or Enyes, scattered along the Red river, neighbors of the Indians on the government reservations. In contact with all these tribes were the Comanches, with their following of small subject or allied tribes, such as the Kiowas, Cheyennes, Arapahoes and others, while the Apaches were then living farther westward, between the Rio Pecos and the Rio Grande, in the Sierra Blanca and Organ

mountains. In the immense region between the Rio Grande
and the Arkansas, these savages were the only inhabitants up
to 1831, when the eastern tribes were removed to the Indian
Territory.

The Santa Fé trade having sprung up just at this time, the
mercantile caravans began to traverse the plains lying between
the outposts of both nations, and were accompanied by escorts
of dragoons from Fort Gibson on the Missouri river. In a
work written in 1844 by Josiah Gregg, which was published
in two volumes, entitled, "The Commerce of the Prairies," interesting details are given concerning the customs of the
Indians, and, what is more important for the purposes of this
Commission, precious data are afforded in explanation of the
causes and origin of the incursions made by the Comanches
and other tribes upon Mexican territory, and at the same time
the motives are explained which rendered such depredations
more frequent from that time forward.

In 1839, Josiah Gregg and other American traders set out
on a fourth or fifth mercantile expedition to Santa Fé and Chihuahua, in order to profit by the closure of the Mexican ports
on account of the war with France. In describing the route,
he says (page 18, vol. II):

"Just at hand there was a beautiful spring, where, in
1835, Col. Mason with a force of United States troops had
a 'big talk' and still bigger 'smoke' with a party of Comanche and Wachita Indians. Upon the same site, Col. Chouteau had also caused to be erected, not long after, a little
stockade fort, where a considerable trade was subsequently
carried on with the Comanches and other tribes of the southwestern prairies. The place had now been abandoned, however, since the preceding winter. * * * We had not been
long at the fort, before we received a visit from a party of
Comanches, who, having heard of our approach came to greet
us a welcome, on the supposition that it was their friend Chouteau returning to the fort with fresh supplies of merchandise.
Great was their grief when we informed them that their favor-
ite trader had died at Fort Gibson the previous winter."

By the above statement, which cannot be doubted when we
bear in mind the time of its appearance and its author, it is

shown that trade with the Comanches and Wachitas was commenced in 1835, on American territory, between the False Wachita and Canadian rivers, near Fort Holmes. The hopes of profit, or the impulse arising from real necessities, engaged the Indians in this trade, which, it must be repeated, was initiated by an officer of the United States army, in the sight of his soldiers, who knew that the articles given in exchange by the Indians were the spoils of their depredations upon a friendly nation.

For the first time the Comanches learned the advantages of this lucrative traffic; for the first time they found sellers of arms and ammunition, and purchasers of their booty; and henceforth they thought only of new invasions and new depredations upon their southern prey, the Mexican settlements then abounding in riches. The general incursion of these savage hordes in 1836, into the flourishing towns in the districts of Villaldama, Monclova and Northern Tamaulipas, had its real origin in the treaties of peace made by Col. Mason, and the mercantile enterprise of Col. Chouteau.

It has been stated by this Commission, upon the faith of undeniable data found in abundance in the archives of the military " Comandancias " of the eastern provinces, the savages had never passed the outer line of posts. If they committed depredations, they all proceeded from their vindictive feeling towards the new settlers, who had gradually driven them northwards to regions not formerly their own. But while the Spanish race was thus repelling these tribes northward, a counter-movement commenced in the northeast, by which the Saxon race, in turn, dislodged their Indian tribes and drove them southward.

A time came when all these tribes were brought together in the same vicinity, in consequence of the counter-movement referred to. The Mexican tribes which had resisted and rejected the benefits of the civilization which the Spaniards had proffered them, and the Northern tribes which, although apparently treated with more policy and justice, were ultimately driven back by a race which disdained to mingle with them, came into contact in 1831, at which time many American tribes were located south of the Missouri and the Arkansas. From this vicinity arose a double peril and a double evil for Mexican settlements, which were menaced on both sides, since the Americans indirectly encouraged robbery by their trade, and placed near the Mexican border other tribes which, though less barbarous and initiated in some of the habits of civilization, were still very dangerous neighbors on account of the natural inclination they all had to pillage and marauding.

It may be seen that not merely the Texan rebellion, but the conduct of the American Government, powerfully stimulated the depredations of the Comanches and their associate tribes. The American officials tolerated, permitted, and, it may be maintained, even fostered and protected these depredations. The Comanches and the Apaches never showed so much energy in evil-doing as was observable from 1836 onward; that is, from the time when American officers had afforded them a market for bartering the spoils of their incursions into Mexico.

In 1840, the irruption of thousands of savages to the vicinity of San Luis Potosi, who also visited the principal towns of Zacatecas, caused enormous damage, desolating numerous *haciendas* and slaying hundreds of victims. This took place precisely when the Mexican Government had on its hands the war in Texas, and when the Comanches were stimulated by the mart opened for their plunder, near the river Arkansas. They had then a motive which had not existed in previous years. Their contact with the whites created necessities they had never known before, and encouraged them to undertakings foreign to the mere spirit of vengeance on account of the seizure of their lands, which was the first cause of their hostilities with the Spaniards, and afterwards with the Mexicans.

The Commission does not here express a simple opinion, but a conviction formed by a careful study of the facts. Notwithstanding the aptness of the Indians for warfare, their knowledge of the country acquired with the greatest ease, and their skill as horsemen, remarkable above all among the Comanches, they had always given way before the arms and dis-

cipline of the Mexican troops, whether led by Spanish officers
before the Independence or by the Mexican officers trained in
their school. The killing of their enemies was their chief object in their early campaigns, and when they had more or less
success at the outposts of our lines, they stopped there, and
returned in triumph, with the scalps of their victims as
trophies.

But as soon as the American trade sprang up, booty became
their chief object, and to obtain it they had to penetrate within the lines, as they began to do, favored by the Texan deserts
and the plains of our frontiers. They invaded an unknown
country, a region they had never traversed, the dangers and
difficulties of which they knew not, and then they began to
collect in large numbers, and organized formal expeditions.
They were the same Indians who had been kept at bay for six
years by Captain Lopez, with 250 men stationed between Las
Moras and San Antonio de Béjar, and repeatedly pursued and
defeated whenever they had attempted an incursion. These
same troops were still there, and in greater numbers, for the
army of operations against Texas was in that vicinity in that
year (1836), but the invasions took place by several distinct
routes.

The reorganization of the defensive companies, which was
decreed in 1826, was carried into effect in 1829, by General
Bustamante. He it was who had stationed the forces above
mentioned, under Captain Santiago Lopez, at Las Moras, San
Sabá and the springs of Leona, which had given six or seven
years of peace to the frontier, during which time all kinds of
cattle had largely multiplied. This organization still existed,
as before mentioned, in the year of the first great Comanche
incursion, but their efforts were fruitless ; the savages kept out
of their reach, or when routed in small parties, fell back upon
the larger masses, and effected all the pillage they could desire.

The great change which was noted in the conduct of the
Indians naturally attracted the attention of military men, and
they could only explain it by the Texan insurrection ; but, as
we have seen, Texas was itself at that time a prey to the
ferocity of these savages.

Much blood had to be shed; thousands of persons have groaned in captivity; immense riches have disappeared, and many years of unheard of calamity have passed, before the real cause was discovered.

The American Government, by driving to the west the Indian nations expelled from several States through greed of their lands, and by locating them on the frontiers of Mexico, gave rise to a new situation, which was imperfectly understood by that government, and a great evil was thereby inflicted upon Mexico, who quickly suffered therefrom. From whatever light this new condition of the Indians in the western plains be examined, their incursions into Mexico, which began at the time of the location of the other tribes on the Arkansas river, were the real and necessary result of that measure. Without it, it is impossible to explain their sudden bravery, or their peculiar comportment in their depredations, utterly different from all that had been previously observed.   •

Before this time, the Indians had made assaults, had spied and surprised the encampments, but they did not approach the towns except at night, and for the purpose of robbing cattle. From this time onward, they formed their camps by day, in open view, besieging the villages, and even carrying off captives. This was done by the Comanches between San Buenaventura and Nadadores, in the district of Monclova, encamping between the two towns, which are less than a league apart; they did the same at Saltillo, approaching that city by the high road, and in like manner at Bustamante in Nuevo Leon, and at Salinas Victoria, before which towns they deliberately encamped, defying the power of the inhabitants and of the government itself, which could only assemble its troops in their rear, after they had all united together to carry off their enormous booty. Then, at last, the soldiers of the military companies attacked them, six leagues from San Fernando, at Pozo, now Zaragoza, routed them completely, recovering all the spoils, and the captives which they had brought from the outskirts of San Luis Potosi.

When General Arista had his headquarters in these towns, the Indians did not hesitate to attack detachments of his army accompanied by the frontier militia, and it was very evident that they were carrying out a regular plan, which perhaps they had not themselves conceived.

In their investigations the Commissioners have collected the facts bearing upon Indian incursions from beginning to end, and the differing phases which this warfare has presented along the entire extent of the frontier. They have foreseen that from this series of facts something would be discovered, which would explain their causes, and that this explanation would be found only by penetrating, as they have done, into the very lodges of the Indians. From such premises, important results have been deduced, and it is believed that the general statements already made will be confirmed in all their fullness by the examination of the period more especially intrusted to the Commission, *i. e.*, the twenty-five years which have elapsed from 1848 to the present time.

The evils suffered during this period are immense, greater even than those which have just been summarily sketched. The Commission, in order to present the picture of the misfortunes of this period, although it has taken the testimony of many witnesses, has employed it merely as a guide to the examination of the archives, in which it has found all that could be asked for. These documents will speak for themselves, and while they show the greatness of the evils, they also prove the strenuous efforts of the authorities to remove them, and their despair at finding themselves impotent to remedy them from causes far beyond their reach. The losses suffered through Indian depredations differing greatly according to their respective localities, and the measures taken for their repression differing in like manner, good order and clearness require that these depredations be treated separately in regard to the States which have come within the scope of the Commission's labors.

INDIAN HOSTILITIES IN TAMAULIPAS FROM 1848.

The great riches which the towns of Tamaulipas had acquired in lands and cattle, between the Rio Nueces and the

Rio Grande, were almost annihilated—first by the Texan war, and afterward by that with the United States.

That portion of the territory of Tamaulipas began anew, after the American war, to be stocked with cattle by the landed proprietors residing on the right or Mexican bank of the Rio Grande. They had barely began to establish their ranchos, when they again experienced the depredations of the Indians.

The town of Reynosa * was one of the first; the judge in charge of one of its ranchos reported that, on the 12th of April, 1849, a cattle station belonging to a citizen of that town had been assaulted by savages from the American side of the river, who had killed two servants, a man and a woman, and had carried captive three men and one woman.

On the 4th of May of the same year, Indians again appeared in the same municipality, robbing cattle, which were carried across the river. Similar invasions were renewed on the 11th of June and the 27th of August of that year, and it appears by the official reports that the Comanches encamped on the Texan bank, cut off communication with Brownsville, to whose inhabitants the Mexican authorities sent timely notice of the presence of Indians in their vicinity. The alcalde of Reynosa addressed the American consul at Matamoros for this purpose.

Hostilities were suspended until 1856, when the mayor of Matamoros, being informed of the presence of Indians near Reynosa, sent a detachment of soldiers in their pursuit. The amount of damage done in this incursion, which was the last, does not appear, but it would seem to have been considerable from the promptitude with which troops and ammunition were sent, and the dispatch of a militia force in aid of the regular troops.

The action of the Mexican authorities in repelling the invasions which had attacked Reynosa from Texan territory was prompt and efficacious, not only in protecting their own citizens, but also those of Texas, to whose authorities notice was

---

* In the Spanish text, reference is made in each paragraph to the " expediente," or collection of documents where the proofs of the facts are found; these references are suppressed in the English version, as unnecessary for the American reader.— *Note of the translator.*

sent, enabling them to guard against a surprise. The solicitude of the government went so far as to urge the sufferers to furnish evidence of their losses, so as to obtain indemnification, but it does not appear that any one took that step. Undoubtedly the sufferers were away from home, and the Commission takes note of their conduct as an evidence of their spirit of honesty.

The city of Camargo, situated farther north, and with greater possessions on both banks of the Rio Grande, suffered greater damage than Reynosa, on account of the greater number of invasions, and the difficulties they encountered at the hands of the American authorities, when they solicited the return of cattle recaptured from the Indians on American soil. In this town, as in Reynosa, the investigation has been limited to an examination of its archives. They afford a good idea of the amount of suffering from Indians, who always came from Texan territory, and have furnished interesting data for the history of the terms of intercourse kept up between the two frontiers, and the manner in which the authorities on both sides fulfilled the duties of their posts.

Camargo having been invaded on the 4th of April and 5th of May, 1849, the Indians recrossed the river to Texas, where they were pursued by Texan soldiers or citizens, and their booty recaptured. The Mexican sufferers having been unsuccessful in reclaiming their property, they made a statement of the facts to the *Ayuntamiento* (Common Council) of Camargo, and that body, in an extra session, voted to address the State government, requesting it to make known the case to the President of the republic, and in this connection asked " that the interpretation of the last clause of the 2d paragraph in Article XI of the Treaty of Peace with the United States, signed on the 2d of February of last year—which guarantees the property robbed by Indians in Mexican territory—may be made known ; and whether this guaranty does not extend to property robbed from Mexicans within the limits of the territory which, by that treaty, was ceded to the United States, which property, although fully guaranteed, is in danger of abandonment, from lack of security ; and whether there is any enactment in the United States which declares the spoils carried off by hostile Indians from Mexican citizens to be a lawful prize when recaptured from them, *since respect for law alone can, in such case, prevent disturbances from occurring between the owners and the recapturers of such property.*"

Soon after these complaints, the authorities of Reynosa requested those of Camargo to inform the military commander in Starr county of these robberies of cattle, and to urge him to take measures for the fulfilment of Article XI of the Treaty of Guadalupe Hidalgo.

The simple statement of a complaint, made in the above extract, is the best commentary that can be made upon the fact of Indian depredations, since it clearly shows a complete neglect of treaty obligation, and a great indifference on the part of the American authorities, as was stated by the First Court of Camargo, on the 11th of March, 1851, in a communication addressed to General Avalos : "The Indians had made an attack upon 'Las Cuevas' from the opposite shore, and had not been pursued, although they had killed a settler, because they were on the territory of the neighboring nation, where they had not been pursued."

With this conduct of the American authorities, in keeping Mexican property recaptured from Indians, or failing to attack them when on American soil, the Mexican towns afforded a striking contrast, distinguishing themselves, although still suffering extreme misery as the result of the recent war, by their zeal in punishing the Indians, for which purpose the armed citizens and the permanent troops marched in every direction.

From Matamoros, where the Avalos brigade was stationed, there were thrown out, by orders of its commander, detachments which hastened to Reynosa, Camargo, Mier, Guerrero and Nuevo Laredo, to aid in all movements against the barbarians. The State Government, with commendable care, obtained arms, ammunition and provisions for the same object, and stimulated the towns to action, and to bear their losses with patience, until a radical remedy could be applied, which remedy, as is seen from all its communications with the local authorities, was to be found in the exact fulfillment of the treaty of Guadalupe.

The inhabitants of the Mexican bank of the river being thus ever on the alert, they did not wait to be attacked before taking every measure of precaution. At the least information of an Indian invasion on the Texas side, orders were sent to the judges in charge of the ranchos, to watch the fords and prevent the passage of the Indians. Speedy communications were sent from town to town with news of every incursion, and since it could not be prevented, as coming from foreign territory, its effects were mitigated by timely warning to those who were immediately endangered.

The superior authority of the Northern District was constantly attentive to the invasions in Camargo and other towns of the line, and in reporting to the State Government those of February 28th and March 1st, 1851, stated that it did so in order that they might be communicated to the National Government, so as to demand of the American Government the fulfillment of the treaty of Guadalupe. Private individuals and authorities clamored daily against that government, for failure to observe the treaty, and for notorious infractions of it, since the Indians were neither forced to return their spoil, nor were prevented from crossing the river to commit their usual depredations.

The leading citizens of our towns on the Rio Grande being proprietors of ranchos in Texas, the prevailing insecurity in that State frequently endangered not only their property, but their lives, and the authorities of the Mexican shore were accustomed to take action in their behalf. A case which occurred to Don Nieves Villareal will illustrate this. It was stated to the First Judge at Camargo, by the justice of the rancho of Fresnos, in the following terms : " At this moment, 1 P. M., Antonio Cano, servant of Don Nieves Villareal, has just appeared on the opposite bank, wounded by an arrow by the savages, this morning, at ' Clavellinas,' a point in Texas a league from the river, and says that he does not know where his master is; and as, in my opinion, the said Villareal may have fallen a victim, I not only inform you, but have taken every step in my power to find and assist him, placing armed men all along the line to protect families crossing the river from the other side."

The above communication being dated August 21st, 1853, it is apparent that the condition of the frontier had not improved in five years, and that the Mexicans residing in American territory found their best protection from the Mexican side. The facts are that the depredations were common to both banks, and in the region in question were more frequent on the Texas side. The natural explanation of this is, that the property of the landowners, though residing on both sides of the river, was chiefly in Texas, and their losses were therefore unrecorded. It is beyond doubt that at this time there were no American stock raisers in this region, they being the only ones who calculate and exaggerate such losses, and the only ones who get any attention.

There was a lull of three years for Camargo, and no further incursion is recorded until 1856, when two men were killed and a boy captured. He was retaken by the energetic action of the forces of Camargo, in conjunction with those of Mier and Aldamas, a town in Nuevo Leon.

The forces of the invaded towns now appear for the first time in joint action, pursuing the retreating Indians as well as the Rio Grande barrier permitted ; and when the savages divided into smaller parties they did the same, even lying in ambush, at times, at strategical points.

In relating above, very briefly, the incursions made in Camargo and Reynosa since 1848, the Commission has not paused to calculate the amount of damages, because it is not fully specified in the documents they have consulted, and which are collected in the proper *expediente*. It will be understood, however, that, apart from the loss of life, the value of which cannot be properly estimated, and apart from the property stolen or destroyed in each incursion, one of the gravest damages has been the suspension of every kind of industry, and the lack of confidence in beginning afresh, arising from the insecurity of the fruits of labors, which if once carried across the river by the savages, would never be recovered, even if recap-

tured from the enemy. Of this fact one sad experience has
been related. Fortunately it was not repeated on account of
the infrequent pursuit of the savages by the Americans, otherwise the anticipated conflict might have occurred between
owners and recapturers of Indian booty. It is a poor satisfaction which one can get from the fact of no such conflict having
ever taken place!

Before passing to the invasions of other towns in Tamaulipas, the Commission feels bound to say in just praise of their
inhabitants, that in view of the evils with which they were
threatened by savages, they always adopted very efficacious
preventive measures, keeping watch for their first appearance,
which they rapidly made known to the herdsmen, enabling
them generally to call in the scattering men and animals, and
that they made great sacrifices for the recovery of stolen property. Neither authorities nor citizens ever bethought themselves of the obligations contracted by the American government, concerning indemnification for or return of stolen property, and whenever any depredations were made it was through
absolute impossibility of preventing it. In consideration of the
power and wealth of the United States, and the justice with
which the American government has almost always tried to
proceed, it will be seen that the conduct of these Mexican
towns is highly commendable.

It should be noted in passing, that during the five years
passed in review, the Indian invasions made in Texas were still
more numerous than in Mexico, and no voice was ever raised
to attribute them to the Seminoles, who then resided in Mexico
with a few Kickapoos, although they traversed all this region,
according to their customs, in quest of game. The cause of
this will be hereafter explained.

As the Commission advances farther north in its examination of the depredations committed by the savages, it will have
to linger longer at each town, to relate evils steadily increasing
in magnitude. This will be manifest at Mier, in which city it
was necessary, as before, to be content with the information
found in the archives. These were not found complete, owing
to local disturbances, but the existing part gives a perfect idea

of the magnitude of the Indian depredations upon the property
on both sides the river, held by those numerous citizens who,
as before remarked, are land owners in both countries.

In this town and the preceding ones, the Commission formed
registers of losses upon affidavits of the sufferers, with the only
object of obtaining a statement of damages which it might
verify by further examination. It endeavored thus to combine
the interests of private individuals, whose complaints could
only be entertained in this way, with the duties of the Commission, urgently summoned to other places, and unable to
devote the necessary time for the study of private losses in
the records.

For sixteen years the city of Mier was constantly struggling
with the calamity of the Indian war. It was four times invaded in 1848, between June and December, although it had
organized a half company of National Guards for the repulse
of the Indians, who in that year killed five persons, carried six
captive, and took all the horses they could find. In the
reports of these losses made to the Mayor of Matamoros, complaint is made that all efforts of citizens and soldiers were
futile, "because the Indians, as usual, repassed the Rio
Grande." The municipality wrote to the member of Congress
for the district, and in summing up the evils then suffered,
said :

"The chief is the constant invasion by savages, who yesterday had the audacity to come within a mile to the south of
this city."

During the above mentioned period the city of Mier was
twenty times invaded. Its citizens were moreover frequently
slaughtered at the cattle stations by assaults from the other side
of the river, where the Indians organized, obtained arms and
ammunition, and passed over to employ them against Mexicans.

The documents examined by the Commission leave no doubt
that, *in all these cases*, the Indians came from Texas. It is
seven times mentioned that their coming was preceded by their
presence on the other side, which was known beforehand, because the inhabitants of Mier, then as now, had many ranchos

in Texas. Several times the Comanches were seen crossing the Rio Grande right in front of the town. Many other times they were seen opposite, and it does not appear that they were ever pursued, or in any way obliged to return their booty to citizens of Mexico. On the contrary, the latter suffered daily outrages which must have been very trying, when they resolved to make a statement to the minister of war, to whom, on the 29th of July, 1852, they wrote as follows:

" It is of public notoriety from daily recurring instances, which have been proven before American authorities, that in the towns on the Texan side of the Rio Grande there are daily brought our horses, mules, cattle and utensils of agriculture, and notwithstanding the proved fact of their having been stolen by Indians, or by well known thieves of both countries, whom we can point out individually ; notwithstanding the aid of the American authorities has been implored for the recovery of our property, they have closed the door to our complaints, in open violation of Article XI, of the treaty of Guadalupe Hidalgo."

The horrible and hopeless condition of affairs depicted by the citizens of Mier, in the preceding paragraph, had been approaching for years, and the State Government had so understood, when on the 23d of March, 1850, it wrote to the *Ayunta-miento* of that city, as follows : " The northern towns, which have always been harassed by Indians, are now in an unusually difficult position on account of the neighborhood of the United States, which country permits the Indians to buy arms and ammunition at low prices to enable them to wage war against peaceful citizens of Mexico."

This assertion was based, by the State Government, on data which this Commission has not seen, but which probably are found in the archives of Ciudad Victoria. It has been confirmed by a dispatch from the Judge of Guerrero to the court at Mier, dated January 23d, 1853, stating the appearance of a party of Indians from San Ignacio, Texas, all armed with carbines, undoubtedly bought in the United States where they resided, and where, only, they *could* have been obtained.

The large number of lives lost during these years, notwithstanding all the precautions taken, and the numerous captives carried to American territory, afford an idea of the cruelty of this warfare. The reports made by the officers sent to pursue the savages, generally state that their efforts had been frustrated by the enemy having recrossed the Rio Grande, and these reports well depict the situation as regards an enemy which appears to have understood the situation, and which certainly profited by it.

In view of the data collected and arranged, the Commission could not omit to mention a circumstance which has had much influence in increasing the loss of life and property in the Mexican settlements on the Rio Bravo. The Indians were not punished, and could not be, except when they penetrated far enough inland to be overtaken before reaching their strongholds. It is thus explained that, although troops were kept in readiness to march at the first news of an incursion, they were able only three times to punish the Indians. These engagements took place near Aldamas and Cerralvo, towns of Nuevo Leon, fifteen or twenty leagues from the river.

As to the conduct of the national and State governments in aid of the sufferers, it should be mentioned that a company of troops was stationed at Mier in 1848, which was soon reinforced by the organization of four more companies of National Guards, which, in connection with the permanent troops, made expeditions against the savages, going in quest of them as far as their places of defense or of assembly on their incursions.

Arms, money, exemptions from imposts, were lavished for the alleviation of sufferers, and as a last resort the lower authorities petitioned for the strict fulfillment of the treaty of Guadalupe, attributing, with truth, their ruin to the infraction of that instrument.

In their solicitude to put an end to intolerable sufferings, the towns associated together by means of their authorities, and appointed special commissioners for their defense, which from 1850, after a careful study of the evil, was systematized with good results. This measure originated in the interior States and towns, and is here mentioned only to show the extent of the evil and the unity of its origin.

In the city of Guerrero, twelve leagues north of Mier, the Commission was astonished at the magnitude of the losses sustained by that place from the outset. Here it was deemed necessary to go beyond the examination of the public archives, and add to their extracts therefrom such information as could be obtained from respectable witnesses, who have suffered great damages, and have passed much of their lives in warfare against the Indians, as officers of the militia companies which have always been organized for that purpose.

The Commission also found here a multitude of townspeople who had recently returned from captivity among the Indians, and resolved to obtain their testimony as to the tribes and places of residence of their captors, and all that they had seen among them, giving especial attention to the means by which they recovered their liberty. With double reason, it was thought fitting to obtain the testimony of many citizens of Guerrero who have taken an active part in the pursuit of the Indians, not only at home, but in Texas itself, in the recent invasions which were made in that State.

Guerrero has experienced more than sixty invasions in a brief term of years, and in the long list of deaths, there was not a single year in which victims of Indians were not registered, some of them killed at "La Costa," in Texas. Seventy-eight persons were killed by Indians between 1848 and 1865, more than half of whom were heads of families. In 1848, 1850, and 1853, it is stated of certain victims that they were killed at "La Costa," in Texas, thus confirming the information sent to the authorities of Reynosa, and by them communicated to the American consul.

The only years since 1848 in which regular incursions were not made were 1860 and 1861, and the registers show murders by Indians almost every month. This, indeed, is readily inferred from the fact that one of the first measures of the government of Tamaulipas, on its reorganization after the war, was to equip a half company of National Guards, which was constantly employed in pursuit of the savages. As these were not enough, the citizens of Guerrero voluntarily undertook a campaign with 110 men, in addition to contingents furnished by other towns on their invitation. A march of sixty leagues to the supposed hiding places of the Indians had no other result than to prove that the enemy was not there, but in Texas, whence it had first come.

An evident proof of this latter fact is found in the persons killed at "La Costa," as above mentioned, in the notice sent by the authorities of Nuevo Laredo to the other towns along the Rio Grande, of the appearance of the Indians at San Ignacio, Texas, armed with carbines, and in their constantly passing the river at the point called "Pan," when coming from the north of Texas. And what removed all doubt as to the sources of these incursions, was the notices sent by officers of the American army to the authorities of Guerrero, informing them that the Indians were crossing the river. On the 21st of June, 1853, General Cruz, in command at Matamoros, was informed by his subordinate at Guerrero, as follows : " On the 18th instant I received from the captain on the *left bank* of the river, information that he had that day overtaken the party of Indians marauding near the rancho Garceño, and that said Indians were crossing the river to the right bank at Golondrinas."

The Commission observes with regret that in five years transpiring from the treaty of peace and the assumption by the American government of the obligation to restrain Indian invasions, the authorities in Texas had not even opened communications with their Mexican neighbors, notwithstanding constant Indian incursions in both countries, and the notice quoted above is the first of its kind.

The losses, however, had been so severe in the preceding years, that the president of the city council, writing to the mayor on the 23d of November, 1850, says : " Since you left this city, there have not passed two days without inroads, killing shepherds and cowherds. * * * Within six days there have been three killed and two dangerously wounded, in addition to the horses and mules carried off by the wretches."

On the 8th of July, 1851, the Garza family was attacked and exterminated by a group of Indians on the road to their rancho ; and on the 31st of the same month the council informed the government that "from January to the end of July the Indians had killed more than twenty townspeople. In July alone they have killed eight, wounded nine, and carried off a boy, not counting seven men wounded and one killed the same day, belonging to the party of Don Juan Manuel Zapata, who was also killed, the Indians losing three killed and two thrown into the river, by crossing which the remainder escaped to the Texan shore."

On the 27th of January, 1854, the rancho "Moros" and others on the banks of the Salado were attacked, a herdsman severely wounded, and all the horses in that region carried off. "At the same time," adds the president, of the council in a dispatch to the Governor of the State, "a large party of Indians crossed the river from the left bank, killed Crisanto Vela, and wounded a wagoner on the road leading to Rome in Texas; on the 25th they returned carrying off many horses."

The same writer, referring to the preceding account, which had also been sent to the prefect of Matamoros, said to that officer on the 4th of February :

"Yesterday the citizen Juan Gonzalez and his son Pablo, who was made captive on the 27th, presented themselves; and the latter says, that he was a witness of the events stated in the communication of the 27th of January; that the Indians concerned were nine in number; that there are twenty-three Indians and two squaws now collected at a place which is probably that called 'La Oracion' that they speak our language very well; that they told him that they are Comanches; that they are dressed like white people with blouses, jackets and pants, with good hats; that they said they were great friends of the Americans; that they had three rifles, a gun and a revolver, and had somewhere near a hundred horses and mules."

These calamities could not be described in more simple and expressive terms. They depict the situation in such lively colors, that when we reflect that it has been the same for almost twenty years, we cannot fully appreciate the sufferings of those inhabitants, except by seeing them, and still more so, when we learn what they had previously suffered from 1836 onward.

The witnesses who have appeared before the Commission,

elderly men, of the best standing in Guerrero, have narrated the hostilities previous to 1848. They say that the Comanches never molested that place until 1836, when they came along the left bank of the Rio Grande, robbing cattle, killing shepherds, and committing many other depredations, until they were routed by Don Antonio Zapata, with the armed citizens of Guerrero, on the spot now occupied by Davis, or Rio Grande City, recapturing many prisoners, recovering the stolen horses, and taking those the Indians rode, so that they escaped only on foot. They state also, that at the rancho called " Mogotes," between Agualeguas and Mier, the Indians, to the number of 500, had taken possession of the houses and corrales, and Zapata dislodged them with great loss; they add that in the same year another numerous party encamped in front of the city, at a time when Zapata with most of the citizens was forty leagues away, engaged in a revolution, and that on learning the fact they hastily returned, and routed the Indians at " Huizachal," near the city, retaking fifty captives who had been carried off from the suburbs. Meanwhile, one of the leading citizens organized a force of eighty men, with whom he went in pursuit of the fugitive Indians, routing them a second time at " La Oracion," and recapturing the remaining prisoners, with one exception. After the death of Zapata, his cousin, Don Juan Manuel Zapata, continued to be the leader of the townsmen on such occasions, until in 1851, he was killed in an engagement. The Indians again attacked the rancho of " Moros," which they burned, and more than fifty persons perished in the flames. They afterwards attacked " China," in the State of Nuevo Leon, killed more than sixty persons at Meco, and were routed on the plain of Ramirez, with the loss of sixty warriors, by the troops of Camargo and Guerrero. The witnesses unanimously state that, previous to 1848, the attacks were made by large parties, which were generally severely punished, and the reason given is quite convincing, namely, that their movements were impeded by the large amount of their booty, so that they were easily overtaken. After the above date, the Indians acted upon a different system, coming in small parties,

which were again subdivided, meeting at and returning to
some place in the desert with their respective spoils. On this
particular, the witnesses were very explicit, since it is stated
in many official reports that such encampments were formed,
sometimes in Texas and at other times in Mexico, and after
this plan was first discovered in Texas, they changed their
point of meeting to a place in the desert of Coahuila, from
which they could depredate either in Tamaulipas or Nuevo
Leon.

Equal truth and exactness is found in the causes which they
assign for the partial cessation of such incursions, which they
attribute to the cattle being nearly annihilated, an evident fact,
and to the tenacity with which the marauders have been punished in Mexico, where all the frontiersmen are now trained
soldiers in this kind of warfare, undertaken by them readily
and systematically.

One of the actors in the wars in Texas speaks of the invasion by Comanches, who entered Mexico in 1836, at a time
when he was retreating from San Antonio de Béjar, after the
capitulation of General Cos. He was a soldier of the permanent companies of Tamaulipas, and fought at Laredo, in Texas,
with the Comanches, who were pursued as far as the Nueces.
After withdrawing from military service, he took part in the
exploits of Zapata at Moros, Huizachal, and elsewhere. He
noted the change of tactics on the part of the Indians after
1848, and attributed it to the same causes as the other witnesses. He relates that before the year 1851, in which Don
Juan Manuel Zapata was killed, that officer and Don José
Maria Benavides Hinojosa became convinced that the Indians
were encamping in Texas and committing murders with impunity. He consequently went over the river with a party of
armed citizens, and by consent of the American commander at
" Ojuelos," attacked the Indians, who had been long encamped
at " Caliches," as was proved by finding in their possession the
spoils of persons killed long before, by the droves of mules recaptured, and, lastly, by the captives who were then set at
liberty.

All the witnesses agree that the only way in which Mexicans could recover their property carried into Texas by Indians was by taking part personally in the pursuit; as it otherwise happened, as in Laredo, that the animals recaptured from Indians would be sold at auction, even before the eyes of the owners.

The President of the Common Council at Guerrero was one of the officers who, in 1850, requested the permission of the American commander to cross the river, and states that he aided with a company of his soldiers, and he adds that four years later, in 1854, the Indians were again pursued in Texas, but this time by Mexicans residing and being organized there, as permission was no longer given to the citizens of Guerrero to participate, and that at the present time even the privilege granted in 1854 is no longer allowed to the Mexicans living in Texas, who in fact cannot now assemble at that place more than sixteen men.

The statements of these witnesses as to the losses suffered by the city of Guerrero being entirely corroborated by the data obtained from the public archives, an irresistible force is added thereto by the testimony which captives have given before this Commission. It is fully confirmed by them that incursions into Mexico are made by crossing the Rio Grande near the Sierra del Carmen, following that range as far as Santa Rosa, scattering thence into the interior States, and on their return recrossing into Texas between Nuevo Laredo and Guerrero. This was done in 1844, when they carried off Sabás Rodriguez, passing by the point called "La Oracion," in the desert of Coahuila, northwest of Nuevo Laredo, above which point they crossed the river, and, passing by San Saba, proceeded forty-three days journey to their settlement, which appears to have been on the Red river or one of its tributaries, according to the description and the Comanche names of the places. And that such is the custom generally followed by these Indians is proved by the two campaigns which the captive made with them, one in 1850, when they came to Salinas, and the other in 1852, when he was forcibly rescued on the hill of "La Oracion."

It is beyond doubt that a residence of eight years among

the Indians enabled him to know their customs, and, in speaking of this point, he averred that they sold all their booty to Americans and to other Indians, and he states that in his own place of residence a drove of mules was once sold. The witness concludes by saying that, in December, 1856, he killed an Indian at the rancho " La Salada," in Texas, and that he was a Comanche, as he knows from having seen him before and heard him talk.

Estevan Herrera and Manuel Villareal were captured in 1868 by Comanches, who were retiring from towns in Nuevo Leon with stolen horses, and near Las Tortillas carried off these two boys. As they have just been rescued by Americans from the Comanches, it cannot be doubted that the latter are the tribe which now commits depredations both in Mexico and in Texas. These captives saw in Texas the murder by Comanches of two Mexicans named Juan and José Maria Benavides ; they saw Indians arrive with cattle, horses, and captives ; they frequently saw them set out on expeditions, and saw Americans from New Mexico come to buy cattle and horses.

That this statement of those captives, although they are very young, is in accordance with fact, is proved by a narrative published this year by a Mr. Hittson, about robberies by Indians in New Mexico, and the sales they make to American citizens. What was stated by Mr. Gregg, in his work already quoted, is fully proved at page 291 of volume I, where the following language is found :

"Such is the imbecility of the local governments (those of Chihuahua and Durango), that the savages, in order to dispose of their stolen property without even a shadow of molestation, frequently enter into partial treaties of peace with one department, while they continue to wage a war of extermination against the neighboring States. This arrangement supplies them with an ever ready market for the disposal of their booty and the purchase of munitions wherewith to prosecute their work of destruction. In 1840 I witnessed the departure from Santa Fé of a large trading party freighted with engines of war and a great quantity of whiskey, intended for the Apaches, in exchange for mules and other articles of plunder which they had stolen from the people of the south. This traffic was not only tolerated, but openly encouraged by the civil authorities, as the highest public functionaries were interested in its success, the governor himself not excepted."

What the American author relates as having taken place in New Mexico in 1840, and censures with good reason, is repeated now-a-days, with the difference that the inhabitants are now American citizens, and what they buy of the Indians is no longer merely property robbed from Mexicans, but from Americans as well, and with the further difference that the partial treaties were made with governments of departments or States, while they are now made with the agents of a powerful government, which permits, tolerates, and protects this scandalous traffic, ruinous to the citizens of a neighboring nation and demoralizing to the Americans themselves.

In September, 1871, when Cecilio Benavides was tending his cattle, with his two sons Juan and José Maria, at his rancho in Texas, called " Prieto," Indians came and took the two boys captive. These boys say that on their journey of twenty-three days to the residence of the tribe, the Indians killed eight or nine persons, and committed other robberies ; that the New Mexicans came to buy horses at the encampment, and that the Indians made frequent expeditions, from which they returned bringing cattle, horses, and captives ; that one of the latter was Manuel Vela, taken in Texas in 1872 by the same Indians, who were Comanches and Kiowas, from whose hands they were rescued in consequence of the encampment being attacked by American troops: these routed them and took many prisoners, who were exchanged for American and Mexican captives.

Juan Vela Benavides, another of the captives, was taken in 1848 ; saw the trade with the New Mexicans ; knew of the trading post where the Comanches went to exchange their Mexican booty ; and, lastly, saw several Germans come to trade, and even availed himself of one of them to effect his own ransom. He states that an American commissioner, accompanied by two other men, came twice to the village and returned. This witness testifies that in the year of his captivity

(1848) the Indians already had their regular place of meeting in the desert, and all his statement fully proves a well combined plan of attack, as well as the understanding of the Comanches with the Americans.

From the multitude of evidence, a clear exhibit has been formed, showing the amount of damages ; that their perpetrators have been Comanches acting with the connivance of American citizens, who have directly or indirectly encouraged them, generally acquiring the booty stolen in Mexico by exchange for arms and ammunition.

When we take into account the pledges usually given by revolutionists when fighting for the triumph of a principle, it will enable us to appreciate two notable facts which show the character of Indian warfare and the importance always given to it. Don Antonio Zapata was, in 1839, accompanying the revolutionary General Canales in his march against Nuevo Leon and Coahuila, when he learned that the Indians had appeared near Guerrero, and he turned back immediately and routed them at Huizachal. Santa Anna, in his last despotic and suspicious administration in 1853, ordered a general disarming throughout the country, and only excepted the frontier States on account of the warfare they were maintaining against the savages.

The amount of attention given to this warfare, even in the most critical times for the country, is sufficiently proved by the spontaneousness with which the menaced towns have undertaken it at their own expense, and especially by the two instances given above, which show the grave nature of an evil which in times of civil strife was regarded as a matter not of fortunes alone, but of life and death.

After the treaty of Guadalupe a new town was built on the right bank of the Rio Grande, opposite the old town of Laredo. The Mexicans born in that town when it belonged to Mexico, who did not wish to endure the cruel fate of being foreigners in their own country, crossed the river and founded Nuevo Laredo on lands originally belonging to the old town. From its beginning this settlement was involved in the same struggle as the other towns on the Rio Grande, and as late as last year has continued to suffer from the Comanches.

Here, as in Guerrero, the public archives and the statements of numerous witnesses, have furnished abundant data to prove enormous damages, and the brief summary which this Commission will now give will show that all the complaints presented to it along the frontier of Tamaulipas represent only a very small part of the real losses, since only a portion of the sufferers have had their losses recorded, and these not the whole, but only that part which they best remembered.

Nuevo Laredo, having been founded during the war, it was directed and enabled, in July, 1848, to organize a half company of National Guards for its own protection against the savages. Nevertheless, its sufferings from their incursions gave occasion to the State government to issue the following order :

" According to Article XI of the Treaty of Peace with the United States, that country undertook not only to prevent Indian invasions, but to punish them severely when made, and to redeem the captives taken in our territory. Consequently, whenever we have to deplore an occurrence like that you mention, you may call the attention of the authorities of old Laredo to this obligation. This government is making the greatest efforts to mitigate the sufferings of your unfortunate town, and authorizes the Ayuntamiento to employ the municipal moneys for the purchase of arms."

As the invasions continued, the citizens of Old and New Laredo combined in a campaign against the Indians at " Laguna de la Leche," in which the troops of the military colony located in that vicinity took part. But as the seat of the evil was elsewhere, nothing came of these expeditions, and the government of the State, pitying the sufferings of the frontier towns, informed them, on the 23d of March, 1850, that "it had urged the signing of an extradition treaty, and would urge it again, since they were at times exposed to Indian barbarity and at other times to depredations by criminals on the left bank of the river." This proposal shows satisfactorily that the Mexican authorities were then struggling at the same time with the savages and the demoralization existing on the left bank, where criminals found refuge, and the inhabitants profited by the purchase of their spoils.

On the 1st of February, 1850, Indians penetrated by night into the town, carrying off all the horses, which were no longer safe even in the yards. It became necessary to set a guard at night in order to enjoy any security, and matters came to the extreme in March, of having to call back a party sent in pursuit of Indians, because other Indians were menacing the town, thus leaving the cattle farms at the mercy of the formidable enemy.

On the 31st of July, the mayor was informed that the Indians had stolen all the horses there were in the neighborhood, that a party of citizens and another of soldiers had unsuccessfully gone in pursuit, and that other Indians had attacked the rancho of Agapito Galvan, and passed on towards Guerrero. There were then in Mexico enough Indians to allow them to go from one town to another, to cross over to Texas to secure their booty, and return to continue their depredations. The alarm caused in Nuevo Laredo by the presence of Indians in their streets, and the unavailing efforts made by the inhabitants to recover their property when hurried across the river, was witnessed by the American town and the garrison in the adjoining fort. But not the slightest step was taken to prevent or to punish these outrages, prepared and consummated in American territory.

The people of Nuevo Laredo did not desist from their efforts to counteract these ferocious assaults. The citizens who had just returned from one expedition, set out again the same year in combination with those of Guerrero, and of several towns in Nuevo Leon, to drive the savages from their pastures, and such was their solicitude to prevent those evils, that they sent notice to the distant town of Monclova of a horde that was taking that direction.

Up to the year 1872, the incursions have continued with more or less vigor. To enumerate them all would take much time, and the objects of the Commission are met by a few citations which afford a complete picture of those which are omitted. In this continuous chain of invasions we find dispatches

18

from the authorities, which set forth in detail the hopelessness of the situation, enabling us by their simple perusal to form an exact judgment of the evil and its origin. After Nuevo Laredo was surrounded daily and nightly by the Indians, murdering and robbing, and evading chastisement by passing over to Texas in full sight of Old Laredo; after it had become notorious that the Comanches were the perpetrators of those depredations, which were tranquilly witnessed by the citizens of the United States; on one occasion when some Lipan Indians showed themselves in the vicinity, the Texans observed a totally different conduct, as may be seen by the following dispatch sent on the 7th of March, 1856, by the first judge to the higher authorities at Guerrero:

"Having been informed to-day, at 8 A. M., by the citizen Rodrigo Martinez, that a body of 80 or 90 armed citizens of Laredo, Texas, have crossed the river into Mexico, at the 'Escondida' ford, near this town, with the object of attacking the Lipan Indians, who have been hunting wild cattle on the Lampazos road, by virtue of a written permit given them by the Governor of Nuevo Leon, Don Santiago Vidaurri; and as this town has not sufficient means for repelling this force, I inform you thereof, requesting you to make the fact known, and to inform me what assistance your city can give us to defend the sovereignty of the nation, whose laws and decorum have been trampled under foot under pretext of the Lipans."

To the grave offense of tolerating the Comanches in their own country, the Americans added this outrage. From this time onward they watched for opportunities to conceal or deny their own offenses, laying the responsibility on Indians who had done no harm. When those deeds are scrutinized in the light of the data collected from many sources, it is palpably seen that this conduct had a crafty purpose, namely, to distract the attention of Mexicans from their own losses to those of the Texans. This object was generally attained by means of a crime, namely, the violation of our territory, which attracted attention, and drove us to reflect on the best means of preventing it. It was not without reason that the authorities asserted that the chastisement of the Lipans was merely a pretext, since

it was well known that those Indians were neither the sole perpetrators of the damages suffered in Texas, nor of those on the
Mexican bank of the river. When the Commission comes to
treat of the Lipans, it will show the real object of this procedure of the Texan people. It will now observe that the Americans were aroused to invade our territory, when they learned
that Indians who were at peace with Mexico were in the
vicinity of Nuevo Laredo. But when the Comanches came
from Texas, passing the rancho of San Ignacio, where they
murdered some Mexicans, being chased to the river bank by
an American officer, our territory was respected.

No rational and satisfactory explanation can be given to
such conduct, which is the more to be regretted, because occurring in the most critical times, when the Indian incursions
were most frequent and the devastations most cruel.

Although the inhabitants of the right bank of the Rio
Grande were kept in continual movement in the pursuit of the
Indians, they not unfrequently laid aside these occupations to
return and defend their towns from the menaced attacks of filibusters, which were organized in the principal towns of Texas,
with the manifest intention of depredating in Mexico. While
they were attending to this new peril, the savages remained in
possession of their pasture lands, and robbed them with perfect
impunity.

Many instances of these piratical invasions are recorded,
which are here mentioned on account of their relation to the
depredations of the savages. They are also mentioned, because
many of our citizens are convinced, with more or less reason,
that the intention was formed of aiding and abetting the robberies of the Indians, with whom they were in partnership.
The Commission does not attach any importance to this belief.
It did not wish even to mention it, and the only motive for so
doing is to show how lamentable has been the condition of the
frontier towns in every respect; that the Indian depredations
have been very extensive, and that the citizens and authorities
of the United States have largely contributed to them, the
former by their menaces of attacking the Mexican towns which

were already suffering from the Indians, and the latter by the aid and comfort they gave to such plans.

From the year 1855 to 1858 there was constant alarm on the frontier, on account of hostile preparations in Texas, and the consequences were disastrous in respect to the spoiling of their property by the Indians. Before this date, other causes, springing from a spirit of positive malevolence, created a situation no less dangerous and threatening for the Mexican towns. The invasions of 1851, which were carefully masked under a different plan, had no other object than the profit of the Texan border at the expense of the Mexican ; the destruction of the latter region in pursuance of a preconceived plan of annexation.

As there are many persons in Texas who still cherish these ideas of conquest, and most of them live on the frontier, the influence they have had in public life has been employed in manufacturing conflicts, increasing the ruin of the Mexican frontier. Hence their indifference to or encouragement of the robberies of the Indians, hence the negro troubles, the complaints against Kickapoos and Lipans, and the recent charges of cattle stealing, for it is seen that when one grievance disappears another is invented.

The Commission does not need to say that this conduct does not proceed from any design of the government of the United States, since it is well known that those evil-doers are hostile to their government, on account of its not countenancing their plans of invasion. These plans, however, have not been put down with the energy and promptitude necessary to forestall the evil, and responsibility has been thus incurred for all that has been suffered.

It is not merely this Commission which condemns the action of the authorities and citizens in question ; their own fellow-citizens have condemned it by contrary action, such as is usual between friendly neighboring nations. It has been said a few pages back that a violation of our territory was committed in 1856 by a body of eighty or ninety Texans, and that this alarmed the Mexicans and caused serious commotion. But recently in 1870, some Indians, who had been marauding in

Texas, crossed the river and were pursued in Mexican territory by American troops. This occurrence gave occasion to Colonel Anderson, commanding at Fort McIntosh, to address the following note, on the 17th of April, to the president of the council at Nuevo Laredo :

" *Sir :* I have the honor to inform you that I sent yesterday a body of troops, made up of soldiers and citizens, in pursuit of the Indians, and that they have followed them across the river. As these savages are common enemies of all civilized people, I hope that this act of pursuing them on the other side will meet with your approval, and I trust it will not be considered disrespectful to your authorities, since our only object is to recover some stolen horses. If, however, your authorities are opposed to pursuing the Indians on your territory, I will send a messenger to recall them."

The authorities of Nuevo Laredo went beyond the suggestion of Colonel Anderson, replying immediately that they had sent a force to co-operate with the Americans in the pursuit of the savages, whom he had so justly called enemies of all civilized people. This act of the American officer is equivalent to a condemnation of the previous conduct of the American authorities and people in Texas, as contrary to the true interests of both nations.

The Commission takes pleasure in narrating another occurrence, which not only proved the zeal of the Mexican authorities in pursuing the Indians, but also the enterprise of private individuals animated by the same spirit. In 1870, while Mexicans and Americans were engaged together in chasing the Indians who had crossed into Mexico, the *rancheros* of " Agua-verde," without notice or order, and moved only by duty, assembled to the number of six, attacked the Indians in the very act of recrossing the Rio Grande with the booty taken on both banks, and recovered the property of Americans and Mexicans, thus proving the activity and good organization maintained in this kind of warfare made only against the Comanches. When the united forces reached Aguaverde in pursuit, they found there the horses recovered by the herdsmen, and all the owners received their property without any conditions, and the Americans returned satisfied to their country.

This good understanding between the authorities of both countries proves, by its favorable result, what might have been done from the beginning, if the operations had been guided by a spirit of concord. This action of the American officer also demonstrates the impropriety of the conduct of all his predecessors since 1848, who have simply kept their posts, and have but once given notice of an invasion made from their territory into Mexico. This same fact shows that the conduct observed in 1856, in invading Mexico to attack the Lipans, when they were hunting wild cattle at a distance from the frontier, was a criminal procedure. It also shows that, with the exception of Colonel Anderson, no Federal authority in Texas has known how to comply with his international duties.

Unfortunately for the preservation of good feeling between the two frontiers, the prevailing spirit among the American authorities has been favorable neither to law nor to justice, but to power and force. When placed in front of unfortified points, they have almost always abused their position. Surrounded by parties interested in the maintenance of abuses by which they profited, the Federal officers have listened to one-sided reports, and have therefore assumed an attitude neither just nor conformable with the true interest of both republics. In most cases an ignorance of English on the part of Mexicans, and of Spanish on the part of the Americans, has prevented their receiving exact information, and has maintained an embarrassing situation.

It will be seen, in the course of this report, that information has been obtained from all possible sources, and that of a nature to inspire the most absolute confidence, since the persons who deposited it in the archives never suspected that it would be used for any special object. The Commission, therefore, confides in such information, and does not doubt that all impartial persons will concede to it that force which it deserves from its authenticity, its simplicity, and its evident truth.

The towns of Tamaulipas visited by the Commission have proven very considerable losses, which are undoubtedly below the fact. These proceed from direct damages to person and property, and indirect losses resulting therefrom.

The calculation of losses which have been proven, although amounting to a heavy sum, is very far from the reality, for not all the sufferers have presented themselves, and those who have done so have not given in the whole amount of their losses. There was such perfect good faith on the part of the complainants that when any one of them had previously presented a claim, he always stated the fact at the outset, and confined himself to mentioning his more recent losses. Not a few of the sufferers have abstained from presenting their complaints, because they had obtained no satisfaction for those presented twenty years before. Aside, therefore, from the justice which is perceptible in the majority of the cases, they have also the further recommendation of supplying evidence for those which are awaiting a decision (by the Mixed Commission) at Washington, since it is plain that no spirit of speculation nor preconceived plan has entered into these complaints.

No one will charge these reclamations with being exaggerated or impertinent, if he considers for a moment the losses which have occasioned them, the long space of time in which they have been accumulating, and the other circumstances already mentioned from which they have arisen. Any scruple on this head will disappear on the slightest examination of the first part of the 2d *expediente*, in which all the invasions of savages in Tamaulipas have been conjointly proven, as well as the immense amount of property carried off to the United States, enriching that country at the expense of Mexico, and, above all, the valuable lives which have been sacrificed. It will there be seen that the claimants have been very moderate, rating neither their property nor their lives at their true value. The Commission has taken care to form a statistical table which represents the incursions in connection with the losses of life and property thereby caused; and it has no doubt that the real losses will thus become apparent, and also the good conduct, nay, the disinterestedness of the sufferers. But if there should be any who still doubt, notwithstanding the authenticity of the documents obtained from the archives, they will undoubtedly be convinced by a parallel drawn between the claimants of the two nations, the Mexicans resting their cases for the losses of twenty years on the public archives alone; while, on the other side, appear incredible tales of imaginary losses during six years only, estimates of which the mere statement suffices, even in the United States, to draw down the ridicule and the condemnation of every right-minded and impartial man.

The morality, and good sense of the Mexican citizens will be still better seen by the fact that nothing whatever has been claimed as compensation for the robberies of horses, which have been made with impunity by American citizens, with perhaps the connivance and protection of their authorities, ever since 1848. The losses from this cause have been incalculable, but owing to the difficulty of estimating them, as well as to the doubt how far the American authorities have become responsible through their negligence, the sufferers have abstained from presenting their complaints, thus affording a criterion of the real value of the American claims for losses of cattle, which are undoubtedly much less than the Mexican losses of horses, since the latter began in 1848, and have continued up to the present time, while the former were unknown until the beginning of the Confederate war.

It being difficult to ascertain the exact losses, the basis of one per cent. per month on the entire amount, as charged by the complainants, will not appear exaggerated. The profit on cattle-farming is calculated by the American claimants at 33 per cent., or one-third of the capital invested, and it will therefore be seen that this point has been equitably determined, as is also the case respecting the valuation of the property stolen or destroyed.

It has been previously mentioned, that many of the sufferers were unable, from sickness or absence, to appear before the Commission; so that the recorded losses, although they afford data for calculating all those which have been suffered in Tamaulipas by Indian incursions alone, do not really represent their full amount, which would be a much larger sum.

No calculation has been attempted of the sums spent by the public treasury in protection of the frontier, because the data are not accessible. It has been ascertained, in a general

way, that the nation, in the midst of its serious difficulties from
internal and foreign wars, has not, for an instant, neglected the
frontier, on which it has fixed its attention, on account of its
importance as an integral portion of the republic, and on account of its relations with the neighboring nation.

Nor has the value of the services of the Mexican frontiersmen, in the pursuit of the savages, been calculated, as in justice it should be. But there have been no accurate data, since
the documents consulted are incomplete, and it has been
thought best to leave this blank, which may perchance be filled
up respecting other of the invaded towns, where such registers
may have been kept.

The Commission has endeavored to give, in the preceding
summary, an idea of the sufferings of the people of Tamaulipas,
on account of the incursions of the savages, but it puts more
trust in the accompanying synoptical table, which gives all the
invasions, along with their dates, the murders and robberies
caused thereby, and the expeditions organized against them.
This table supplies all that has here been omitted, and will
prove the accuracy of the Commission's statements, for it
should be distinctly remembered, that nothing has been
affirmed which does not rest on some public document, or been
placed beyond doubt by the unanimous testimony of numerous
witnesses.

DEPREDATIONS OF SAVAGES IN NUEVO LEON.

Nuevo Leon being separated from the American frontier by
Coahuila on the north, and by Tamaulipas on the east and
northeast, it would seem to be sheltered, by its position, from
the depredations of savages who had other towns nearer at
hand on which to satisfy their greed of rapine and bloodshed ;
but unfortunately this has not been the case.   The evils, damages and sufferings of its neighboring States have been here experienced on a still greater scale, in proportion to the greater
riches accumulated by the well-known industry of its citizens,
who, having enjoyed domestic peace ever since the independ-

ence of Mexico, had devoted themselves to stock-raising and agriculture as the sources of their prosperity, until the savages, by their incessant warfare, involved them in ruin.

It will be remembered that Spanish civilization, in its laborious task of peopling these regions, and civilizing the native tribes, had, at the close of the last century, advanced its settlements in this direction as far as Lampazos, Laredo and the *Presidios* (military colonies) of San Vicente, Bábia, Aguaverde, Alamo and Bahia; that soldiers and missionaries had preceded the first settlers of these regions, who did not occupy them until reports of their beauty and fertility aroused a spirit of enterprise, after they had been completely reduced to peace by the force of arms or of proselytism.

The origin of San Antonio, of Laredo, of Guerrero, and all the other towns on the right-bank of the Rio Grande, was due to the same causes, and most of them were colonized by Indians of Haxcala, who by their adhesion to the Spaniards, by their bravery and industry in the most indispensible arts of civilized life, contributed to facilitate the work of the conquerors. Thanks to these expedients, most of the Indians were brought to order and Christianity, the remainder were driven northward, and in the middle of the seventeenth century the struggle which still continues was begun.

The superiority in arms and discipline which the Spaniards communicated to the Christianized Indians overcame all resistance, and it is to be noted that the Spaniards who lived in those establishments always preserved their influence over those Indians, whom they did not fear to arm for the conflict with the savages.

These discoveries and settlements went on progressing during the seventeenth and the greater part of the eighteenth century, at the end of which their decline commenced. It was then seen that the colonies remained stationary, weighed down by the war with the savages, and the colonial companies were then organized upon a plan so sagacious that eight of them, conveniently located, kept at bay the immense multitude of Comanches and other Indians who roamed over the deserts of New Mexico and Texas, then belonging to our nation.

It is true that no step was taken in advance, but it is also true that from the organization of the said companies all the frontier towns were greatly relieved from their previous struggles, and those farther south enjoyed complète peace up to the year 1836.

The frontiers of Tamaulipas and of Coahuila, as being more open and extended, were garrisoned by seven companies, and but one was destined to Nuevo Leon, which was placed near Lampazos to guard the approaches to the center of the State. The experience of forty years showed that this system, combining attack with defense, was well devised, for except in one or two instances, neither the Comanches nor any other Indians penetrated within the extensive lines defended by the colonial garrisons, from Bahia on the Gulf coast to San Vicente, near the old post of San Carlos in Chihuahua.

Santa Rosa, San Fernando de Aguaverde, Presidio de Rio Grande, Lampazos, Laredo and San Antonio, which were the outposts, are the only towns which preserve in their annals the details of the depredations committed by Indians, who rarely failed on such occasions to be severely punished, and even pursued into their native deserts.

Travelers passing to the south of the above mentioned posts enjoyed the same security as within the towns themselves. This peace and tranquility was still better secured from the year 1829, when General Bustamante reorganized the colonial garrison, as before mentioned, creating a situation of prosperity which will seem wonderful and even incredible without an investigation of the position of the Indians at this period.

The work of Josiah Gregg, already mentioned, which was written at a time when it was not even imagined that it would ever supply evidence in international questions, solves the enigma of the formidable invasions made by the savage hordes inhabiting the frontiers of Northern Mexico and the western territories of the United States. Its data are the more precious because obtained in the Indian country, and precisely at the time when they were effecting their great movement towards the Mexican settlements, and because while the author criticises the Mexican authorities for their dealings with the Indians, he has written down the condemnation of his own country, furnishing a criterion by which to pass judgment upon this complicated Indian question.

It has already been stated that the government of the United States, yielding to the pressure applied by some of the States, dislodged the Indian tribes which led an independent existence in the midst of that republic, the inhabitants of which never intermarried with them, leaving them to preserve their savage manners and customs. That government being, according to the expression of De Tocqueville, impotent to protect the Indians, it transplanted them to the frontier of Mexico, and at the close of 1831 ten thousand had been placed at the nearest point to Mexico, at a great distance from all American settlements.

Some of the observations made by Mr. Josiah Gregg in his travels across the prairies to Santa Fé and Chihuahua in the spring of 1839, have been quoted at the beginning of this report for the purpose of explaining the origin of the great eruption made into our three States in 1836, the precursor of so many later ones. It must be here explained that Camp Holmes, mentioned as the place where the first trading post with the Comanches and Wichitas was established, was situated in American territory, in the Creek country, near the Canadian river, at about latitude 35° 5'. This trade must have been important, since the author expressly says, " as far as Holmes we had a passable wagon road, which was opened on the occasion of the Indian treaty before alluded to, and was afterwards kept open by the Indian traders."

This statement, written in 1839, proves that for four years in succession the Comanche trade had been kept up, since though the trading post of Colonel Chouteau had been abandoned since 1838, the road to Camp Holmes had been kept open by the Indian traders, which shows that the Indians either sought out the traders, or that the latter came to Camp Holmes, following the road which had been " kept open."

Our author next relates an interview he had with an Indian chief, who talked a little Spanish, that language being more or less known by the Prairie Indians. Tabba-quena, the Indian chief, showed by his talk that he was well acquainted with all the Mexican frontier from Santa Fé to Chihuahua and thence to the Gulf, as well as with all the prairie region. He gave proof of this by making a map which well represented the principal rivers, the plains, the road from Santa Fé to Missouri, and the Mexican posts were better located in this Indian sketch than in the printed maps.

This fact proves the continual intercourse of the Comanches with the American establishments, since they knew them well as far as the Missouri. It is added that Tabba-quena had with him about sixty persons, including squaws and boys, and also some Kiowa chiefs and warriors, who, although belonging to another tribe, are frequently found living with the Comanches. Tabba-quena said that his companions had gone to see the "Great Captain," which he had not done, because he turned back to get better horses, and the author afterwards learned that the Kiowas had really been at Fort Gibson, and had received a considerable present. This Indian captain was living on the False Wachita, in territory then and now belonging to the United States :

" We succeeded in purchasing several mules, which cost us between ten and twenty dollars' worth of goods apiece. In Comanche trade, the main trouble consists in fixing the price of the first animal. This being settled by the chiefs, it often happens that mule after mule is led up and the price received without further cavil. The Santa Fé caravans have generally avoided every manner of trade with the wild Indians, for fear of being treacherously dealt with during the familiar intercourse which necessarily ensues. This I am convinced is an erroneous impression, for I have always found that savages, are much less hostile to those with whom they trade than to any other people. They are emphatically fond of traffic, and being anxious to encourage the whites to come among them, instead of committing depredations upon those with whom they trade, they are generally ready to defend them against every enemy."

The Commission has extracted these details concerning the trade with the Indians, their fondness for and eagerness to maintain traffic, in order to point out the connection between this free intercourse with American citizens and authorities, and the robberies and butcheries perpetrated on Mexican towns. The great Indian irruptions can only be explained by these antecedents. There must have been a cause for the change which took place among those savage hordes in 1836, and that cause cannot be other than the trade which was begun the previous year at Camp Holmes by an American colonel, and was actively continued by other Americans, in order to enrich themselves by the fabulous gains of this traffic. Another cause may be found in the removal of the Southern Indians to the remotest corner of the American territory, in contact with the savage tribes of Mexico. A brief sketch of the avocations of the said tribes on their last reservations will hereafter be given, and will show the truth of the inference which has just been drawn.

As the especial object of this Commission, according to its instructions, is to investigate the damages caused by Indians from the United States since 1848, the Commission will proceed to state the results obtained, as regards the State of Nuevo Leon, and will do so with greater minuteness than heretofore, because the depredations have been immense and incalculable, and because this State being the central one of those which have suffered this great plague, the narrative will necessarily include much relating to the neighboring States, and from it may be derived authentic conclusions as to the right of the citizens to indemnifiation, and the responsibility of the United States to make it. The depredations previous to 1848 will first be summarily treated to show the origin of the responsibility, aside from all treaties, according to natural law.

As in Tamaulipas, the public archives have been the main source of information, but with the important difference that in Nuevo Leon they have been found nearly complete, not having suffered the same spoliation as in the former State, which has frequently been a victim of piratical or filibustering expeditions, and of local revolutions, which have caused the destruction of very important documents. Another source of valuable information has been the statements of the most respectable citizens of all the towns visited, especially those who have held public positions, or have been leaders of expeditions against the Indians. The Commission is therefore certain of having ascertained the truth upon this interesting topic, and feels sure that the results will attract public attention through their importance, not less than their novelty to most readers, though the facts themselves are of remote occurrence.

The government of Nuevo Leon had barely been reinstated, about the middle of the year 1848, in the midst of the difficulties incident to the evacuation of the posts held by the American troops during the war, when its attention was called, not merely to the evils committed in the towns by the disorderly troops of the retiring army, but to the invasions of the Comanches, which were made with a violence never before seen. From the 15th of July, 1848, when the authority of Cañas (now Mina) reported the first Comanche incursion, there was not a single day of rest for the government, for Villaldama, Lampazos, Vallecillo, Valenzuela and Salinas continually reported other and repeated invasions. From these communications, which have all been compared in order to form the annexed statistical table, it appears that 104 Comanches penetrated into the center of those towns, besides four other parties of which the numbers are not given, but calculating them at only 15 each, they bring up the total number of invaders to 164.

Eleven persons killed, three wounded, two captives, and droves of horses and mules carried off, were the consequences of these incursions, which were resisted by more than 200 men of the towns attacked, and by a few regular troops sent in pursuit by the commander-in-chief. Six combats with the Indians, resulted in taking from them saddles, a captive and some cattle, proved that they were Comanches, and that the local and federal authorities complied with their respective duties.

The year 1849 was ushered in by an attack upon Agualeguas by a party of Comanches, which extended its foray to every one of the northern towns, including San Nicolas de las Garzas, three leagues from Monterey. More than 500 Comanches made during this year thirty-four incursions, killing thirty-four persons, wounding fourteen, and capturing four, besides the usual robbery of horses, which may be safely calculated, in accordance with official data, at more than one thousand.

The parties of citizens and soldiers organized to resist them equaled the number of invasions, and more than 1,000 men were this year engaged in pursuit, fighting the Indians in three engagements, recapturing some horses, though but few, for while some were fighting others were engaged in hurrying off the stolen animals. It was thus noticed in all the engagements that their principal care was to preserve their booty, making the greatest efforts to accomplish this object, and generally succeeding in distancing pursuit by the rapidity of their retreat.

The memoir presented to the Congress of Nuevo Leon, in 1850, speaking of "public security," said : "that of this State would be complete, were it not for the incursions of the savage tribes," which although less numerous this year than in the other frontier States, presented the horrible picture of 800 Comanches, who killed 21 men, wounded 20, captured four children, and robbed more than a thousand animals. The forces employed in resistance, besides the permanent companies, amounted to 1,520 men, organized in 16 towns.

The Commission cannot refrain from mentioning the names of these towns, and the number of assaults they experienced this year, for this will give an exact idea of their sufferings. Villaldama was nine times attacked by Comanches, Agualeguas seven, Sabinas Hidalgo eight, Cerralvo two, Marin four, Mina nine, Salinas Victoria eight, Bustamante four, Lampazos nine, Vallecillo ten, Pesqueria Chica one, Pesqueria Grande six, San Nicolas de las Garzas two, Abasolo three, San Nicolas Hidalgo three, and China once—making a total of 86 incursions upon 16 towns of Nuevo Leon, in a year when the governor informed Congress that their forays were less frequent than in the other frontier States. This was a fact, and if the proofs have not been found, through the incompleteness of the archives, it was nevertheless well known to all when the said memoir was published. This shows in what manner the investigation of depredations in Nuevo Leon discloses what took place in other States.

Nine regular campaigns were undertaken by order of the government, besides the partial pursuits made by the National Guard of each invaded town, some of which mustered 80 or 100 men. The situation produced by these occurrences attracted the attention of the press in the capital of the republic, and in announcing the events of the frontier it was said:

"The first thing that meets our eyes is always something about savage Indians. Why is it that these unhappy towns can never free themselves from this horrible plague? Plans of defense are devised, funds are raised for the war, but the result always is that, although the savages are sometimes beaten, the towns never have a moment's rest. Their inhabitants perish at the the hands of the savages, or are carried into a fearful captivity. Agriculture, industry and commerce relapse into insignificance, the revenues cease, tranquility is lost by constant fear of the peril which threatens life, honor and family interests; all, in short, presents the most doleful picture of misfortune and desolation."

Everywhere people wondered that the frontier did not enjoy a moment's rest, in spite of all the plans and systems devised to repel the savages; the desolation of the beleaguered towns was felt at hundreds of miles' distance. Information of these calamities must have reached the government at Washington, for the Indians who ravaged Mexico lived in the United States, and they paraded their spoils in full view of the military chieftains. It was, then, their duty to prevent this mischief, since they had expressly contracted by treaty to do so.

In the midst of the ruin and desolation which befel a great part of the republic, the general government of Mexico prepared to unite its efforts with those of the United States to carry into effect the solemn engagement of the latter to prevent such invasions. With this object, the inspectors of the East, Chihuahua and the West, and the commanders stationed in Coahuila, Nuevo Leon, Tamaulipas, Durango, Chihuahua and Sonora, and the prefect of Lower California were instructed:

"1st. Under their own strict responsibility to grant no peace

19

and to wage vigorous war with the savage Comanches, Apaches, Lipans and other tribes who roam through the American territory, without forming settlements or cultivating the ground like other tribes, but devote themselves entirely to hunting and warfare of an atrocious character, not only when they emigrate from the United States under an appearance of peace, but also when they may be driven thence by force of arms. 2d. To make no truce, peace or agreement with any other savages, not included in the above category, without awaiting the decision of the supreme government, to whom a report must be sent as to the circumstances and the condition of the tribe which may desire to make peace."

When the supreme government, on the 10th of September, 1850, forwarded the above rules for the guidance of its officers in their dealings with the savages, it treated all agreements for peace as imprudent, because they would weaken the force of the unquestionable obligation undertaken by the United States to put down and chastise the Indian incursions.

The statesman who formed the above resolutions took into consideration all that was occurring along the vast extent of the Mexican frontier, and knew that, in spite of all the efforts of government and people to suppress Indian depredations, there was no other means of success than in the fulfillment of the solemn obligation of the United States. While awaiting such action on the part of the American government, he arranged and prepared everything to facilitate it, and took care, above all, that no act should weaken the binding force of the obligation. That the savages should cause greater ruin and sacrifice more victims was preferable to losing the rights given by nature and by solemn compact. The war was, therefore, to be accepted and waged at whatever sacrifice.

The State governments acted in harmony with that of the Federation, and at the time the above measures were taken a plan of defense was published in Nuevo Leon, declaring a war of extermination against the savages.

Taking into account the deserts, the hiding places offered by the mountains, the agility of the savages, their endurance, astuteness, and dexterity in their peculiar mode of warfare, rules were drawn up to meet all these requirements; a decree was promulgated and carried at once into effect. It was high time, for, as has been seen, the evil had assumed enormous proportions, which engaged at once every sentiment of pride, dignity, and honor ; and the government could therefore say in the circular which accompanied the plan of defense, " Who, in contemplating this picture which would horrify the most apathetic citizen, does not hear the imperious voice of duty and honor demanding that a remedy be found for all these evils ? "

All the elements and resources of Nuevo Leon, having been brought to bear upon the remedy of the situation, the Indian war presented a more favorable aspect in 1851. The memoir published by the government in this year contained the following words :

" The idea, which was roughly suggested in the previous memoir, concerning the means of defense against the savages, was carried into effect. The towns were provided with a sufficiency of arms, ammunition, and pecuniary resources, and the ferocious savage learned to his surprise and his cost that the State will not quietly endure the evils he is accustomed to inflict."

Nevertheless, the Commission found sixty-eight incursions recorded during this year, made against the same towns by about 600 Indians. The losses were 36 killed, 33 wounded, and 12 captives, besides about 300 horses.

By order of the government, and in accordance with the plan of defense approved on the 20th of September of the preceding year, four expeditions were organized, and the pursuit of the Indians was more active and effective than ever. The greater number of the killed was the result of eight engagements, which took place either in the immediate pursuit or in the desert fastnesses, where the Indians brought together their booty, and whence they sent out small parties into the northern districts of Nuevo Leon.

The severe punishment and loss of life inflicted on the Indians in the active campaign everywhere undertaken, is fully set forth in the official reports, and it was seen that united action and a proper distribution of the forces, which were the chief elements of the plan of defense, would produce favorable results, after a little experience. The forces employed this year amounted to more than 1,000 men.

The savages acted as if they comprehended that they were the object of a combined action on the part of the government and people, and meant to prove their valor and real power, coming, in 1852, in greater numbers and more frequently than ever. There were, consequently, more killed, more wounded, more captives, and greater robberies. Ninety-two attacks were made upon herdsmen, laborers, and travelers by parties of greater or less size, and it is authentically shown that more than 1,000 savages were concerned in them.

About 2,000 men were employed in a pursuit which was carried into the rudest fastnesses of the mountains, at a sacrifice of 62 killed, 30 wounded, and 16 captives, and the usual accompaniment of horses and mules stolen, amounting to more than 500. A real war was now being waged ; eight large expeditions were sent out on formal campaigns, ten engagements took place, in all which the Indians were beaten with loss, and over 200 horses and mules were recaptured.

In the following year, 1853, the Indians were distributed in smaller parties of fifty, thirty, twenty, ten, or even five, and thus made 77 incursions in the north and west of the State, causing a loss of 35 killed, 23 wounded, 6 captives, and some 300 horses stolen. About 1,500 men belonging to the companies already organized in the towns were employed in pursuit; four engagements took place, with notable loss to the savages, and, there being 800 of them scattered in small parties, many minor chastisements inflicted upon them escaped official notice.

To the list of towns which had been annually, and sometimes daily, assailed since 1848 without a moment's intermission, there must now be added, for the year 1854, the names of towns which had never before been attacked, such as Linares, Montemorelos, San Pedro de Iturbide, Galeana, Doctor Arroyo, and Rio Blanco, the two former situated to the south of Montery, on the road to Victoria, at the foot of the Sierra Madre, the third in the heart of the Sierra, and the rest on the other side of the mountains, a hundred leagues from the State capital.

This change of tactics on the part of the Indians was undoubtedly occasioned by their conviction that they could no longer overcome the resistance made to them in all quarters, and also in great measure to the fact of the diminution of the number of horses in the towns they had so frequently visited. They thought it possible to obtain a larger number, which they wanted for their system of exchange, by attacking other districts, as yet unaccustomed to their spoliations, where they might satisfy their thirst for blood.

Although the Comanches are astute in robbery, dexterous in self-defense, and daring in attack when in sufficient force, all which qualities they have acquired during several generations of border warfare, they nevertheless had not shown therein any knowledge of real military science, carrying on their early wars, as has been said, rather from vengeance than for the sake of spoils. Tactical warfare was not known or practiced by them until after 1840, and its date may be more correctly assigned to about the year 1848. On their ancient system they staked the success of their campaigns upon the number of forays; they sent forth one or two thousands of prairie warriors, appeared at many points at once, robbing immense numbers of horses and mules, which they carried off in triumph to their chosen retreats; but they never once failed to be defeated in their larger masses, as happened at the "Llano de Ramirez," at Huizachal, at El Pozo, and, as will be seen hereafter, at La Oracion, Rosita and other places.

A superior intelligence, an intelligence not native to the Indians, must necessarily have suggested to them their change of tactics. As their object was to steal horses and conduct them in safety to their market, another plan was devised, which consisted in meeting together in large numbers at a given rendezvous within Mexican territory, at some place advantageously located for defense, far away from settlements and unknown to their victims; to fortify themselves therein with all possible secrecy and precaution; from these headquarters to carry out their simultaneous forays, returning there with their booty, and repeating the operation as often as possible, until the time came to carry off at once their immense booty to the United States.

Those who know something of the Indians; those who have

studied their habits and followed step by step the incidents of their nomadic and warlike life, must agree that such combinations could not originate with them, and that they have been taught them by civilized men, without heart or conscience, who desire by their means to realize gigantic speculations.

In August, 1854, the Indians had passed that massive range of the Sierra Madre, which would seem to be an unsurmountable wall of defense, and the towns of San Pedro de Iturbide, Galeana, Doctor Arroyo and Rio Blanco suddenly beheld the sanguinary tomahawk of the savages hurled at the heads of their inmates. A hundred and ten Comanches, in a single body, attacked those unsuspecting settlements with the result which is shown in the following communication, which is textually inserted here:

"GALEANA, August 15th, 1854.

"*To the Governor of the Department of Nuevo Leon:*

"MOST EXCELLENT SIR :

"By the inclosed original reports, your excellency will learn that the savages, to the number of about 100, have invaded this municipality, committing acts of the most horrid cruelty at the place called 'Peñuelo,' where they murdered all the inhabitants, consisting entirely of defenseless women and children, the men being all in the country tending their cattle, which they were taking to the Department of Zacatecas. These lamentable occurrences have thrown this town into the greatest consternation, and the commissariat under my charge in these sad circumstances, has, by making use of every resource, armed and mounted twelve men of this town for the speedy relief of the hacienda 'Potosi,' where the arrival of the terrible enemy is momentarily expected, and which is exposed to all the devastations of the savage, it being without men and without arms. It would be difficult, excellent sir, to describe the lamentable picture presented by the estate where the tragic event occurred, and the sentiments of Christian men are horrified at the sight; but it appears to me that at present our attention should be exclusively given to the more important duty of burying the dead, and aiding other places exposed to the same fate as the ruined hamlet of Peñuelo. Yes, most excellent sir, the innocent blood of more than 200 victims is still reeking in the fields of Peñuelo calling aloud for vengeance;

and this municipality, being unable from its poverty, to arm and mount even one hundred men, earnestly and respectfully implores your excellency to impart your paternal protection in the manner you may find most expedient, supplying us with arms and. ammunition for our defense against so atrocious an enemy, and for punishing him if possible, whenever he shall again appear within this district.

"PEDRO PEREYRA."

While these disasters were occurring at such a distance from the capital that it was impossible to render timely aid and succor to the hapless sufferers, many other districts of the State were overrun by small parties of ten or fifteen Indians, and by larger ones of two or three hundred each, killing in this year fifty-six persons, wounding thirty-five, taking captive nineteen, and carrying off 600 animals. An active pursuit of these scattered parties through mountains, plains, and forests, with the greatest zeal, by 1,500 men, gave no better result than the recapture of sixty animals and a small amount of other booty, effected in four engagements against more than 400 Comanches.

On account of the ever-increasing energy displayed by authorities and people in the pursuit and chastisement of the savages, who were worsted in every encounter, there were in 1855 only twenty-seven forays, two of which were upon towns to the south of the Sierra. In that year there were only forty-four killed, three wounded, and two captives. The invaders numbered more than 200, and the six towns assailed sent against them 500 men, who, however, only once overtook them.

In the next year, 1856, there were seventy-three forays against the northern towns of Nuevo Leon, but the losses were less, amounting only to twenty-five killed, fifteen wounded, three captives, and barely 100 animals stolen. The government and people, stimulated by the successful result of their systematic and well-combined defense, were more active than usual. Ten expeditions were sent against the Indians, and although no regular battle took place, the savages perceived that they were awaited and vigorously pursued, and that they could no longer commit their usual depredations with impunity. More than 2,000 men were employed against about 500 Indians.

It should be stated that all that was done against the savages, in 1855 and 1856, was at a time when Nuevo Leon and all the frontier was engaged in a political war, defending their principles by means of armies which were sent into the interior of the country, and which were kept there until the conflict was decided in favor of the liberal cause they had espoused. The Indian war was not, however, neglected, but, on the contrary, it was undertaken more vigorously than ever, so as to keep in the interior of the republic that army of citizens which would instantly have returned at the first news of danger to their families.

The Commission relates this circumstance, because it is honorable at once to the government and to the people, and shows the real importance always given to the war with the savages, which was never neglected either by government or people, even in times of civil or foreign wars.

In 1857, the invasions followed the ordinary course of previous years; there were eighty-nine forays upon the northern towns, which lost forty-five men killed, twenty-six wounded, thirteen captives, and three hundred horses. Parties of National Guards, composed of from seventy down to ten men, were constantly sent against the invaders, 2,000 men having been thus employed. With the exception of thirty Lipans, who attacked Mina, the other assailants were Comanches. It was noticed that in the same month, and almost at the same time, they fell upon six different towns, all of them being remote from their usual theater of operations. During this year, as in the preceding, the parties of Indians who gave occupation to an army of 2,000 Mexicans were never larger than thirty, and sometimes consisted of only three or four.

It seems incredible that so small a number of savages could cause so much woe and escape punishment, even when constantly pursued by the combined forces of the towns surrounding the theater of their depredations. Yet this was generally the case, and can only be explained by the nature of the ground, which offers rare facilities for guerrilla warfare through its almost impenetrable forests and its many rugged mountains.

These considerations may explain the comparative impunity of the Indians themselves, but not their success in carrying off their booty; it has, however, been mentioned that their first care is to secure their spoils, by sending a portion of their number in all haste to place them beyond reach, while the remainder, concealed in the mountains, await other opportunities for new depredations.

The grand total of the ten years examined, from 1847 to 1857, shows as the result, 652 persons killed, wounded, and carried captive, although the services of more than 12,000 men were employed in their pursuit, attacking them whenever it was possible. During this period the savage invaders numbered more than 5,000, an average of 500 each year.

The preceding calculation having been formed upon the reports made to the government, in which the number of hostile Indians is not always mentioned, as is also the case respecting the parties of citizens sent against them, the Commission feels sure that even double the number both of enemies and of armed citizens would fall short of the real truth. But the numbers given above suffice to prove the persistency of the war, and the immense extent of the evils thereby caused. In ten years the State of Nuevo Leon lost 650 of her best sons, and in each year 1,500 of her citizens were constantly under arms to hasten to the relief of the places attacked, which comprised, at one time or other, almost all the towns of the State. Even the few which have not been directly ravaged, have suffered their share of the robberies and butcheries which marked the path of the barbarians.

The solicitude of the State and general governments could not exceed the requirements of the afflicting situation. The plan of defense of the 20th of September, 1850, provided measures so prudent and efficacious, that, without them, the ruin would have been complete. The supreme government created new military colonies, and put into operation the same scheme of warfare established by the ancient *presidios*, which were now replaced by these colonies. Nothing that could tend to the extinction of the Indian war was omitted, and if it still exists, the reason is obvious—the aggressors live in the territory of another nation, where they are encouraged, befriended and almost impelled to wage this warfare with the persistency they have shown therein.

The national Congress appointed a committee of its members to draw up a project containing suitable measures for putting an end to the growing evil of these invasions ; and the argument of their plan contained the following declaration :

"The 11th article of the Treaty of Peace between Mexico and the United States, if carried into effect carefully and in good faith, would supply the means of radically terminating the Indian war. The exact fulfillment of this article would suffice to invigorate the defense of the frontier States, and would soon extirpate the war which is devouring them. The Junta ought never to lose sight of that article, and we therefore propose that the general government be requested to furnish a report upon this important point, as a basis upon which to predicate the action most expedient for the welfare of the States in question."

In the same year (1849), the Junta of Congress, being desirous to perform its task faithfully, called upon the military commanders in the frontier States and the inspectors of the colonies to emit their opinion upon the best means for the defense and security of the border. The commander-in-chief in Nuevo Leon, who was also inspector general of the eastern colonies, gave his report on the 8th of July of that year, and, among other things, he wrote as follows :

"In the midst of the necessity and despair which so great sufferings have produced, the idea has several times occurred of imitating the conduct of the Spanish soldier, Don Juan de Ugalde, by carrying the war into the deserts, and attacking the savages in their own haunts. Some State governors, who have heretofore tried this plan separately, found that the barbarians forestalled their efforts by carrying their families far to the north, to hiding places unknown to the Mexicans, and then followed the footsteps of these exploring parties, falling upon them and wreaking vengeance at unguarded moments. This plan is out of the question at the present day, because our frontier being now the Rio Grande, it is incumbent upon the government of the United States to restrain the incursions of the Indians, in fulfillment of the obligation contracted by the 11th article of the Treaty of Guadalupe Hidalgo, and under these circumstances, how could the war be carried, without danger of reclamations, into a desert which is not our property ?"

After the careful examination which Inspector Jauregui made of all the plans devised for the defense of the frontier, under the new situation, so different from that of 1772, when the plan of *presidios* was adopted; after depicting with excellent judgment the differing aspect of affairs at a time when the savages were always punished by the forces which garrisoned the frontier, nothwithstanding their excellent arms and their dexterity ; he concludes that their present abode being on foreign soil, and consequently beyond reach, the only means of preventing their depredations would be to obtain from the Government of the United States, the fulfillment of the 11th Article of the Treaty of Guadalupe Hidalgo, and to combine some new civic militia with the reestablished military colonies.

The brevity of this report will not permit the Commission here to enumerate separately all the measures adopted by the General or the State Government for remedying the evils caused by the Indian invasions. No absolute success was attained, but a situation more favorable than that of the United States was reached, as may be seen from the following article, found in the official newspaper of Nuevo Leon of the 31st of May, 1849 :

" MATAMOROS, May, 14th, 1849.

"On Thursday, the 10th instant, at 11 o'clock, P. M., two or three merchants came to the house of General Francisco Avalos, bearing a communication from the first judge of Cameron county (Brownsville), Mr. J. B. Bigelow, in which he requested that some cavalry be sent to his aid to repel a party of savages which was marauding near Palo Alto, and which, it was feared, might approach Brownsville and other towns on the river. General Avalos, as was natural, called together the necessary forces, but at the same time replied to Judge Bigelow, that inasmuch as Mexican soldiers ought not to cross the river without the express consent of the American military commander, he should wait for an official invitation, to avoid all pretext for future complaint or reclamation. Many American and Mexican families living on the left of the Rio Grande have crossed to this city to escape danger from the ferocity of the savages. Judge Bigelow, in another communication to General Avalos, said that the American commander had declined to interfere in the matter, and that he was therefore obliged to dispense with the aid which the general was kind enough to afford him. Consequently, the Mexican troops withdrew from the river bank to their respective barracks."

This incident, thus recorded in the newspaper "*El Bien Publico*," printed in sight of the city of Brownsville, needs no comment, and shows how well the stipulations of the treaty of Guadalupe Hidalgo were complied with in the second year after its signing. The American Government, up to that time had taken no measures to protect its own citizens, much less those of Mexico, from the ravages of savages dwelling within its territory.

The newspaper already cited affords information that the rancho "El Capote," within the jurisdiction of Matamoros, was invaded by Indians, and that another party was seen across the river. The Mexican ranchos were protected by cavalry troops immediately sent out.

This unprotected condition of the American frontier still continued in 1853, and undoubtedly led to greater activity on the part of Mexicans in the ensuing years, in organizing and directing a real army of operations, which always obtained favorable results in the pursuit of the savages.

Within the period under consideration, the authorities of Nuevo Leon took the initiative in carrying out the new plan of defense, efficiently aided by the military colonies, and organized a coalition of the frontier States, by means of Commissioners, who met together and drew up a scheme similar to that already adopted by Nuevo Leon. Notwithstanding these efforts, the lives sacrificed, the captives carried off to be trained up as enemies of their own kindred, and the property stolen and destroyed could not be repaid by many millions of money, for beyond the material loss was felt the paralyzation of all industry, especially stock-raising and agriculture, which were completely abandoned when it was found by costly experience that the efforts of both State and National governments were ineffectual to prevent the depredations of the savage.

Before continuing the narrative of the events of the second decade, and having already summarily related the losses suffered by the State of Nuevo Leon up to 1857, it will here be fitting to give a slight idea of the operations directed by the military headquarters established at Monterey under the auspices of the War Department.

It appears from the archives of the said headquarters, that from the month of September, 1848, it sent troops for the protection of Lampazos; that it placed a force of dragoons at Mamulique for the defense of the adjoining towns; that it had an officer employed in operations at "Ceja Colorada," beyond Ciudad Guerrero; that it executed an order from the Department of Foreign Affairs to remove the "Taracanhuaces" Indians from Laguna de Lara, whither they had come, escaping from pursuit by American forces in Texas; that it provided Lampazos with a piece of artillery for its defense, not only against Indians, but also against American adventurers who threatened to attack it; that for the same purpose it sent 100 men under Commandant Pozas to defend that town from 80 Americans discharged from the retiring army; all which measures were approved by General Miñon, who was at Saltillo.

While watching over the safety of a portion of the frontier, the troops of the general government routed a body of Indians in January, 1849, recapturing considerable booty; and, lastly, while penetrating into the desert in search of the common enemy, they united with the civil authority in selecting lands suitable for a colony.

Still more vigorous action was displayed in 1850. The military colony of San Vicente, located in the desert 120 leagues north of Monterey, routed the Lipan and Mescalero Indians, killing five and wounding twenty-two. In Lampazos, two parties were sent against invading Indians, two others in Salinas; the Comanches were attacked at "Pajaros Azules" in combination with the local militia, and an expedition was equipped in union with the military colonies to penetrate the desert as far as the "Laguna de Jaco."

Certain information was given by the officers of Fort Mc-Intosh to the military colonies at Monterey Laredo in January, 1851, that the American government had made peace with several tribes of Comanches, and this news was corroborated in March by the fact of eight Indians of that tribe soliciting peace with Mexico.

Four captives, natives of Nuevo Leon, were this year ransomed by American troops, and the State government refused to pay the eighty dollars advanced for this purpose, on the ground of the obligation contracted in the 11th article of the treaty of Guadalupe Hidalgo. The year terminated with a peremptory order from the War Department to send a respectable force to the hill of Pánico to dislodge the Indians there collected, thus proving that even in the capital of the republic the occurrences on this remote northern frontier were noticed.

In February, 1852, the commander-in-chief at Monterey was informed by the government of Nuevo Leon that a party of Comanches had killed every inhabitant at Bajan, in Coahuila, and at the same time learned from the authorities at Vallecillo that a party of 200 Americans and Texan Mexicans were preparing an invasion of that municipality under the same leader who had made a similar attempt two months before. The situation presented to the governor and to the commander in Nuevo Leon by such menaces was embarrassing and cruel. Ferocious hordes of savages were desolating the towns, and were abetted by native and adopted citizens of the United States, in whose territory they were openly organized. Notwithstanding, both those authorities attended to the double menace, and in September a party of Indians was totally destroyed at Capulin, where more than 200 animals were recaptured.

During the year 1853, in accordance with the instructions of the supreme government of the republic, the commander in Nuevo Leon extended a protecting hand to the State of Coahuila, in whose capital he placed a garrison, which was immediately employed in the pursuit of the Indians who appeared at San José and at Florida.

Once more the tidings of attacks designed by filibusters

obliged the governor and the commandant of Nuevo Leon, the latter of whom was now at Mier, to act at the same time against two enemies. The forces of Colonel Zuazua, employed exclusively against the savages, were ordered to fall back to the south, so as to protect Salinas, Vallecillo and other towns along that line, while Colonel Caso was, for the same reason, ordered to proceed to Villaldama. Such was the anxiety of the government to stimulate the war with the Indians, that the commandant was ordered to watch closely the movements of the filibusters, and should they desist, as was probable, to send his National Guards into the desert in search of the Indians, which was accordingly done and duly reported to the War Department.

While the permanent forces of the republic attended to the danger from filibusters, other forces were operating against the Indians at Aguanueva, near Saltillo, at Patos and at Santa Rosa, where in two engagements a party of Indians was severely punished after killing several and recapturing much booty.

As to Nuevo Leon, during this year, when the danger from filibusters had ceased, the commandant provided Galeana with arms, and allowed its citizens to carry them, visited the northern frontier of the State at Parras and Vallecillo, sent 70 regulars on an expedition to Huizaches, and finally sent the entire State forces, then first placed under his command by virtue of a revolution, into the desert as far as "Laguna de la Leche," notwithstanding the fact that there had been no recent Indian invasion to repress.

The Seminoles presented themselves this year to the commandant general, soliciting agricultural implements in order to cultivate the lands which had been assigned them, and in the same month the commander at Marin and Colonel Zuazua respectively reported successes achieved against the hostile Indians. All the army officers were indefatigable in their combinations and in the distant expeditions which they undertook, at the slightest word of the Indians having appeared even in the mountain fastnesses. The general government meanwhile did not forget the interests of the peaceful Indians, the

Seminoles, and Mascogos, with whom it had made treaties on the 16th of October, 1850, and the 26th of July, 1852; and now ordered that these agreements be carried into effect. It was also ordered that special defensive armor be prepared both for the infantry and the cavalry employed upon Indian service.

In the course of this same year the commander at Marin repulsed an attack by the Indians in his own district, aided the militia of Apodaca and Mina, and located a flying section of twenty dragoons at "Minas Viejas," to attend to the security of the adjacent district. About this time, the War Department established, at Doctor Arroyo, a fifth cantonment for the better defense of the frontier. The Lipans had been admitted to live in peace at "Mesa de Catujanos," in Coahuila, but were to be watched by a detachment placed near them by the commandant general of Nuevo Leon.

In 1855, Captains Menchaca and Ugartechea received especial instructions to go in pursuit of the savages, wherever they might be found. The former, a native of San Antonio de Bejar, who had been in the Mexican service since 1836, traversed a great part of the desert, as may be seen by the diary of his operations, and expressed the opinion that most of the invasions are made by Texan citizens disguised as Indians. The latter, who took another direction, followed the Indians to the Rio Grande. He simply expressed his opinion that *some* white men disguised as Indians committed frequent robberies of horses, and carried them for sale to the adjoining republic.

Although the frontier was engaged, in 1856, with a vast political question, and was maintaining an army in the interior of the republic, a new force was nevertheless organized in January at the town of Muzquiz, and by order of the commandant general immediately undertook a campaign. Forces were also sent against the remnant of the Lipans, who attacked some shepherds at San Diego, and escaped punishment only by recrossing the Rio Grande. A little before this time a so-called massacre of some Lipans had taken place, an act considered as just and well deserved by the military commander of the frontier. The Tancahue Indians were also pursued on account of their having abandoned their reservation without the knowledge of the authorities. Elsewhere, a body of Comanches was attacked, and six captives, 200 animals, and much booty were recovered from them, as is circumstantially related in the diary of operations kept by the officers in command. There were also movements of troops near Lampazos, Parras, and Mondova Vieja, in pursuit of Comanches. It was also in this year, 1856, that an American Commission, professing to be properly authorized, visited the Mexican frontier and conferred with the authorities concerning the damages which the Lipans were causing on both sides of the river.

The Commission desired to present a compend of all the operations during the time of the *comandancias generales*, in order that it may be seen what the supreme government of the republic was doing through its agents, for the security of the frontier and the maintenance of good relations with the adjoining country. Their action was so constant and efficacious that it became superior to that of the United States, and for five years there was more security against Indian invasions and depredations in Mexico than in the United States. The Commission has also felt bound to examine the conduct, both of the civil and military authorities which have represented Mexico in this great question of Indian invasions, because it was necessary to show that neither the immense extent of the evils nor the notoriety of the fact that they proceeded from the United States, a country bound by treaty to prevent them, ever led to any violation of the territory of that republic.

In continuing the thread of our narrative of Indian depredations upon the northern towns of Nuevo Leon, from 1857 onward, it will be seen that many years and vast efforts were necessary to obtain some respite from those invasions, which at this time began to diminish in number.

Only thirteen towns were attacked, in 1858, in forty invasions; the same towns having been assaulted four or five times by more than 700 Comanches. Thanks to the vigorous resistance and an active pursuit by 1,000 citizens, only 18 persons were killed and four wounded. Of the former, several lost

20

their lives in the eight engagements of this year, which resulted
in recovering more than 200 animals and two captives, besides
killing many Indians. In spite of all this activity, they succeeded in carrying off a large number of horses. In the invasions of this year, mention should be made of the daring
and audacity of the Indians in approaching the suburbs of
Monterey, climbing on foot the steep mountains to the South,
and reappearing at Guadalupe, two leagues away, and that
.the 30 Indians who performed this feat called out in pursuit
nearly 1,000 men who followed them into the mountains without being able to reach them. It was, however, learned that
the greater portion of them perished of hunger and thirst
among the rocks where they found refuge.

Eight towns in the north, and one in the south, beyond
the Sierra Madre, suffered in 1859 the accustomed scourge,
eleven citizens being killed, six wounded, and many children
and horses carried off. The number of the Indians had de-
creased to 300, but several parts of the State were simultaneously attacked. On the the 20th of January, three parties of
Indians entered the district of Lampazos at different points,
and on the 30th, others attacked Galeana, more than 100
leagues distant. This tactics was intended to attract all the
defensive forces to the north, while the invaders of Galeana
might meet with no impediment. In view of these operations,
and of the opinions of intelligent officers, such as Ugartechea
and Menchaca, who had grown gray in Indian warfare, it may
be deemed certain that these Indians were aided, materially or
morally, by citizens of Texas.

In all the year 1860, but one person was killed, four wounded,
and two made captive by the Indians. Although they appeared
four times near Lampazos, and five times at Villagarcia, great
vigilance was displayed both here and at seven other places
where they showed themselves, they being repulsed in five engagements. Their number was about 150, and their booty
insignificant.

In the thirty-one invasions of the year 1861, the loss of
horses was considerable, though not exactly specified in the
reports of the *Alcaldes*. Ten of the northern towns had to

deal with about 400 Comanches, losing eight persons, an insignificant number as compared with previous years. Great dexterity was displayed by the invaders in eluding pursuit, and in placing their booty in safety in their chosen hiding places.

But one person killed and one wounded are recorded for the year 1862. Ten incursions were made against seven of the northern towns, by less than 100 Indians.

In 1863, only 100 Indians appeared, making seventeen incursions, and being pursued by more than 300 citizens, who lost six killed and four wounded, without being able to recover the few stolen horses. Each year since 1861 has shown a decrease in the numbers of the killed, of the invaders, and of the amount of booty. The year 1864 presents but four persons killed and two wounded, and a small number of animals stolen from five of the northern towns. Still less were the losses in 1865. Only eighty Indians were seen in this year, who killed two citizens and wounded several in an engagement, and carried off a few horses from four towns, which were the only ones molested. In 1866 not a single Indian returned.

The Commission will leave for another place the many important considerations suggested by this review of the eighteen years warfare with the Indians in the three frontier States of Nuevo Leon, Tamaulipas, and Coahuila. At present it will confine itself to a fact which has attracted its careful attention.

From the breaking out of the Confederate war in 1861, it began to be noticed that the invasions began to diminish year by year, until they totally ceased in 1866, when that war had also been concluded. The natural order of events would have been that on the withdrawal of the Federal garrisons from the Rio Grande in the former year, the savage hordes would pour through the gap thus left open and devastate the north of Mexico. But the fact was directly the converse of what every one expected, and it needs explanation.

This explanation may be found by first taking cognizance of the prior fact that the American garrisons on the Rio Grande and the Colorado, though presumably established for the defence of both Texans and Mexicans from Indian invasions, were ineffectual for that object, as has been sufficiently seen in the long lists of calamities suffered by both countries, but especially Mexico. Very few cases of recapture of horses from the savages occurred up to 1861. During the same period the invasions were constantly increasing in number and in importance, and they almost ceased with the withdrawal of the Federal troops—a fact attested by all the inhabitants of the frontier. Taken by itself, a participation or a direct influence of the Federal troops in those depredations might naturally be deduced from these premises.

This Commission is very far from drawing such a conclusion. It has already shown that in 1835 an immense trade with the Comanches was established by American speculators, and that this was the origin of the great movement against the Mexican frontier. The testimony of American witnesses, especially that of Gregg, has so confirmed this fact that it has acquired an irresistible force. The later fact of the cessation of the Indian invasions simultaneously with the withrawal of the Federal troops, supplies another proof that the invasions had no other origin than the traffic in question. On the day when the cause disappeared, the depredations ceased, because the motive no longer existed. The withdrawal of the Federal troops removed the occasion of such a criminal traffic.

Two very powerful reasons co-operated for this change so beneficial to Mexico and to humanity. The first was the rupture between the North and the South, which divided the great Republic into two hostile camps, and monopolized the activity of all its citizens, both the men of principle and the speculators, in the service of their respective parties—the former devoting themselves exclusively to the triumph of their own cause, the latter looking after the result of the speculations for which an enormous field was opened. The Indian traders, whether Unionists or Confederates, saw before them this great opportunity, and hastened to utilize it, leaving the Indians without the stimulus which alone had induced them to undertake such dangerous and fatiguing campaigns. The other fact, which contributed in a smaller degree to the change in question, was the mercantile current which sprang up during the confederacy between Texas and Kansas, the latter State becoming a great center of the cattle trade, which could no longer be carried on through the blockaded ports, but became possible in this direction through the rapid extension of railroads. The Indians could no longer be competitors; they did not comprehend the revolution which was taking place against their interests, and they thus became isolated from their former customers. It was thus that mercantile calculations and the new use of capital solved, in a measure, one of the gravest questions which had so long defied the more or less intelligent and energetic action of two governments.

The few years which remain to be examined down to the present time, show a slight increase in the number of incursions until 1869 ; they are reduced to two in 1870, and then completely cease. In 1867, 80 Indians appeared in seven of the northern towns, causing two deaths and carrying off a considerable number of horses. In 1868, four towns were robbed of but few animals by about 200 Indians, who, however, murdered no one. In 1869, the incursions were 25, the deaths nine, the wounded four, and but one captive. The horses carried off were in considerable numbers, and but few were recovered in three engagements. One town only, Lampazos, was attacked in 1870, by two different parties of Indians, one of which killed 30 persons, and both carried off many horses. They were chased by both regulars and militia until they repassed the Rio Grande at different points.

From this examination of the annals of twelve years, from 1857 onward, it appears that there were in Nuevo Leon 105 persons killed, wounded, and carried captive. The warfare was almost insignificant during the six years of American war and reconstruction, and the spoils, though less than in previous years, was beyond all proportion to the number of aggressors.

As has been seen and proved by the tables formed by the Commission from official records, the losses in the entire period embraced by its researches have been enormous in lives, liberty and property, as well as in the destruction of commerce and agriculture. Nevertheless, these official data do not represent the full amount of the losses ; they are but the proofs of their

existence which the authorities of the towns were able to produce at the outset, before the full particulars in each case were
revealed by the result of the pursuit of the invaders, and by
the recounting of the remaining stock. The object of the
earliest official reports having been simply to give notice of
the incursions, so as to enable the government to take speedy
measures for their repression, it was a secondary consideration
to give the losses, which were barely mentioned, as a proof of
the appearance of the savages.

In such moments, the citizens of all the towns thought only
of meeting the danger, and in view of the trouble and delay
incident to making out full proofs, they did not take care to
place them in the archives. Notwithstanding this, the losses
have been so great that in going over the records the chief con-
tents are found to be the daily reports sent to the authorities
of the various phases of Indian robberies and murders.

The inhabitants of the frontier being obliged, in the way of
business, to make long journeys to Chihuahua, Sonora, Durango, and Texas, it oftened happened that they were attacked
by large parties of Indians, lost their property, and left their
companions buried in the deserts, far away from their homes.
None of these numerous disasters are recorded in the archives,
but the testimony of witnesses and of captives has thrown light
on this other source of enormous losses of life and property.
Such evidence from ocular witnesses is very interesting in
details, reliable in point of facts, and important for the understanding of many official reports, whose authors have amplified
and illustrated them by personally appearing before the Commission.

In the towns of Nuevo Leon visited by the Commission,
forty-two witnesses have been examined, ten of whom have
been captives. From their statements have been learned the
dates of many incursions, the tribes which made them, the
amount of damages, the persons who chiefly suffered them, and
the steps taken by the towns for the recovery of their property.
These witnesses have been persons of the best standing in their
respective places of residence. Many of them have been persons of capital, who have held office, especially in the organiza-

tion of the National Guards for Indian campaigns, and they have thus been able, in many cases, to fill up the blanks as to losses and sufferers, so frequent in the public records.

These witnesses being from seventeen different towns, they have shown, according to their geographical distribution, the gradual advance of the invasions southward. They have proved that the depredations did not begin until after 1836 to pass through the line of the towns which, like Lampazos and Salinos, are close to the military colonies. No one of these witnesses has failed to give a particular account of the atrocities perpetrated by the Indians, as personally seen, or learned on good authority. The truth of the official reports has thus been ascertained and corroborated; and while the interested parties have brought witnesses to prove their losses, the new testimony has generally been confirmed by the less specific evidence of the archives.

It has been a remarkable fact noticed in this investigation, that the greater part of the Indian outrages which occurred in any one State have found proof in towns of other States. Thus, for example, reports made in 1852 by an officer at Lampazos, who participated in the engagement between the citizens of Guerrero and the Indians at "La Oracion," has placed beyond a doubt the truth of the statements made by the citizen Benavides Hinojosa, and the captive Sabas Rodriguez.

The incursion of Indians upon Laredo, Texas, in 1869, as described by citizens of Nuevo Laredo, who united with the Texans in pursuing the marauders as far as the boundary of Nuevo Leon, has been fully corroborated in all particulars by the statements of General Naranjo, of the citizen Manuel Rodriguez, and the official reports. The same conformity exists between multitudes of the *expedientes* drawn up in different States, and some of them have been confirmed by evidence obtained from Texas.

Citizens of San Francisco (Nuevo Leon) testified before the Commission when it began its labors at Salinas Victoria, that in 1860 they drove their stock to Texas for sale, because they had become convinced that they could not profitably carry on stock raising in Mexico, on account of insecurity and the impossibility of hiring herdsmen at any price; that having penetrated into the interior of Texas on account of the war then breaking out, they found they could not dispose of their stock, and therefore resolved to stay there; that they suffered great losses from an invasion by Comanches, who had taken several captives on both sides of the river Nueces, and at this time carried off a boy who was the son of one of the Mexican herdsmen.

At the same time, General Quiroga made a similar statement about Indians whom he had fought when living on a ranch in Texas, near Laredo, mentioning an occasion when a party of eighty Indians attacked some wagons with families traveling from Laredo to San Antonio, whom he with five of his herdsmen rescued by a stratagem, but were unable to deliver a captive woman previously taken by them.

These witnesses could not know, when they made their statements, that the said captives would soon after confirm what they said. Two months later, when the Commission was approaching the Rio Grande, all those captives arrived from Fort Sill, where they had been ransomed from the Comanches and Kiowas, who had committed the depredations referred to on the Rio Nueces, whence they had been carried captive. This incident, properly belonging to the section relating to Texas, is here narrated to show the character of the witnesses examined by the Commission, and illustrate by this instance the truthfulness of others not less competent and intelligent, and who deserve equal credit.

It has been stated that ten captives have given testimony. These are to be divided into three classes; some were taken before Mexico became independent, others in the period about 1848, and still others in recent times. On each of these periods they furnish interesting information, which must be considered in order to understand many points which would otherwise have remained obscure.

It has been thought important to know the routes followed by the Comanches, Lipans and Mescaleros in Mexico and the United States, as well as their relations to each other; and on this subject only the captives could afford light. Ventura Garza states, that he was captured in 1858, at Bustamante, by the Mescaleros, who in this incursion killed 20 men and carried off 150 mules. Their retreat was made crossing the river near Laredo into Texas, and following up the Rio Grande to Paso del Norte. They again crossed the river near that town, and at Sierra Rica, in the State of Chihuahua, met with the rest of their band, composed of Mescaleros, Lipans and Gileños, then at war on both sides the Rio Grande. Their system was to depredate only in the United States when they lived in Mexico, and *vice versa*, which did not prevent them from marauding in either republic at a sufficiently remote distance from their headquarters. By this deceit they kept their haunts unknown and kept clear of pursuit on both sides. They would suddenly go to New Mexico, says the captive, treat for peace, open trade, exchanging their Mexican booty for arms, and afterward, probably in 1861, broke their engagements, committing horrible atrocities and spoliations. This witness was ransomed in 1865 at Paso del Norte.

By this narrative, it is plainly to be seen that the treachery of the Indians has either not been understood, or it has been tolerated in order to gain temporary advantages which, in the long run, cost dear.

The Comanches carried off another captive from Villaldama in 1851. His testimony is useful only for the enumeration of the murders and robberies which they committed during the few days he was with them, for the proof of the tribe to which they belonged, and for the confirmation of the fact that they used to encamp on the tops of mountains to go down and rob in the valleys. On comparing the statement of this captive with documents from the archives of the State Government, it is found that, on the 31st of March of that year, the alcalde reported the murder of two persons and the captivity of two others, and a drove of horses. This illustrates the light thrown upon official reports by testimony such as this.

Another captive states that Comanches carried him off from Potrero, after killing his companion Dominguez; that a little way off they killed another man, and two more before reaching Baján, from which place they came. The Indians were only four in number, and in a few days they had collected a considerable booty, with which they got away to the North, passing near Monclova. This witness confirms other statements as to the passes by which the savages crossed the Rio Grande.

In a foray of the Comanches upon Sabinas, in 1848, they carried off a boy who remained among them three years, and was then sold to the Lipans. From the latter he was ransomed by the Americans, along with other Mexican captives, at the trading place for the sale of their horses in Texas. The Comanches and Lipans were then at peace with each other, committed their depredations together, and traded in the United States their booty. Official documents prove that at this time the Lipans were waging an atrocious warfare in Mexico, as proved by reports found in the army headquarters at Monterey. The captives above mentioned were from Durango, Coahuila and Nuevo Leon, which fact shows the extent of territory over which they marauded.

Cornelio Sanchez was taken captive in 1839. He was taken across the Rio Grande above San Fernando; was at San Saba, where there were then some Comanche huts; visited the Lipans who were on good terms with them, and during eight years that he lived among the Indians saw the dealings between the Comanches and other tribes, the latter of whom traded with the Americans. Just at the time when this captive escaped from Santa Rosa, the last-mentioned witness was captured at Sabinas. Their evidence agrees in depicting a good understanding between Comanches and Lipans, and also as to the location of their several villages or encampments.

The frontier town of Lampazos—the same where a colonial company was founded at the close of the last century—experienced, in 1820, an incursion of more than 200 Comanches, who captured nearly fifty children, two of whom escaped, some years later, from their detention near the Rio Colorado; one of them belonged to a prominent family at Lampazos, and still holds a high social position there. He says that during the six years of his captivity he was constantly a witness of traffic

existing between these Indians and the Americans, as well as
the New Mexicans; that the Lipans lived in harmony with the
Comanches; that although they sometimes quarreled on matters relating to elk hunting, this only resulted in separation,
and never in hostilities, which they only had with the
"Washas," a tribe living farther north; that he became acquainted with the Kiowas, Yamparicas and Sarigtecas, who
belong to the same group as the Comanches, and who also, together or apart, used to make forays upon Mexico; that he
saw the Tuj-ka-nayes, agricultural Indians who lived as permanent settlers at points on the same river, and that he became
acquainted with the Lipans, Mescaleros and Gileños, who
were known by the common name of Apaches. He mentions
the Tahuacanos, and says that all these tribes lived and dressed
nearly alike, and that the chief difference observed between
the two great families of Comanches and Apaches was in the
arrows—those of the former being shorter and better made;
that the Comanches may also be known from the Apaches by
their wearing the hair in three braids, while the latter form
only one tress, or cut it even with the shoulder. He was aided
to escape to New Mexico by a native of Santa Fé; returned
home in 1826, enlisted as a soldier in the colonial companies in
1828, and served in the detachments stationed at "Las Moras,"
under the orders of Captain Santiago Lopez. He states that
the frontier enjoyed peace from 1829 to 1836, through the
active pursuit of the Indians every time that they approached
the line of garrisons; that he has often fought against the
Indians, who have almost always been Comanches, and that he
estimates the losses caused by them to have been very great.

On a comparison of the statements of this captive and of
another who was his companion, with the descriptions given by
Mr. Gregg in his work so often quoted, there is found to be an
absolute agreement in the two accounts of manners and customs, and a certain knowledge is obtained of the places where
they lived, of the beginning and progress of their incursions,
and of their traffic, since we learn from the work in question
that certain American adventurers penetrated for the first time
into those immense prairies in the year 1821.

However this may be, these captives clearly prove that the marauders upon the right bank of the Rio Grande have always been Comanches and Lipans; that previous to 1848, these two tribes lived only to the North of that river; that they have maintained a traffic in Mexican booty, chiefly with Americans, but sometimes with Indians of the reservations, obtaining by barter arms and ammunition, and that this trade has been since 1836 the most effective stimulus for their work of pillage and devastation.

The towns of Nuevo Leon have lost much more than 1,000 souls in killed, wounded and captives, since the official documents alone mention 935. If the damage to life, health and liberty, be estimated at the inadequate sum of $10,000 for each individual, it would therefore amount to ten millions of dollars. Nevertheless the people of Nuevo Leon do not claim so great a sum, and the moderation and equity displayed by the sufferers needs no clearer proof.

During twenty-two years of continual assaults, the towns of Nuevo Leon have been devastated by the savages eighty-nine times, as may be seen by the tables accompanying this report. In each of these incursions the damages may be calculated at $5,000, and in the majority of the cases the documents of the archives show that they were greater. Upon this insufficient basis, the loss would amount to $4,045,000.* The losses stated in the town records as examined by the Commission, are evidently but a small part of the real loss. Such as they are, the amounts stated have been proved by the sufferers in legal form, and with unimpeachable evidence. Indeed, the reflections lately made in this report would suffice to establish their truth, even if they were only affidavits of the interested parties.

In the section devoted to the State of Tamaulipas, sufficient reasons have been given for the amount of interest charged on the sums representing losses, and it is unnecessary here to insist upon the extreme justice and equity of that calculation.

In closing this examination into losses, another important element should not be overlooked, which should naturally in-

---

* Later documents increase this sum.

crease the amount, but for which no estimate has been made. It is well known that when a town was invaded, the citizens took up arms and started at once, at their own expense, in pursuit. It is evident that in many cases this abandonment of their ordinary avocations must have occasioned irreparable losses, but none of them have ever calculated even the value of their time while thus employed.

To understand the consequences of this omission, and to appreciate the moderation displayed in this matter, it will be enough to state that for 22 years the forays average three per month, and in their repression more than 12,000 citizens have been engaged, not counting the forces employed by the Supreme Government. The services of these citizens would amount to nearly a million and a half, calculating only for the third part of each year. These services have been compensated in part by small amounts of money, exemption from taxes, and distribution of the booty recaptured. The State of Nuevo Leon has suffered a real and positive loss of more than three millions of dollars, not a cent of which has been entered in the Commission's register of damages.

It was necessary to make these explanations, for only in this way can a complete idea be formed of the situation of the frontier towns, whose fate has been for more than a century to struggle with savages, especially during the last fifty years, since our savages first came into contact with those of the United States. Could Mexico ever have foreseen this result, when she ought rather to have expected that the influence of the sister and friendly republic upon the savage would be a well-spring of blessings for both countries?

The trade which was begun in 1821, which was carried on with greater activity ten years later, originated mutual necessities in that quarter, and should have brought about an intimate connection between buyer and seller, for such is the nature of commerce. Yet it was not the United States, not the republic which carried it on, but only a small number of its citizens; and in this case the observation of a profound writer is verified, that the spirit of trade separates private individuals, and produces a different result from that which ensues from inter-

national commerce. The relations of individuals in the United
States with others of Mexico have proved the truth of this remark, for those relations were followed by a war of extermination, because they were not based upon the general interests of
the two countries. The removal of Indian tribes of the United
States to the southwest (contrary to the desires of a government which regarded them with favor, but according to De
Tocqueville was impotent to protect them), rendered the condition of affairs worse, and prognosticated evil results for
Mexico.

INDIAN DEPREDATIONS IN COAHUILA.

Coahuila was originally united with Texas, forming a single
province, under the name of "New Philippines," the principal
colonists having come from those islands. Its immense territory, bounded on the east by the Gulf of Mexico and Louisiana,
and on the west by Durango or Nueva Viscaya, stretched to
the north beyond lat. 37°. Its features were mountainous to
the south, while immense sea-like prairies in the north afforded
sustenance to vast numbers of cattle and horses, which multiplied from the animals abandoned there by their owners in
consequence of Indian invasions.

When the Spaniards were extending their discoveries northwards, their most advanced posts in this direction were Saltillo
and Chihuahua. These conquests were suspended in 1670, on
account of the immense numbers of Indians, some of them
original inhabitants of this region, others driven hither by the
progress of the conquest in other parts.

As there were no insuperable obstacles for the iron-framed
men of that age, and their spirit of enterprise carried everything before it, a century did not pass before these Indians
were subdued and forced to live in villages, while the refractory
had to retire northwards to a great distance from the settlements.

Most of the existing villages in Coahuila were thus established. The wise policy of the conquerors overcame the resist-

ance of the natives, and the indigenous element became the basis of their power in all the provinces which formed New Spain. The butcheries and other cruelties of which the Spaniards have been accused have thus had their compensation.

In 1688 Candela was already settled, and one of the missionaries located there was informed by Indians from beyond the Rio Grande that settlements were being made on the Gulf of Mexico by white men who were not Spaniards. This news was sent to Mexico, and resulted in the exploration and conquest of Texas, a very easy task, according to the chroniclers, on account of the mild character of the Indian natives. San Antonio de Béjar was the capital of the province. Up to the year 1719 there were more or less disturbances in dealing with the resident Indians and in keeping off hostile tribes. At that date the Marquis of Aguayo, Don José de Valdivieso, carried there troops and more missionaries, and order was restored. New colonists from the Canary Islands added to the security of those settlements, and Spain advanced her boundaries to the river Empalizada, afterwards called Red River, which became the boundary with Louisiana. Military colonies and outposts were placed along the immense line of defense, and a general tranquility proved that the Marquis of Aguayo had accomplished his object.

The characteristics of the ensuing wars of conquest have been given in the sections on Nuevo Leon and Tamaulipas, and there is no occasion to add anything here. The position of the province called Coahuila-and-Texas, being the farthest advanced, engaged it more deeply than its neighbors in such struggles, in which it was always triumphant, because security was fully established on the right bank of the Rio Grande.

The year 1836 came and this situation was completely changed. The savages on both sides of the Rio Grande ravaged all the plains, enjoying impunity through their numbers. The accumulated riches in cattle was too great to be carried off in a single incursion, and there was so much in the districts nearest to the military posts, that they more than sufficed for the earliest incursions, which did not therefore extend beyond Monclova, Lampazos, and Guerrero until the year 1840. In this year the marauding hordes fell upon the three frontier States at once. One column penetrated by Santa Rosa, taking the high road, which it lined with corpses, encamped near San Buenaventura, and again in a stronghold near Saltillo, defeating the militia of both towns, and continued their progress into the State of San Luis Potosi, robbing and murdering at every step. They passed through Agua Nueva, Ventura, San Salvador, Salado, and many other places, as far as Morterillos, fifteen leagues from the city of San Luis, all which towns suffered enormous losses, and some of their families still mourn their members carried into captivity.

At the same time another horde penetrated through the center of the State, encamped near Bustamante, in Nuevo Leon, killing or wounding more than 100 persons, passed on to the important and wealthy town of Salinas Victoria, defeated the regular troops and militia combined, and, carrying off an immense booty, effected on their retreat a junction with the other column which was carrying away the rich plunder of San Luis. A third column at the same time visited Ciudad Guerrero, in Tamaulipas, causing horrible destruction. This was the first time that these barbarians presented the order and aspect of an army.

The towns above mentioned having been surprised when they had no reason to expect such a daring attack, the great losses suffered were inevitable. For the chastisement of such audacity, hurried orders were sent to the detached parties of the colonial companies to assemble and cut off the retreat of the savages. These veterans, well acquainted with the country and with the habits of Indian warfare, correctly calculated from the data given them, the line of march and the movements of the Indians, whom they surprised in turn at El Pozo, eight leagues west of San Fernando de Aguaverde. They completely routed the savages, recovering all the horses and freeing the captives, except a few who fled along with the Indians, through fear of their intending liberators, of whom they had heard unfavorable reports. The armed citizens of the entire frontier co-operated in this notable feat of arms. The third section of invaders was meanwhile pursued by the assembled citizens of Guerrero, Mier, and Camargo, and was routed with great loss.

As has been mentioned elsewhere, the order of march, the formation of the encampments, and the tactics in battle observed by the Indians in this colossal campaign were entirely novel, and far too scientific in their strategy to make it credible that Comanches, Lipans, and Mescaleros were the devisers of such combinations. From that time it was generally believed that some Texan-Americans, hostile to Mexico, were mixed up with them, their object being to keep off the war with which that insurgent State was then threatened. Even if this were not the case, another cause for this Indian campaign may be found in the fact that on the American frontier these savages were stimulated by army officers, and were brought into contact with Osages, Kaws, Delawares, Shawnees, and other Indians of the reservations, with whom they traded, and who perhaps accompanied them in their incursions. It was beyond doubt that American citizens from that region, and officers at the forts on the Arkansas river, were the directors of this incursion.

The corruption of these officers, and of the speculators who went from village to village on the reservations, looking out occasions to cheat the Indians, had an important bearing upon the incursions on our frontier. The Indians experienced a sudden change, which does not admit of any other explanation than the removal of the civilized American tribes to the southwest and the employment of immoral agents who betrayed their trust and brought about the ruin of a great part of Mexico. It is to be noted that such proceedings were made known to the American Government, but no remedy was applied.

From this negligence in superintending the Indians of the reservations, and from the corruption of the agents employed in dealing with them, sprung the great organized invasions of Mexico by Indian tribes. There is no other rational explanation, nor can any be found, especially if attention be given to the gradual development of their mode of warfare.

At the outset, only the outposts were attacked. After the war had become an object of speculation, from 1836 onward,

21

the first elements of an organization became perceptible, the Indians having now a well-defined object, *i. e.*, to get as much booty as possible. They had formerly destroyed great numbers of animals, carrying off but few ; they now took pains to collect and carry off as many as possible. On perceiving that the system of invading in large bodies did not work well, they abandoned it, and fixed their encampments near San Saba and on the river Pecos, making those places their headquarters for their expeditions ; this change was the result of the severe chastisement they had received. From about 1848, they began to send out guerrilla parties separately from their encampments in Texas.

The ravages suffered by Coahuila, which presents an immense frontier extending for 100 leagues along the Rio Grande, have been innumerable, for the invaders could cross at any point. Many incursions have come from the North, crossing the river above or below the ancient " Presidio de San Carlos," and passing through the " Bolson de Mapimi," to attack the southern settlements of Cuatro Cienegas, Párras, Viesca and Laguna.

Depopulation, poverty and ruin have been the natural consequences of so many irruptions, and this is the present condition of a State which is one of the most important of the republic in extent, fertility of soil and salubrity of climate. It was once very wealthy in cattle, but its flocks and herds have disappeared on account of this warfare. During many years the sons of Coahuila have fought the Indians merely to defend their own existence, since their cattle no longer afforded a temptation to the enemy, who nevertheless had to cross the State on his route to the more wealthy estates of San Luis and the south of Nuevo Leon. The wayfarers and the country residents were exposed to destruction on these excursions of wide range, and it was necessary to live always with arms in the hand, although there was no more property to secure or defend.

The narrative of the invasions experienced in Coahuila will confirm the above statement, and will excite wonder, for it will seem impossible that towns which have experienced such great and long-continued sufferings could have been kept together.

The Mexican territory had not been fully evacuated after the peace, of which the principal condition had been the repression of the savage tribes and indemnification for their depredations when not checked, ere the towns of Coahuila were attacked. During the months of August, September and October, 1848, three bands of Indians ravaged several towns, and led to an expenditure of more than $3,000 from the public coffers for repelling them. The State government, foreseeing an irruption of Comanches and other Northern tribes as the consequence of the war which the United States has agreed to make upon them, employed all its funds in equipping troops for the contingency. The proofs found in the archives of that government show that during the year 1849, over $24,000 was spent for that purpose.

The Indians, meanwhile, continued their usual incursions, which numbered this year eleven, the invaders being estimated at 800. Having perceived that they could no longer be pursued across the river, they established their villages nearer to its left bank, as headquarters for perpetrating their devastations with impunity. Thanks to the activity of the State forces and the colonies, their murders were, however, less numerous than on some former occasions. The loss amounted to 22 persons killed, wounded and taken captive, and several hundred horses stolen.

In 1850, the Comanches, Mescaleros and Lipans, sometimes in union, and sometimes separately, marauded over the whole vast area of Coahuila, ravaging the greater part of the ranchos and *haciendas*, and even attacking the town of Santa Rosa, which only escaped being occupied by them through the timely warning given by a recently escaped captive. More than 600 savages were engaged in skirmishes with the militia of Santa Rosa, Morelos and Guerrero, at the same time that others were marauding at Palomas, a hundred leagues to the south, and at Viesca, a hundred leagues to the west.

In the 36 places which they attacked this year, they killed 28 persons, wounded 14, and captured the same number. Five battles resulted in liberating half the captives and a part of the horses stolen. About 1,000 men were employed in the campaign, at an expense on the part of the government of Coahuila of $3,824.

The citizens of Santa Rosa, in connection with the colonies of Monclova Viejo and San Vicente, undertook a campaign during the closing days of the year, and in January, 1850, ten scalps had been taken from the Indians, and eight more were killed, but carried away by their comrades. The citizens of Cuatro Cienegas made an expedition to Lake Jaco, in quest of a party of Indians supposed to be encamped there. The statements of a captive, who escaped from a band of Gileños, after an engagement at Rosita, furnished evidence that the Indians had already carried their stolen horses across the Rio Grande.

The general government, in its solicitude for the welfare of the frontiersman, ordered that the widows and orphans of the killed in the battle just named should receive the 'pensions fixed by law. Permanent sections of troops were stationed at Saltillo and Párras, whose citizens cooperated in defense, so that their vigilance extended throughout the north, south and west of the State, while the eastern line was protected by the detachments of national troops placed at Lampazos, Mina and Mamulique.

When in the month of June the savages invaded the district of Párras, causing immense losses over a hundred leagues of territory to the northward, the authorities at Guerrero wrote to the government on the 14th of June : "These misfortunes occurred on the 12th instant; on the following day this corporation sent out a party of 15 men, which returned to-day, after having pursued the savages until they recrossed the Rio Grande." From the western extremity of the State, the authorities of Cienegas thus described the situation in the same month : "We do not know to-day which way to pursue the savages, for they are seen in every direction, and traces of them are seen even in the suburbs of this place."

Communication between the frontier and Zacatecas and San Luis having been cut off by Indians on the high roads, the government of Coahuila informed the National Government of the fact, requesting that 100 men from the colonies might be sent to protect the roads. The war department, unwilling to call off troops from the frontier, refused the request, but authorized the equipment of 150 more men at the cost of the federal treasury. The governor immediately raised such a force from among the most experienced Indian fighters. During this whole year the State Government was untiring in its organization of elements of defense, especially for the district of Párras, where hostilities were of daily recurrence.

The picture presented by the year 1851 is frightful. Coahuila suffered 94 incursions, which occasioned a loss of 63 persons killed, 35 wounded, 11 captives, and an immense number of horses plundered from almost every rancho, hacienda and settlement in the State, which was literally inundated by more than 3,000 Comanches and Lipans. The number specified in the reports alone was over 1,000, while in 41 reports they were not numerically estimated otherwise than by speaking of a "large" or a "considerable" body.

More than 2,500 soldiers were constantly occupied throughout the year, for not a week passed without an appearance of the enemy in some quarter. The engagements numbered 16, a large number when it is remembered that the Indians avoid fighting and prefer to murder defenseless victims. The efforts of the soldiers and citizens effected the delivery of three captives, the killing of 11 Comanches, and the recapture of 400 animals. In order to fully understand the desperate nature of the situation, it will only be necessary to peruse a few extracts from the reports written under the impressions of the moment by civil and military authorities.

The towns of the Rio Grande district, situated in front of Fort Duncan, suffered 14 invasions, and concerning one of them the mayor of Guerrero wrote on the 7th of February in the following terms:

"At this moment (3 P. M.) the citizens whom I sent in pursuit of the Indians have returned, and they inform me that the savages have been engaged for two nights in driving across the river the horses stolen from this vicinity, being probably occupied during the daytime in ranging along the hills across the Rio Grande, watching where the horses were kept on this side, so as to come for them by night.   The citizens did not cross the river in pursuit, because they had no orders to do so. This new system of strategy affords very little hope of our being able to preserve the very few animals left to us, and when they are all gone the invaders will no longer have to fear the pursuit which they have hitherto experienced from us."

The combined efforts made by the authorities to restrain the overflowing torrent of invasion were proportionate to the gravity of the evil.   The governor wrote to the governors of Durango, Chihuahua, and Zacatecas to inform them that the frequent onsets of the savages had forced him, notwithstanding the small amount of his resources, to project a campaign in combination with the sub-inspector of colonies, and those governors were requested to take appropriate measures.   The legislature of Coahuila imposed extraordinary taxes for the same purpose, and commissioned one of its members to attend to the organization of the State's defense in this disastrous war. The sub-inspector of colonies gave instructions to Colonel Galan, which it is proper to quote in part, as showing that the origin of the depredations was then as it is now, and always has been, on the left, or American side of the Rio Grande.

After naming the points called San Vicente, Noche Buena, Jaco, San Antonio de los Alamos, Bolson de Mapimi, and Laguna de Tahualilo, as localities to be visited, forming a complete circle of 400 leagues from the starting point at Piedras Negras, the sub-inspector gave the following direction :

" On the route above designated there are some places which need to be carefully explored.   The first of these is the bank of the Rio Grande from the mouth of Pecos river to the ford of Ahogados, near which last point *the Indians who devastate this department generally cross the river, having their villages near by on the opposite bank.*"

It was also ordered, in pursuance of instructions from the War Department, to make no peace with the Comanches, Apaches, Mescaleros, and other tribes which lead a wandering life on the American territory, exclusively occupied in hunting and in warfare.

The campaign was organized, consisting of troops from the colonies, along with some Seminole and Kickapoo Indians, who had recently arrived in the country. The latter abandoned the expedition during its return march, in order to attend to their families, which had been left unprotected. The party was engaged for two months in traversing the desert, and twice gave battle to the savages. The commander, in his report, dated August 4th, said:

" I continued my march up the Rio Grande, and Sergeant Candido Guerra had another engagement on the river with the savages, who were returning with their plunder to their villages *situated across the river.* He succeeded in recovering a boy who was captured from the hacienda of Hermanas. I then detached an officer to pursue the fugitives to the Rio Grande. On his return he stated that he had traced the trail of the enemy, numbering 87, across the river, and that when once on the other side they moved slowly, knowing that the Mexicans were not allowed to pursue them on that side."

The experienced officer, Colonel Juan Galan, who made this report, added some highly important information, as follows:

" I continued my march the next day (July 4th, 1851) up the river, and, examining as many places as possible, I found on the left side several trails along which the savages had lately passed in small parties, with their booty from our frontier. I was satisfied that for more than a year no savages have lived on this side the river between the colonies and the junction of the Sierra, and that they have their villages not far from the latter point on the river Pecos."

In the careful examination which was then made of the canyons of the Sierra del Carmen, it was ascertained with equal certainty that the savages no longer inhabited those mountains as formerly. The deserts of Chihuahua were also explored, and there were found, near San Vicente, the trails of savages conducting the spoils of the interior States across the Rio Grande to their villages.

All efforts for the due chastisement of the savages having proved futile, on account of their residence being in American territory, and the evil being beyond remedy so long as this situation should last, the sub-inspector was careful to so inform the commandant-general, which he did in connection with submitting the report of Colonel Galan, in the following terms:

"By the testimony of Col. Galan, in confirmation of the documents I sent you on July 27th and the 3d instant, it is shown that the savages set out on their campaigns against us from the head waters of the rivers Colorado and Nueces, from the junction of the Pecos with the Rio Grande, and other points in Texas where they live; *that our spoils and captives are sold to speculators and traders* who live among them, increasing their brutal covetousness, and making this warfare interminable; that therefore Mexico cannot expect the protection offered her by the treaty of Guadalupe Hidalgo, and must take measures of her own to secure such protection."

Colonel Maldonado, the sub-inspector of the eastern colonies, did not confine his attention to the reports of his subordinate when he affirmed that the Indians resided exclusively in the United States, but referred to other proofs already forwarded, which showed, as he said, that *our spoils and captives were objects of traffic in the United States,* in spite of treaties, and that the war had become interminable in consequence of the stimulus given it by that criminal traffic.

All the governors of the frontier States responded to the cry of alarm raised on the banks of the Rio Grande, not so much on account of the non-fulfillment of a treaty as on account of the protection given to their enemies in Texas and other parts of the United States, and the alliance made with them for the plunder and annihilation of Mexico. The States of San Luis, Zacatecas, Durango, Chihuahua, Coahuila, Nuevo Leon and Tamaulipas formed a coalition, and prepared for the conflict by uniting their troops and their resources.

From every side outcries were made against so flagrant a violation of treaties and of natural law. The official gazette of Durango copied, this year, the text of the 11th article of the Treaty of Guadalupe, and narrated the fruitless efforts of the Mexican Minister, Señor La Rosa, to obtain from the Government at Washington its fulfillment, which subject was brought before a committee of the American Senate. The writer exclaimed, in conclusion: "That government which is the readiest to raise an outcry when any breach of treaty is committed by other nations, is itself scandalously and unscrupulously breaking the faith which it pledged in the name of God Almighty!"

It was despair which burst forth in this cry and this invocation. From this time it was currently said that since the United States had no settlements along the 750 leagues of its frontier from the mouth of the Rio Grande to the Pacific, it took no care to fulfill its agreements, and that it overlooked them because the sufferers were Mexicans. From that time the writers at Durango, guided by the soundest principles of natural law, maintained that nothing could be more just and reasonable than the demand made by the Mexican Government upon that of the United States, on account of those depredations, even apart from the treaty of Guadalupe Hidalgo.

The Government of Coahuila, in inviting that of San Luis to unite its forces and resources for an effort to restrain the invasions, stated the necessity of maintaining troops in the Bolson of Mapimi and other points, to prevent the savages from maintaining there their places of deposit for booty and centers of operations during their inroads. The situation imperiously demanded such a concert of action, and the governor added: "This, in my opinion, is what is most urgent to be done, until the Supreme Government can properly defend the frontier, and the United States carry out the obligation it contracted to restrain the incursions of the Indians." No one failed to see that the evil could not be remedied without the intervention of that republic as being the source whence it proceeded and was fomented.

Not a single day passed without some confirmation being given of the neglect imputed to the United States, and even the most simple minded fully understood the bearings of the situation, and depicted it as perfectly as words can express it.

The chairman of the common council of Guerrero, on the 8th of October, 1851, after enumerating the murders and robberies of the day before, employed the following language in a dispatch to the government:

" This continual recurrence of murders and robberies, for

which no remedy can be found, is a sad omen, and the more so since we are prohibited from taking effective action for driving away the marauders from our homes, through fear of the United States. That country offered in the treaty of Guadalupe to restrain such inroads, whereas its own territory now affords a secure refuge for the marauders. In this afflicting situation, where can we find a remedy for the sufferings which overwhelm us? Our only resource is to send our complaints to your government, and to inquire whether the governor will kindly allow us to pursue the savages (into American territory) so as to punish them and drive them from their headquarters; and if this cannot be done, although according to natural law it would seem proper and urgently necessary to do it under the circumstances, I would request him to authorize me to solicit from the American commander near Piedras Negras the fulfillment of the 11th article of the said treaty of Guadalupe, sending a force to the residence of our Indian enemies to punish them and return us our property."

The sub-inspector of the colonies had written the day previous in a similar strain, relating his recent observations. He stated that having pursued the Indians until they crossed the river, the citizens who accompanied him were exasperated at seeing the enemy leisurely halting on the other side, and proposed to go over and punish them, which he had some difficulty in preventing, by adding persuasion to command.

This honored commander, who carried to such an extreme the strict fulfillment of the orders of his government, was obliged to place infantry every night to guard the fords of the river. All this took place at only ten leagues from Fort Duncan, the commander of which took no notice of these occurrences and employed no measures for repressing the Indians. It was a settled policy to permit them to do as they pleased, so long as they did not injure American citizens. The sub-inspector had perceived this from the time of the revolt of the Kickapoos, which had occurred a few months before, when, as will be seen in the proper place, the requests made to the American commander produced no result.

The culpable negligence of the American government was proved by daily observation on the frontier. The governors of Coahuila and Nuevo Leon therefore addressed separate notes to the minister of foreign affairs, requesting him to arrange with the government at Washington for the Mexican troops to be allowed to cross the river in pursuit of the retreating marauders, or for that government to place on the frontier sufficient forces to prevent their incursions in the name of common humanity.

These petitions and demands from the frontier States show clearly that at the close of the year 1851 all the incursions came from the United States, that the booty was carried thither, and that the American government had not properly garrisoned the border. The State authorities did all in their power to promote a mutual understanding between the two nations, while the national government, in the belief that such understanding existed, had taken its measures to deal with the fugitive tribes, which it was supposed would be driven into Mexico by pursuit on the part of the Americans. Never was there a more costly deception, nor one less merited from the responsible party.

To fill the measure of the woes of the Mexican frontier, there was only lacking a menace of filibusters. The colonel commanding at Fort Duncan, on the 3d of November, 1851, came over to Piedras Negras to advise the inspector of the western colonies that he had learned by express of the approach from the direction of Béjar of a group of adventurers intending to deprecate on the frontier, and that Adams, the negro hunter, was at Leona with seventeen men. All that he offered to do in the premises was to prevent them from crossing the river at the places where he had any forces stationed, and the terms of this offer showed that the action of the Federal authorities did not extend to the disarming of the bandits. The State authorities of Texas acted in the same manner.

Under such circumstances, the warning could not be considered as any service. Its only effect was to draw off from the Indian war all available forces, and place them in readiness to meet the new perils which it will be remembered menaced Tamaulipas and Nuevo Leon at this time, producing the same result. In fact, both savage and civilized enemies only did the same work, and that work was the ruin of the Mexican frontier.

After the heartrending picture of murders and desolation which characterized the year 1851, it could not have been anticipated that any greater misery was in store for the ensuing year. Yet such was the case. During the year 1852, more than 2,000 Indians appeared 110 times in the towns and ranchos of the State, causing a loss of 73 persons killed, 48 wounded and 32 captives. The effective loss was five per cent. of the whole population, which was then less than 70,000 souls. Property was almost extinguished, all industry was destroyed or paralyzed. It will now be understood why the governor of Nuevo Leon, in his message to the legislature, said that although the misfortunes of the State had been frightful, they had been less than those suffered by other frontier States.

This Commission is not in the habit of making calculations, but of simply presenting official data. In the present instance, however, it will venture, in consideration of the perfectly evident deficiencies of the official reports in giving account of losses of life and property, to double the official statement of killed, wounded and captives for the year in question. The result shows an amount of destruction greater than that caused by the most dreaded scourge of mankind, the cholera.

In sixteen engagements with the savages, three captives were recovered and a small number of horses. Besides the constant assaults of the accustomed foe, the filibusters also kept the border in continual alarm.

In 1853, all four of the districts of Coahuila were overrun by great numbers of Comanches, who killed 28 persons, wounded 24 and carried captive six children. In seven engagements, although a few horses were recovered, none of the captives were freed.

During the ten years, from 1854 to 1864, the inroads of the savages were incessant, and none of the inhabited points in Coahuila escaped the consequences. During this period, according to official data, there were 124 persons killed, 43 wounded and 20 carried captive. In the numerous engagements twelve of the captives were recovered, and more than 800 animals. There were occasions when the same town was simultaneously approached from three or four different directions. The farmers were obliged to grasp with one hand the plow and with the other the rifle, and they were not unfrequently laid dead in the furrow. Wagon trains were abandoned on the high road after the murder of the wagoners and seizure of the mules. The raising of sheep was entirely abandoned from the unusual peril to which the shepherds were exposed, and this prosperous industry of the frontier States completely disappeared.

Other serious evils were first felt during this period. The robbery of cattle had now become an object for the Indians, who had heretofore taken only horses and mules. The coincidence of the new settlements made at the same time in the western part of Texas, adjoining the Indian country, gave reason to suppose that the cattle were stolen for the ulterior benefit of these fresh customers.

The authorities never displayed greater zeal, activity and energy than now in the pursuit of the savages, expeditions being repeatedly sent into the desert as far as the Laguna de Jaco. On such an expedition in 1856, a captive was recovered named Crescencio Santiago, who was a boy at school in Durango when carried off, fourteen years before. He stated that his captors and all the Indians who marauded in Mexico resided in Texas, between the Rio Grande and the Colorado, where they left their families, and where they traded their booty for arms, provisions and clothing at an American settlement.

In March, 1856, in consequence of depredations committed by the Lipans, who resided in villages in Coahuila, and had been regarded as at peace, stringent measures were taken with them, as will be more particularly related in a future section devoted to this tribe. The result was the extermination of a great portion of this tribe, and the flight of the survivors into Texas, where they established themselves on the Rio Pecos, and thence continued, in combination with the Mescaleros, their depredations upon both countries, as will be proved by the statements of captives. But from this time the tribe may be considered as having disappeared, and it would scarcely be necessary to mention them were it not for charges made against Mexico of protecting their depredations in 1861, at the time of the beginning of the American civil war.

Early in that year the Lipans, in union with the Mescaleros, came from the river Pecos (Texas) and attacked the Mexican town of Resurreccion, the most northern settlement of Coahuila, on the Rio Grande. Several of the inhabitants were killed, and five children were carried captive, who were not recovered until seven years later, all which time they passed with their captors in American territory.

Under pretext of rendering assistance to the suffering town, Captain H. A. Hamner, commander in the neighboring Fort Clark, committed an outrage upon the laws of Mexico. Without any authorization, he brought over some troops and accompanied the citizens in pursuing the Indians a few leagues, without result. On his return to the town, he demanded the surrender of a negro whom he claimed as his slave. Happily, he did not gain his object, on account of the firmness of the citizens.

In May and June, 1861, Colonel John H. Baylor, commander at Fort Duncan, complained, to the First Alcalde of Piedras Negras, of outrages committed in Texas by numerous parties of Indians, whom he supposed to be Lipans, coming from Mexico. He also wrote to the Mexican military commander of the frontier, and to the governor of the State, to the same purport, sending these letters by Captain Hamner, as a special commissioner to treat of this subject, and also to propose a combined action against the tribes of Mescaleros, Apaches and Comanches, whom he characterized as " common enemies." At the same time he enlarged upon the necessity of a good understanding between Mexico and the Confederate States, in view of the increased trade which would be the result of " the unjust war which Abraham Lincoln has commenced against us."

The governor of the State replied to Colonel Baylor, under date of June 29th, showing the impossibility of the aggressors in Texas being Lipans, that tribe having been reduced in 1856 to a small number of individuals, known to be poor and without horses. He expressed his conviction that the real culprits were Comanches and Mescaleros.

In December 1861, January and March 1862, the Lipans gave further evidence of their sentiments towards Mexico by coming with the Mescaleros and robbing again near Resurreccion, and at Villa Muzquiz, whence they carried off more than a thousand cattle. They were pursued by two bodies of troops until they reached the Rio Grande, *en route* for their villages on the Pecos, taking with them the Indian inhabitants of " Burro," who had heretofore been considered as peaceably disposed.

In Coahuila, as in the other frontier States, the Indian hostilities diminished rapidly after the outbreak of the American civil war. This phenomenon was undoubtedly due to the same causes which have been mentioned in another place. Since the re-establishment of order, hostilities have again been resumed, though with less activity than before. The invasions have generally been by the lower fords of the Rio Grande, from Guerrero to San Ignacio (Texas). The aggressors have invariably been Comanches or Kiowas, who have first marauded in Texas, have crossed to Mexico with their booty, and again recrossed at another point. This tactics has contributed to throw suspicion on the Kickapoos, and has also aided the marauders to carry off their booty, though it has sometimes been taken from them in Mexico and returned to the owners in Texas. Sometimes these invaders, returning from their raids in Mexico, have been attacked by troops from Fort Clark, and the booty taken from them, though Mexican property, has been regarded as a lawful prize.

The continual expeditions organized in Coahuila, as may be seen in the journals of their commanders, have always stopped at the Rio Grande, and testify that all the booty has been carried across. On the few occasions when, by invitation of American officers, the forces of the two nations have been united in pursuit, the line of march has always been on the left bank, up to the mouth of the Rio Pecos, where the hostile Indians have been found, with a few exceptions, when, in order to deceive the American troops, they have hastily crossed the Rio Grande to the right bank, but have returned when the danger was past.

On reflecting upon the long duration of Indian warfare in Coahuila, it is easy to see that the losses must amount to a very large sum. Very few, however, have been registered, for a multitude of difficulties has prevented the citizens from appearing before this Commission. One of these difficulties arose from the uprising of the Lipans, in September last (1873), and the murders committed by them in revenge for the attack made upon them by American troops (the McKenzie raid) in Mexican territory. This cause operated on all the frontier towns, and local political disturbances had the same effect in Monclova, Saltillo, Párras and Viesca. Such considerations as have been advanced respecting the claimants of Tamaulipas and Nuevo Leon, induce us to form a favorable judgment upon the claims which are set forth in an accompanying table, and which amount to a considerable sum.

The victims sacrificed have been innumerable, especially on the three occasions when the American troops have chastised Indians who were living in peace in Mexico, and which led the Lipans ultimately, after perpretrating great depredations, to retire up the Pecos river into the heart of New Mexico.

In concluding this general review of Indian incursions in Coahuila, it is needless to mention that it completes those relating to the other two frontier States, inasmuch as the points of crossing the river, and those which served them as headquarters during their raids were generally in this State.

The reclamations collected in all three States have been mainly presented as evidence before this Commission, though some of them have been received by local judges, by virtue of powers given by it, and in conformity with the rules published at the commencement of the investigation. These evidences and the extracts made from the local archives will prove the sufferings of the frontier towns of Mexico, and that the protection extended to them, though greater than that existing on the American border, has been far from meeting the necessities of the case, and the demands of national interests, arising from the proximity of the towns of two Republics. Great embarrassments on the frontier must be ascribed to the negligence of both Governments, who have never heretofore properly examined this important subject.

INDIAN DEPREDATIONS IN ZACATECAS AND SAN LUIS POTOSÍ.

The same robberies and horrible butcheries which have been narrated in the cases of the frontier States, also took place in Zacatecas and San Luis. The sufferings of these States were equally grave, although of less duration, because the savages did not carry their inroads so far, until they had already desolated the vast area which lies between them and the frontier. Publications made in 1849 and succeeding years afford sufficient data for forming an idea of their magnitude, although the Commission has not visited any of the localities in question. The account now given of these depredations will therefore be brief, and is chiefly introduced as being confirmatory of the opinions already expressed as to the motive of such distant incursions, namely, the criminal traffic begun in 1835 by American citizens with the savage tribes. After 1848 this traffic, instead of being abandoned, as was required by the good faith pledged in a solemn treaty, was extended, and resulted in the desolation of these rich States.

The superior authorities of Zacatecas and San Luis, knowing well that the savage tribes of the North, had to traverse Nuevo Leon, Coahuila and Durango before reaching their own borders, had recourse to a union of all the States in question,—the first proposal of such a coalition having been made by the governor of San Luis. That functionary, on the 25th of August, 1851, after informing the Government of Nuevo Leon, that three parties of Indians were raiding in the north of the State, went on to say :

"It would seem proper under the circumstances, for the governments of Zacatecas, Chihuahua, Coahuila, Nuevo Leon,

22

Tamaulipas and San Luis Potosi, to unite in a common plan of defense, each State affording the resources in its power, and acting in combination with the greatest energy for the punishment of the savages."

The result of this proposal was the appointment of commissioners from the several States named, who drew up a plan of defense. This measure proves not merely the generality and importance of the danger, but that it proceeded from the United States, whence the invaders came, and whither they returned with their booty ; it also shows that the evil had become extreme, as was recognized by the Governor of Nuevo Leon in accepting the invitation.

While the Commissioners of the invaded States were assembled at Saltillo, their natural center, and were engaged in the formation of a plan of defense, horrible scenes were enacted in the State of Zacatecas, where the haciendas and ranchos of Sombrerete, San Andrés del Teul and Fresnillo were devastated by a multitude of savages. During this year, 1852, the ravages reached the State of Jalisco, which thereupon joined the coalition, and gave $10,000 *per annum* for the expenses of the campaign.

In July, 1852, more than 50 persons were murdered near Fresnillo. The districts of Sombrerete and Jerez were next attacked, and though the government sent more than 400 men in pursuit, it was rendered fruitless by the fact that white robbers accompanied the Indians, guiding and directing their movements very skillfully.

It was not in Zacatecas alone that it had been observed that the Indians were guided in their work of murder and robbery by intelligent white men. Three years before the same observation had been made in Nuevo Leon, by a director of the colonies, who informed the inspector-general that citizens of San Antonio, Texas, accompanied the Indians, as he perceived by their dress and other pecularities, which left him no doubt on the subject. The same discovery was made by the authorities of Agualeguas, in Nuevo Leon, and the fact was confirmed by the testimony of a captive from Nuevo Laredo, in Tamaulipas.

In view of news received by express, that 700 Comanches

were approaching through Durango, the whole State of Zacatecas rose in arms to repel them. At this time the hostilities reached ten States, including, besides those previously mentioned, those of Sonora and Sinaloa. All these aggressors were either Comanches or Apaches, of which tribes there was not a single village located on Mexican soil, as was declared this year by the experienced Colonel Galan, in his report of an extensive exploration of the Mexican deserts.

If, in addition to what has been said respecting the frontier States, separately, we sum up the results in each year, and take note of the immense number of regular troops and militia constantly employed in the Indian service, we shall, after all, only be able to form an insufficient idea of the vast amount of the losses. In illustration of this statement, it may be enough to refer to the sufferings of a single one of the districts of Zacatecas. In Marzapil there were more than 400 persons killed, wounded and taken captive—a fact which will startle even those most accustomed to the bloody scenes of the frontier.

No one will be surprised to learn that in Zacatecas, troops were ultimately recruited to be *exclusively* employed in pursuit of the savages. This was done in 1857, under the direction of Colonel Francisco Treviño, from whose skill in this warfare the best results were obtained. In one of his numerous engagements, he recovered from the enemy 8,000 horses, and on another occasion a quantity of bars of silver. Such facts demonstrate the great number of the invaders, and indicate the vast amount of life and property which must have been sacrificed in this State from 1848 to 1857. The preceding data respecting Mazapil, are the only ones which have been furnished the Commission, but it is evident that other districts which are wealthier and more populous must have suffered more severely.

As to San Luis, only very general information has been obtained, but the simple fact of that State having been the first to propose a coalition against the savages, shows that its sufferings must have been cruel. It has already been mentioned that San Luis had first become a prey to such hostilities in 1840, shortly after that great impulse which precipitated the tribes of the plains against the Mexican frontier. Horrible butcheries and extensive robberies were then perpetrated, as appears by the records of that period, but these former ravages were undoubtedly surpassed by those which gave rise to the coalition of 1852.

In the conferences for drawing up a plan of defense, it was recognized that the enemy resided in the United States, and it was for this reason that the governors said in their notes to the Supreme Government, that nothing practicable could be devised unless the privilege of pursuing the savages on American soil could be obtained, or the American Government could be induced to attack them after crossing the Rio Grande. The latter alternative, it was added, was out of the question, through the scarcity of troops along the entire line of the American frontier, and till more forces were placed there, the desolation of the Mexican border was inevitable.

When, therefore, the Plan of Defense was published, under date of the 22d of February, 1852, its 78th article was in the following terms:

"The governments of the coalition will earnestly urge the supreme national authorities to obtain from the government at Washington permission for Mexican forces to cross the Rio Grande, and attack the nomadic tribes which reside in that territory; without omitting to demand constantly and vigorously the fulfillment of Article 11th, of the Treaty of Guadalupe, and an indemnification for the losses which the frontier has heretofore suffered from the non-fulfillment of that article."

The national coffers, the donations of States which were free from such ravages, the fortunes of private individuals, all aided the border States in their warfare against the savages. But the American government did nothing to comply with its natural and prescriptive obligations. Ten years after the treaty of Guadalupe, the frontier was still ungarrisoned, and later, the inefficient organization of the troops stationed there, their small number and miserable armament, neither afforded security to the American settlements nor impeded the incursions of the Indians into Mexico.

Now that this plague has extended to Texas itself, and other parts of the United States, it is seen that the Mexicans have displayed a great superiority over their neighbors in their mode of Indian warfare. The brief narrative, which follows, of depredations by Indians in Texas, will show the mode of pursuit there adopted, and will confirm the opinions heretofore expressed as to the complicity of the authorities and people of the United States in Indian robberies and butcheries, for the fact will be revealed by military officers, by the citizens robbed, by captives and by the Indians themselves, all agreeing that government agents have supplied them with arms, thus inciting them to commit these depredations, in which, moreover, they have been directly aided by American citizens.

INDIAN DEPREDATIONS IN TEXAS.

The Commission has already made a brief statement of the occurrences which took place in 1831, in regard to the savage tribes inhabiting the territory of the United States, and also to those settled in Mexico at that date, when Texas was included in the republic of Mexico. At said period, as before stated, the removal of Indian tribes from the northeastern to the far southwestern portion of the United States was effected, thereby placing said tribes in contact with the savage hordes of Mexico.

In sundry portions of this report the Commission have given their opinion as to the great evil which this measure caused to the republic of Mexico, basing said opinion upon extracts taken from a history of all these tribes, written forty years ago by an American citizen, who crossed the plains several times, was acquainted and had intercourse with the majority of said tribes, those living on the reservations included, and who for this very reason was enabled to give a very minute account of their habits, and to prove the same by the testimony of captives and other men, so well versed in Indian affairs, that full credit cannot but be given to the greater portion of said history.

Neither the author nor any of his countrymen could have imagined that this work would become the most unimpeachable witness, upon the testimony of which we might rely to judge successfully all questions relating to the savages, which might in time present themselves, on account of the frequent depredations committed by savages both in Mexico and in the United States.

The waste lands of both countries were, in those regions, very extensive. There, the Indians being free to hunt, it is an unquestionable fact that no one molested them; besides which, they did not carry hostilities into American settlements, because these were too far removed from said regions, and in the places nearest to the savages there were military camps established as advanced posts to guard the reservations.

None of the officers of the United States government, and none of those engaged in commerce with New Mexico and Chihuahua, which commerce was begun about this time, could help knowing that the Comanches and the other tribes, not subject to the jurisdiction of the United States, were in the habit of robbing and committing other crimes in the Mexican settlements; and, according to Gregg's narrative, this knowledge was never a hinderance to prevent traders from dealing with Indians, but, quite on the contrary, Gregg himself advised all merchants who, out of fear, abstained from trading, to go into the business at once, as he knew by his own experience that the Indians were fond of trading, and always defended those who were in the habit of bartering with them.

This author was so utterly selfish upon this question, that his judgment was entirely led astray. Whilst condemning the authorities of New Mexico and Chihuahua as imbeciles and criminals, on account of the treaties of peace entered into with the Apaches, notwithstanding their depredations in other sections of Mexico, where they were wont to steal and then convey their plunder to those States, he did not perceive that he was committing himself, for he had stated previously that the Indians lived by plunder in Mexico, and that he never thought it was wrong to trade with them on American soil, as if the stolen property became legitimate merchandise by transfer to the neighboring country. If his censure of the

Mexican authorities was just, the public functionaries of his own country deserved it still more for violating the first principles of law and justice, by establishing trading stations and bartering with tribes of Indians who they well knew were robbers and assassins, and opening by this iniquitous behavior a deep chasm wherein one half of the wealth of Mexico would be engulfed, and, sooner or later, a great portion of his own country also.

Regarding these two facts stated above, viz : First, the establishment of Indian reservations in close proximity to the Comanches and Apaches ; and second, the mercantile trade started since that time and continued up to the present, it can easily be perceived that the Commissioners have not been misled in their opinion, when they point them out as the unique cause to explain the depredations committed by the Indians, both in Mexico and in the United States. The Commission deems it unnecessary to expound reasons of their own to corroborate that judgment, but will limit themselves to narrate the depredations committed in Texas, copying literally some opinions of the Texans themselves, and of the officers of the United States army, who have been compelled to acknowledge a glaring truth, in recognizing that these facts (including the negligence of the United States Government) are the cause of the Indian devastations in Mexico.

The Commission thought that a report of the depredations committed in Texas, made at a time when the minds of the people were unprejudiced, would place the Indian questions in their true light, and the best arguments that could be made might be based upon it. Through the Mexican consul at San Antonio, Manuel Maria Morales, who has given notorious proofs of his energy and laboriousness, the Commission has just received data relating to the depredations of the Indians in that State, from 1857 to the present, with the only exception of those committed during the Confederate war, which were not found mentioned in army newspapers.

Said data having been received just when the Commission were about to consider this matter, acting on information which had been obtained on the Mexican frontier, and when they had already written that portion of the report relating to the States of Tamaulipas, Nuevo Leon and Coahuila, it was with positive satisfaction that they saw their opinion; corroborated by private and official documents published in Texas. There the press has made efforts to misrepresent the Indian question, and now it comes to show the true cause of the trouble, and to acknowledge the justice of our complaints. The Commission quote these opinions because they are the researches of Texans themselves, and also because they are vouched for by the best authority, that of the United States officers of the army, so that partiality in an opinion on this question cannot be attributed to the Commissioners.

They have always been fortunate in the investigation of the different points aimed at; in many instances, the best information and very best proof wherewith to throw some light upon the question, were procured in Texas, as if this State had been charged indirectly to show the inculpability of the Mexican frontier. It thus occurred with a message of the Governor of Texas, at the close of the first part of this report,* and also with a report of the grand jury of Kerr county, in regard to the discovery of a large party of American citizens, who, under the disguise of Indians, have been perpetrating, for the last five years, the most atrocious crimes, killing defenseless persons and stealing horses and cattle.

These scandalous and unprecedented crimes which were committed on a very large area of the territory of Texas, have been commented upon by the newspapers, which, when publishing some of the depredations actually committed by the Indians, have expressed doubts as to whether the perpetrators of the crimes were Indians or not, and in fact, suspected them to be dispersed members of a band of outlaws, who concealed themselves in caves along the banks of the Guadalupe river, where they took refuge for a long time. This discovery was made in one of the border counties, in fact the very one which has been most clamorous against Mexico, through state-

---

* Cuadernos, No. 8, of Vouchers, fol. 8.

ments which they often caused to be published, relating to the injuries caused by Kickapoos acting in conjunction with Mexicans; and these publications are very important as relating to all questions concerning the Comanches, Kickapoos, and horse and cattle thieves. In a word, it explains in a great measure the true source of the violation of Mexican soil by General McKenzie, at the head of some Federal troops, in order to chastise Indian criminals.

Even this has not been sufficient to disabuse the Texan press, for a spirit of invasion predominates in the minds of a majority of Texans, to whom a large portion of Mexican territory would be an easy prey. The Commission will, in the examination of these invasions, consider the fundamental principle of prejudice, for as such they qualify sentiments of those who still shelter irrealizable and pernicious ideas to the welfare of both frontiers, tending to keep them in perpetual disorder, and to retard progress and the acquirement of wealth. In the enumeration of the depredations committed in Texas, the Commission regret not being able to present so clear a statement as that which they were able to make in regard to the frontier settlements of Mexico. Nevertheless they have a complete account, covering several years, which will enable them to make some comparisons, and by this means give another illustration of the immensity of the evils Mexico has had to suffer.

Before undertaking this task, however, the Commission think it advisable, in order to be fully understood, to point out with precision the ordinary abiding places of the Indians, both savage and independent tribes, and also those who live on reservations subject to the government at Washington.

The savage Indians are the Comanches, Cayugas, Apaches, Arrapahoes and Cheyennes; they neither till the ground nor live in towns, but dedicate their lives to hunting and stealing; these constitute what are properly called Prairie Indians, who roam over the country from " false " Wachita to Santa Fé. Near this river, and living sometimes in United States territory and at others on Texan soil, the Wacoes, Whitchutas, Takuakanoes, Towyash, Kerchies, Cadocs and others were found. As to the second class of Indians, those who live on the reservations, are the Cherokees, Choctaws, Chickasaws, Creeks, Seminoles, Florida Indians, Shawnees, Pottawattomies, Kickapoos, Delawares and others, who inhabited the country from the Arkansas to the Red river in the acknowledged limits of Mexico.

As soon as these Indians were transported to those remote regions, they began plundering. In Gregg's * often quoted work we read the following passage:

"Three or four days after this, and while crossing the head branches of the Osage river, we experienced a momentary alarm; conspicuously elevated upon a rod by the roadside, we found a paper purporting to have been written by the Kansas agent, stating that a large band of Pawnees were said to be lurking in the vicinity. The first excitement over, however, the majority of said party came to the conclusion that it was either a hoax of some of the company who had gone ahead, or else it was a stratagem of the Raros (or Kansas Indians) who, as well as the Osages, prowl about the prairies and steal from the caravans whilst on the route, whenever they entertain the slightest hope that their deeds will be attributed to others. They seldom venture farther."

It is not only true, as stated in the above quoted paragraph, that the Kansas Indians alone committed robberies in the hope that their evil deeds might be laid to others, but the Shawnees, Delawares and Kickapoos were also in the habit of leaving their reservations, and going to the prairies to hold intercourse with other Indians.†

"Though the Shawnees, Delawares and Kickapoos are amongst the most agricultural of the northern Indians, yet a few of these spend their time on the prairies in hunting, and in trading with the wild tribes. Whether because the vicious inclinations of the Indians rendered their residence in the States of the American Union dangerous to the inhabitants, with

---

* Commerce of the Prairies, Vol. 1, fol. 4.
† Commerce of the Prairies, Vol. 2, fol. 275.

whom it was difficult to make them live in peace, or whether to prevent the anomaly of sovereign nations, as the Indians were considered, living within the limits of the United States, eighty thousand were transported to the Red river, in the acknowledged limits of Mexico."

As soon as the Indians were removed to the southwestern portion of the counties of Mexico and the United States, they commenced the depredations alluded to, although more inclined to the craft of agriculture than other tribes.

Ever since then, the policy of the government has been greatly censured, because they undertook to maintain the Indians in peace by giving them money in the shape of annuities, which served only to keep them in idleness and to corrupt their habits without giving them strength, energy, or any industry by which to live. Since then the contractors or government agents, who in reality deserve the name of harpies, have acted in such bad faith as to merit the following criticism upon their conduct : *

" It is one of the calamities incidental to the state of ignorance in which some of the poor Indians remain, that their intimate and, indeed, political intercourse with the more civilized people of the United States does not spare them from being preyed upon by these unprincipled harpies, who are continually prowling about their reservations ready to seize every opportunity of deceiving and defrauding them out of their money and effects. The greatest frauds practiced upon the frontier Indians have been perpetrated by contractors and government agents. The character of these impositions may be inferred from the following instance as it is told, and very generally believed, upon the southwestern frontier : It had been pretty well known that some of those who had been in the habit of contracting to furnish with subsistence several of the southern tribes in the year 1838 *et seq.*, had been imposing most grossly upon the Indians as well as the government in the way of short rations and other delinquencies, which resulted in the gain of a very large sum to the parties concerned. About the close of their operations, one of the employees, who was rather more cunning than the principals, took it into his head, on account of some ill treatment he had

---

* *Ubi supra,* vol. 2, p. 262.

suffered, to make an exposé of their transactions. He happened to hold a letter of instructions (which were of course of a confidential character), wherein were set forth the processes by which these frauds were to be practiced. And to turn the affair to his particular profit, he threatened the parties with a complete exposure unless a satisfactory gratification should interpose. A compromise being indispensable to the welfare of all whom it concerned, a negotiation was soon set on foot, but the 'noisy customer' was not silenced until he was paid $13,000 cash, whereupon he delivered up the obnoxious papers and agreed to abscond. Some notice of the facts of this case are said to have been brought to the notice of the government, and how it has escaped an investigation, and more especially how it escaped the attention of the superintendent of that immediate district, have been matters of great surprise to those who had a knowledge of the particulars."

When we see immorality practiced on such a large scale by the very commissioners and agents appointed to take care of the Indians, and we find these subject to such misery and suffering, we can hardly consider it strange that they should hunt on the prairies, and, associating with the Comanches, yield to their natural propensities, and participate in the depredations committed by the latter on the Mexican settlements. The history of the reservation Indians will show that this opinion is well founded.

We must bear in mind that, on the other hand, those men who at the same time were robbing the Indians were speculating with the government of their own country, and that their acts of criminality were never punished, notwithstanding that these were notorious; they could have no scruple whatever after the United States reduced the annuities to the Indians to make up for the profits they could no longer realize by trading with property plundered by Indians from Mexico.

Such conduct on the part of the United States, which at first passed unnoticed, makes their responsibility all the greater, and this is not only the opinion of the Commission, but of the very agents and citizens of the United States who, victims of this tortuous policy, adopted ever since 1831 and continued up to late years, when a remarkable change has occurred, have repeatedly asserted these facts.

The Commission will in the first place cite the Texan news-papers, organs and interpreters of public opinion in that State, and afterwards proceed to give the result of their own investi-gation. By following this plan, the credibility, good faith and honesty of the witnesses who have given their depositions can be the better appreciated, and will be better understood by bearing in mind that the Commission had already ended their investigations and written the greater portion of this report before they received the data referring to the injuries caused by the Indians in Texas, which, as has already been stated, have confirmed and strengthened their opinions.

One of the most reliable periodicals of Texas, *The Herald*, by request of the Commission, furnished the Mexican consul at San Antonia with a literal copy of the articles taken from the files in the office, and certified to by the editor, relating to all the facts which had been published concerning the Indians. The source is unimpeachable. By this means the Commission is enabled to follow the incursions of the Indians, step by step, from 1857, from which year these data were collected, although for the purposes of the Commission the data of any would have sufficed. The facts are as follows:

On the 4th of August, 1857, some troops from Fort Mason pursued a party of sixty Indians as far as " Devil river " (alias San Pedro), where they attacked them, killing ten Indians and losing only two soldiers.*

Prior to said date, on the 27th of July, 1857, the second lieutenant of the 2d cavalry, stationed at Fort Clark, reported a fight with the Indians. They were at first supposed to be Tancahues, who, judging from information received from Fort Mason, were coming for their families, but it was soon discov-ered that they belonged to another tribe. Nine Indians were killed, with a loss of two soldiers, and as the tribe dispersed and the force was not considered sufficient, further pursuit was abandoned. †

Mr. Brackett, captain of cavalry at Fort McIntosh, sent a

---

* Cuaderno, No. 7 of Vouchers, fol. 1.
† Cuaderno, No. 7 of Vouchers, fol. 2.

squad of cavalry, by way of Laredo, in pursuit of a party of Indians who had approached that camp and stolen some horses from the town. The Indians, who were thought to be Comanches or Lipans, abandoned in their flight twelve animals to the troops. *

On the same spot, a skirmish occurred on the 3d of November, between the soldiers and a party of Indians, in which the latter lost their horses and equipage.†

About a month before, on the 16th of October, in the same year, some troops belonging to the 2d cavalry, under command of the second lieutenant, left the fort in pursuit of a band of Indians who had murdered two men ; the Indians made their escape on foot, but all their horses and clothes were captured.‡

About the same time, the 25th November, § the *Herald* published some letters received from the town of Santa Rosalia, State of Chihuahua, referring to the invasion of some four hundred Indians, who had encamped in front of the town, stolen horses to the value of five thousand dollars, and killed a great many cows. The Indians returned to the United States by the same route they had come, crossing the line at a point a short distance above San Cárlos and by way of Fort Lancaster, from which place they had stolen twenty-five bushels of corn on their way into Chihuahua.

Governor Runnels, finding the frontier line of northeastern Texas entirely exposed, ‖ applied to General Twiggs, in command of the department, for some regular troops, stating that in that district the Indians had killed one white and one colored ·man, and wounded a boy, besides stealing property to a large amount ; and as about one-half of one of the three companies which the State had organized to protect that line, was the only available force, and by no means sufficient for the emergency, aid was earnestly requested.

---

* Cuaderno, No. 7 of Vouchers, fol. 5.
† Vouchers, Cuaderno, No. 7, fol. 6.
‡ Vouchers, Cuaderno, No. 7, fol. 7.
§ Vouchers, Cuaderno, No. 7, fol. 9.
‖ Vouchers, Cuaderno, No. 7, fol. 10.

This occurred on the 14th of January, and the day before the *Herald*, under the head of " Protection to the Frontier," said : *

" An intelligent person of Waco informs the commander of the department of the depredations committed by the Indians near Camp Colorado, where they have assassinated two of the inhabitants and stolen a great many horses. *The writer states as his opinion that the Indians in these depredations were led, or instigated, by the Mormons.*" †

At the time of these occurrences, and whilst the facts and opinions were being published in Texas, the press there were in receipt of information from Laredo, Texas, that in the interior of Mexico some of the northern tribes, very likely the Comanches, had destroyed a wagon train and killed three teamsters, adding that the Indians, thirty in number, were armed with rifles.‡

From a research made by the San Antonio *Herald*, on the 2d of February of said year 1858, it appears that in the department of Texas § during the two previous years the troops had had sixteen engagements with the Indians. In these, twenty-six Indians had been killed, twenty-three wounded, and six taken prisoners, besides the losses sustained by the Indians in almost every engagement by the capture of their horses. Most of these combats had been fought on the banks of the Colorado, Brazos, and Concho rivers, and in one of the combats that occurred on the banks of the Rio Grande the Indians, said to be Comanches, were pursued on the right bank. In another combat, which took place under command of Lieutenant Hood, on the San Pedro river, the Indians were of the Comanche and Lipan tribes.

Several bands of Indians were seen at Medina. ‖ From this place the Herald received letters which brought information that persons who had accompanied the troops in the pur-

---

* Vouchers, Cuaderno, No. 7, fol. 11.
† Repetition of quotation.
‡ Cuaderno, No. 7, p. 11.
§ Cuaderno, No. 7, p. 11 to 16.
‖ Vouchers, Cuaderno, No. 7, pp. 16–18.

suit of the Indians as far as the mountains, stated *that a squaw before dying, had declared that her party belonged to the reservation,* and that several other bands had left there without the knowledge of Major Neighbor, the Indian agent.

In another publication dated February 17, 1858,* it was said that the duty of the companies organized by order of the State legislature was to operate against the Indians at once, without waiting to chastise them for robberies committed, and thus avoid a useless excursion which would not remedy the evil. It was also said that General Twiggs was powerless, and that the time had arrived for the Federal government to take into their own hands the defense of the country. By timely help, the Indians would be repulsed as far as the reservation, and the atrocities and depredations committed on the frontier and the suffering endured by the inhabitants would immediately cease.

The special agent of the Comanches wrote the same day that he had captured two Comanches and two Mexicans who had stolen from the reservations and in Texas; that as the Mexicans had fled, he had caused the two Comanches to be tried by a court composed of their chiefs; that having been sentenced to death, they were examined and revealed the fact that several bands of Comanches, Kickapoos and Caiguas, commanded by Shanico's son, were the perpetrators of the robberies, and that Kickapoos and Comanches lived together towards the north of Red river. Mr. Ross, the agent, concluded by promising that he would soon go and examine personally the camp of the Indians.†

On the 14th of April, the Indians appeared near Laredo, and on the 20th, between camp Hudson and Fort Clark, where they wounded two men on San Pedro river, who stated that the Indians were armed with rifles and belonged to the Comanche tribe. Another party of Indians followed, within view, a train of wagons as far as Puerco river in order to attack it at their convenience; and that Mr. Rome, by whom

---

* Vouchers, Cuaderno, No. 7, pp. 18, 19.
† Vouchers, Cuaderno, No. 7, pp. 21, 22.

the report was made, observed that the road to El Paso was strewn with Indians who apparently were bolder and more hostile than ever before.*

On the same day, two parties of soldiers left Fort McIntosh in pursuit of a party of Indians who were driving some horses in the direction of Nueces river.†

On the 24th of August, four men, two Americans and two Mexicans, were assassinated near El Paso, seventy-five miles below Fort Davis, by a party of Comanches coming apparently from Mexico, as they were driving a large herd of horses. ‡

According to news received from northern Texas, which was published on the 28th of said month, the Comanches were then on the Arkansas river on the agency of the Osages, making their preparations to fall on the frontier of Texas. §

The assassination of several families and the robbery of cattle at Denton and Clear Creek, perpetrated in September, caused a great deal of excitement, and the neighboring towns commenced to arm themselves. ‖

During the early part of October, footprints were noticed on the banks of Devil river, and on the 12th of the same month, the *Gazette of Austin* said that, on account of the complicity of the renegade Kickapoos and Kichees with the Comanches, who showed themselves very hostile, one hundred men were to be armed, by order of the governor, to recover the stolen property wherever it could be found.¶

In the month of October, Wise county was invaded by Indians, believed to be Kickapoos, and three of the inhabitants of the county were killed.**

On the 22d of October, a long article was published in the *Herald*,†† showing the state of alarm in which the people of Texas lived, because the Comanches and Wichitas, their enemies, were ferocious and blood-thirsty savages, and powerful enough, on account of their large number, to destroy any town they might choose to attack. The frontier, it was said,

---

* Vouchers, Cuaderno, No. 7, p. 23.   † *Ibid.* 24.
‡ Vouchers, Cuaderno, No. 7, p. 26.   § *Ibid.* 27.
‖ Vouchers, Cuaderno, No. 7, p. 27.   ¶ *Ibid.* pp. 28, 29.
** *Ibid.* p. 30.   †† Vouchers, Cuaderno, No. 7, pp. 30 and 31.

was exposed to all the horrors of rapine and murder for many miles along the line, because the government troops could only give protection to those who were within reach of the post parapets; besides the troops were few in number, and not competent to maintain the kind of warfare necessary to subdue the savages who defied them, and fearlessly crossed the lines of the camps, and penetrated into the central part of the State. As a proof of this, it was said that, a month before, eight of the most influential citizens of Brownsville had been murdered, and by letters from that city it was known, that from Fort Duncan to Ringgold Barracks, a distance of over three hundred miles, there was not a single soldier to be seen.* Such a state of affairs looked somewhat like criminal indifference on the part of the authorities at Washington, who had promised to send troops to check the Indians. It was added that all the Indians were well armed with bows and arrows, lances, axes and rifles, and it was recollected that a very short time previous an American by the name of Chism,† a trader, had sold to the Indians seventy-five boxes of arms and ammunition, on agreement that they should go to Texas and steal horses and whatever other property they could, which would be paid for with arms and provisions, thus establishing a regular trade of stolen goods.

The governor of Texas reported to the commander of the department the depredations committed in Brown county by twenty Indians, who had killed four men and taken two captives. ‡

The assassinations just referred to caused great alarm at Lampazos and its vicinity. The letters were unanimous in saying that the Indians were on the war path throughout the country, obliging the families to abandon their houses, cattle and all other property. It was said, however, that the Indians, authors of these assassinations, had been punished, and this

---

* " Surely this is all wrong, and shows something like criminal neglect on the part of the authorities at Washington."

† Vouchers, Cuaderno, No. 7, p. 31.   ‡ Vouchers, Cuaderno, No. 7, p. 32.

was proved by the property rescued from them, which had belonged to the persons they had killed. *

About the end of December, three bands of Indians overran the vicinity of Bandera, and retreated after having stolen some horses ; they were pursued by troops ordered to the rescue by General Twiggs. The opinion then was that the Indians were more bent on robbery than on anything else. †

The Commission will now bring to an end these extracts of the depredations committed by Indians in the State of Texas during the years 1857 and 1858. It may readily be observed that whilst in Texas the Indians committed twenty-two assassinations, wounded five persons and captured two others ; in the State of Nuevo Leon they killed forty-five persons, wounded twenty-six and captured thirteen during 1857 alone, and in 1858 they killed eighteen and wounded four persons, forming a total of sixty-three killed, thirty wounded and thirteen captured, i. e. four times as many persons sacrificed as in the State of Texas.

It will also be observed at a glance, that the operations of the Indians in Texas and on the frontier States of Mexico, were all based on the thorough knowledge which they possessed of the respective situations of these States, and also of the indifference of the Texans in regard to the depredations perpetrated in Mexico. For this reason, whenever they stole horses in Texas, near the places where they lived, they took good care to drive them in small lots, so as to facilitate their own flight, whilst the reverse was the case whenever the robbery was committed in Mexico, for although in the towns of the interior they proceeded in like manner, yet, whenever they came near the Texan line they always formed in one body, and did not mind passing in view of the military camps posted on that line.

The spirit of the public press during all these years tends to show that the injuries caused by the Indians were attributed partly to those living outside of said reservations, because the line was uninhabited ; there were very few soldiers, and the

---

* Vouchers, Cuaderno, No. 7, p. 33.
† Vouchers, Cuaderno, No. 7, p. 35.

military posts were easily avoided. Such conduct on the part of the government was censured, qualified as bad and criminal, and the government was urged to furnish sufficient troops to repress the Indians.

This same view was expressed by the Commission when they endeavored to explain the cause of the horrible depredations committed by the Indians from the very commencement of the trouble. The *sorties* of the Indians from their reservations, as was ascertained by a squaw and confirmed by the report of the official agent of the Indians; the concentration of the Comanches in places inhabited by the "Osages" (transported in 1831), in order to concert their attacks upon Texas and other States; the connivance of the Comanches, Kickapoos, Wichitas and Juyes in the depredations committed upon the settlements; the participation of the Mormons, they being not unfrequently accused of sometimes instigating and at others leading the Indians on to warfare, as was discovered in the case of Chism, an American trader, who furnished arms and ammunition to the Indians; and the very remark that the Indians were more inclined to robbery (which requires abettors) than to any other crime; all this now published in the face of Texas is only a repetition of what occurred in 1835, with the only difference that they who fell victims to those depredations, *i.e.*, since 1836, were Mexicans exclusively, but from 1836 to the present, the Texans have likewise suffered, although on a far minor scale, as is shown by the comparison drawn before.

This result, as has been before said, is the effect of the general cause of trouble on the banks of the Arkansas river, in 1831, when the northeastern Indians were put in intercourse with those of the southwest, and also by the encouragement given their natural propensity for stealing, by American citizens who bought from the Indians the spoils which they brought from their incursions into Mexico, until the live stock being exhausted in that country, they were forced to extend their raids into Texas, where everything fell easy prey to their rapacity.

Even without the acknowledgment made by Texans in late

years, it was generally surmised that it was their own fellow-citizens who either led or incited the Indians to plunder, and it is easy to trace this fact, that whether by Mormons, or Indians from the reservations, who were in constant business relations with American citizens, the Indians were incited and even led at different times by such persons. The simple fact that these tribes have had no other occupation for more than half a century, during which time they have carried away from Mexico an immense number of horses which they could not employ, not having any need for them, is of itself a proof that they disposed of them, either to the Indians on the reservations, with whom they were in daily communication, and through them to Americans, or to the latter directly. Nevertheless, it is a great step in relation to this criminal traffic, that the discovery has been made that all the depredations committed by Indians, have been by those living in a savage condition, and by those supported by the government on permanent establishments.

The Commission might here close this report, considering their opinion as to the origin, progress and actual condition of the Indian depredations to be well grounded, and established by the extracts heretofore set forth; but as such persistent efforts have been made of late to impute all the depredations committed in Texas to a part of the Kickapoos, now living in Mexico, they deem it advisable to give further details of the depredations committed before the settlement of these Indians in Mexico, noting the remarks then made whilst, pending the hostilities, the case was likely to be better appreciated and understood.

In February, 1859, some soldiers from Fort Quitman,* situated between El Paso and Presidio del Norte, had a rencontre with the Mescaleros, who fled to the mountains of Chihuahua, in Mexico. In the same month the troops from Fort Inge, in Uvalde county, in conjunction with some citizens, pursued a party of Indians and recovered nearly all their horses. The depredations in Uvalde † continued, and it was thought that

---

* Vouchers, Cuaderno, No. 7, pp. 35 and 36.
  † Vouchers, Cuaderno, No. 7, pp. 36 and 37.

they had been committed by the same Indians, who had been beaten, reinforced by others.

Through letters from El Paso and San Elizario, it was discovered that on the 7th of February, there had been another rencontre with the Mescaleros, in the Cañon del "Peno";* some heads of neat cattle and a few horses had been stolen from San Elizario; a posse of residents and troops pursued the Indians, killed from twenty to thirty, and wounded quite a number.† In the same month some Indians were seen near "Pedernales" and "Bandera," with the apparent intention of stealing.‡

The *Herald* published, on the 24th of March, an account given by two Comanches, taken prisoners in the combat near Fort Arbuckle, in October, 1858. Amongst other things, it was said that all the Indians were ready for war with the whites; that they had over four hundred Mexican captives, men, women and children, and two white men in the Comanche country; that they got their arms and ammunition from other Indians who received such from the Americans; that a few Comanches went to the vicinity of Bent's Fort, and procured arms and ammunition from the agent; that the Indians go at pleasure to Mexico, across the Rio Grande, and are not afraid of the Americans on the other side of that river.§

After this, the troops had several engagements with the Comanches ‖ near Fort Arbuckle, and they pursued them actively for several murders committed by them, and for the capture of two young girls above Boston. On the following day, they were overtaken and the captives rescued ; one, a girl of about twelve years of age, said that the Indians spoke English.¶

The citizens of Young county ** had a meeting in April, with a view to petitioning the Federal Government to remove the Indians from the reservations, and in case of the demand

---

* Vouchers, Cuaderno, p. 39.　　　† Vouchers, Cuaderno, pp. 38 and 40.
‡ Vouchers, Cuaderno, p. 39.　　§ Vouchers, Cuaderno, No. 7, pp. 41 and 42.
‖ Vouchers, Cuaderno, No. 7, p. 45.
¶ The little girl says that the Indians spoke English.
** Vouchers, Cuaderno, No. 7, pp. 45 and 46.

not being granted, to join with the neighboring counties and force compliance with their desires.

The following was written from Fredericksburg, in the month of April : *

" It is certain that the Indians are aware of the movement of the troops, and if care is not taken to guard the passes from Concho, Kickapoo, San Sába and Llano, they will be able, without much difficulty, to open war on the frontier, having an open field from the Colorado river to the Guadalupe."

On another occasion in Fredericksburg and Kerr, † there was another incursion of Indians, and robberies were committed which caused the greatest anxiety to the inhabitants.

In the following month, May, 1859, ‡ about seven hundred Indians, of various tribes, attacked a body of troops in Colorado. § Meantime, the Indians from the southern reservations had abandoned their fields, encamped in the grounds of their agent, Mr. Ross, and declared a war opened, the results of which were greatly to be feared.

At the very time that a man was killed in " Frio," ‖ and that animals were being stolen and wrested from the Indians, news came that Van Doren had obtained a recent victory over the very Comanches whom he had routed in October of the preceding year.

From a report ¶ made by Lieutenant Hazen, of the infantry, it became known that the Indians were encamped near Uvalde and its vicinity. They were in possession of papers signed by persons purporting to be officers of the army, and were guaranties of good conduct, &c., &c. It was thought that if the papers had really been given to those in whose possession they were found, it would be dangerous for such papers to fall into the hands of others. It was also inferred from the papers, the antiquity of which was remarkable, that the bearers were Kickapoos.

---

* Vouchers, Cuaderno, No. 7, p. 47.   † Vouchers, Cuaderno, No. 7, p. 48.
‡ Vouchers, Cuaderno, No. 7, p. 50.   § Vouchers, Cuaderno, No. 7, p. 50.
‖ Vouchers, Cuaderno, No. 7, p. 51.
¶ Vouchers, Cuaderno, No. 7, pp. 52 and 53.

In June,* they committed robbery and a murder in the county of "Llano;" and shortly before they repulsed Baylor, an officer, who attacked them at the head of over one hundred men, on the reservations of the agency at Brazos.

According to letters from San Elizario, published in the Herald † of June 9th, two hundred Indians had passed by Camp Stockton with a number of horses, bound north, evidently on their return from Mexico, from whence the horses had been stolen.‡

During the months of June and July, the counties of "Blanco" and "Frio" § were invaded by small bands of Indians; on one of these occasions, the stolen property was all recovered, and one Indian killed.

In August, the counties of "Mason" and "Bandera" were invaded; and in the following month, those of "Kerr" and "Blanco;" the damages consisted of the killing of cattle and the stealing of horses in small lots.‖

In September, they appeared in "Webb" county, and killed a Mexican boy near Palafox; about the same time, in the county of "Maverick," not far from "Eagle Pass," at a place called "Pendencia," they committed the most horrible atrocities on a family residing there.¶ They were pursued by a party of Americans from "Eagle Pass," but were not overtaken; and believing that they had crossed into Mexico, the authorities of Piedras Negras gave a written permit to the commandant to pursue them, in case of necessity, to their own territory, and otherwise lending aid to the pursuers with a reinforcement of seven men. **

---

* Vouchers, Cuaderno, No. 7, p. 54.

† Vouchers, Cuaderno, No. 7, pp. 54 and 55.

‡ "These Indians were, no doubt, just from Mexico, where they had stolen the horses they had with them.

§ Vouchers, Cuaderno, No. 7, pp. 55 and 56.

‖ Vouchers, Cuaderno, No. 7, pp. 57, 58 and 59.

¶ Vouchers, Cuaderno, No. 7, pp. 60 to 65.

** "Captain Stone started soon in pursuit. Seven of the company were from Mexico. The merchants in Eagle Pass threw open their stores, and generally told the volunteers to help themselves to supplies. Captain Stone obtained a written permit from the Mexican commandant to go into Mexico in pursuit of the Indians, if necessary."

During the months of September and October,[*] the counties of "Webb" and "Frio" were invaded, and on the 5th of October the *Herald* published accounts received from San Sába, through a Mexican captive who had made his escape from Comanche county, and who stated that he had been captured in Santa Clara, Durango, by the Comanches, who took him north and put him to take care of horses, in connection with other Mexicans, who were retained as servants to the Indians.

He further stated, that after the battle with Van Doren, the Indians [†] retreated towards the northwest, making short marches and hunting buffalo in order to maintain themselves on the journey. They did not encamp until they arrived at a large camp of white people; the place was situated on the banks of a wide river, near a grove of tall pine trees and high mountains; that at that place the Indians received liquors, clothing, sugar, blankets, and they were promised that Van Doren and the Texans should not fight against them, and that they should encamp at two days' journey farther on. He also stated that the white men furnished the Indians with guns, clothing and ammunition in exchange for horses, and that carts were constantly being removed laden with various articles; that the Indians were united for war, and that this was the first time they had taken him towards the South to rob; that after the Indians left the establishment of the white men, where they had procured all they desired, they marched for a whole moon together, and afterwards separated into small bands, the one with whom he traveled being composed of six Indians.

On account of the frequent incursions of the Indians near Castroville during the month of October,[‡] troops left Fort Inge in pursuit of the savages, whom they overtook between Fort Terret and Fort Clark, and seized one hundred and thirty horses.

Captain Samson found an old Indian encampment in Nueces,

---

* Vouchers, Cuaderno, No. 7, pp. 65 to 67.

† Vouchers, Cuaderno, No. 7, pp. 67 to 70.

‡ Vouchers, Cuaderno, No. 7, p. 71.

which had served as a refuge to the Indians in the spring of 1859, and when he made his report in October, he remarked, "that in his opinion the greater number of the bands * who invaded that part of the country came from the north and created disturbances on the frontier on either shore of the Rio Grande. In case of pursuit, if they succeeded in crossing the river, they considered themselves safe in Mexican territory." †

News of atrocities committed by the Indians came from Fort Stockton on the 27th October,‡ that not far from the fort two men had been killed and a number of horses stolen. On this occasion, the editors of the *Herald* asked : How long will the lives of men be exposed through the criminal economy of the government? How long will the present administration depreciate the lives and property of its citizens? §

In November,‖ troops from Forts Clarke and Inge, with citizens from Uvalde, started in pursuit of the Comanches, whom they routed near Fort Terret. This was the official report made by the expedition. In the same month, preparations were made to await the Indians at the Springs of Leon, that being the point from which they had made their entrance.¶ Official intelligence from Fort Clark, relative to the encounter referred to, stated that the Indians with whom they had fought near Fort Terret, carried guns, revolvers, and bows and arrows.

During the three months ending November, 1859, in which Captain Samson ** and his company had been scouring the county of "Kerr" and the vicinity, he is said to have discovered various trails leading to the settlements, but as the Indians were on foot, it was almost impossible to discover and punish

---

* Vouchers, Cuaderno, No. 7, p. 75.

† " I am of the opinion that most of the parties that visit our part of the frontier come from the north, and whip around to the Rio Grande on their return. In case of pursuit, if they can cross that stream, they feel safe in Mexican territory."

‡ Vouchers, Cuaderno, No. 7, p. 77.

§ How long will human life be a prey to the puny economy of the government? How long will this utter disregard of life and property characterize the present administration?

‖ Vouchers, Cuaderno, No. 7, p. 78.   ¶ Vouchers, Cuaderno, No. 7, p. 79.

** Vouchers, Cuaderno, No. 7, pp. 82 to 85.

them. At the end of the year the Indians invaded the county of Blanco, from whence they stole a few horses.

From all the reports of Indian depredations in Texas during the year 1859, it will be observed that the murders committed by them were few, and the damages from robbery small, since the stolen goods were nearly always recovered, and a number of Indians reported as killed. Those who could never be punished, according to reports from Fort Quitman, were the Mescaleros, on account of their taking refuge in the mountains of Chihuahua. Nevertheless, these did not altogether escape, for at a later date they were whipped at "Cañon del Perro," Texas, to which place they had returned, which is conclusive evidence that the Mescaleros lived in Texas.

The incursions along the whole left bank of the Rio Grande, clearly demonstrate that those who made the war were Comanches and other northern tribes. The encounters which took place near Fort Arbuckle, in the Chickasaw territory, leaves no room for doubt on the subject, and the belief is confirmed by important revelations made by two young Comanches, as for instance : the fact of the number of *Mexican* captives and the scarcity of Americans, and the trade with the reservation Indians, who furnished them with arms, as did also the agent at Fort Bent. This fact is sustained and confirmed, as well as the other report that there were American leaders amongst the Indians, as was stated by the girl of twelve years of age, who was rescued near Belton, and who heard the Indians speaking English. Still greater force is lent to these statements by the testimony of the young Mexican captive, who had been held in the same settlement or encampment with the two Comanche prisoners, and who reiterated the fact of trade with the whites, and exchange of horses for arms, and participation of the authorities and citizens in this merchandise of human blood and stolen property.

The observations of army officers, who were in pursuit of the savages, as to the revolvers in their possession, the opinion of Capt. Samson (Chief of the Rangers), that the bands who carried hostilities on both banks of the Rio Grande, came from the north, and when pursued, took refuge in Mexican territory, and in fact, the very situation of the counties in which the depredations were committed, all go to form incontrovertible proof that the ills endured by Texas, originated on its own soil, where the Indians dwell, and through its own citizens, who furnish the savages with arms and incite them to robbery and murder.

It is worthy of notice, that during this year all the depredations committed were attributed to northern tribes; it is not concealed that those who assailed the county of Kerr and other frontier counties, came from the north and returned there by the same route, and it is fully acknowledged that it was they who were the authors of the injuries sustained on both banks of the Rio Grande. At that time, then, Mexico harbored none other Indian tribes but the Seminoles, and at this very time, there were American agents employed in trying to effect their transportation or return to the United States.

As regards the damages sustained by Mexico, apart from those before mentioned and proved, later data collected in Texas, by means of the official reports from Fort Quitman, as well as from letters written from the frontier, and through the statements made by the very Comanches themselves relative to the great number of Mexican prisoners retained by them, it is unquestionable that these do not proceed from any other source than by way of Texas or the United States.

A glance at the map of that State and of the frontiers of the United States and Mexico, compared with the official information given, and the statements of citizens who have pursued the Indians, all afford another material proof of the source from whence the Indians come. It is useless, therefore, to enumerate facts to establish this opinion, except perhaps the expression of feeling in the invaded counties, from which may be traced the point from whence the Indians came.

During the year 1860,* they appeared by way of Mason, Brady Creek, La Leona y Frio, Laredo, Camp Colorado and Fort Lawson. It was somewhat remarkable that in these invasions the Indians were generally on foot, and that those who

---

* Cuaderno, No.7, pp. 84 to 101.

were pursued from Laredo passed by Fort Clark on their way northward, which indicates the extension of their wanderings, and shows that there is no reason to blame other Indians than the aborigines of Texas.

In the same year the San Antonio Herald of February 22, published intact an official report from Captain Richard M. Richardson, in command of cavalry troops stationed at Fort Mason, addressed to Capt. John Withers, adjutant. The report was dated February 16, and, after referring to the operations against the Indians pursued by the troops, and the results thereof, he concluded the communication with these remarkable words : *

" There can be no doubt but that white men were engaged with these Indians. When I charged upon the camp I heard two persons within, speaking the English language too fluently to be Indians. This party was mounted, and armed with rifles and six-shooters."

Meridian, Palo Pinto, Mason, Bosque, Hil, Brazos and Belknap, all suffered depredations, and some of them were of a horrible character. In mentioning these, the *Herald* of March 20 quotes the Houston *Telegraph :* †

" The Indians killed ten persons, carried some off captive, and horribly abused others, especially two young ladies, whom, after abusing with all the brutality which Indians and white outlaws know so well how to practice, they stripped them of their clothing and turned them loose to die of cold and hunger, or to fall again in the hands of the brutes who infest the country, or to be torn to pieces by savage beasts of prey."

Other incursions followed, and Castroville, Eagle Springs, Boerne, Fredericksburg, and Laredo suffered considerably. New proofs that the Indians were led by Americans who used this mask to obtain plunder through the medium of the savages, whom they aided in their work of pillage and murder. On the 16th March, 1860, after a skirmish with the Indians, intelligence came from Castroville to the *Herald* as follows : ‡

" The chief spoke good English and Spanish, and said that

---

* Cuaderno, No. 7, p. 95. † Cuaderno, No. 7, p. 97.
‡ Cuaderno, No. 7, p. 98.

he knew a great deal of German also. The Indians carried rifles and six-shooters."

On the 16th of March, 1867, this same paper published a letter from Mr. Henry Redmond, owner of the ranche of this name, giving valuable information of the depredations from which the towns were suffering, and, amongst other things, remarked : *

"In January, a Mexican boy was captured by the Indians about twenty-five miles from this place, in Mexican territory ; he escaped a few days since during a battle between the Indians and the troops from Fort Clark, and has returned to his home. He says that the Indians are at war with Mexico and Texas, and that there are a great many above here in the Pecos and Independence Creeks, composed of Kickapoos, Comanches, and Lipans."

The paragraph concluded as follows :

" A short time since, we saw an account in one of our Missouri exchanges of the lynching of five of these Indians who were captured, with a lot of horses in their possession, by a company of settlers. They turned out to be bogus Indians, painted white horse thieves and murderers, and they admitted, at the time of their execution, that they had just come over from Texas, where they had stolen all the stock they had with them."

From 1861 to 1865, the emergencies of war prevented the periodicals from giving the details of the doings of the Indians, and it was not until 1866, that intelligence upon this subject reappeared in. their columns.† These depredations had been continued up to 1867, when nine hundred Comanches attacked Fort Lancaster, and continued there marauding through the following year in Bandera, Fredericksburg, Llano, Camp Atkison, Hondo, Frio, Sabinal, San Márcos, Middleton, Fort Mason, San Sába, Leon, Pedernales, Guadalupe, New Braunfelds, Boerne, Fort Davis, Concho, Loyal Valley, Kickapoo Springs, and Camino del Paso.

The depredations committed in 1860 and the following years, on the margin of the Rio Grande and the central counties

---

* Cuaderno, No. 7, p. 105.   † Cuaderno, No. 7, pp. 105 to 125.

of Texas, the official report that Americans were in league with the Indians, the confirmation of these reports by the " Galveston News," and the statements received from Castroville, all present horrible pictures of deeds committed, which were not attributed to Mexican Indians or to those residing in Mexico, but to those of the United States who were in collusion with white men. It was well known in Texas that these same Indians who committed robberies in Mexico, crossed the Rio Grande, and, on their return by way of Fort Clark, they released a captive whom they had taken on Mexican soil. This having occurred in 1867, three years after the coming of the Kickapoos to Mexico, it was not considered strange that the captive denounced said Indians as associates of the Comanches, since it was believed that the tribe of Kickapoos, to whom he referred, belonged to that portion of the tribe who had remained in the United States.

· On perusing the information sent to the press from the above mentioned places, the attention of the Commission was attracted by several very important features of the case. First, that from August, 1868,* after the Kickapoos came to Mexico, no mention is made of them as participators in the depredations committed, yet, notwithstanding this fact, the writer from Fort Mason alludes somewhat dubiously to this omission ; second, in reporting the encounters with the Indians, they are said to have been armed with bows and arrows and shields, arms not used by the Kickapoos ; and, in the third place, that they understood English, as was noticed in one of the skirmishes had with them.

From the examination made, which covers eight years, exclusive of the years of the war, we have as a result the fact that, up to 1868, there were considerable losses in Texas through murders and robberies committed by the Indians, and up to that time there was no doubt whatever that the perpetrators were Comanches in league with other Indians from the reservations, and other tribes known as Wild Indians. These acts, corroborated by the instigators of the bloody struggle

---

* Cuaderno, No. 7, p. 118.

which was sustained, and from whom important confessions were forced, not only serve to explain what was actually taking place, but also to foretell what was likely to happen in the ensuing years.

It being indisputable that white men instigated the Indians to robbery, and furnished them with arms and ammunition, sometimes directly, and at others through the reservation Indians, it is easy to believe that one step further would convert them into guides and commanders of the savages on their marauding excursions; and the fact was soon discovered through various sources, that white men or Americans accompanied and led the Indians in these invasions. The most absolute proofs have been obtained of this criminal act, which words fail to characterize, for there are official reports, statements of released captives, of innocent maidens, and of men of veracity and clear judgment, all going to prove that there have been cases, like those of the Missouri, in which white men—Americans—disguised as Indians, conducted horses stolen in Texas.

It being only five years since these atrocities were consummated, and no proof existing that any energetic measures on the part of the Federal Government or of Texas have ever been taken to discover the criminals, who associated with Indians and disguised themselves in savage garb, it will not be difficult to surmise that the evil increased from day to day.

The acts committed in Kerr county this year prove this clearly, and the Commission will make no commentary on the following report of the grand jury, presided over by the Hon. Judge Everet, from which a plain idea will be formed of the effect of the negligence or apathy of the authorities : *

"Report of the grand jury, presided over by the Hon. Judge Everet: We, the grand jury of the county of Kerr, elected and sworn in for the present session of court, respectfully submit the following report of the condition of our county : With care and diligence we have inquired into the facts relative to the execution of Jamison and the dragging of James Ratcliffe and George Graffenreid from the prison, followed by the immediate execution of the men, and after the most careful

---

* Vouchers, Cuaderno, No. 7, pp. 13, 14 and 15.

investigation of the case, we have been unable to discover, or even to get a trace of the persons who infringed the law in this respect.

"Our county is situated on the frontier; and a short time previous to this, it was invaded by fugitive criminals coming from the more populous counties of the northeast. These persons have taken up their abode on the Rio Guadalupe, a region almost uninhabited, covering a great extent of mountainous country, in which numerous caves abound, forming a secure and easy refuge; the valleys are rich and the pasture excellent, serving for the sustenance of their flocks. From these almost inaccessible mountains, the outlaws have swooped down upon the towns and villages, robbing cattle, and effacing the brands by substituting their own.

"It is also discovered and proved, by good and reliable evidence, that, not content with stealing cattle, they have disguised themselves as Indians, the natural enemies of the white men, and, under this garb, have added, not unfrequently, to their innumerable crimes, those of murder and incendiarism.

"It is unfortunate that some unknown persons have applied prompt punishment to these criminals, without awaiting the action of the courts. As the act was secret, it has been quite impossible to discover the perpetrators or those who took any part whatever in it. We honestly believe that this state of affairs has ended, and that in the future affairs will return to the peace and quiet heretofore enjoyed. Respectfully submitted, this 31st day of July, 1873, by the president,

"CHAS. SCHINER."

The application of the terrible "Lynch Law," and the abuses of it by whomsoever it may have been put in practice, and for whatever other crimes it may have been applied, goes to show the popular feeling in Kerr county in respect to assassinations and robberies of cattle and horses by persons under the disguise of Indians, and the little confidence had in appeal to judicial administration. This case also proves the exactness of the before named articles and other evidence which accuses white men, disguised as Indians, of being the actual perpetrators of these crimes, of which they were accused since 1855, by officers of the Mexican army, as has been previously stated.

It will be remembered that this state of affairs in Texas was the result of acts committed by their own citizens in league with the Indians, and that at that time the Federal Govern-

24

ment had almost surrounded Texas by forts and military posts, covering the boundaries towards the northeast, and guarding it on the north by the Red river. The boldness of the Indians in daring to force their way through a line so garrisoned, for, though but poorly defended, it still formed a very formidable barrier, can only be accounted for in the fact previously noted, that Americans were the guides and leaders of the savages, furnishing them constantly with the number of the forces and all other information which would serve to render their expeditions successful.

It will be well, just here, to note that the line of United States forts and military posts extends from 100° to 101° parallel of west longitude, and on the north, from Eagle Pass, their number includes Forts Duncan, Inge, Clark, Campo Verde, Terrett, McKavett, Campo de San Sába, Concho, Campo Colorado, Chadbourne, Phantom Hill, Griffin, Campo de San Marcos, and Camp Cooper. These two last posts * are situated on one of the branches south of Brazos river, on the 33° of north latitude, and directly on the route to the reservations of the Comanches, Kiowas and Apaches, lying on the left bank of the Red river, in the 35° of latitude. Thus, there is over forty leagues over which the Indians could roam and enter Texas from the reservations and the prairies on which they dwelt, with scarcely any obstacle, in spite of the numerous forts situated in the center.

Although the object of the Federal Government in establishing such forts and military stations was the protection and security of the populated portion of Texas, it will be seen that it was not successful, and that the Indians have overrun Texas from all directions, passed through the line of military posts into Mexico, and returned with captives and other fruits of their plunder, as is proved by occasions when they were attacked near the forts and the Mexican captives released.

The Indians had by this time prepared another market; they robbed in Mexico and Texas and carried their plunder to New Mexico to dispose of it, and the trade in this was so extensive there, and so barefaced, that the "Borderer," a periodical

---

* See map of Texas.

of "Cruces," New Mexico, attempted to defend it by upbraiding a wealthy stock raiser of "Palo Pinto," who endeavored to recover his cattle which the Indians had stolen and sold in that territory, perhaps in connection with the white outlaws from Kerr, dwelling on the Guadalupe river.

Mr. Hittson, the stock raiser of "Palo Pinto," above referred to, wrote on the 10th February of said year to the president of the Committee on Indian Affairs; and the matter of which he treats is of such grave importance that his letter cannot be omitted. It runs as follows:

"Sir: Your letter dated January 3d, in which you request a detailed account of my expedition to New Mexico in search of stolen cattle, is at hand, and it gives me great pleasure to accede to your wishes, as far as my memory will permit me, not having at hand all the minutes of my operations, which would make a complete report. You and the other members of the committee are well aware that the stock raisers of the northwest portion of Texas have been subjected to immense losses from the frequent invasions of the Comanches, Caiguas, and other tribes of Indians, and that through their constant and unrestrained depredations, the large flocks and herds of past years have been exhausted in this section of the country. In order to put a stop, as far as was possible, to these acts, and to recover the stolen property, I went to New Mexico last summer, and in consequence of not having any aid, and on account of the limited period of my stay, I was only able to accomplish a part of my object. There are a great many difficulties in the way of recovering stolen property, because so many persons in the territory are implicated, directly or indirectly, with the Indians in the robbery of cattle on the frontier. They also furnish them with arms and ammunition, with which numbers of our people have been murdered and mutilated. From this cause, I met with great opposition, with which I had to struggle in my endeavor to recover the stolen property. * * * I was enabled, however, to vanquish the majority of the obstacles put in my path, and I was put in possession of five or six thousand head of cattle which had been stolen; but the herd was recovered only at the cost of enormous expenditures almost equal to the value of the property. The number of stolen cattle bought from the Indians and disposed of by those implicated in this illegal traffic, in the territories of Arizona and New Mexico, is far greater than is supposed by the people of Texas. I am convinced, from personal observation, that it will be no exaggeration to estimate the number of stolen cattle, disposed of in the manner above stated, at one hundred thousand head during the two last decades. Until some measures are taken by either the general government or the State, these depredations will continue."

This criminal trade with the Indians presents itself on every hand; it has been denounced from all parts, and this fact being notorious, it has not escaped the attention of the Committee on Indian affairs, the president of which asked for the information contained in the above quoted letter, in which, as is seen, the Comanches and Caiguas are expressly accused as the principal authors of the depredations committed in northwestern Texas, and implicitly of those committed in Mexico, it being known that on their route the same tribes attack Mexico, and carry off large numbers of horses and cattle, which, together with those stolen from Texas, find a market in New Mexico.

If, in spite of the great number of forts and military camps situated on a direct line from Eagle Pass to Los Brazos, the sole object of which has been to protect Texas on the line of the prairies, the central point of habitation of the Indians, the savages have been able to cause great evils to that State, it will be easy to calculate and understand the amount of damages sustained on the Mexican frontier, constantly invaded since 1848 up to one year ago, from within this line, and also from the vast unprotected lands in the northwest, from Fort Clark to Paso del Norte; over this vast tract, from the time you leave Fort Clark, there are no other posts save Hudson, Lancaster and Stockton, at great distances from each other and from the Rio Grande. After these on El Paso road, there is Fort Davis, far distant from the river, and above Presidio del Norte is Fort Quitman, and no other defense until you reach El Paso.

The immense open tracts lying between the posts have made incursions easy, and served as a refuge for Nuxcaleros, Lipans and Comanches, who have always dwelt on Puerco river. From this source and cause come many of the evils of the Mexican frontier, and many of those of Texas, as is proved by the robberies committed at "Palo Pinto."

Without having any military information, the Commission will risk an opinion, based on a comparison of the military posts of to-day and those established and maintained by the Spanish Government, and preserved by that of Mexico, that the latter were better calculated to obtain the desired object, even as to the location of the forces, which, without being numerous, maintained peace and security. But their lives were not inactive, and, besides, there were none to incite the Indians to robbery at that time.

The depredations of the Indians during the last five years, between 1869 and 1873, differ very slightly from those committed previously, for they have not changed the theatre of their pernicious acts, nor the manner of committing them. The robbery of horses and cattle has been constantly maintained in the invaded counties, and in order to execute their design with security, they employed the same tactics as in Mexico, dividing in small groups and attacking many places at the same time, thus diverting attention and escaping easily with their booty—another proof that the thieves and assassins in Texas and Mexico were the same people.

Worthy of notice and special consideration is the difference of the proceedings taken in Texas and in Mexico. The authorities of the former do not seem to have taken any measures for organizing the citizens and arming them against the enemy who devastated their property, but on the contrary, the action seems to have been individual and without system. The injured parties have assembled and, without order or leaders, have started in pursuit of the criminals, and if in some instances they have been successful, far more frequently they have utterly failed.

This absence of concerted action and unity on the part of the counties springs, without doubt, from the reparation which they expect to receive for their losses through the Federal government, which owes them security; and this feeling crops out in all the actions of the people,—in the statements made by individuals, who not unfrequently contradict themselves, not having really witnessed the acts, and in the notorious exaggerations of others who, not fearing any public authorities who could force them to tell the truth, present things in a manner suitable for a claim, or for a sensation in the newspapers.

For this reason, no great confidence can be placed on the number of the depredations asserted; but it is, nevertheless, well proved that they have been frequent, because the commanders of the forts have published, from time to time, an account of their operations, which were sometimes corroborated here by the sufferings of Mexicans, transient and permanent residents in Texas.

If, after the precaution suggested, evidence is admitted or reports considered not having an official source, it will still appear that the counties of Texas have suffered greatly from invasions on the part of the Comanches and Caiguas from the reservations, and other tribes, not living on the reservations, distinguished by the name of wild Indians.

There are indications in the places where they have been encamped, and in others where the Indians have approached near enough in broad daylight to be clearly seen, to convince the observer that the invaders have been none others than the Comanches and Caiguas. Other vestiges noticed in the northwest in the combats had in that district with the Indians, indicate that the Apaches and Comanches are the ones who attack that portion of the State, sometimes together, and sometimes separately.

In designating the tribes who have committed the depredations, the correctness of the data heretofore given is corroborated by the testimony of persons living at the forts. One of these persons,* writing from Fort Griffin on the 12th of June, 1869, affirmed that the Indians from the reservations were the authors of the depredations, and that the reservations were nothing more than a rendezvous and depot for the stolen animals. These Indians, said the letter, " are an organization of thieves, whose object is to make money by the purchase of stolen animals. There can be no doubt (it continued) of this fact on the part of persons who are aware of the proceedings of

---

* Cuaderno, No. 7, p. 139.

the past three months, but it is somewhat astonishing and peculiar that the robbery of horses and mules in the vicinity of this locality coincides with the arrival of certain persons from 'Cash Creek,' who have no known occupation or mode of livelihood, and it is worthy of notice that Texans were not admitted to the reservations."

The same writer * gives an account of frauds existing in the reservations, enumerating the cases of stolen property carried over this route, and concludes by saying that it was easy enough for them to do this, " because the white friends of the Indians kept them posted as to the number and movements of the troops."

The investigations made in Guerrero City by the Commission confirm some of the articles published by the papers of San Antonio, which remarked, referring to letters of September 26, 1871, received from Uvalde, that the Indians had approached Eagle Pass not far from that place, and had killed two negroes at Fort Clark. This was also mentioned by Servando Gonzalez,† whom the Comanches and Caiguas had captured from the rancho del " Prieto," Texas, in that month. The captive added, as a confirmation of what Mr. Hittson had declared, that persons from New Mexico went to trade with the Indians, and exchanged cattle and horses for arms and other goods.

From letters dated Friotown, January 29th, 1872, ‡ it was known that the Indians who had been seen at the head of the Nueces, and who had proceeded to the county of Llano, were Comanches, as was certified by experts who had examined the arrows. Wherever an effort has been made to discover the truth, none other tribes have been found, save the Caiguas, who almost always accompany the Comanches.

Mention is also again made of the Kickapoos,§ residing in Mexico, implicating them in the robberies committed on the banks of the Rio Grande. The writer throws out this suspicion, which springs from having seen these Indians roaming

---

* Cuaderno, No. 7, p. 193.   † Expediente, No. 3, p. 24 to 26.
‡ Cuaderno, No. 7, of Vouchers, p. 197.
§ Cuaderno, No. 7, of Vouchers, p. 193.

over the lands near the river. Up to the close of 1872, no formal accusation nor acts of notoriety had been alleged, that would serve to implicate the Indians referred to, in the depredations committed in Texas. It being necessary to treat of these separately, it has been considered as well to call attention to the fact, that until last year the sufferers themselves in Texas recognized the reservation Indians and the other savages inhabiting the neighboring plains as the authors of the robberies and murders committed.

After having referred, with such detailed minuteness, to the depredations committed in Texas from 1857 to 1868, the Commission will explain why they did not proceed in the same manner in regard to the ensuing years. The reason is obvious. It was necessary to expose the evils which had existed in Texas at the time when no Indians were living in Mexico, and this had to be done in detail, in order that the causes of the troubles assigned might be properly understood and appreciated, and that they might serve to explain the acts committed in following years. At that time there being no Indians in Mexico, and those living on American soil being the only ones known, no others could possibly be accused of committing the depredations. At that time the truth was told, but afterwards, for reasons which will be hereafter noted, it was not convenient to acknowledge the same causes, and therefore accusations were indulged in against Mexico.

The total depravity of hundreds of individuals living in Texas and the contiguous States has become so patent since 1858, that a great many Americans commenced to allude to this state of affairs in the newspapers, denouncing, for the first time, the criminal intercourse of American traders with the Indians, as has been stated in the case of Chism. That accusation was confirmed by reports of captives, Comanches, women, children, officers of the Government, and the stock-raisers, all of whom, year by year, have revealed some act or another putting this alleged crime beyond a doubt. And yet neither the Government of Texas nor the General Government, nor even the people, in spite of repeated denunciations, have taken any measures to discover and punish the criminals, who have grown so bold as to establish themselves almost in the heart of Texas, disguised as savages, and more to be dreaded on account of their superior intelligence and audacity.

From the number of men who have given themselves up to the horrible crimes alleged and proved against them, an estimate may be made of the low stage of morality in Texas, and the reason why the Kickapoos have been blamed in latter years for the depredations committed in that State may be found in the fact that a few of the tribe have been surprised and inveigled by the criminals, who doubtless intended in this manner to conceal their own horrible crimes by laying the blame on others, and to stimulate feeling and prejudice against Mexico in the minds of the Texan people, in order to seek a quarrel with the Mexican frontier.

The correctness of this judgment is verified on considering the proceedings of the present year, and connecting them with the invasion of Remolino, whilst in pursuit of the Kickapoos.

The following will explain the means that were used to call the attention of the public by grave acts, in order to divert the minds of persons from the criminals who lived in Texas.

On the 9th January, 1873,* the " Galveston *News* " published reports from Live Oak county of murders and robberies committed by the Kickapoos a short distance from Oakville, saying that the Indians had been killed after a valiant defense, and that they were armed with pistols and bows and arrows. They also asserted that the Indians were Kickapoos, and drew this inference from the fact that they bore chimales (shields), and that the shepherd who was wounded, himself a Mexican, so affirmed. The statement itself possesses the elements why it should be rejected, because the fact is well known that these Indians do not use bows and arrows, nor shields nor pistols. This invasion was by the Comanches and Caiguas, the same as the one of the previous year, by which the stock-raisers of San

* Cuaderno, No. 8, p, 1.

Diego, a rancho farther south than Oakville, had suffered terribly the previous August.

Besides, these statements were contradicted a few days afterwards by a publication in the San Antonio *Herald*,* referring to information given by Mr. Diamond, who had seen, in the county of Bandera, Indians dressed in the United States army uniform; they were armed with bows and arrows, and he had heard them speaking English during the combat.

A United States army guide, who had been employed in this capacity for eleven years, to lead the troops whilst in pursuit of the Indians, destroyed this report in regard to the Indians residing in Mexico. On the 1st February of this year, after referring to the evils suffered by Bandera, this guide declared that after eleven years experience he felt authorized to give it as his opinion, that in the first place the mode of making war with the Indians would be inefficacious unless soldiers, either regulars or volunteers (rangers), who would be always ready for the march, were employed ; and in the second place, he suggested as an effective means of defense the fortifying of the line from Red river to Rio Grande, which was all the more necessary now that the Indians were more audacious and better armed than the whites, having received needle guns from the American government.*

And that no doubt should exist that the Comanches and Caiguas were the invaders of Mexico and Texas, and in order to deny, officially, the private intelligence received from Laredo, Oakville and other places on the southern portion of the Rio Grande, concerning depredations of the Kickapoos, there appeared on March 31st of the present year † a statement from the headquarters of the army in Texas, giving information that Mr. Tatum, the Indian agent, had notified the recovery by him of six more captives from the Comanches and Caiguas. The names of the released men, who had been captured in Mexico and Texas, were Servando Gonzales, Manuel Vela, and those before mentioned, all of whom have been examined by the Commission.

---

* Cuaderno, No. 8, p. 1.   † Cuaderno, No. 8, of Vouchers, p. 1.

From February, when they appeared in Bandera and provoked the above expressions from the guide, nothing is heard of the Indians until May 24th, when they appeared in Las Nueces, and afterwards four hundred more, who had crossed the Rio Grande near Eagle Pass.

Other incursions followed in June, and the appearance of the Indians near Fort McKavett, caused the correspondent of the San Antonio *Herald*,* to write from Menardville that the Comanches and Caiguas continued their work of devastation. †
A thousand of these Indians, according to advices from Fort McKavett, were encamped on the Colorado, and it was feared that they would attack the escort who was conveying prisoners, made by McKenzie, to Fort Sill. ‡

The foregoing had scarcely been published, when advices came from Bandera that the Kickapoos, and their allies, the Mexicans, were revenging themselves for the attack made by McKenzie, commencing by the assassination of the family of Mr. Moore, dwelling not far from that place. It was very soon discovered that that family had fallen victims to the ferocity of disguised whites, or bogus Indians.§ Without any mistake whatever, the spirit of the letter referred to proved that the writer belonged to a party of banditti, who had been prosecuted in Herr county.

The presence of the Indians at Fort McKavett, in July, ‖ clearly indicated the source from whence they came, and the person who wrote to the San Antonio "*Herald*," stating that the Counties of Brown, Coleman and Camp Colorado had been invaded, mentioned that the reservation Indians were not quiet, and that they and the wild Indians were the perpetrators of the evils committed.

In June, one month previous,¶ a decided proof was obtained at Fort Concho, that the invaders of Texas were none other than the Comanches. The military held at that post one hundred prisoners of that tribe, including women and

---

* Cuaderno, No. 8, of Vouchers, p. 4.   † Cuaderno, No. 8, of Vouchers, p. 6.
‡ Cuaderno, No. 8, of Vouchers, p. 4.   § Cuaderno, No. 8, of Vouchers, p. 1.
‖ Cuaderno, No. 8, of Vouchers, pp. 4 and 11.
¶ Cuaderno, No. 8, of Vouchers, p. 7.

children, and it was supposed that the hope of effecting the release of their people had restrained them from invading Del Paso road during this period.

In view of the depredations committed * at Frio, Dogtown, Bandera, Atacoso and Hondo, the "Galveston News" stated, in July, that the punishment inflicted by McKenzie had produced no benefit whatever, and that there was now no doubt that the sufferings endured had proceeded from the Comanches and Kickapoos of Fort Sill. The unjustness of McKenzie was enlarged upon, and the falsity of the accusations against Mexico maintained.

In this same month the Indians also appeared in the counties of Uvalde and Sabinal, and, fifteen miles from Fort Sill, the postmaster † was obliged to ask protection against the Caiguas, who conducted themselves in an insolent and threatening manner.

Whilst these occurrences were taking place, intelligence came from Uvalde that the Mexicans and Indians were the perpetrators of the murders, and that they ought to be exterminated in order to put a stop to so terrible a situation; but the editors of the "Herald," ‡ on the same day, expressed a different opinion, pointing to the reservation Indians as the authors of the murders and robberies which had occurred, and expressing an opinion that in all of these the reservation agent had a part; and that the postponement of the conferences, which were to have taken place to decide the fate of Satanta and Big Tree, chiefs of the Caiguas who were detained in prison, was owing to the fact that the Indians were absent on a robbing expedition, and that the agent wanted to gain time for them to return.

Every day brought news of incursions in other places; and as the disturbances were in counties contiguous to the Mexican frontier, the conclusion arrived at was that the Kickapoos and Lipans, residents of Mexico, were the authors of

---

* Cuaderno, No. 8, of Vouchers, p. 9.
† Cuaderno, No. 8, of Vouchers, p. 37.
‡ Cuaderno, No. 8, of Vouchers, pp. 16 and 18.

these atrocities, forgetting that a portion of these tribes resided in Texas, and were more likely to commit these deeds than the others from whom they could not be distinguished, and who were closely watched, which was not the case with the Texan Indians.

But the " Weekly Express," * in an article of the 24th July last, put an end to all these theories by declaring that there was conclusive proof that the Indians who invaded Texas came from the reservations of Fort Sill, as was indicated by their dress, arms and ammunition—strong corroborative evidence.

" Besides," continued the article, " none of the trails were directed towards the Rio Grande, and had the invaders come from that section, the fact would soon have been discovered. The military," it was added, " held the same opinion, and they were very well informed."

At this very time the discovery was made in Kerr, that the hordes of criminals who, under the disguise of Indians, had committed the most horrible atrocities, were white outlaws, and the press being occupied with these, it neither admitted nor published any further accusations against the Mexican frontier, for after these disclosures, it would have been barefaced and ridiculous to have propagated reports which no one would have credited.

During the succeeding months, the papers were filled with news of incursions, but they limited themselves to a judicious observation on the state of the Indian war, and what is still more worthy of notice, a general belief that the marauders came from the reservations.

After enumerating the invasions made in Texas by Indians who have sometimes been designated as Comanches or other northern tribes residing in the United States, and at other times as Kickapoos living in Mexico, the result of all the data, collected from the public press in Texas, and those procured in Mexico, may be summed up as follows:

---

* Cuaderno, No. 8, of Vouchers, pp. 10 and 35.

First. The depredations committed in Mexico, in the States
of Nuevo Leon, Coahuila, Tamaulipas, Zacatecas and San Luis
Potosi, since 1848 to the present year, have been perpetrated by
the Comanches, Caiguas and others of the tribes residing in the
United States. This fact has been fully established : first, by
means of the testimony given before the Commission by the
residents on the banks of the Rio Grande, who have witnessed
the Indians crossing from the left to the right bank of the
river, and returning with the fruits of their plunder to American
soil ; second, by documents collected from the public archives,
in all the towns on the right bank of the river, from Reynosa
and the lower portion of said river to "Resurrection," one
hundred miles above, said documents being corroborated by
archives of old military posts, and those of the government of
the States referred to ; third, by the official reports of the military commanders of the United States, advising those of Mexico of the invasion of Comanches, who when pursued in that
republic, or even watched, crossed over into Mexico ; fourth, by
the permits solicited by the authorities to pursue bands of Comanches, who after having committed depredations in Texas
took refuge in Mexico, to do as much or still greater damage ;
fifth, by reports of those officers of the reprisals of captives
and horses stolen in Mexico by the Indians, the captives being
generally ransomed in the United States by the troops and
citizens of that republic; sixth, by the statements of Mexican
captives who have escaped from the Indian encampments, or
ransomed, and also by the evidence of the very Indians themselves.

Second. The immense amount and value of the articles
stolen or destroyed by the Indians in the three States above referred to is incalculable, and this fact is confirmed by official
documents and the unanimous testimony of a thousand witnesses, including the history of the frontier towns.

Third. The robberies and murders which have been the
result of these depredations have been committed, not only
by the Comanches and other northern tribes, but also by some
American officials and private citizens, who instigate the savages
to pillage, by purchasing from them the stolen property with arms

and ammunition, and who stimulate them by accompanying or guiding them on their expeditions. The proof of this may be seen : 1st. In the history of the Indian nations, written by an American citizen; 2d. In the testimony of witnesses who have been in the Indian agencies and observed the illicit traffic, which has been continually carried on, in stolen goods; 3d. From public denunciations, such as that of Mr. Hittson and the Texas press in general, on the complicity of some officials and entire towns of the United States, in the robberies and murders committed by the Indians.

Fourth. The depredations committed in Texas may be attributed exclusively to the reservation Indians and various other roaming tribes not confined to the reservations, and also to hordes of criminals who, disguised as Indians, have invaded different counties, and not by any means to those tribes residing in Mexico, who have had no participation in said damages. The evidence of this, according to the proofs given, is as follows : 1st. The official communications of the American authorities addressed to their superior officers and to those of Mexico. 2d. The daily press commenting on the operations of the American and Mexican forces against the savages, whose arms they described, and who made description of the places invaded by them in pursuit of the Indians, thus putting their statements beyond a doubt. 3d. The unanimous declarations of American and Mexican captives, prisoners of the Indians, as well as those of the residents and officers of the forts. 4th and lastly. The report of the grand jury, who stated that for over five years a numerous band of American outlaws had been committing the atrocities for which the Kickapoos and Mexicans had been blamed.

ROBBERY OF CATTLE AND HORSES.

Having explained in all its details the cause of the complications on the frontier, and accounted for the robbery of cattle in Texas for the Mexican market, and the robbery of horses in Mexico for the United States, the Commission has but little more to add upon this subject. Another mode of stealing cattle and horses, not considered at the time the first report was rendered, because it was not in practice at the points then visited, will require some explanations.

In all the towns, sufficient data were collected to give a thorough knowledge of this question. In every locality an investigation was made as to whether there were any persons there engaged as cattle traders who went to Texas and brought cattle for consumption in that or other towns, and the result always went to show that there were no such traders, and that the cattle introduced into Mexico were brought there by Americans, who frequently pass with droves for Monterey and Saltillo. Mention is everywhere made of those speculators, who live at "San Nicolas de los Garzas," of whom it has been said that they make their importations by way of Nuevo Laredo and Piedras Negras, under custom-house documents regularly registered.

The witnesses mention various *rancheros* of Leona, Pendencia, Nueces, and other points of Texas as the principal vendors; they specify the modes of making the sales, drawing up the registers, and the frauds, which, in spite of the strictest watchfulness, are committed by these *rancheros* to the prejudice of the legal owners of the animals exchanged; they demonstrate the barrier which the use of the register presents for the discovery of theft, which is consummated under protection of law and the force of habit permitting cattle raisers to dispose of animals of any brands whatever; they explain how many American dealers, in order to avoid the registration, which is usually made in the place where the inspector resides, accompany the purchasers to the bank of the Rio Grande, and aid them to pass the droves, which are not stolen except by the vendors themselves.*

In Guerrero City † there are persons who, since 1855, opened the cattle trade with Texas, and who furnish interesting

---

* See " Expedientes," 1, 2, 4, and 5.
† See " Expedientes," 1, 2, 4, and 5, pp. 37 to 40.

information relative to the origin of this branch of traffic. They were merchants trading in national goods with the central portion of Texas. An inundation of the Nueces river caused them to delay their journey, and in the "ranchos" they exchanged their merchandise for fat cattle, which they brought and sold in Mexico to great advantage. This fountain of profitable commerce once discovered, they devoted themselves exclusively to it, and have continued the business up to the present date.

These witnesses are too well known, both in Mexico and Texas, for their integrity, and do not need, in order to be believed, that their evidence be substantiated by other testimony. Nevertheless, their declarations have been well sustained ; and besides enumerating the diverse modes of stealing practiced by the rancheros at the branding places, and in the sales of droves for Kansas and Mexico, which droves are composed of animals of different owners, they contain judicious observations relative to the robberies committed for the Mexican market, placing the number at a low figure.

Persons well acquainted with the markets of Monterey and Saltillo, the only points where sales of cattle can be effected, declare that the thieves would not be able to find purchasers for large numbers, and it is clear that without the incentive of quick and easy sales robberies would not be perpetrated. Honest traders, having maintained constant relations with the butchers of Monterey, affirm that the cattle legally imported are quite sufficient for the consumption, and that there is no reason, therefore, for robberies on an extensive scale.

The data obtained at the municipal treasury of the city of Monterey, prove the exactness of these observations ; * it is found that in a period of ten years, the consumption of cattle in the city referred to, amounted to thirty-six thousand four hundred and seventy-two; averaging three thousand six hundred and forty-seven head of cattle a year.

If this result is compared † with the bills issued by

---

* Expedientes (Vouchers), 1, 2, 4 and 5, pp. 64 to 66.

† Expedientes (Vouchers), 1, 2, 4 and 5, pp. 27, 28, 42, 43 and 60.

25

the custom houses of Guerrero, Nuevo Laredo and Piedras Negras, it will be seen that during the last four years in the two former, and in ten months in the latter place, there were legally imported twenty-three thousand three hundred and forty-one head of cattle, which is equal to five thousand three hundred and thirty-five a year, corroborating the evidence of the traders of Guerrero city, and showing that the legal importation furnishes a full supply for Monterey, and leaves enough for the consumers in the other towns, which are Saltillo and Parras.

If we consider, as is the truth and is fully proved in the respective "expedientes," that a great amount of the consumption by the towns referred to is supplied by cattle raised in Tamaulipas, in Coahuila and in Nuevo Leon, we shall see that the legal importation of Texan cattle, according to the custom house permits, covers the demands of the markets, and the stolen cattle would find no purchasers, save at prices so low that the thieves would lack all incitement to commit the crime.

Information which the Commission has received from the towns through which the cattle pass on their way south, is uniform as to the fact that the cattle drivers make periodical journeys to Monterey, Saltillo and Parras; they are for the most part Americans, and the sales they make, at the points where they stop, are insignificant on account of the small consumption, and because, as they express it, the cattle raisers of the vicinity are able to supply the demand.

It should be noted * that, amongst the reports received, this general fact is testified to by some American citizens living on the frontier, who further state that these cattle drivers have been frequently pursued by Texans, as thieves, and that they have been followed as far as Sabinas Hidalgo.

Bearing in mind the inefficacy of the system of registering done by the inspectors in Texas, for the better security of the proprietors, who never receive the value of their animals registered and sold, sometimes because the marks are so altered that the witnesses can easily swear unanimously, sometimes

---

* Expedientes, 1, 2, 4 and 5, pp. 11, 12, 15, 16, 169 and 170.

because this legal requirement is omitted, and sometimes for other reasons, it will be no exaggeration to affirm that of the six thousand· head of cattle annually imported from Texas into Mexico, five-sixths of the number are stolen, from the fact that their legal owners have never sold them ; but this is the system of legal robbery practiced in Texas for many years since the confederate war, as is stated by the traders. ·

That this is the true cause of the cattle stealing, has been clearly demonstrated by the Commission in their first report through the enumeration of abuses, each one of which was thoroughly investigated by means of testimony from competent witnesses; with the statistics published in Texas ; with the records of the criminal courts, and with the articles constantly published in the newspapers, to say nothing of the well known and notorious acts that prove conclusively, so to speak, the cause of the diminution of the cattle, and the folly of attributing the same to a scheme for robbing, organized in Mexico, to supply the markets.

The movement which has lately been put into operation by the cattle raisers of Texas, of holding a convention, which will open its session on the 3d November, and the causes which have led to the formation of their society, will prove a mortal blow to the claimants against Mexico on account of cattle stealing, and be a confirmation of the correctness of the judgment formed by the Commission, since early this year, as to the true nature and importance of the cattle depredations.

" The Western Stock Journal," a paper organized in Texas for the defense of the stock raisers,* issued its first number in Pleasanton, Texas, in August last, and No. 20 of the issue, dated September 16, contains an exhortation to the cattle raisers, in the following words :

" At the last meeting of *The Stock Raisers' Association of Western Texas*, they passed a resolution to hold the next regular meeting of the association in Pleasanton, on the 3d of November. This notice has been put in possession of every-

---

* Cuaderno, No. 8, of Vouchers, p. 64.

one from the coast to the mountains, and from the Colorado to the Rio Grande, and according to the advices we have received, the decision of the Assembly has been adopted, and those interested are desirous of attending the sessions.

"It is to be hoped that the whole west will be vigorously represented at the coming sessions, as questions of the greatest importance, as affecting the interests of stock raisers of western Texas will be fully discussed by the association, and on the resolutions of that body will depend, in great part, the future success of the cattle business in our country.

"The custom or practice of selling cattle without the authority of the owner, which has existed for a long time in this country, opening the door to abuses which have caused incalculable injuries to the interests of the cattle raisers, ought to be stopped; the cattle thieves and hide purloiners should disappear, if to do this it is necessary to call in the gallows to enforce the rights of property, even though this be only cattle. It is also essential that the *grab game* should cease, if we do not wish to renounce the prosperity which cattle raising promises.

"But, in order to accomplish these important objects, it is indispensable to secure unanimity of thought and action amongst the stock raisers, and to do this they must combine and *discuss* the means of remedying the evil before applying them.

"Serious fears are felt that there is an impending conflict between the stock raisers on account of the existing evil practices, and it is believed that there will soon develop a serious state of affairs. When they meet in November, the stock raisers will be in position to calm these troubled waters; first, by adjusting their own differences, grown out of the sales of cattle, quietly and fairly, and afterwards agreeing not to sell nor interfere with any but their own cattle, except in the case of having a written permission from the owner to do so. Besides, the stock raisers will bind themselves to prosecute to the last extreme any infraction of the law relating to cattle, remembering that this law, properly enforced, is sufficient to protect the interests of stock raising in all its ramifications. Unity of action and a rigid observance of the law on the part of the stock raisers will preserve public tranquility and achieve the protection and security which their interests demand.

"If the association unanimously adopt these measures, and it is seen that the stock raisers are earnest in inaugurating a more equitable mode of doing business, public confidence will be restored and the cattle business will receive a new impulse which will elevate it to a better position than it has ever before possessed."

After three years of unjust and irrational complaints against Mexican thieves, the vicious system (" malpractice ") which has so greatly injured the interests of the stock raisers of Texas has been discovered; they condemn the custom of selling cattle without the consent of the owner, recognizing the fact that by this means the door was left open to a thousand abuses which have occasioned incalculable injuries to the proprietors; they see that immense and scandalous frauds have been committed, and they even suggest punishment on the gallows to those who commit these crimes in the future.

The Commission has already expressed an opinion relative to these abuses, which they discovered through the investigations practiced by them in Matamoros in the latter part of the past year, and are now convinced that they were correct in their judgment, since the whole force of Texan stock raisers, through their organ, " *The Western Stock Journal*," so declare by the important confessions they make, and no matter what solution the association of stock raisers may arrive at to account for the grave difficulties they are about to consider, they have at least established the fact of the disorder, the amount of the incalculable losses sustained and the general abuses which exist, from their own confession, from the " coast to the mountains, and from the Colorado to the Rio Grande."

The disorder having been introduced in 1861, twelve years of constant abuses have been hardly sufficient to furnish a perfect knowledge of the causes, and, perhaps, the circumstance which has most contributed to drawing aside the veil which concealed them has been the coming of the American Commission. As in Texas there are several persons acquainted with the source of the fortune of Richard King and other *rancheros*, on seeing the anxiety with which many presented themselves to register injuries they had never sustained in losses of cattle, but had in reality caused them to a great number of their neighbors, the attention of the poor men of Texas, who are numerous, was attracted by an act of such barefacedness, and from thence proceeded the reaction which has been observed.

It is true that the estimates of damages sustained through

the loss of cattle was accepted in the proportion given by the claimants, and attributed to bands of Mexican criminals, and that such fabulous claims were presented to the United States Government, through the report of its Commission; but their amount, so enormously exaggerated, and the causes assigned by the claimants, offended the public sense of justice; they were at once denounced, classified as absurd, and people sought other causes which were quickly found.

The fears entertained that conflict might ensue on account of the abuses committed, reveal the existence of a great and profound evil, and there are symptoms that tranquility will be disturbed, unless they who have introduced the evil make an effort to check it in the interest of the future of business. The honest portion of the stock raisers have leagued themselves against the dishonest ones, and if the simple initiation of their work has resulted in the vindication of Mexico, it is to be hoped that a full discussion of the matter will lead to a full reparation.

But the evils which seem to be the base-work of the Stock Raisers' Association of Western Texas, are not the worst phases of the question, and probably they do not know all their details, which differ according to the localities in which the frauds are perpetrated. All these varieties the Commission have carefully weighed, and will here specify what they discovered very lately in the county of Kerr. The bandits who have a refuge there dress like Indians, when sallying forth to rob and assassinate in all directions; and they were, under this disguise, engaged in the robbery of cattle and horses. The jury who made this declaration after careful investigations, did not include it in their report, although it was not doubted that the persons engaged in the scandalous trade with New Mexico found allies in the banditti of Kerr.

The present condition of Kerr county, the civil authorities of which are unable to defend it against the attacks of thieves and murderers, is sufficient proof of the truth of this statement. The "*Weekly Express* of October 2," from that county, contains the following statement:*

---

* Cuaderno, No. 8, of Vouchers, p. 64.

" For several years Kerr has been the point of union of criminals, who are compelled to flee from other places, and who devote themselves there to their profession."

In view of this condition of affairs, a company of cavalry, by command of General Augur, marched to Kerr to preserve peace, but notwithstanding this, a correspondent of the *Daily Herald* wrote from that county, the nest of criminals, an article published August 20th, as follows : *

" We maintain that the only solution to the question of the defense of the frontier, is the establishment of our line beyond the Rio Grande, and, if necessary, to the Sierra Madre."

Previous to this, on the 7th of the same month, the " Weekly Express," of San Antonio, published an article stating that the counties of De Witt, Goliad, Karnes, Victoria and others were infested with bands of robbers and highwaymen† —

" Because the authorities are incapable of restraining them. And what do we see in Kerr ? The citizens of that place, in order to defend their lives and property, are compelled to neglect their business and organize themselves into companies of militia. What a state of society is this ! Is the law a dead letter? In some other parts of the State, the court houses have been burned and the towns pillaged by bands of armed criminals."

Some time later, on the 4th September, the same paper, in referring to De Witt county, remarked that there existed there two large bands, well armed, who threatened the public tranquility, and that the sheriff, through either fear or inability, was unable to cope with them ; the article concluded as follows : ‡

" This condition of things is not peculiar to the county of De Witt ; it is the same throughout the State, and is the result of the abolition of the State police."

---

* Cuaderno, No. 8, of Vouchers, p. 47.
† Cuaderno, No. 8, of Vouchers, p. 49.
‡ Cuaderno, No. 8, of Vouchers, pp. 52 and 63.

The state of affairs described by the newspapers as general throughout the State of Texas, was also alluded to in *The Daily Herald*, of San Antonio, of the 31st of May, relating that Martin S. Culver, of Corpus Christi, had been in the office, on that date, and had said : *

" I am the bearer of sworn affidavits and statements of a great many of the most honorable persons, showing the manner in which they have been robbed, *not by persons who reside on the other shore of the Rio Grande, but by people living on this side*. The chief of the band conducted a train of seven cars in which the hides of the animals they had stolen were openly conveyed to a *rancho*, and that in view of such acts it was absurd to even suggest that the thieves came from Mexico."

About the same time, a band of Americans and Mexican Texans † made an assault on Corpus Christi, according to a publication in the *Galveston News* of the 6th of July last.

Martin S. Culver, one of the claimants against Mexico, before the American Commission, on account of cattle said to have been stolen by the Mexicans, has damaged his claim by the petition which he has presented to the governor of Texas, asking protection against the thieves who live in Texas, and not in Mexico; he must be aware that he has prejudiced his own claim and that of his companions, but very likely preferred this to seeing his ruin consummated by the legion of banditti who were quartered there.

Still greater disorders have occurred in other counties. In the county of Dimmitt, for instance, which is situated on the Rio Grande, north of Webb and south of Maverick, the inhabitants are for the greater part thieves and murderers. ‡ The stealing of horses is committed by them in the most barefaced manner ; they hire escaped prisoners from the jails in Mexico, and employ them in stealing horses from Mexico, and not content with this, they murder the Mexican travelers who stop at their ranchos to sell horses, take possession of the ani-

---

* Cuaderno, No. 8, of Vouchers, p. 58.
† Cuaderno, No. 8, of Vouchers, p. 58.
‡ Expedientes, 1, 2, 4 and 5, pp. 102 to 173.

mals and enjoy the benefits of their guilt in the face of the populace, who are well aware of the manner in which such property is acquired.

Some of these bandits have crossed over into Mexican towns, contracted for valuable horses, and the owners, on going to leave the animals at Carrizo, Dimmitt county, have been murdered. These banditti appear as claimants against Mexico for large sums on account of cattle said to have been stolen by Mexican citizens and soldiery directly and indirectly under protection of the Mexican authorities. The investigations pursued have done nothing less than demonstrate the double robbery which the inhabitants of Carrizo have been indulging in ; first by the sale of animals of all kinds of brands, and then, after having aided in the transportation of cattle across the Rio Grande at points not authorized by law, they receive the animals again as stolen property whenever the Mexican authorities have voluntarily rescued them from the thieves.

It has been said of these inhabitants of Texas, by their fellow-citizens * who know them well, and are acquainted with their habits and mode of living, that all the crimes of which they are accused can well be believed, because they are quite capable of any crime in the calendar. They were the first who introduced cattle into Mexico for sale, and they are the ones who have continued the traffic. The fact of being a stock raiser in Texas is a passport for robbery, as one who sells animals belonging to another is not considered a thief provided he is also an owner, and nothing is more frequent than the sale of large lots of cattle in which there is not a single animal belonging to the vendor.

It is an old habit in a certain rancho that some of the stock raisers themselves, or the Mexicans whom they employ, drive in large herds of cattle, formed of animals from Leona, Medina, Frio and las Nueces, and divide the profits after the sales are made.

It has been frequently observed, that when the thieves have been apprehended with cattle stolen from the above-named

---

* Expedientes, 1, 2, 4 & 5, pp. 102 to 173.

ranchos,* and escaped from the jails in Mexico, they seek refuge in the aforementioned county, where they live as herdsmen to the stock raisers, notwithstanding that some of these very stock raisers, on recovering the stolen cattle, have seen them in irons in the prisons of Mexico.

These acts, which are referred to amongst the many that have been proved by means of the investigations instituted on the right bank of the Rio Grande, are sufficient to form an idea of the extent of the demoralization on the opposite shore. Nor is there any intention to deny that it also exists, in a measure, on the Mexican bank; it certainly exists in the majority of the places, but, unlike the case in Texas, criminals do not control the towns, intimidate the action of justice, nor are the headquarters of their machinations established in Mexico.

It has already been shown of what these banditti are capable. Kerr county alone, whose nearest point is situated forty leagues from the Rio Grande, gives ample food for thought and deep reflection in the late horrible acts committed there, not only on account of the criminality of the principal actors, but because of the demoralization existing amongst the masses of the people. The banditti are not afraid to live amongst them; on the contrary, they attended the investigations of the jury which sat in the case of Madison, who was murdered in order that his house might be appropriated by one of the chiefs of the band who had fancied it. So great, indeed, was their confidence that most of them sent for their families.†

These details prove that there were intimate relations and a life in common between the banditti and the rest of the inhabitants of the county, where they first engaged in the stealing of hides and the transportation of cattle, and then perpetrated other atrocities in the counties of Brown, Medina, Boerne, Sabinal, Pedernales, and other points, it having been clearly proved that for five or more years they had been committing these depredations.

The same person who, in the month of July, informed the

---

* Expedientes, 1, 2, 4 & 5, pp. 102 so 160.
† Cuaderno, No. 8, of Vouchers, pp. 14, 15, and 28.

Daily Herald * of the acts of the banditti whilst disguised as Indians, wrote, on May 3 : " that there had been incursions of Kickapoos, Lipans, Seminoles, &c., with their not less brutal allies, the *Mexican Greasers*, to whom the assassination of the Terry family was attributed." This family, as was afterwards discovered, and reported by the same correspondent, had been sacrificed by the disguised banditti who infested Kerr, and who were not in reality the Kickapoos, Lipans, Seminoles and their allies the Mexican Greasers. Thus is truth perverted, and thus she punishes those who belie her, discovering their guilt at once, condemning them out of their own mouths, and branding them as inconsistent and destitute of common judgment.

And in order to make the calumny more glaring, it will be well to copy the letter which this same writer caused to be published, on the 17th of July last, two months after he had furnished the previous information : †

" Up to the present it has been almost impossible to believe that a great part of the depredations attributed to the Indians were committed by white men, but there is now no doubt whatever upon this subject. The statement of young Baker is fully corroborated. A great many of the details cannot yet be published, but from what is already known it would seem that these banditti do not number less than from fifty to seventy in this part of Texas. The atrocities committed by them under the guise of Indians, have been numerous. Our readers must recollect the murder of Mr. Alexander in this county about five years ago ; the assassination of the daughter and grandchildren of Mr. Coe in Brown county ; and later, that of the Terry family, near Zanzemburg, ten miles from Kerville. All these murders were, at that time, attributed to the Indians (and as it will be remembered, to the Indians resident in Mexico, and to their allies, the Mexicans), but to-day there is no doubt whatever that these horrible deeds were perpetrated by those disguised white devils."

These acts described by the same person, were attributed at one time to the Mexican Indians, because it suited his purpose to do so, and afterwards, in defense of the truth, to the real

---

* Cuaderno, No. 8, of Vouchers, p. 14.
† Cuaderno, No. 8, of Vouchers, p. 14.

criminals. He gives at the same time a sketch of the horrible condition of things on the Texan frontier, and declares that all the charges against Mexico are as unfounded as those of the above named murders, which were attributed to residents of that country.

All sense of justice is completely ignored, and the administration of law so lax that one of the bandits of Kerr, at the point of being lynched, " cursed those who had not perjured themselves to save him." Another asked how many witnesses were needed to establish his innocence, and this, as the *Herald* naively remarks, needs no commentaries.*

Whilst the Texan frontier was being devastated by the means and the people referred to, the Mexican frontier was suffering like injuries from the very same sources.

The relations between the two places are so intimate and so closely connected, that it would be impossible for the injuries suffered by the one not to be felt by the other. And, as if to make the evil unendurable, these relations are based upon the poorest kind of foundation, consisting; 1st. In the inequality with which justice is meted by the authorities in cases of robbery : the Americans invariably urge immediate restoration of cattle stolen in Texas, without previous investigation as to whether the same have been transported to Mexico, and make it a positive obligation on the part of the Mexican authorities to recover the property and capture and punish the criminals. Quite the contrary happens when the Mexicans reclaim horses stolen from Mexico ; no attention whatever is paid to these demands, nor are the proceedings of the Mexican authorities in the case accepted as proof of the act. Action taken by individuals must be subject to the laws of the country, and, as every one knows, proceedings of this kind are expensive, and it generally ends by the owner renouncing his rights and losing his property.

2d. The lack of reciprocity, arising from the different customs of the two countries : whilst in Mexico official warrants are accépted in the course of the proceedings which may be

---

* Cuaderno, No. 8, of Vouchers, p. 13.

had in a foreign country, the United States rejects them, trusting to the investigations made by its consuls.   *   *   It is believed that this practice influences the conduct of the American authorities, and causes them to reject as evidence the warrants of the Mexican authorities; holding that the crime demands a trial in the place where the stolen property and thief are found, they also require the evidence to be given at such place.

The Commission finds no other rational explanation of so irregular a proceeding as that practice by the American authorities without exception, no matter what precedents be offered them, notwithstanding that the law of Texas, as has been stated above, qualifies as theft that which has been committed in another place, even though it be in a foreign country.

It has been observed that the Mexican stock raisers on the right bank, in order to facilitate somewhat the recovery of their stolen animals, are compelled to register their brands in Texas, a circumstance which indicates that no confidence is given to the certificates of the Mexican authorities. Besides, that nullifies the beneficial effects of the law above quoted, which qualifies as theft that act which would be so considered if committed in Texas.

Following this unequal course, the proprietors of Texas have greater facilities for recovering their stolen property, because they are aided by the civil and military authorities, without other proofs being required save a notice of the robbery and a description of the property. The Mexicans almost always lose the property stolen from them.

Since the year 1848, after immigration commenced in Texas, the losses of cattle have been incalculable, for in order to stock the *ranchos* they stole all the animals from Mexico. From that time, when the stealing of horses commenced which exists to the present date, there has evidently been no successful effort on the part of the Texan authorities to put a stop to that evil. It has permeated that State under other favorable causes, and helped to develop the principle of immorality which has been fostered for years, like disease, and spread into Mexico, inciting and stimulating the robberies committed there. The receivers were converted into thieves, and that explains the existing question of the stock raisers. The serious discord existing amongst them arises from a pernicious system, allowing the appropriation of another's property, which, as a natural and logical consequence, gives room for the illegal traffic of these men with the thieves of Mexico.

The first case of cattle robbery which presented itself in the upper part of the Rio Grande, took place in San Felipe rancho, Texas, and was committed by Americans; afterwards a few of the residents of the towns in the district of Rio Grande stole from the same rancho some cattle, and by a simple notification of the act, without a warrant from the owner, the commandant ordered the apprehension of the delinquents, the entering of suit and the return of the stolen property, giving immediate notice to the Governor of Nuevo Leon and Coahuila, who approved the resolution and action taken, and agreed with him to adopt in the future the following regulations : *

First, That all robbery perpetrated in the United States, does not cease to be such because the stolen property is conveyed into the territory of Nuevo Leon and Coahuila.

Second, An act of this kind once proved, the civil authorities were bound to proceed, either *ex officio* or by request of some person, to the capture of the thieves, the recovery of the stolen property from the person with whom it is found, and who holds it either as deposit or by purchase, and the return of the same to its owners or the legal representatives thereof who prove ownership.

Third, The delinquents to be sent to the capital of the Government.

Fourth, When, through default of proofs, proceedings are instituted against suspected parties, a brief of the proceedings (*acta*) must be drawn and sent with the accused to the capital.

Fifth : In respect to property stolen in the State, and conveyed to the opposite shore of the Bravo, like proceeding will

---

* Cuaderno, No. 14, of Vouchers, p. 51.

be instituted against the culprits, according to the spirit of the preceding regulations, reserving to the interested parties the right to recover the stolen property in a neighboring State, by any means which is possible, although the authorities cannot act *ex officio* in this respect. Nevertheless, they can furnish to the parties the certificates or documents necessary to establish the fact of the injuries received.

In issuing these regulations, the Governor took care to express that they referred to the robberies being perpetrated, with scandalous effrontery, on both shores of the Rio Bravo, the stolen goods consisting principally of horses and cattle, which were publicly sold on either shore, in utter heedlessness of the crime, which was no less one because they crossed the lines with the goods.

It was also set forth that the crime was in its infancy, and that on account of the pernicious effects likely to result from it it was necessary to suppress it in the beginning. The draft of these regulations is alone sufficient to show opposition of the Mexican authorities to the depredations committed in Texas. When in the exercise of ample authority, such as the government at that time enjoyed, every effort was made to prosecute the criminals, who, be it remembered, appeared simultaneously with the Confederation. Such was the zeal of the authorities that excesses ensued ; they trampled all tutelary forms of justice, forced judgments from judges competent to act, and in the abhorrence of the crime and the criminals, they constituted themselves defenders of the interests of Texas, without caring for or expecting reciprocity.

The Mexican authorities have latterly employed their energies, under various regulations, to put a stop to this most scandalous traffic. The arrest of various parties along the line from Guerrero to Resurrection, and the punishment of some of the thieves, is the fullest demonstration that they know how to fulfill their duties, and this is the more conspicuous, when it is reflected that neither the Texan rancheros nor the United States troops have arrested any thieves, notwithstanding that they might have easily done so, from the knowledge they must necessarily possess of their grazing lands, and

because of the time and labor employed by the thieves to collect a herd of fat animals, which, as is well known, are not
always to be found together.

These and other circumstances enumerated by the witnesses, and the fact that the Mexican authorities gave spon-
taneous information of the places selected in Texas* for
collecting the herds, and the passes of the river likely to
be used in their transportation, which information the stock
raisers of Carrizo, Dimmitt county, never availed themselves
of, leave room for belief that it is with their concurrence and
participation that the robberies are committed.

In order to present at a glance a practical demonstration,†
so to express it, of the groundlessness of the charges against
the authorities in regard to the cattle stolen, the Commission
have caused to be made a map showing the course of the Rio
Grande, from its mouth, in the Gulf, to San Vicente, a point
on the boundary between Coahuila and Chihuahua, a distance
of about two hundred leagues. Men well versed and familiar
with the country have determined the localities of the ranchos
on both banks of the river, the distances between them, the
passes of the river at ordinary times, the points at which there
are ferries or boats or other means of crossing, and finally the
moorage on the margin of the river. The ranchos are so situated on either bank that if there existed good police regulations, and these were vigilantly executed, the inhabitants might
be maintained in peace and security. The fact that for a great
distance along the bank of the river the ranchos are in such
close proximity that one can be seen from the other, added to
the certainty that it is at these points that the robberies are
oftenest committed, compels one to believe that there is great
neglect either in the enforcement of the laws, or the framing of
such as would most effectually put a stop to these abuses.

In the course of their investigations, the Commission placed
this latter supposition beyond a doubt, since in Texas every one
is at liberty to kill cattle in the pastures without being com-

---

* Expedientes, 1, 2, 4 and 5, pp. 146 and 147.
† See foregoing "*Expedientes*," pp. 74 to 261.

pelled to notify the authorities, a circumstance which, from an exaggerated respect for the rights of property and individual liberty, has given rise to the existing disorders. They would be difficult to occur in Mexico on account of the excellent police regulations, which, although observed only partially, serve to maintain a degree of established order.

If, furthermore, it be observed that the boats across the river are for the greater part in possession of the *rancheros* residing in Texas, and that generally these vessels have to be employed in the transportation of the cattle, it being a slow and difficult proceeding to make them swim, it cannot but be admitted that the frequent robberies which occur could never take place except through the carelessness or connivance of the Texans with the thieves. Both exist, and greatly contribute to the perpetration of the crime, and account for the fact that the arrest of thieves in Texas is so rare.

The difficulties arising out of the robbery of cattle and horses, it will be seen, are reciprocal, and have their points of contact, for it not unfrequently happens that the ones are exchanged for the others. The *ranchos* of Texas swarming with fugitive servants from Mexico, whose habits and inclinations are not of the best, have always fostered an element of demoralization which, added to that already existing in Texas, has caused evils on either bank of the river. The Mexican shore has suffered a triple loss: in the absence of men, considered as an instrument of labor; in the capital, which at the time of his flight the servant owes his master (a positive loss of capital), for in order to secure the services of these men it is necessary to advance their salaries; and lastly, through the depredations committed by these men, who after their flight dedicate themselves to the theft of horses from the grazing lands with which they are well acquainted, in order to dispose of the animals to speculators, who purchase the stolen goods without scruple, and even hire these men to commit the crime.

The immense losses suffered by the Mexican frontier, through the flight of servants, may be computed at over one million a year.* The result of the information collected in Nuevo Leon and Coahuila, authorizes the fixing of this amount.

From less than one half of the municipalities of the two States referred to,† which have furnished data upon this matter, there appears to have fled into Texas, since 1848 to the present, two thousand eight hundred and twelve servants, who have transported thither their families numbering two thousand five hundred and seventy-two persons. The liabilities of two thousand and twenty-eight of these fugitives from proprietors of Nuevo Leon, amount to a sum of two hundred and fifty-five thousand nine hundred and ninety-five dollars and eighty cents ($255,995 80), and that of the others, who are from Coahuila, amount to one hundred and twenty-three thousand one hundred and twenty dollars and twenty cents ($123,120 20).

Nearly half a million of dollars of actual loss; but it is not so much the loss of money that attracts the attention of the Commission, as that of labor to places where the population is sparse, the lack of men being a loss of capital to the country, considered as they are instruments of labor.

Dr. Engel, a famous German statistician, calculates that it requires the sum of one thousand one hundred and twenty-five dollars to place a person of either sex in a condition to become a producer. If, under this rule, an estimate is made of the amount lost by the Mexican frontier, including the debts of the fugitives, we have a sum of fifteen millions four hundred and twenty-nine thousand six hundred and twenty-three dollars ($15,429,623), an amount which does not include any elements except those which ought to be considered and which refers to the double character of producers and consumers borne by the five thousand two hundred and eighty-four persons emigrating from Mexico, to escape the labor to which they were in duty bound.

The United States, whose prosperity is in a great measure accountable to this personal capital or labor furnished by other countries to augment its wealth, cannot have benefited

---

* Cuaderno, No. 9, of Vouchers, pp. 1 to 108.
† Cuaderno, No. 9, of Vouchers, pp. 1 to 108.

much by that acquired from Mexico, for, unfortunately, they bring with them a vicious element which, added to that of the floating population congregated there from all parts of the world, and composing a considerable mass of the inhabitants, imperils the preservation of good habits of order and peace, as is demonstrated by the existing demoralization in the State of Texas.

The fugitive servants referred to are for the most part criminals, for they always steal before fleeing or have already been prosecuted for other crimes, and it is only reasonable to suppose that in the United States, where they take refuge, they do not maintain any better conduct. These criminals and others of another class, especially the cattle thieves who have managed to escape, all reside in Texas, having a permanent or transitory nationality in the United States, and in the crimes they commit, as is clearly shown, neither the inhabitants nor the authorities of Mexico can take any part. The evil is plainly the result of a lack of good police regulations which would impede the combination of evil disposed persons such as the classes above mentioned.

Freedom of labor having been established as a constitutional principle, the institution of *servants*, once a specialty and considered necessary on the frontier, cannot to-day be sustained, nor would it be advisable, either morally or economically considered. But the annoyances endured, and the evils involved are of the most paramount interest to both frontiers, as regards the peace and harmony of each. The matter deserves consideration, and a stop should be put to the abuses, by laws, which properly enforced, would close the door to the system of roaming, which is indulged in by the people of the States of Nuevo Leon, Coahuila and Tamaulipas, towards the frontier of Texas.

The institution of field labor having undergone a radical change, by action of law and a better knowledge of true economy, the old system is fast disappearing. Whilst this change is taking place, the energies of the authorities should be employed in causing, directly or indirectly, the return of servants, by means of extradition, when they have committed robberies or other crimes, and by the collection of debts in Texas. This last might be effected through the public agents charged with facilitating extradition, agreeably to the principles proposed by the Commission.

When it will be known to the fugitives that Texas is no longer a place of refuge where they can flee with impunity, after swindling their creditors, the tide of emigration will be diminished on the part of men who, by their habits of idleness, are no less pernicious to the State of Texas than to the frontier of Mexico, and beneficial effects will be enjoyed by all parties through the advantageous measures which may be adopted, to produce this result.

A BRIEF SKETCH OF THE INDIAN TRIBES WHICH HAVE LIVED IN MEXICO.

It having been affirmed in a public document that the Kickapoos, Lipans, Seminoles, Carrizos, and other tribes were sheltered in Coahuila and Chihuahua, and enabled thereby to invade Texas with impunity, this Commission undertook to collect from the archives all the information to be found concerning the said tribes, knowing that the propagators of such statements could be satisfactorily refuted, inasmuch as the Kickapoos only of the above mentioned Indians, have ever lived in Mexico.

Valuable information communicated by General Augur, in command of the Department of Texas, to the American Border Commission, proves the fact of Indian depredations in Texas, along the whole line of the Rio Grande to Paso del Norte; but as that Commission did not visit the regions which suffered such evils, it declared the evidence to be imperfect. It nevertheless deemed the data sufficient foundation for a charge against Mexico, which is found in the report of the said Commission, rendered to its government on the 10th of December, 1872.

In order to ascertain the facts concerning the Carrizo

Indians, and the others who were said to have their hiding-places in Mexico, and to use them as points of departure, and of asylum in the perpetration of inroads upon Texas, this Commission has spared no labor, and has sought for the truth, rather in documents of ancient date, than in the evidence of witnesses.

These researches were commenced by examining the archives of Reynosa, and it was fully ascertained, that not a single one of the tribes mentioned, had any existence in that district.

The Carrizos were the original inhabitants of that region, when it was discovered and occupied by the Spanish Government. They were formed into missions, were partially civilized, and became the basis of the population of the present towns along the Rio Grande. Very few individuals of the tribe persisted in maintaining the customs, language and name of the tribe; but even these have disappeared, and their descendants are now blended with the mass of the population in all the towns on the right bank as far as Guerrero. They are employed chiefly as domestic servants, for which they are in great request on account of their proverbial honesty. Evidence obtained at Camargo fully confirmed these facts, and documents were found, which put an end to all question on the subject.

In 1857, the Governor of Nuevo Leon having received complaints against the Carrizos, as being the perpetrators of the depredations suffered that year at Agualeguas and Cerralvo, transmitted them to the authorities of Mier and Camargo in Tamaulipas. The reply made from the latter point, under date of August 5th, contained the following statement:

" If your excellency was surprised to hear that this class of Indians had committed the ravages generally attributed to the Comanches and Lipans, how great must have been my surprise on reading your communication, since *I positively know* that the said tribe known as Carrizos in the time of the missions, became extinct several years ago; their descendants having abandoned the manners, customs and peculiar language of the tribe, and become blended with the people at large. Your excellency may therefore rest assured, that you have been

incorrectly informed, concerning the *supposed Indians* residing
hereabouts, and it is scarely credible that the enemies of peace
should employ such wicked means for stirring up discord."

This paragraph, written in 1857, is the most convincing
reply that could be made to the accusation made sixteen years
later by the American Commission. The Judge of Camargo
could scarcely believe, in 1857, that the Carrizos were accused,
inasmuch as they had not existed for many years, and he
lamented that any hearing had been given to persons who
wanted only a pretext for stirring up discord. What can be
said now of those who present similar charges? The same as
was then said by the Judge of Camargo, *i. e.*, that enemies of
public peace and the fraternity of nations are employing per-
verse means for accomplishing their objects. The complainants might also be invited to come and point out the Indians
whom they accused, which would be impossible, because they
do not exist.

The Commission wished to carry the investigation to an extreme, although it was no longer necessary, and it obtained the
same result at Mier and Guerrero. The tribe of Carrizos did
not exist; it had disappeared, and its descendants testified to
this fact before the Commission at Guerrero.

The Carancahuases, Indians from Texas, were mentioned at
Reynosa by some witnesses, who testified that this tribe had
been driven into Mexico by American troops since 1848, and
had obtained an asylum. In 1688 this tribe lived on the Bay
of Espiritu Santo, where it was found by the governor of Coahuila, Don Alonso de Leon, when, by order of the Viceroy of
Mexico, he marched with troops to that point to drive away
the French, who had gained a footing there. It was found
that these Frenchmen had already been massacred by the
Carancahuases, who remained in the same region even after
the colonization of Texas by Don José Valdivielso, Marquis of
San Miguel de Aguayo, who, in 1719, penetrated as far as Red
river, the boundary between Texas and Louisiana. The colony
brought soon after by the marquis from the Canary Islands did
not disturb these Carancahuases, otherwise called Tampacuases.

These Indians, few in number when Texas ceased to belong

to Mexico, were driven thence, and were, in 1852, located within the jurisdiction of Reynosa at "La Mesa" and other points. Yielding to the habits of their vagabond life, they soon manifested their inclination to plunder, obliging the authorities of that town to organize troops and reduce them to order. General Avalos interfered in the case by virtue of instructions from the general government, took them under his protection, and removed them to the center of Tamaulipas, not far from Burgos. There they gave occasion to dispute between the governments of Nuevo Leon and Tamaulipas, which led to their being carried back to their former place of residence near Reynosa. Being again attacked on account of robberies, the tribe removed to Texas, and on the 26th of October, 1858, the judge of Rosario sent the following report to the mayor of Reynosa:

"In pursuance of your orders of the 23d instant, for the arrest of the Carancahuases, I took measures for that purpose, but finding that they are now on the left bank of the Rio Grande, beyond the limits of my authority, at the place called 'Uresteña,' I informed the authorities at Rosario and Bañon, to the end that they on the American side and we on this side may combine for their arrest, since, besides the horses they have carried off, they have committed other robberies at La Mesa. With the inhabitants of this district, I have explored all this region in their pursuit."

The history of these Indians terminates with an attack made upon them in the said year 1858 by Juan N. Cortina, then a citizen of Texas, along with other *rancheros*, when they were surprised at their hiding place in Texas, and were exterminated.

These Carancahuases were undoubtedly the "other Indians" referred to by the American commission in connection with the Lipans, Kickapoos, Seminoles and Carrizos. They were the only ones known in Tamaulipas of whom information could be had at Brownsville, and the accuracy of such information may now be readily inferred.

Shortly after the establishment of the military colonies, in 1850, certain Seminoles, Kickapoos and Muscogees presented themselves in the district of Rio Grande, in the State of Coahuila, soliciting lands on which to settle, since they truly affirmed that the Americans had appropriated their own lands. The sub-inspector of colonies reported the fact to his immediate superior, and the latter signed on the 26th of July an agreement by which they were given lands on the rivers San Rodrigo and San Antonio, of equal extent to those usually set apart for colonies, and in recompense they promised their services against the savages, upon the same conditions as the Mexican colonists. The rights of citizenship were to be conferred upon them upon renunciation of American nationality.

During the same year, by direction of the Department of Foreign Affairs, the compact was amended by adding the following clauses, as obligations of the Indians:

" 1st. To obey the authorities and observe the laws of the republic. 2d. To preserve harmony with the nations friendly to Mexico. 3d. To prevent in every possible way the Comanches and other barbarous nomadic tribes from making their inroads through the region they inhabit; to punish and pursue them in case of invasion. 4th. To have no traffic with the barbarous tribes. 5th. To preserve the best harmony with the citizens of the United States of America, in accordance with the treaties of peace between that republic and Mexico."

These conditions were annexed to the favors extended by the government to the Seminoles, Kickapoos and Muscogees, were read and explained in presence of the officers of the colonies to the chiefs of the said tribes, and were accepted by all of them, after which they received gratuities from the inspector, and were promised the lands they had solicited.

It appears by a communication dated the 14th of July, 1851, from the sub-inspector of the colonies, that the Kickapoos had committed an act of treachery by suddenly withdrawing from a campaign which they were making along with regular troops against the Comanches, robbing at the same time the horses recaptured from the savages. Being then located at " Tulillo," they crossed to the left bank, instigated by the people at Eagle Pass. Of the large number of Kickapoos who the year before had sought the hospitality of Mexico, there only remained nine men, seven women and four children under the command of the chief Papicua, who reported the robberies committed by the remainder of the tribe from their new location on American soil. Colonel Maldonado, the sub-inspector of the colonies, lost no time in transmitting these facts to the commander of the American forces at Fort Duncan, invoking all the stipulations of the treaty of Guadalupe, but in vain. The American authorities took no measures, and the Kickapoos continued their depredations.

The lands set apart for the Indian emigrants were on the right bank of the Rio Grande, but the events above mentioned showed that it was inexpedient for the Seminoles, Muscogees and the nine Kickapoos to continue to occupy them, the neighborhood of the United States being dangerous in every respect. The remaining tribes were therefore persuaded to remove to the mountains of Santa Rosa, thirty leagues to the westward.

The Seminoles and Muscogees undoubtedly found the new location an advantageous one, for the next year, in July, 1852, Wild Cat, chief of the Seminoles, and Papicua, chief of the remnant of the Kickapoos, were in the city of Mexico soliciting as a reservation the locality called "Nacimiento," which was granted them under a new compact celebrated with the War Department, as also a similar reservation in Durango, in recompense for the good service they had begun to render in the war against the savages. Papicua settled near Villa Morelos, where he devoted himself to agriculture, and finally died.

As to the Seminoles we will now briefly narrate their history and comportment in Mexico up to the time when they all returned to the United States. While the chiefs of the Seminoles and Muscogees were negotiating in Mexico for their grants of land, several parties of those tribes were accompanying Colonel Langberg in his campaign against the Comanches, as far as the "Laguna de Jaco;" the remainder were engaged in agriculture and in hunting. A later campaign made by the Seminoles against the Comanches earned for them the thanks of the government, which, however, ordered that in future expeditions they should be accompanied by some Mexicans, as was done in 1853 and 1854. The next year they had a battle with the Mescaleros, inflicting upon the latter a loss of sixteen killed, 6 prisoners and 52 animals recaptured. Up to the close of this year, according to the reports made by the authorities at Santa Rosa, the Seminoles had given no occasion for complaint; they were industrious, warlike and desirous of education and religious instruction for their families.

Several expeditions were made by them in 1856 and 1857, with favorable results, but in the latter year many Seminoles died of small pox. Among the victims were the chiefs Wild Cat and Coyote. The authorities of Santa Rosa had occasion to report bad conduct on the part of the Muscogees, especially in refusing to co-operate with Col. Langberg for the defense of the frontier against filibusters.

Robberies made by the savages from these tribes in 1858 led to two combined expeditions. Differences between Seminoles and Muscogees about water privileges occasioned the appointment of a Mexican as a justice of the peace among them. A school had been maintained by the government for three years past.

Early in 1858, two chiefs who had gone to the United States to see their kinsmen, returned and tried to induce these tribes to go back to their former homes. This action was regretted by the Mexican authorities on account of the good services they were rendering against the savages. They were temporarily diverted from their purpose by a new campaign into the desert, but afterwards most of them were persuaded by two Americans, living at Santa Rosa, to set out for the north. On the 26th of February, 1859, there only remained at Santa Rosa 60 Seminoles, 22 of whom were fighting men, and the rest women and children.

Shortly afterwards the government directed that the Muscogees be removed a hundred leagues to the south to prevent their being carried off by filibusters.

On the 25th of August, 1861, the rest of the Seminoles went to Texas, in charge of members of the tribe who came to Nacimiento for that purpose, provided with passports from an American officer.

To understand fully the causes of the return of the Seminoles from Mexico to the United States, it will be expedient to remember that in 1857, an American named Barnard, residing at Corpus Christi, made a contract with the governments of Nuevo Leon and Coahuila for bringing the Florida Seminoles to Mexico. This contract was published at the time, and undoubtedly influenced the subsequent conduct of the agents of the American government.

On the 12th of March, 1859, a representative of the United States agent for the Seminoles came to Villa Guerrero, and informed Colonel Blanco that his object was to bring about the removal of the two tribes in question to their reservations. This person was given a passport and an escort to Monterey, and was accompanied thither by the Seminole "Tiger," this mission leading to the removal which took place two years later, as above mentioned, to the general regret of the inhabitants of Santa Rosa.

The measures taken at this time for the return of the Seminoles to the United States did not spring from any misdeeds committed by them in Texas. No accusation of the kind was brought against them. The motive may have been to reunite the dispersed members of the tribe, or the fear that the Mexican portion would attract their American brethren, and thus leave the agents without the gains of their official posts. At all events, the action was not a just one, for it damaged legitimate Mexican interests, on which considerable sums had been spent.

At the close of 1861, not one of the tribes in question lived in Mexico, except the so-called Black Muscogees, at Parras; numbering from 40 to 60 persons. The Seminoles and Kickapoos were all gone, except nine of the latter, who lived at Morelos and Allende as farmers and teamsters, several of whom, however, had already been killed in Texas in 1859, when they went thither to sell deer skins and furs.

In the heat of the Confederate war and our war against the French intervention, the Kickapoo chief, Tobacco, asked from the military commander of the district of the Rio Grande, permission and an outfit to go to the north and bring back many of his tribe who wished to come to Mexico. It appears by a communication from the government of Nuevo Leon, dated

December 6th, 1863, that the expenses incurred in complying with his request were approved.

On the 13th of October, 1864, the first alcalde of Santa Rosa reported that five days before, more than 200 Kickapoos of both sexes had presented themselves, asking for subsistence and permission to remain in that municipality, until they could solicit a permanent place of residence from the president of the republic. It was observed that they presented no passports from the authorities of Rio Grande district, but their journey had been along the high road, and they were presumed to be acting in good faith.

No other document on the subject appears in the archives of Santa Rosa until January, 1866, when the alcalde of that place acknowledges receipt of a decree of the 11th of that month, which granted to the Kickapoos the location of Nacimiento, formerly abandoned by the Seminoles and Muscogees.

From communications found at Rosa, Nava and Guerrero, it is found that in 1865, some of these Indians were engaged in hunting near Remolino, where they solicited and received rations of meat. They were also charged, about this time, with stealing horses at Resurrection, which led to secret investigations and precautionary measures. A circular order was sent to the ranchos near Piedras Negras, by the prefect of that district, directing the greatest vigilance in preventing the Kickapoos from going over to Texas to rob, as had been attempted by a party of eleven warriors at Pacuache ford. This attempt was prevented, and gave rise to strict injunctions from the government of Coahuila, to watch and report their conduct, accompanied by a threat of expulsion, in case of a repetition of the grievance.

The action of the Mexican Government in watching over the interests of Mexicans and Americans was loyal, prompt and efficacious, and for three years thereafter, no further complaint was made against the Kickapoos. It was stated in the account of depredations in Texas, that up to 1868, the Kickapoos had not been mentioned, even as the *probable* perpetrators of outrages. This fact proves the good result of the warnings given and the measures of precaution taken in

1865. It should also be noted that the first charge made against the Kickapoos, of robberies in Texas, proceeded from Mason county, adjoining Kerr, where about this time bandits disguised as Indians had taken refuge. These same bandits had been accused of being in alliance with the Comanches in 1858, before the Kickapoos came to Mexico. Moreover, as Mason county is equidistant from the American and Mexican Kickapoo reservations, there is greater reason to attribute such depredations to the larger fraction residing in the United States, than to the smaller in Mexico.

It is nevertheless true, that the conduct of the Kickapoos was not always unexceptionable. A few isolated cases of robberies of cattle occurred, but the sufferers were almost always Mexicans, although in one or two instances, the depredation was committed on the Texan side of the river. The government of Coahuila and the military authorities of Rio Grande district were ever on the alert to discover and punish such depredations as were actually accomplished. On different occasions, several of the malefactors were killed in the act, others were imprisoned, and the stolen animals returned to their owners on both sides of the river. In February, 1866, the measures of repression adopted were so vigorous as to lead to a fear that the whole tribe might become hostile. A commissioner was appointed to reside among the Kickapoos for the special purpose of watching their conduct and recovering property supposed to have been stolen. On the 5th of July, 1867, that officer forwarded to the prefect of the district of Rio Grande, a description of the animals he had seized, giving their brands, and suggesting that the losers of animals be invited to reclaim their property. The leaders of the tribe were assembled and solemnly warned of the dangerous consequences which would ensue from any renewal of such depredations. The complaints from Mexican sufferers ceased in 1868, and the authorities of Santa Rosa, who had hitherto been conspicuous in accusations against the Kickapoos, defended them from the charge of collusion with the Comanches, alleging that the Kickapoos themselves had just been plundered of all their horses by that tribe of notorious marauders.

Alliances between the Comanches and the American section
of the Kickapoos, living on their reservations, had been made
before 1868. If the Comanches and Kiowas living in the same
region have marauded in every direction in Texas, as is known
to be the fact, there was nothing to prevent the American
Kickapoos from imitating their conduct. Many reasons combine to show that such was really the case. The Mexican
Kickapoos never numbered above 150 fighting men.. Of these
the greater part have been constantly employed in agriculture at
Nacimiento and San Blas, remote from the frontier. No
Mexican Kickapoo has been killed or captured by the American
regular forces, nor by the Texan militia in their numerous
engagements with the marauders.

The claims brought by American citizens and authorities
before the authorities of Muzquiz (Santa Rosa) have been attended to and their property returned in the few cases when
the losses proved to, be real. American complainants have
been allowed to go to the Kickapoo settlement in search of
their property, and the solicitude of the Mexican authorities
has been carried to the extreme of seizing horses from the Kickapoos on suspicion of their being stolen. In such cases, information has been sent to Texas for the benefit of the presumed
owners. The infrequency of such seizures and the small number of animals found, sufficiently proved that very few Indians were engaged in this criminal occupation.

This Commission does not undertake the defense of the
Kickapoos, for it is true that some individuals have committed
robberies. It maintains, however, that their inroads in Texas
have been insignificant, and this is shown by the fact that none
of the witnesses examined in the numerous places visited, have
seen Kickapoos offer horses or cattle for sale.

It is worthy of note that just at the time when these Indians had been reduced by earnest effort to lead a more orderly
life, an American commissioner, Mr. S. Brown, arrived at Santa
Rosa for the purpose of inducing them to remove to the United
States. He was allowed to propose the matter to the Indians,
but in spite of his offers of land and rations, they refused to

remove. The offer was renewed at Brown's request, by the authorities of Santa Rosa, with the same negative result.

It was now apparent that there would be complaints against the Indians, and the authorities, who a few months before had risked their existence in their repression of all misconduct, were indirectly threatened with the charges of complicity which have since been brought against them.

It may not be presumptuous, in view of the known fact of the multiform speculations carried on among the Indians of the reservations, to attribute to the private interests of agents and traders, their labors for the removal of Seminoles and other Indians who have sought refuge in Mexico. This conjecture is strengthened by the fact that in March and April, 1870, three or four different commissioners came to Santa Rosa for the common object of effecting the removal of the negroes and Kickapoos of Nacimiento. They succeeded in respect to the negroes, and the poverty of the Kickapoos made it probable that they would follow the example.

Such energy shown by private individuals in this matter, shows that depredations were not the cause of their action. Moreover, the poverty of the Kickapoos convinced the several commissioners of the falsity of the sweeping charges made against them in Texan papers, which represented them as committing murders and robberies on a grand scale, aided and abetted by Mexicans who publicly bought their booty.

In order to attend to the urgent wants of the Indians residing at Nacimiento, a census was taken in June, 1870, and they were found to number 500. The authorities of Santa Rosa then appealed to the philanthropy of the towns in the districts of Monclova and Rio Grande, for the relief of their wants, and the State government also succored them in consideration of the services they had rendered against the savages. It was just at this time that the commander of Fort Duncan and the commercial agent at Piedras Negras came to Santa Rosa, offering the Kickapoos great inducements and all kinds of guaranties for removing.

The excessive vigilance with which the Kickapoos were watched by the authorities of Santa Rosa, from 1867 onward, was on account of certain notorious losses suffered at their hands by Mexicans, and not on account of any forays into the United States. None such had occurred, and but rarely had a few thefts taken place on the left bank of the river. This vigilance will sufficiently acquit those authorities of the charge of collusion with the Kickapoos in any depredations.

The evidence gathered by this Commission in the towns it has visited, and the testimony of the archives conclusively show that the greater part of the Kickapoos have conducted themselves well. The exceptions have been very few in number, and their robberies have been of insignificant value, and chiefly in Mexico. The Commissioners, Messrs. Atkinson and Williams, who have again visited the Kickapoos this year (1873), have expressed a belief that they were not the perpetrators of any depredations in Texas. This conviction was the result of extended conferences with the chiefs of the tribe relative to their removal, in which those chiefs earnestly alleged that they had given no provocation for the McKenzie invasion, in which so many of their kinsmen had been massacred.

At this stage of the negotiation the Commissioners offered to go and obtain the release of the captives taken in the Mc-Kenzie raid before continuing the conferences. They set out for that purpose, but were obliged to return without having obtained that object. As the result of the final interviews, four hundred Indians agreed to return to the United States, while the remainder, numbering about two hundred, set out, some on foot, others in carts drawn by oxen, for a new place of residence farther to the south, on the boundary line between Durango and Coahuila.

This is the history of the Kickapoos during the eight years that they have lately resided in Mexico. Poverty, spoliation of their lands and persecution forced them in 1864 to abandon the territory of the United States, and the same causes have now led to their return. Their destiny—the destiny of the Indian race—pursues them everywhere. They are now divided and no longer form a people, but isolated families, whose names will soon be forgotten.

The difficulties under which the authorities of Mexico

labored in 1851, when this tribe first presented itself, were repeated on the second occasion, although assuming a different character. It was inevitable that semi-civilized tribes, foreign to our soil, would occasion such difficulties, which were due to a forgetfulness of the lesson taught on the earlier occasion, and to the violation of the wise rules laid down in September, 1850, prohibiting all negotiations with such tribes of Indians without the express approval of the supreme government.

The second immigration of the Kickapoos into our republic took place during the war with France, and was not known to the supreme government, unless, perchance, by means of complaints. It was a State government which received them and gave them lands near the American frontier. Recent occurrences have proved the great wisdom and prudence of the resolution taken in 1850, concerning the manner of regulating and directing Indian affairs.

AN ACCOUNT OF THE LIPANS.

The Lipans, one of the tribes composing the Apache nation, have for many years committed horrible depredations on the frontier of Mexico. It was they who, after having been defeated in 1789 and 1790, in the two famous campaigns directed by the celebrated Don Juan de Ugalde, first brought their allies, the Comanches, to this side of the Rio Grande, in 1813, when a long period of peace had filled the pasture grounds to overflowing with all kinds of cattle.

In the general summary of Indian invasions, a sufficient account has been given of their misdeeds up to 1854, at which date a peace was made with them by the governor of Coahuila. This act brought about difficulties with Texas, and also with Nuevo Leon ; the governor of the latter State refusing to admit the Lipans into its towns, on account of the ingratitude they had always shown to all similar favors. On this occasion again the wise rules of 1850 were broken by admitting within our borders a savage tribe, which was formidable not so much

27

from its numbers as from its familiar knowledge of our territory.

In the accounts of depredations in Nuevo Leon and
Tamaulipas, it has already been mentioned that the Lipans
were followed by parties from both those States, to ascertain
whether they had been the perpetrators of any of the outrages
suffered therein. On this errand Colonels Zuazua and Frutos
penetrated from Lampazos and Ciudad Guerrero to Villa de
Rosas, where the authorities aided their investigations, giving
them guides to the Indian encampments. Although no positive proofs against the Indians were found, the suspicions were
not quieted, since it was ascertained that some of the tribe
had previously disappeared, carrying away numerous horses.

These suspicions and other new complaints made by towns
in Mexico and Texas very properly engaged the attention of
the governor of the frontier, who, in December, 1855, wrote as
follows to the minister of war:

" The Lipan tribe which, in the time of the immortal
Iturbide, numbered nearly a thousand warriors, has suffered an
incredible diminution, owing to its wandering life and savage
habits; since its chiefs lately made peace with governor Car-
dona, the fighting men number only eighty-eight. Notwithstanding the treaty, the Americans and some of our frontier
towns have made complaints against these Indians, and the
military authority, therefore, appointed an agent to watch
their conduct and report their expeditions, so as to prevent or
punish them. The Lipan chieftains, who were not well pleased
with such supervision, which they attributed to Colonel Langberg, came to this office to complain of that measure; but
when they learned that it was by my order, and when I showed
them that it was a guaranty for them as regards both Americans and Mexicans, they went away satisfied, promising to
keep the treaty of peace. There is nothing to fear from this
tribe, which is located at a place which it cannot leave without
being observed, but as it is really composed of savages, it needs
a director who shall care for its education, and lands for cultivation."

The character of these Indians, their number, their situation,
the damages they had caused to Mexicans and Americans,
the necessity of watching over them and of stimulating their

inclination towards civilized life, are all described by the governor who exercised such strict supervision over them. A month later, in February, 1856, the Lipans were subjected to a searching investigation, in consequence of certain robberies in Coahuila and murders in Texas, when an order was given " to notify them for the last time, that the least complaint for damages caused on either side of the Rio Grande would be the signal for their extermination without discrimination of any kind." It was not until a month later, in March, 1856, that investigations were made in Texas, resulting in charges being made against the Lipans for the acts already mentioned. Appeal was made to the friendship and good will existing between the two countries, and co-operation was offered for putting an end to the depredations of the Lipans.

In replying to the note of Colonel Ruggles, of Fort McIntosh, in which the above mentioned complaint was made, the Governor of Nuevo Leon and Coahuila took occasion to make a demand and to remind the American officer of an unfulfilled duty. Under date of March 16th, 1856, he wrote as follows :

" I have the satisfaction to inclose copies of communications sent to the military commanders on the frontier. In them you will see that before you informed me of the murders and robberies committed by the Lipans, I ordered the arrest of the malefactors, and in case of resistance, to wage a war of extermination against them. I trust, Mr. Commander, that this conduct on the part of the Mexican authorities will be imitated by those of the United States, in respect to the Comanches, Kiowas and other barbarous tribes who, in large numbers, cross the Rio Grande to rob and devastate the territory of Mexico, and who sell their spoils to American citizens, as is fully proved by the kind of arms they employ, and the known existence of trading posts on the left bank of the Rio Bravo. It cannot be believed that the government of the United States will tolerate such traffic in the blood and fortunes of the citizens of a friendly nation, nor that when it learns the existence of this shameful and inhuman traffic, it will fail to instruct the commanders of detachments along the line to prevent the Indians from crossing, and the white settlements from supplying them with arms, as has heretofore been done from Moras up to Paso del Norte."

Under date of March 26th, the governor and commander-in-chief communicated to the war department the result of his proceedings against the Lipans, as follows:

" The auxiliary troops of Rio Grande and Lampazos having been placed under arms by my orders, the former surprised on the 19th instant, a party of 63 Indians near Villa Gigedo, and was conducting them to Rio Sabinas to act in concert with Colonel Zuazua; but before arriving there, the savages undertook to escape, while their women commenced killing their infants, rather than see them deprived of liberty. This unnatural action enraged the troops, and after Captain Miguel Patiño had in vain attempted to prevent the flight and this horrible butchery, he was forced to appeal to the last remedy, by putting to death 41 persons of both sexes. Meanwhile Colonel Zuazua was engaged in carrying out his own instructions, with a respectable force, and without awaiting the arrival of Captain Patiño, he attacked and disarmed the enemy, capturing 74 persons of all ages and both sexes."

Five days later, these events were communicated to Lieutenant-colonel Daniel Ruggles, in command at Fort McIntosh, in the following terms:

" My orders for the chastisement of the Lipans were carried out on the 21st, 22d and 23d instant, with such exactitude that the result surpassed my hopes, the whole tribe having been made prisoners, most of the warriors killed, and the small remnant so dispersed that their insignificant number cannot inspire any fears for the future. * * * I trust that the civil and military authorities of the United States will correspond to the desires and expectations of those of Mexico, who have now afforded a rare example of the interest they take in the misfortunes of their fellows, by imitating their conduct in regard to the Comanches and Kiowas, of whom I spoke in my note of the 16th instant."

It may be said that the history of the Lipans is brought to an end by the official notes above transcribed. The Commission might here close this subject, for the tribe disappeared in 1856, and the miserable remnants do not deserve the name of a tribe. But the charges which are still made against Mexico on their account, have forced the Commission to trace all their steps, even after the above date.

The statements of captives have supplied interesting data concerning the dispersed remnant of the Lipans. From their concurrent testimony, it appears that since 1856, the Lipans have lived on the banks of the Pecos river, united with the Mescaleros, and have marauded on both sides of the Rio Grande, maintaining traffic with the Comanches and with the people of New Mexico. Their residence on the Pecos river has also been abundantly proved by the combined expeditions of Mexicans and Americans made against them in that locality. They have not lived in Mexico except for a short time in 1868, when the vigilance over them was so strict that they soon decamped and returned to the Pecos. In April of the present year (1873), they presented themselves again, but the massacre of the Kickapoos frightened them away, and they went murdering and robbing on their retreat.

From 1856, when this tribe was nearly exterminated, to the present time, the remnants have presented themselves in Mexico three times, always with unmeaning offers of peace. The first time was in 1861, when they remained four months. Again in 1868, a fraction of them came and lived two years at Remolina. Finally, in April of the present year they again came, but withdrew in May on account of the McKenzie raid. Two years and a half of residence in Mexico against fourteen and a half in the United States.

This Commission finds itself bound to censure the procedure of the governments of Coahuila in this respect, since no amount of experience has been sufficient to teach them the impropriety of accepting propositions of peace from Indians who continually violated its stipulations and acted with evident duplicity. The exercise by that State of a faculty which belongs exclusively to the supreme government of the republic merits not merely censure but condemnation. The same may be said of the grants of land to the Kickapoos. The frontier needs settlers of a very different class, who are repelled by the presence of semi-barbarous Indians. This imprudent conduct, however, involves no offense against the United States, nor has that nation experienced any grievance from the short sojourn of the Kickapoo and Lipan Indians in Mexico.

INVASION OF MEXICAN TERRITORY BY FORCES OR CITIZENS OF THE UNITED STATES.

A profound sensation ought to have been caused, and was really caused, by the conduct of General McKenzie, when, without notice to any authority in Mexico, and without just cause, he invaded our territory with a detachment of the army of the United States, surprising a small encampment of Kickapoos which was living at Remolino engaged in the ordinary labors of agriculture.

The conduct of that officer has been reviewed in a separate document, in which this Commission believes that it has stated all the circumstances which explain it. It may here be mentioned that the judgment of the Commission differs entirely from that of the Texan press, which attributed that step to instructions left by the American secretary of war when he visited the Rio Grande frontier shortly before.

By the facts set forth in the sections devoted to Kickapoos and Lipans, the value of the accusations against the former may be correctly estimated. The name of the latter was never mentioned in this connection, it being well known that they resided in American territory. All the accusations were brought against the Kickapoos, for no other reason than that they lived in Mexico, and not a single proof of any depredations by them in Texas was alleged.

The abundant evidence collected by this Commission shows that the invasion was intimately connected with the recent arrival of a band of Lipans numbering thirty warriors, who had been admitted, as being peaceably inclined, by the government of Coahuila. They had settled at Remolino, adjoining the Kickapoos, with whom some of them lived, while others were engaged in tending their horses and cattle in the pastures of the Sierra. One of the Lipans had with him a Texan boy taken captive years before, whom the American commercial agent at Piedras Negras undertook to ransom.

Outrages had been committed in Kerr county and vicinity for a term of years by American bandits disguised as Indians, and their depredations were currently attributed to Kickapoos or Mexicans. Forays had in consequence been made by Texans of the frontier into Mexico, one of which, from its grave character and consequences, must be here narrated.

Under pretext of recovering stolen property, a party of fifteen or twenty Texans crossed the Rio Grande on the 27th of September and murderously assaulted the house of the alcalde (Aguilera) at Resurreccion or Villa Nueva. The aggressors had painted their faces black ; they were headed by a " notorious assassin " named McWeber, whose sole object was the murder of Aguilera, and among them were several wealthy citizens of Uvalde county. In the encounter the house was burned down, a woman and a boy were severely wounded, and Aguilera himself was killed after a heroic resistance, in which he killed three of his assailants. The horrible nature of this crime forced the Texan authorities to take cognizance of it. Several of the criminals were imprisoned, and the press loudly condemned the act, though writers were not wanting who defended it.

A person named Strickland wrote to a Texan paper a letter dated April 20th, from San Felipe, a rancho on the Rio Grande, 25 leagues above Eagle Pass or Fort Duncan. In it he charged that the surrounding region was being constantly plundered by Indians and Mexicans disguised as Indians, and complained of the impediments offered by the authorities to the pursuit of the robbers into Mexico, under pretext of the laws of neutrality, "which had," so he said, "become a dead letter, and been nullified by the continual incursions of people from the other side."

This letter undoubtedly produced considerable effect, which was strengthened by another written from Kerrville on May 3d to the San Antonio *Daily Herald*, accusing the Kickapoos, the Lipans, the Seminoles, red or black, and their *Mexican allies* of constant forays and murders in that district, as well as in Kendall and Bandera counties.

Close upon these letters came a dispatch from the commercial agent at Piedras Negras dated May 8th, quite as false and exaggerated as the above statements, which was undoubtedly the immediate cause of the McKenzie invasion.   It was textually as follows:

" *Editor of* EXPRESS :

"I have been 'informed that the Mescaleros have in their possession another boy who was taken captive five years ago at Olmos, near San Antonio and Bandera.   A messenger I sent to the Indian encampment to ransom him has returned, bringing word that the Indian who holds the boy is away on an incursion in Texas, and the captive cannot be given up until his return."

An agent or public officer of the United States should naturally be considered too discreet and prudent to propagate falsehoods.   The dissimulation with which it was done produced its full effect.   From the above dispatch it was inferred that the Mescaleros were living in Mexico, and this was false, for there was but a single one of them in Mexico, who was married to a Lipan woman, and lived on a rancho of his own. The falsity of the statement about the Indian whose absence on a foray in Texas delayed the ransom, is obvious to all who know the mysterious and reserved manners ‚of the Indians. Nevertheless, this item served as a text for a general explosion in the Texan press against Mexico, and these inflammatory appeals were speedily followed by the McKenzie raid, which took place just at a time when the new American Commissioners for the removal of the Kickapoos had passed through San Antonio, on their way to Monterey and Saltillo, at which latter place they were at the moment of its actual occurrence.   This circumstance adds force to our friendly construction that the raid was not directed by the American Government, but was due to a sudden resolution of General McKenzie, acting on his own responsibility.

According to official data, General McKenzie set out on the 17th of May, with six companies of the 4th regiment of cavalry and 25 Seminoles.   His force is estimated at 500 men. Crossing the Rio Grande with the utmost secrecy and advancing with great rapidity, he reached the Kickapoo village of Remolino, between 8 and 9 A. M., on the 18th of May, surrounded and burned it without resistance, killing 19 Indians, capturing 41 women and boys, and about 50 horses. The men were mostly away from the village, engaged in their agricultural occupations. The settlement of Lipans escaped attack, on account of a deep creek which separates it from the Kickapoos. After a hasty breakfast, for which they killed four cattle, the invaders retreated with the utmost rapidity, and had recrossed the Rio Grande before the militia of the Mexican towns could be assembled to avenge this audacious violation of Mexican territory.

The few horses which formed the only booty could not be identified as American property, and were accordingly distributed among the Seminole guides. The Lipans who had so narrowly escaped from a blow which was principally intended for them, speedily retired to a more secure encampment in the Sierra del Burro, and early in September they withdrew from Mexico, after murdering three persons and stealing more than two hundred horses.

Had it not been for the extreme swiftness of McKenzie's march, a conflict with the Mexican militia would have been inevitable. The forces of Piedras Negras, Moral and Resurrection, as well as all the other towns of the district were called to arms, but before they could be assembled the invaders had disappeared.

As to the pretext alleged for this violation of Mexican territory, the statements of two Americans concerned in it show that no one believed in any recent depredations by the Kickapoos, but that the Lipans were the intended objects of the attack. This fact clearly shows the injustice of the action taken, for the Lipans had been for many years, and until a month preceding, residents on the Rio Pecos in American territory.

Elsewhere this Commission has severely condemned the conduct of the Government of Coahuila, in granting terms of peace to the Lipans and permitting their residence within that State, but this condemnation does not at all justify the conduct of the American officer. So far as the United States are concerned, they cannot object to that procedure, for they had permitted the Lipans to reside quietly on the Rio Pecos, whence they had made repeated forays into Mexico. As long ago as 1861, they had carried off five boys as captives from Resurreccion, who were not recovered until 1868, when the tribe momentarily returned to Mexico. The surrender of captives, who could not otherwise be obtained, afforded a strong inducement to negotiate with them, and such negotiations were in no respect an offense against the United States, where they had so long been tolerated in the midst of the federal forts.

It has been observable for many years, that the Americans do not consider these Indians as public enemies, *except when they come to live in Mexico.* No one remembers them when they are within the United States; they are never mentioned nor attacked, nor are they thought to be capable of committing any outrage. But when they are living in Mexico, even under the severest vigilance, they are transformed into perpetrators of all the injuries suffered in Texas, where it would seem that people wish to enjoy the exclusive privilege of harboring hostile Indians.

If the presence of the Lipans at Remolino influenced the invasion, it becomes thereby less excusable, for no recent crime was charged upon them. If they had committed any outrages, they were not known in Mexico. The division of the horses captured at Remolino, among the Indian guides because they did not belong to any citizens of Texas, is the surest proof that there was no real motive for the insult offered to Mexico.

The conduct of these Indians in September last (1873) in murdering several Mexicans at Remolino, Moral and Resurreccion, and carrying off their property to the United States, shows how far they are in complicity and good fellowship with the citizens of the towns in question. These depredations have been the inevitable consequence of the act of General McKenzie. The Lipans cannot believe that the American forces could have made the attack without the connivance of the Mexican residents at those places, on whom they have therefore wreaked vengeance as the supposed accomplices in the McKenzie raid.

THE INDIAN POLICY OF THE UNITED STATES.

Out of 300,000 Indians now living in the territory of the United States, according to the last census, less than half are civilized. Only 130,000 support themselves, while the government maintains 115,000 and 55,000 are savages who live by the chase and by robbery.

This single fact, transpiring in the midst of one of the most powerful nations of the earth, shows that the races which formerly possessed the northern part of our continent have gained nothing by contact with the whites, since for three centuries their situation has been worse than it was before the coming of the Europeans. Formerly they could support themselves, to-day the government maintains them as if they were beggars.

Whether such a protectorate over the Indians be necessary or the reverse, the system observed in regard to Indian affairs is a bad one. Persons competent in the matter, have long since censured it, expressing wonder that the United States have been able, in an easy, tranquil and even legal manner, almost to exterminate the Indian races from their primitive domain, which they have gradually appropriated without the employment of material force.

The isolation in which the Indians were placed, the contempt with which they have been treated, and the perils with which they were surrounded by immoral "agents," have produced their fatal results. The partially civilized tribes have not advanced in the path of enlightenment, nor have the savage tribes entered upon that path. It has already been mentioned, that the contact between the agricultural and the nomadic tribes has been for both a source of corruption, and the origin of a delicate question which cannot now be solved by the united efforts of policy and justice.

From the time of the colonial government in New England, there was declared against the Indians, under a peaceful and apparently just form, what was virtually a war of extermination. This circumstance naturally attracted the attention of the founder of the United States, the best man known to have existed in our hemisphere, who pitied the fate of the aborigines, and used, in one of his messages to Congress, these noble words:

"We are more enlightened and more powerful than the Indian tribes; we are bound in honor to treat them with kindness and generosity."

In these words Washington condemned the policy which had been followed with the Indians, and expressed the necessity of a change which the honor of the Republic, represented in him, demanded in behalf of men who had not been treated according to their just deserts. His counsels were not adopted, and the greediness of the whites for the lands of the Indians soon lost sight of the demands of honor. Enjoying no repose, and kept in constant agitation, the Indians soon lost all faith in their own prosperity, and when they had taken a step towards civilized life they retrograded as much on being driven to the West and surrounded by savages.

Having already indicated the immense evils for Mexico and for the United States which sprung from this measure, it is unnecessary here to recapitulate them. It is enough to note that a sad and very costly experience has taught the American Government that the customary policy was pernicious and inhuman, and that it should be replaced by that which Washington recommended. The present administration took this great step, but on undertaking to put in practice the so-called Quaker policy, the obstacles in the way of execution and first application of the new system, have been so great that the results appear to condemn it. Many have even preferred the system of extermination, although so evidently condemned by morality and justice.

The Federal Government having no efficient support in the States nearest to the Indian reservations, at issue with the plundering habits acquired by these tribes, and the new system of peace and order being opposed to the interests of the speculators who have profited by the ignorance of the natives, it is natural that during the few years since the introduction of

he new policy very few advantages had been obtained. Yet
; is undeniable that some good results have already been per-
eived, and this Commission takes pleasure in admitting this
act, inasmuch as it recognizes the excellent intentions of the
overnment at Washington, in its present effort to substitute a
acific for a warlike policy.

Having heretofore, in this report, expressed an unfavorable
pinion as to the Indian policy of all the American adminis-
rations anterior to the present one, this Commission will ab-
tain from any criticism of the actual government, knowing
hat it has to struggle with rooted abuses and prejudices with
which it often has to temporize, in order to terminate them with-
n a given period. It observes, nevertheless, the existence of a
areful and profound system which is revealed by many acts,
ome of which it may be well to indicate.

The general government now desires to prevent the States
rom dealing with the Indians. It is trying to locate them
upon reservations, so as to obviate the inconveniences which
esult from their wanderings. It has recognized the evils re-
ulting from the lack of education among the Indian youth,
nd there is an effort on the part of the government to edu-
ate the rising generation which will soon take the place of
heir semi-barbarous parents. It is thus attempted to place
hem beyond the control of the States whose influence has
been hostile to the improvement of this unfortunate race.

In this respect it is observed that the Federal government,
rue to its principles, has not attended to the repeated requests
made by the State of Texas for the enlistment of troops to be
employed in defense against the Indians. The abuses and excesses of every kind which irregular troops have committed
whenever they have been employed, have not been forgotten;
they are too well remembered to admit of employing instruments which would result in destroying a work which is being
carried out with patient wisdom in the midst of formidable
obstacles.

This Commission believes that it has divined that the object to which the efforts of the government are directed, is to
accomplish the union of the Indians, to make of them a people,

to admit them ultimately to the full enjoyment of the rights of citizenship, and thus put an end to the old policy which tended towards extermination. Though having to endure sharp criticism as to the means employed, it steadily pursues its course. It is already seen that since the new system was begun, there has been a real revolution in the habits of the Indians, who are more pliable and less ferocious than they were before ; in the action and influence of the speculators who controlled them ; in the methods of life among the Indians which have improved by subjection to law ; and lastly, in the spirit displayed by the Indian agents.

That an extraordinary vigilance is now employed is a fact beyond all doubt, as also the disappearance of many of the causes which kept the Indians in constant movement by affording to their marauding forays the stimulus of a certain market for their booty. The cessation or paralyzation of Indian hostilities in Mexico and their diminution in Texas, are the immediate result of this energetic action by the government. Even the incursions still made in Texas prove the same fact, for they show that the Indians do not venture far away from their ordinary places of residence, so as not openly to violate their agreements. These depredations in Texas indicate, moreover, that the criminal traffickers, who induced them to commit robberies, have not entirely disappeared, but that their numbers are diminished, and that the vigorous action of the government will ultimately force them to abandon their nefarious occupation.

It is true that other causes have been at work in the same direction as has been hinted elsewhere by this Commission. It is certain that material improvements, which have been finished within a few years past, have changed the aspect of those mercantile exchanges which are the soul of nearly all operations in the neighboring republic, and that this circumstance has had an important bearing upon the change of conduct both in the Indians and in the speculators ; but it cannot be denied that the action of the government has been the most efficient influence at work for the realization of the work in question.

If this line of conduct had been observed from 1848 onward, or if even the points on the Rio Grande where the Indians generally cross had been garrisoned, the list of their depredations would not be so long. But care was taken only for the security of Texas and the American establishments, and Mexico was handed over as a prize for the rapacity of the savages, who speedily invaded and desolated our country. Nor could the exclusive intention of protecting Texas, which was shown by the new distribution of forts and encampments, be fully successful, since the American garrisons, from their numerical feebleness, their deficiencies in horses, and many other causes, were useless for any pursuit of the Indians. It thus came to pass that more than once greater security was enjoyed in Mexico than in Texas, and that American authorities requested aid from Mexico for their own defense against hordes of Comanches who encamped in front of their towns.

The protection of the American frontier, for more than ten years from 1848, was so completely neglected, that in several central points in Texas, entire settlements of savage Indians were made with the object of serving as headquarters for their raids upon Mexico, and from which they also marauded on a smaller scale in Texas itself. The Federal authorities, meanwhile, remained indifferent, viewing with tranquility the organization within their own country of expeditions to invade a foreign republic. They showed the same indifference when the nomadic hordes returned with the cattle they had robbed, and even when they drove them in front of their military posts, never attempting their recapture. At other places, officials who represented the American Government in its relations with the Indian tribes, secretly fomented a traffic with the robber tribes, which were exclusively engaged in the plunder alike of Mexico and of Texas. Employees of the Federal Government shared the gains of that illicit traffic, while they directly or indirectly, and with full knowledge of the fact, sacrificed the good name of their country, by stimulating the Indians to continue their depredations on the Mexican frontier.

What has recently transpired in Texas in this respect, is of so serious and noteworthy a character, that it alone will suffice for the condemnation of the policy observed towards Mexico, on this delicate and grave Indian question. For, if the spoils captured within that State can be publicly exposed for sale, as occurred in the case of the cattle stolen from Mr. Hittson, during the present year, it is evident that the spoils of Mexico, amounting to an enormous quantity, must with greater reason have constituted a still more lucrative and scandalous traffic.

Without here entering upon the circumstances of the notorious Howard-Cochise treaty, which placed the Apaches, of Arizona, upon the frontier of Sonora, and left them at liberty to pursue their horrible career of outrages upon a friendly country—a proceeding which has been energetically condemned by leading American journals, it may be observed that with slight differences the occurrences in Sonora are just the same as those of the Rio Grande. In the former case the reservations are on the very frontier, and what passes in them may be seen from both countries. On the lower Rio Grande, the reservations are at a great distance, in Northern Texas, but the conduct of the Indians is quite as fully proved by trustworthy evidence. In both regions alike, the agents on the reservations have looked on with indifference, while robberies and kidnapings have been the order of the day, and have rewarded the criminals by the distribution of their annuities.

Indifference, neglect and duplicity at once have characterized many of the officers who have held command in the Federal forts and outposts. From their very encampments they have seen the Indians from the reservations on their way to Mexico, and they have not hindered them. They have seen the savages return laden with an immense booty, and have not tried to recover it, even when they have seen Mexican troops reach the Rio Grande in pursuit. The consideration that all these Indians are subject to the United States has availed nothing for the prevention of such outrages, and none of the commanders of American forces on the frontier have ever remembered that they had any duties to perform in behalf of Mexico.

In other places the entire absence of garrisons has facilitated the incursions of the Indians. In 1858 there was not a single soldier along a line of 300 miles, from Ringgold Barracks to Eagle Pass. Along another line of nearly 1000 miles, from Eagle Pass to Fort Davis, the military posts were so weak that the Indians sometimes attacked and destroyed them. Frequently the garrisons had no other occupation than to serve as spectators of the depredations committed in Mexico, whither the Indians would set out from their villages on the Rio Pecos, located in the midst of American forts. The commanders of those forts failed to report the facts, or when they did their reports were neglected by the government at Washington, which thereby incurred a responsibility equal to that arising from the devastation of Sonora.

The Texan newspapers, which certainly do not favor the Mexican frontier, admit the reality of the devastations in Sonora and along the Rio Grande. The *Daily Herald*, of San Antonio, under date of the 23d of July last (1873), after enumerating the suffering of Texas, and condemning the criminal protection given to marauding Indians on the Fort Sill reservations, said that—

" This neglect does not surprise us, for the same thing occurs on the Chiricahua reservation in Arizona, where the government made peace with the chief Cochise, leaving him free to wreak his hate upon the Mexicans by devoting all his attention to plundering them ; for which end he was withdrawn from military control, exempted from roll-calls, and handed over to an agent who had no instructions to watch him, nor to prevent those forays into Mexico which commenced immediately after the Howard treaty. There can be no doubt of the fact, for the marauding Indians were tracked to the reservations where all the booty was found, and where the agent admitted the depredations in Mexico.

" Indeed, it is circumstantially in evidence that free forage on Mexican territory was relied upon as the chief inducement for Cochise to keep the peace on our side of the line. The newspapers raised their voices for very shame, but the interior department made no change and took no steps to prevent these outrages, and was satisfied with Gen. Howard's assurance that Cochise was innocent."

The complaints of Gen. Pesqueira to Gen. Cook, on the

28

same subject, had no other result than an offer to consult his superiors with a view to obtain permission to subject the Indians to roll-call, but this permission was refused, according to the explanations which Col. Velasco furnished the government of Sonora.

Texas being, according to the writers of that State, in the same position as Sonora, whose sufferings they related as parallel to their own, it is easily seen that the depredations in Mexico were notorious, as well as the obligation on the part of government to suppress them.

"As the government had refused to restrain the Indians on the Sonora line, so on the same principle it declined to impede their robberies in Texas where a frontier of more than a thousand miles was unprotected."

About this time the case of two Kiowa chiefs, Satanta and Big-Tree, in whose behalf the general government intervened, when they had been arrested, tried and condemned by the Texan courts, gave rise to an acrimonious debate, in which the Indian policy of that government was bitterly denounced. Making due allowance for exaggeration on the part of political opponents, this case still throws great light upon the principal question at issue.

The depredations of the Kiowas in Texas were clearly proved, but although the right of the Texan courts to punish criminals is recognized, the policy of the Federal government, represented by Secretary Delano, required the liberation of the Kiowa chiefs. The ultimate decision is still (1873) to be reached by a conference with the Governor of Texas.

This question has been discussed from the opposite standpoints of the extermination of the Indians and their pacification by humanitarian methods. In this connection the former and present conduct of the Federal government has been passed in review. The charge has been distinctly made that the government itself or its subordinates has supplied arms to the Indians from the Mississippi to the Pacific coast, as shown by the Modocs who, in fighting the American troops, used rifles of recent invention.

"The people and government of the United States," it was alleged, "are the real causes of these crimes, they having first murdered and robbed the Indians."

A delegation of Comanches, Kiowas and Apaches went to Washington to solicit the liberty of the imprisoned chiefs. The legislature of Texas declared against such a step, and although the *World* stated that the protest was the reflection of the sentiments of the Texan frontier and of almost all the Texan papers, it nevertheless maintained the policy of the government.

The Texan papers have ransacked the published reports of the board of Indian commissioners for several years, and have thus brought to light important documents in which that board has expressed its weighty opinion against the scandalous means by which Indian agents formerly acquired splendid fortunes. While it is not denied that the same abuses still exist on a smaller scale, an official proof is thus afforded that the Federal government has always been and still is responsible for the misdeeds of the Indians. It is admitted that all the past Indian troubles have been caused by a failure to observe the treaties.

In rejoinder to these opinions of the board about the sanctity of treaties, and the value of peaceful measures in Indian questions, the same papers brought forward again the horrible butchery of Lipans and Kickapoos committed by McKenzie, and observed that the War Department had approved his conduct, thus presenting in a strong light the inconsistency of the government.

It has always been the fate of all important and salutary plans of governments to encounter thousands of obstacles even in their purely economical details. This is what is now taking place in the United States, in regard to the Indian question. Nevertheless, the responsibilities contracted under the former vicious system cannot be repudiated by the change, any more than those arising from the misconduct of its present agents.

To extirpate the inveterate abuses involved in the administration of Indian affairs is a herculean task, in which the government at Washington is likely to fail, in case its humane views be not seconded by the agents, who should therefore be chosen with extreme care. Otherwise the prophecy of Tocqueville will be fulfilled: " the Indians are condemned to perish, and must resign themselves to their fate."

It is a painful duty to remark that in practice the humanitarian policy of the American government has been far from an unmixed benefit to the Mexican frontier, and in notable instances has been exercised at our expense. Sufficient proofs of this fact will be found in the conduct of General Howard and Agent Jeffards in Arizona; in the conduct of the commanders of Forts Quitman, Davis, Stockton, Clark, and Duncan, who have allowed parties of Comanches and Mescaleros to pass by them unmolested, when they were known to be on their way to ravage the Mexican frontier; and in the recent refusal of the commander of Fort Clark to deliver to their Mexican owners, who personally claimed them, a number of horses taken by his troops from a party of Indians on their return from a foray into Mexico, a procedure in direct contrast with that of the Mexican authorities a few months before, as already related.

The facts stated and proved by this Commission respecting the horrible depredations of the savages, conclusively show that Mexico deceived herself when she expected the United States to fulfill their natural and treaty obligations. Mexico has suffered the horrors of the most atrocious warfare that any nation can register in its annals, and all in consequence of her strict observance of a solemn treaty. Confiding in the power of the neighboring nation to effect the pacification of the Indians, she regulated her conduct in conformity with that view. Hence the establishment of military colonies to hold in check the Indians who might be driven by hostilities in the United States to take refuge in Mexico; hence the strict orders issued to make no terms with nomadic tribes, and hence the zeal with which the frontier towns were garrisoned and supplied with arms, for the last brief struggle which, it was anticipated, would be made by the Indians.

The course of events was far different—Mexico became the protector of the American frontier. The inhabitants of Texas came to Reynosa and Matamoros in 1849 and 1853 for protection against the hordes of savages who were encamped around their towns, and their authorities called for help from those of Mexico. That help was granted, and the Comanche encampments were put to flight by the efforts of the Mexicans, who availed themselves, in their own interest, of a permission to fight the common enemy upon American soil. The inhabitants of Guerrero took the first step in this direction, and they were several times imitated by the settlers in the district of Rio Grande in Coahuila. As a recompense for these good offices, the Mexicans living in Texas have been denied the privilege of assembling together in a number greater than ten individuals!

While Texas was thus the rallying-point of all the Indians who desolated Mexico, and while those tribes were almost permanently encamped in that territory as a base of operations against Mexico, neither the people nor the army of the United States prevented their actions. That people and that army were witnesses of the depredations, and took no action, unless to increase the horrors of the situation by threatening the Mexican frontier with invasions on their own part, and even effecting them on the most futile pretexts.

For example, at a time when Nuevo Laredo was besieged by the Comanches, it suffered an invasion headed by one Benavides, under pretext that the Lipans, then at peace with Mexico, and under strict vigilance, had approached the line of the Rio Grande. It had been thought right and proper for Texas to make peace with them in 1854, without any conditions as regarding hostilities in Mexico; but is was *not* to be tolerated that Mexico should make any treaty with those Indians, even when, as in this case, it was stipulated that they should refrain from incursions into Texas.

We have already given the history of the Lipans—that wretched and miserable tribe whose ruin was brought about by the Texans, and whose warriors do not now exceed thirty. It seems incredible, that living as they did, not in **Mexico** but in Texas, their name should have been used as a reproach to the Mexicans, when Texas has thousands upon thousands of other savages who roam in every direction, and are the real perpetrators of all the depredations she has suffered. Nevertheless, certain special agents of the American Government have preferred charges against Mexico for harboring the Lipans, and this is one of the principal chapters of the grievances which have lately been proclaimed to the world!

At the present time, fortunately, the outrages formerly committed upon Mexican towns, on account of fugitive slaves, no longer occur. In the same degree that this conduct was dishonorable and criminal on the part of the persecutors of those unhappy refugees, the course of the Mexican authorities and people, in defending them on all occasions, at the hazard of life and property, and at the risk of invasion by filibusters, will ever be a title of honor to our country. An indelible stain will rest upon that army which then gave its support, at Piedras Negras, to the bandits who trafficked in human blood.

CONCLUSION.

The sketch which this Commission has endeavored to draw of the calamities suffered by the Mexican frontier, does not do justice to the reality, for a complete picture would require more time and a more exhaustive consultation of documents. The present report gives, however, an idea of the immense extent of the evil, of its varied forms, and of the continual losses to which it has subjected the frontier, decimating its inhabitants, preventing every useful enterprise, converting it into a military encampment, and forcing it to lead a nomadic life, like that of the savages in whose pursuit our inhabilants have spent their days in toil, dangers and misery.

Having summed up the incalculable losses occasioned by Indian incursions, this Commission believes, after a careful study of this warfare from its beginning, that the evil had its origin in the wrong policy of the United States, in their treatment of a question which involved the future of thousands of the Indian races, as well as that of several millions of the residents of Mexico.

After a long period of neglect, the question of the civilization of the Indians has now attracted the serious attention of the government of the United States. This fact is a most explicit recognition of the right of Mexico to demand and obtain indemnification for the losses suffered on account of failure to restrain the Indians from committing depredations.

The right to such indemnification, moreover, is established not merely by the history of the Indian tribes, but by the conduct of the government to which they are subject, independently of all treaties, as a consequence of the duties which the Government at Washington now recognizes and endeavors to discharge with honorable solicitude, in spite of all the hindrances thrown in the way by the bastard interests which its own negligence has created. All these considerations prove the reality of the grievances experienced by Mexico, as proceeding from American territory, in which the invasions have been prepared, and whose citizens have been, with the connivance of their authorities, the receivers of Mexican booty.

On her part, Mexico has done all that the situation demanded. She has facilitated the action of the American Government in the fulfillment of its agreements; she has contributed more than her revenue has warranted, towards the extirpation of an evil which was not a common one, and for that very reason was not suppressed by the government responsible for its existence. She has exhausted the measures of prudence, of convenience, of necessity and of utility, to prevent the desolation that was being wrought upon a great part of her territory, and all without result, as has been seen from the conduct of the American Government in this question, which has been treated not merely with disdain, but perhaps with intentions openly contrary to the demands of justice.

Every where and at all times the violation in the first instance of the Treaty of Guadalupe, and secondly, of the principles of natural justice between nations, has been apparent. When it is recognized that the observance of those principles is essential to preserve the life and tranquility of nations, it cannot be believed that the United States will sanction so many injuries by refusing to make proper reparation for what it failed to prevent and to punish.

In no case of international controversy have the facts been more evident than in this matter of Indian depredations. The honor and the reputation of the American people, as has been recognized by just men of that country, are involved in the indemnification of the Mexican sufferers, and this report contains but a few of the many reasons which concur in establishing the justice of such a demand. It should also be recognized by the United States, as being interested equally with Mexico in the observance of that natural law which enjoins nations to lend each other mutual assistance in their efforts for genuine progress.

The equality of rights between Mexico and the United States as sovereign nations, aside from all considerations of relative wealth and power, which do not affect intrinsic justice, is another powerful argument in favor of the claims of Mexico. The United States in presenting claims of its citizens for grievances said to have been suffered from Indians living in Mexico, will place itself upon a ground which necessarily presupposes its own obligation to satisfy the just claims of the same nature presented by Mexican citizens, for which the evidence both of fact and of responsibility has been shown to be so complete and so convincing. The undeniable obligation on the part of Mexico to prevent, as far as possible, all aggression by Indians living within her borders, upon the Texan frontier, has been faithfully discharged. When the small tribe of Lipans and the semi-civilized tribe of Kickapoos have resided in Mexico, it has been upon the express condition of refraining from all outrages upon the neighboring nation. Extreme vigilance has been used in enforcing good behavior, and every dereliction has been followed by prompt and severe chastisement.

In the necessity of taking action for the future security of her territory from similar incursions from the United States, Mexico has to contemplate two objects, viz: the prevention and the punishment of such outrages. The former object can only be attained by agreement with the United States, which is under an evident obligation to prevent all such incursions.

The latter object demands from Mexico the cantonment of forces sufficient to repel all aggressors of whatever class. It is believed that the presence of disciplined troops along the line, will avail not only as against the Indians, but to prevent invasions by parties of bandits, such as those who in September last (1873) attacked La Resurrection, adding to material outrage, insult and calumny.

A convenient distribution of troops, and their being commanded by honorable and educated officers, would go farther than a mere display of numbers, towards effecting a change of opinion among the Texans of the frontier, who might perhaps be thus brought to abandon their traditional system of invasion and indiscriminate hostility, and cultivate those fraternal relations which the two peoples so urgently need.

It will much contribute to this result, if the policy announced by the Supreme Government of Mexico, in its circular of the 10th of September, 1850, shall be rigorously pursued, by refusing all terms of peace to the savage tribes. Even respecting the semi-civilized tribes, after the difficulties which have arisen with the Seminoles, Kickapoos and Muscogees, a similar policy should henceforth be adopted.

It is one of the first duties of Mexico, and one which the Commission cannot sufficiently urge, to place herself in a condition to repel every act of violence which can be anticipated from her numerous enemies in the United States, whether they be real Indians, disguised white men, filibusters or simple bandits. The sending of sufficient troops to protect the national territory from all outrages, will not only afford security to the inhabitants, but will stimulate the colonization of the vast deserts which urgently demand industrious settlers for the material welfare of the country, and as a check to the unbounded ambition of filibusters.

Four detachments of 150 men each, distributed between San Vicente and Las Vacas, would close the doors through which the savages have penetrated into the three States of Coahuila, Nuevo Leon und Tamaulipas, and would also protect the greater part of Durango. Three encampments or military colonies placed at Bábia, Zorra and Pico Etéreo, would complete the defense, and would open to settlement a region rich in mines and abundant in pastures.

The old and modern history of Texas, filled with calumnies, outrages, invasions and ambition against Mexico, is a lesson which should attract towards the frontier all the energy of the Mexican government, in order to afford its long-suffering inhabitants a respite from their continual struggle against open and secret enemies. As the Commission has said elsewhere in this report, it is only the creation of material interests superior to those they could expect from an increase of territory, that can put an end to the restless spirit of the floating population of Texas, which, in the absence of lawful resources to employ the energy of its will, is ever dreaming of revolutionary enterprises inconsistent with the maintenance of peace and harmony between the two nations. To meet this exigency a prolonged and vigorous effort is necessary.

It is not a fear, but the proved existence of important facts, which impels this Commission to insist again and again upon the protection of the Rio Grande line by suitable forces. The spirit of invasion, still dominant in Texas, does not forget the tactics which secured the separation and loss of that territory. This spirit lives and is nourished upon the ideas of Sam. Houston. It is necessary to oppose to it not only the barriers of justice, but those of force, the greatest of which would be the rapid settlement and consequent prosperity of the Mexican frontier. No law, no special measure for that end is requisite; nothing but the stationing of the most select portion of our army along the frontier. In a secondary degree, the vigilance of the supreme government is required in the formation of laws and police regulations respecting the intercourse between the settlements on the opposite banks of the Rio Grande, for which measure the same reasons and the same rights may be presented as for similar action in our sea-ports. All communications, even in private, with a foreign nation, demand the attention and vigilance of the federal authorities.

The administration of justice in the remote districts of the frontier States, in immediate contact with the United States, is far from satisfactory, owing to the ignorance of its officers, or the listlessness of their agents. This fact has had no small influence upon the demoralization and decline of that region. It would, therefore, be a public benefit if the supreme government, through the means open to it, could exercise an influence for the better discharge of judicial functions which may imperil our relations with the neighboring republic.

This Commission, in the discharge of its duties, has been careful to collect documents whose study will tend to the promotion of its important objects. It believes that in so doing it has acted judiciously, and contributed to realize the intentions of the Congressional law of October 2d, 1872, to which it owes its existence. The examination of these questions, whose importance is greater than the capacities of the members of the Commission, has been purposely confined within certain limits, so as to leave to the sound judgment and wisdom of our statesmen, the task of deducing the important consequences which flow from the facts so carefully collected and proven.

In fine, in order to crown the just, grand, necessary and befitting work of elevating the frontier of Northern Mexico to that degree of prosperity which the security of the republic demands, and to which nature has destined it, the difficulties and obstacles are neither insurmountable nor relatively great. If care shall be taken that the laws be observed and executed with all strictness; if the security of the frontier shall be diligently and vigilantly maintained; if prompt remedies shall be applied to difficulties arising from a long period of disorder; the frontier will soon, very soon rise to a prosperity which will be reflected from all the other States of the federation. Thus the real power of Mexico will be cemented, as the peace now enjoyed and the preparatory measures already taken happily forebode.

MONTEREY, *December* 7th, 1873.

IGNACIO GALINDO.
ANTONIO GARCIA CARRILLO.
AGUSTIN SILICEO.

FRANCISCO VALDÉS GOMEZ,
Secretary.